Recruitment and Selection Law for Local Government Employers

Diane M. Juffras

2013

UNC
SCHOOL OF
GOVERNMENT

The School of Government at the University of North Carolina at Chapel Hill works to improve the lives of North Carolinians by engaging in practical scholarship that helps public officials and citizens understand and improve state and local government. Established in 1931 as the Institute of Government, the School provides educational, advisory, and research services for state and local governments. The School of Government is also home to a nationally ranked graduate program in public administration and specialized centers focused on information technology and environmental finance.

As the largest university-based local government training, advisory, and research organization in the United States, the School of Government offers up to 200 courses, webinars, and specialized conferences for more than 12,000 public officials each year. In addition, faculty members annually publish approximately fifty books, book chapters, bulletins, and other reference works related to state and local government. Each day that the General Assembly is in session, the School produces the *Daily Bulletin*, which reports on the day's activities for members of the legislature and others who need to follow the course of legislation.

The Master of Public Administration Program is a full-time, two-year program that serves up to sixty students annually. It consistently ranks among the best public administration graduate programs in the country, particularly in city management. With courses ranging from public policy analysis to ethics and management, the program educates leaders for local, state, and federal governments and nonprofit organizations.

Operating support for the School of Government's programs and activities comes from many sources, including state appropriations, local government membership dues, private contributions, publication sales, course fees, and service contracts. Visit www.sog.unc.edu or call 919.966.5381 for more information on the School's courses, publications, programs, and services.

Printed in the United States of America

17 16 15 14 13 1 2 3 4 5

ISBN 978-1-56011-730-8

∞ This publication is printed on permanent, acid-free paper in compliance with the North Carolina General Statutes.

Printed on recycled paper

Summary Contents

Table of Contents

Preface

Like my previous book, *Employee Benefits Law for North Carolina Local Government Employers*, published in 2009, *Recruitment and Selection Law for Local Government Employers* grew out of my School of Government experiences in teaching and advising local government employers. It is the first in a series of books that will replace the School of Government's general employment reference work, *Employment Law: A Guide for North Carolina Public Employers*, the third edition of which is now out of date. Rather than write a book that surveys employment law, I have decided to write a series of books about distinct topics in employment law, including the hiring process, the Fair Labor Standards Act, constitutional issues, privacy in public employment, and discharge and discipline. This book addresses the process of recruitment and selection, which can be particularly challenging for employers as it is governed by a patchwork of federal and state laws. Although many discussions are applicable to community college and state government hiring, the book focuses on the recruitment and selection issues that face local government employers.

I had two main goals in writing *Recruitment and Selection Law for Local Government Employers*. First, I wanted to answer some of the basic, recurring questions about what federal and state law requires of public employers with respect to advertising openings and interviewing applicants. These are topics about which I receive regular inquiries from local government employers by telephone or email. I also spend considerable time discussing these topics with participants in the School of Government's Introduction to Public Employment Law course and its Municipal and County Administration course. Second, I wanted to bring some coherence to an area where the many different sources of law sometimes leave human resources personnel and local government attorneys feeling concerned that one or another legal consideration may have been overlooked. I have seen how committed North Carolina's local government and community college employers are to achieving a workforce composed of individuals who have excellent training and skills, have a commitment to public service, and also reflect the diversity of the communities they serve. My broader goal is to help them do this by providing a more in-depth look at the legal issues that typically arise at each stage of the hiring process than a survey of employment law is able to do.

I would like to thank my School of Government colleague Bob Joyce for a detailed reading of the manuscript and for his many helpful comments and suggestions. I would also like to thank Mike Smith, Dean of the School of Government, for supporting this project by approving me for a writing leave during the 2011–2012 academic year.

Diane M. Juffras
Professor of Public Law and Government
March 2013

Introduction

Introduction

A North Carolina town manager once said that hiring was the hardest part of his job. Given the high cost of training and of turnovers, he felt enormous pressure to find and choose the best applicant for every position. Learning enough about applicants to make an informed decision about whether they would be a good fit for the position would be difficult enough if there were no limitations on the questions that could be asked and the factors that could be taken into consideration. The process of finding a seemingly best candidate is that much harder given the number of rules and prohibitions governing the hiring process. Included in that list of rules governing recruitment and selection are the following:

1. Unless the law has created a specific exception, all employees are at-will employees. In the hiring context, the employment-at-will rule means that employers may generally hire whomever they please, even if the person selected is not the most qualified applicant for the position.
2. Notwithstanding the employment-at-will rule, federal and state antidiscrimination laws prohibit employers from making hiring decisions based on race, color, gender, religion, national origin, age, disability, or military status.
3. Unintentional discrimination is as illegal as intentional discrimination.

4. There are no general federal or state laws that require public employers to post, advertise, or otherwise seek applicants for vacant positions in any particular way, but an organization may adopt policies that establish procedures for hiring. Where such policies are adopted by statute or ordinance, the policies have the force of law and must be followed.
5. An employer may not reject a job applicant because that applicant is a member of the Armed Forces or Armed Forces reserves and may be subject to a call to duty.
6. No applicant may be automatically disqualified on the basis of a criminal conviction.
7. No applicant may be automatically disqualified on the basis of poor credit history or bankruptcy.
8. Employment tests of various kinds are permitted so long as they are not used to discriminate on the basis of a protected category and do not unintentionally discriminate by disproportionately weeding out members of one or more protected classes.
9. An employer may not ask any medical questions or require any medical examinations of an applicant until a conditional offer of employment has been made.
10. No public employer may hire a person without verifying that he or she has registered with the United States Selective Service.
11. All employees must be eligible to work in the United States.
12. An employer who uses a third-party vendor or agency to do a background check on an applicant must comply with the requirements of the Fair Credit Reporting Act.
13. Most rules governing initial hiring also apply to promotions.

The list set forth above is not exclusive, and these and other rules that govern hiring cannot be found in any overarching federal or state statute. The law of hiring is instead a patchwork of rules. Some are directly stated in federal or state statutes and regulations, some are interpreted or derived from statutes, and others are rules of common law. In the public sector, still other rules derive from the federal and state constitutions.

North Carolina Local Government and Community College Employers: Who Are They?

This book covers the law of recruitment and selection as it applies to North Carolina local government and community college employers. Cities and counties are the units of local government that people most commonly associate with the term "local government," and the law of hiring as it applies to North Carolina cities and counties is a major focus of this book. But in North Carolina, and for the purposes of this book, local government employers also include area mental health authorities (sometimes known as local management entities or LMEs), water and sewer authorities, public health authorities, local Alcohol and Beverage Control (ABC) boards, and regional councils of government (COGs, which are created to provide technical assistance and assistance in economic development and grant administration to local governments in multi-county areas). The practices of cities and counties will be discussed more frequently than those of other forms of local government and will be the subject of numerous examples. But unless specifically singled out for exception, the term local government employer and discussions of recruitment and selection law will apply equally to area authorities, water and sewer authorities, public health authorities, local ABC boards, and COGs.

Community Colleges

The North Carolina Community College System was created by the North Carolina General Assembly and made a joint responsibility of the state and of local government. Both the operating authority and decision-making power and the expense of running a community college are shared. The State Board of Community Colleges and the board of trustees of the local community college have each been delegated a share of operational and decision-making responsibility, and the state provides the bulk of the funding for educational programs while the counties a college serves bear the cost of building and maintaining its facilities. For some purposes, a community college functions more like a state agency (as when it participates in the Teachers and State Employees Retirement System and the State Health Plan of North Carolina), and for others, more like a local government (as in its close relationship with the local public schools and the role of the local school board and the board of county commissioners in choosing the college's trustees).

For the purposes of this book, community colleges are much more like local governments than they are like state agencies or local boards of education. In general, community colleges are subject to the same law as local governments when it comes to hiring. For this reason, community colleges are included among the units of government covered by this book.

Local Government Entities Not Covered by This Book

Other forms of local government entity exist in the State of North Carolina, including housing authorities, airport authorities, public (usually county) hospitals, sanitary districts, and local fire protection districts. These units of local government, to the extent that they exist as local government employers separate and independent of the cities or counties where they are located, are not covered by this book.

In North Carolina, the public school systems, like the state's community colleges, receive funding from the counties in which they are located and are closely tied to their local communities. Indeed, local boards of educations are generally considered to be units of local government. But the structure, authority, and rules governing public school employment are substantially different from those of other forms of local government employment. For this reason, public schools are not considered local government employers for the purposes of this book.

Small Employers

Some of North Carolina's smallest municipalities have only a handful of employees, while the state's larger cities and counties may have over 6,000 employees, as does the city of Charlotte. While most employment laws apply to most employers, many have exceptions for small employers. The difficulty is that different statutes' coverage is triggered by different numbers of employees. Federal antidiscrimination statutes such as Title VII of the Civil Rights Act of 1964, the Americans with Disabilities Act, and the Genetic Information Nondiscrimination Act, apply to employers with 15 or more employees, but the Age Discrimination in Employment Act applies only to employers with 20 or more employees. The Fair Labor Standards

Act and the Family and Medical Leave Act (neither of which regulates the hiring process) apply to employers with a single employee and 50 employees respectively. The North Carolina law prohibiting discrimination in employment against persons lawfully using lawful products applies to all public employers. To assist small local government employers in understanding the extent of their obligations under the law, Appendix 1 sets forth the number of employees that a local government employer must have before each of the statutes discussed in this book applies.

Initial Hiring versus Promoting from Within

The book's title, *Recruitment and Selection Law for Local Government Employers*, can refer to two different ways of filling a vacant position; namely, by hiring from outside the organization and by promoting from within the organization. Although many of the book's examples, hypotheticals, and discussions focus on the more common of the two circumstances, hiring from without, the book is also meant to be a resource on the law as it applies to the selection of existing employees for promotion. Promotions are not treated in a stand-alone chapter. Instead, except where noted or where the law or discussion is obviously inapplicable to promotions, everything that is said about initial hiring should be understood to apply equally to promotions.

Entry-level positions are usually advertised outside an organization. But every time a vacancy occurs in any other type of position, an employer faces a choice of whether to advertise the position or to promote an already existing employee into it, either by soliciting applications from those eligible for promotion or by making an executive decision solely by reference to the employee's performance and conduct on the job. Whether interest in a promotion is solicited or not, employers may not choose who to promote on the basis of race, color, gender, religion, national origin, age, disability, military status, or lawful use of lawful products, just as they may not make an initial hire on that basis. Additionally, the same restrictions on criminal background and credit checks and on the use of written examinations, physical agility tests, and assessment centers apply to evaluation of current employees just as they do to evaluation of new applicants.

A Summary of the Book's Contents

The initial chapters of the book survey the patchwork of rules that comprise the law of hiring for North Carolina public employers. Later chapters look more closely at the different stages of the hiring process. This book is guided throughout by the need and desire of North Carolina's local government and community college employers to achieve a workforce composed of individuals who have excellent training and skills, take initiative, are reliable and motivated, have a commitment to public service, and reflect the diversity of the communities they serve. What follows is a brief description of the book's contents.

Chapter 1, "An Overview of the Laws Governing Recruitment and Selection," surveys those laws other than antidiscrimination statutes that govern the law of hiring for North Carolina public employers. It begins with a discussion of the way in which the North Carolina General Statutes grant hiring authority to cities, counties, and other units of local government. It then discusses the rule of employment at will before turning to some provisions of law that may be less well known to local government employees with human resources responsibilities—the Fair Credit Reporting Act, the Immigration Reform and Control Act, North Carolina's own E-Verify requirement, and state laws prohibiting discrimination on the basis of tobacco use (lawful use of lawful products), requiring U.S. selective service registration, and prohibiting employers from charging applicants for the cost of employment-related examinations and records.

Chapter 2, "Discrimination Law in the Recruitment and Selection Context," surveys federal antidiscrimination laws (Title VII, the Age Discrimination in Employment Act, the Americans with Disabilities Act, the Genetic Information Nondiscrimination Act, and the Uniformed Services Employment and Reemployment Rights Act) and their North Carolina state law counterparts. The chapter contains an in-depth discussion of the theory of adverse impact, which underlies many of the legal issues that arise during the recruitment and selection process. It also introduces and discusses the constitutional concept of equal protection.

Chapter 3, "Defining and Advertising the Job," begins with a discussion of job descriptions and focuses on the ways in which they can help or hurt an employer's defense to an employment discrimination claim. It then uses a draft job advertisement for a hypothetical position with a North Carolina local government to illustrate the legal issues raised by the content of a job advertisement. The chapter concludes by considering the legal implications of promoting a current employee to a newly created position without posting or advertising, offering a position to an outside candidate without posting or advertising, and using word-of-mouth recruiting in lieu of advertising.

Chapter 4, "Personnel Policies Related to Recruitment and Selection," analyzes the legal issues raised by three policies that North Carolina public employers frequently adopt: residency requirements restricting employment to residents of the hiring jurisdiction or its surrounding area, anti-nepotism policies restricting the employment of members of the same family or household, and policies limiting consideration of former employees for rehire. In the case of residency requirements, the North Carolina General Statutes expressly authorize local government employers to adopt them, and the chapter therefore explains how they may nonetheless violate federal constitutional and statutory antidiscrimination law, drawing on the discussion of equal protection and disparate impact in Chapter 2. Anti-nepotism policies are also prevalent in North Carolina local government employment. This section of the chapter discusses equal protection challenges and whether a public employer can prohibit spouses and family members from working in different departments in the same organization or prohibit employees from dating one another. Neither of these issues has been considered by courts having jurisdiction over North Carolina.

Chapter 5, "Lawful and Unlawful Questions: Applications and Interviewing," is divided into two sections. The first section discusses the explicit prohibitions against medical inquiries and examinations under the Americans with Disabilities Act and the Genetic Information Nondiscrimination Act. The second section discusses questions that are not unlawful on their face but could lead applicants, the Equal Employment Opportunity Commission, and juries to question whether the employer had discriminatory intent in asking them. Both sections discuss possible ways to rephrase a question that looks unlawful or improper but is actually seeking relevant and lawful information.

Chapters 6 and 7 turn to the use of scored testing in making decisions to hire or promote candidates. Chapter 6, "Testing of Applicants and Candidates for Promotion: Written Examinations," discusses written examinations for entry-level and promotional positions in public safety, because that is primarily where they are used, although scored written examinations may be used in hiring for other local government positions as well. This chapter focuses on the potential for disparate impact that scored testing poses. Through a discussion of cases, it explains methods of test construction validation that can support an employer's disparate impact defense of job related and consistent with business necessity. The chapter concludes with a discussion of the United States Supreme Court case *Ricci v. DeStefano* and how public employers should handle testing results that have disparate impact. Chapter 7, "Testing of Applicants and Candidates for Promotion: Physical Ability Tests and Assessment Centers," looks at scored testing in the context of physical ability tests and assessment centers and the difficulties that are unique to them. It also considers the perils inherent in introducing local modifications to the North Carolina Police Officer Physical Ability Test (POPAT), a common practice among small employers.

Chapter 8, "Background Investigations of Applicants for Employment: Criminal Records, Credit History, References, and Internet Checks," looks at the four most common types of background checks used by North Carolina local government and community college employers: criminal history checks, credit checks, reference checks, and Internet background checks. The sections on criminal history and credit checks focus on the disparate impact that use of arrest and conviction records and credit histories may have on minority applicants and on the Equal Employment Opportunity Commission's new initiatives to combat misuse of that information. The discussion on reference checks incorporates North Carolina statutory provisions and the development of North Carolina's common law rule of negligent hiring. The law governing the use of the Internet to develop background information on applicants is still in its infancy, and this section focuses primarily on information found through the use of search engines such as Google and social media sites like Facebook, with particular emphasis on the need to balance an applicant's First Amendment rights with the government employer's needs. The chapter concludes with a discussion of the Fair Credit Reporting Act's requirements governing the use of a third-party agency for uncovering criminal history, credit, and other background information.

Chapter 9, "Hiring Employees versus Engaging Independent Contractors," turns to an issue in which the Internal Revenue Service and the U.S. Department of Labor have taken renewed interest of late. As tight budgets force public employers to cut personnel costs, many are tempted to bring on workers as so-called contract employees, more properly known as independent contractors. Employers who engage independent contractors are not required to pay FICA taxes on them or to make statutory contributions on their behalf to the North Carolina retirement system. Employers also save money because independent contractors do not have to be paid overtime or included in the employer's health insurance group plan or under its workers' compensation or general liability insurance policies. But the misclassification of an employee as an independent contractor is fraught with risk. This chapter sets forth the tests for determining employee and independent contractor status under the Fair Labor Standards Act and the Internal Revenue Code.

Chapter 10, "Applicant Records: Confidentiality and Retention," begins by discussing the confidentiality requirements imposed by the North Carolina General Statutes on applicant information. It then turns to the requirements of the Americans with Disabilities Act and the Genetic Information Nondiscrimination Act that medical information be kept confidential in the context of the hiring process. The chapter discusses the data retention required for Equal Employment Opportunity Commission reporting purposes and concludes by surveying federal and North Carolina law governing the retention and disposition of applicant records.

The book also contains five appendixes that summarize or contain more in-depth discussions of material found within the text proper. Appendix 1 sets out in chart form how the employment laws discussed in the book apply to small local government and community college employers. Appendix 2 provides an in-depth discussion of the history and current status of affirmative action in public-sector hiring. Appendix 3 summarizes what it means to validate a practice, test, or process used in recruitment and selection of employees. Appendix 4 provides a model summary of consumer rights for use by local government and community college employers who use third-party companies to perform background checks. Appendix 5 contains the Equal Employment Opportunity Commission's Form EEO-4, which public employers must file with the agency.

Chapter 1

An Overview of the Laws Governing Recruitment and Selection

Chapter 1

An Overview of the Laws Governing Recruitment and Selection

The first two chapters of this book survey the laws that affect hiring and promotion for North Carolina public employers. This chapter covers federal and state statutes other than antidiscrimination statutes, as well as common law rules applicable to the employment relationship. Antidiscrimination law will be surveyed in the second chapter. We begin with a look at the foundational rule of American employment law, the rule of employment at will.

1.1 The Common Law Rule of Employment at Will

Absent a statute, ordinance, or employment contract that confers some sort of right to continued employment, all employment in North Carolina is employment at will. The term "employment at will" is a shorthand way of saying that employment may be ended at the will of either the employer or the employee. An employer can fire an employee for any reason or for no reason at all. An employee can quit for any reason or for no reason at all.[1] The at-will rule also applies to disciplinary actions that fall short of termination. An employer who can fire employees at will can also refuse to

---

1. *See* Kurtzman v. Applied Analytical Indus., Inc., 347 N.C. 329, 331 (1997) ("This Court has repeatedly held that in the absence of a contractual agreement between an employer and an employee establishing a definite term of employment, the relationship is presumed to be terminable at the will of either party without regard to the

hire any given applicant, set the terms of employees' work, raise and lower employees' pay, and demote, suspend, or transfer employees, all at will.

The employment-at-will rule is what is called a "common law" rule; that is, a law developed in the courts, as opposed to laws found in statutes passed by legislatures or rules promulgated by agencies. Common law is case law, created by judges as they apply legal principles to various facts. This is in contrast to statutory law, which is created by the United States Congress or the North Carolina General Assembly. The employment-at-will rule applies to both public and private sector employment in North Carolina and in every other state in the United States except Montana. In the public sector in North Carolina, the at-will status of employees is in some instances explicitly stated in the General Statutes. For example, Section 160A-147 of the North Carolina General Statutes (hereinafter G.S.) states that a city manager is appointed by the council "to serve at its pleasure." Similarly, G.S. 153A-103(2) provides that sheriff's deputies "serve at the pleasure of the appointing officer."[2] But even where the at-will status of a particular position or group of employees is not expressly stated, the presumption is that employment at will applies unless it is stated otherwise.[3]

In the hiring context, the employment-at-will rule means that employers may generally hire whomever they please. There is no legal requirement that the person be the most qualified applicant, have relevant experience, or even meet the minimum stated qualifications. The decision about whom to

---

quality of performance of either party"); Soles v. City of Raleigh Civil Serv. Comm'n, 345 N.C. 443, 446 (1997).

2. *See also* N.C. Gen. Stat. (hereinafter G.S.) § 160A-147 (authorizing a city council to appoint a city manager to serve at its pleasure); G.S. 160A-173 (the city council appoints the city attorney, who serves at its pleasure); G.S. 153A-81(1) (authorizing a county board of commissioners to hire a county manager to serve at its pleasure); G.S. 153A-111 and G.S. 153A-114 (the county clerk and the county attorney, respectively, are appointed by the board of commissioners and serve at its pleasure).

3. *See, e.g.,* Cannon v. Town of Long View, 1989 WL 117820 (4th Cir. 1989) (holding that the plain language of G.S. 159-24, which provides that "each local government and public authority shall appoint a finance officer to hold office at the pleasure of the appointing board or official," made the plaintiff finance officer an employee at will). *See also* Blair v. Randolph Cnty. Bd. of Educ., 2011 WL 2206690 (2011) (unpublished disposition) (plaintiff was employee at will in absence of any policy or document to the contrary); Roberson v. City of Goldsboro, 564 F. Supp. 2d 526, 530 (E.D.N.C. 2008) (same); Wuchte v. McNeil, 130 N.C. App. 738, 740 (1998) (same); Woods v. City of Wilmington, 125 N.C. App. 226, 229 (1997) (same).

hire is completely within the employer's discretion. To put it starkly, where the at-will rule applies, employers may hire whomever they please, even if the person selected is unqualified or offensive.

The notion that the decision about whom to hire is completely within the employer's discretion is, however, qualified by the employment-at-will rule's status as a common law rule. Common law is made by the courts one decision at a time, with each decision building on decisions that came before it. At any time, however, a legislature may overrule a rule of common law by passing a statute to the contrary. The employment-at-will rule is thus subject to a number of exceptions that have been created by federal and state statutes. It is therefore more correct to say that under the employment-at-will rule, an employer may hire and fire employees for any reason or no reason at all—just not for a reason made unlawful by federal or state law.

Those sections of the North Carolina General Statutes that set forth who has the authority to hire in North Carolina local government and community colleges sometimes accord employees at-will status and other times make it lawful only to hire persons with certain credentials or by following certain procedures. These same statutes sometimes allow employers to hire at will but only permit termination of employees for good cause. The statutory sections applicable to each kind of local government and community college employer must be read carefully.

1.2 Hiring Authority in North Carolina Local Government

1.2.1 Hiring Authority in North Carolina Municipalities

1.2.1.1 The Mayor–Council Form of Government

G.S. 160A-155 states that the council in mayor–council cities shall appoint the heads of all city departments and all other city employees. Under the General Statutes, the mayor has no individual hiring authority. The council may, however, delegate to any administrative official or department head the power to make the hiring decisions for employees assigned to his or her department. The council also has the power to create offices, positions, and departments and to organize municipal government as it sees fit.[4] This

4. *See* G.S. 160A-146.

power includes the power to create a position not found in the General Statutes—namely, that of city, town, or village administrator—and to hire a person to fill the position. An administrator performs all of the functions that the council assigns to the position, and the council's delegation of authority may include the authority to hire, the authority to fire, or both. For cities with populations of 5,000 or more, neither the mayor nor any member of the council may serve as the head of any city department, even on an acting or interim basis.[5]

1.2.1.2 The Council–Manager Form of Government

G.S. 160A-147 authorizes a city council to appoint a city manager to serve at its pleasure. Irrespective of the size of the city, neither the mayor nor any member of the council may serve as the manager, on a permanent or temporary basis.[6] For cities with a city manager, the General Statutes delegate the authority to hire employees to the manager. G.S. 160A-148(1) provides that the city manager shall appoint, suspend, and remove all city officers and employees "who are not elected by the people and whose appointment or removal is not otherwise provided for by law" in accordance with such personnel rules as the council may adopt. City officers and employees whose appointment is otherwise provided for by law include the city attorney and, in some jurisdictions, the city clerk. The city council appoints the city attorney, who serves at its pleasure.[7] The General Statutes direct cities to appoint a city clerk but do not specify who is to appoint the clerk.[8] Instead, the hiring authority over the city clerk is usually found in the city charter, with some charters providing that the clerk serves at the pleasure of the council, while others grant hiring and firing authority to the manager.

A question that frequently arises is, what happens if the city council orders the manager to hire someone? The legal answer is a straightforward one. The city manager (like the county manager, discussed below) serves at the pleasure of the governing board—that is, the manager is an at-will employee. In the manager–council form of government, the council has

5. *See* G.S. 160A-158.

6. *See* G.S. 160A-151.

7. *See* G.S. 160A-173. Sometimes the city attorney's appointment is as a city employee; sometimes it is as an independent contractor on a retainer.

8. *See* G.S. 160A-171.

no authority to hire anyone other than the manager, the city clerk, the city attorney, and the city tax collector. The council therefore cannot hire the desired individual. As the supervisor of the manager, however, the council can request that the manager hire a particular person. That does not violate the way in which the General Statutes have delegated hiring authority. And, as a practical matter, if the manager hires someone other than the person desired by the council, the manager may well be fired: the council can fire the manager for any reason or no reason, just not for an unlawful reason. It would not be unlawful for the council to fire the manager because he or she did not hire the person the council desired. A savvy manager will probably do as the council suggests or directs.

1.2.2 Hiring Authority in North Carolina Counties

In counties that have adopted the manager form of government, the board of commissioners appoints the county manager, who serves at its pleasure, and the manager is vested with general hiring authority.[9] Although a city council member may not serve as city manager, the General Statutes permit a member of the board of commissioners to serve as county manager.[10] The county manager's hiring power is subject to the approval of the board of commissioners unless the board passes a resolution permitting the manager to act without first securing the board's approval.[11]

There are certain county officers and employees whose appointment and dismissal are required by law to be made by the board of commissioners, even in counties in which the county manager form of government has been adopted. The clerk of the board and the county attorney are appointed by the board and serve at its pleasure.[12] The tax collector is

---

9. *See* G.S. 153A-81 and G.S. 153A-82(1). As of this writing, all but one of North Carolina's one hundred counties have managers; Tyrrell County has an administrator rather than a manager. G.S. 153A-87 provides that in counties not having a county manager, the board of commissioners shall appoint, suspend, and remove all county officers, employees, and agents except those who are elected by the people or whose appointment is otherwise provided for by law.

10. *See* G.S. 153A-81.

11. *See* G.S. 153A-82(1).

12. *See* G.S. 153A-111 and G.S. 153A-114, respectively. As is the case with the city attorney, the county attorney may be a full-time county employee or an independent contractor with his or her own legal practice whose services are provided on a retainer.

a board appointee who serves for a term determined by the board.[13] The county assessor is a board appointee who serves a term of not less than two nor more than four years. The county assessor may in turn hire listers, appraisers, and clerical assistants.[14]

Unlike a city council and its manager, a board of county commissioners and its manager do not have hiring authority over all those who work for the county. The North Carolina General Statutes have established multiple hiring authorities within county government. Although many positions are under the control of the board of commissioners and the county manager, others are under the control of elected officials. Still others are under the control of various county boards and are subject to the State Personnel Act. This makes human resources administration at the county level more complicated than at the city level.

1.2.2.1 Hiring Authority of the Sheriff and the Register of Deeds

Article VII, Section 2, of the North Carolina Constitution provides that each county shall have a sheriff elected by the people for a four-year term. G.S. 153A-103(1) states that each sheriff has the exclusive right to hire, discharge, and supervise the employees in the sheriff's office, except that the board of commissioners must approve the appointment of a sheriff's relative or of a person convicted of a crime involving moral turpitude. Employees of the office of the sheriff are employees at will.

The register of deeds is also an elected officer, with a four-year term. As is the case with the sheriff, each register of deeds has the exclusive right to hire, discharge, and supervise the employees in the register of deeds' office, except that the board of commissioners must approve the appointment of a relative of the register of deeds or of a person convicted of a crime involving moral turpitude.[15] Employees of the office of the register of deeds are employees at will.

---

13. *See* G.S. 105-349(a).
14. *See* G.S. 105-296.
15. *See* G.S. 153A-103(1).

1.2.2.2 County Library Employees and County Board of Elections Employees

Public library employees are appointed either directly by the board of commissioners or, where the commissioners have appointed a library board of trustees and delegated hiring authority to it, by the library board. The board, not to exceed twelve members, is appointed by the board of commissioners for a term set by the county.[16] If the commissioners have granted hiring authority to the board, the trustees may appoint a chief librarian or a director of library services. The trustees appoint other library employees upon the advice of the chief librarian or the director of library services.[17] G.S. 153A-267 states that the employees of a county library system are, for all purposes, employees of the county.

County boards of elections are composed of three members appointed by the State Board of Elections for two-year terms. The board's clerk, assistant clerks, and other employees, including precinct transfer assistants, are appointed and dismissed by the county board of elections.[18] The county director of elections is appointed by the executive director of the State Board of Elections, upon recommendation by the county board of elections.[19]

1.2.2.3 County Employees Subject to the State Personnel Act

The State Personnel Act (found in Chapter 126 of the General Statutes) governs recruitment, selection, and dismissal in four county departments: health, social services, mental health, and emergency management. These departments receive federal funds that require the use of competitive recruitment and selection procedures as a condition for their receipt. Thus, these employees are sometimes called competitive service employees.

Health department employees are competitive service employees. They are appointed by the county or district health director in accordance with the rules of the State Personnel Commission.[20] The health director is also subject to G.S. Chapter 126 and is appointed by the county board of health in consultation with the board of commissioners.[21] A county board of

---

16. *See* G.S. 153A-265.
17. *See* G.S. 153A-266(4).
18. *See* G.S. 163-33(10).
19. *See* G.S. 163-35(a).
20. *See* G.S. 130A-41(b); G.S. 126-5(a).
21. *See* G.S. 130A-40.

health is composed of eleven members appointed by the board of commissioners to serve three-year terms.[22] A district health department including more than one county may be formed instead of county health departments, upon agreement of the county boards of commissioners and local boards of health having jurisdiction over each of the counties involved.[23]

Social services department employees are competitive service employees. They are appointed by the county director of social services in accordance with the rules of the State Personnel Commission.[24] The county director of social services is also subject to the State Personnel Act and is appointed by the county board of social services.[25] The county board of social services is composed of three or five members, appointed for three-year terms.[26]

Emergency management employees are the third and least well-defined group of county employees subject to the State Personnel Act. G.S. 166A-7(a) states that the governing body of each county is responsible for emergency management within the county and is authorized to establish and maintain an emergency management agency. This grant of authority is permissive, and counties are not required to establish a separate agency or department. Some counties have stand-alone departments, but the more common model is to have the emergency management function co-located with other public safety functions, such as 911, the emergency medical service (EMS), or the fire department (the emergency management function is not usually situated within county law enforcement because of the sheriff's status as an independently elected official).

The governing body of each county that establishes an emergency management agency is to appoint a coordinator who will have direct responsibility for the organization, administration, and operation of the county program and will be subject to the direction and guidance of the governing body.[27] Although the appointment of an emergency management coordinator is not required unless a county creates an emergency management agency, the practical effect of federal rules and regulations governing the use of funds for emergency management purposes has been that almost

22. *See* G.S. 130A-35.
23. *See* G.S. 130A-36.
24. *See* G.S. 108A-14(2).
25. *See* G.S. 108A-9 and G.S. 108A-12.
26. *See* G.S. 108A-1 through G.S. 108A-5.
27. *See* G.S. 166A-7(a)(2).

all of North Carolina's counties have appointed an emergency management coordinator.[28] Only about 25 percent of the coordinators spend all of their time on emergency management duties, however. The more common model is to appoint the head of 911, EMS, or the fire department as the emergency management coordinator.

The General Statutes do not specify who has the appointing authority over emergency management employees. Given the absence of a provision granting hiring authority to any other person or body, the county manager presumably has the hiring authority.

Whether or not county employees with emergency management duties are subject to the State Personnel Act depends upon whether their primary duties are in emergency management or another area.[29] County employees who have full-time emergency management duties or who work for a free-standing emergency management agency should be considered employees covered by the State Personnel Act. Employees whose primary duties are in another field and whose emergency management duties are incidental are not covered by the State Personnel Act.[30]

The State Personnel Act authorizes local governing boards that establish personnel systems in compliance with the federal standards attached to federal funding for health, social services, emergency management, and mental health activities to petition the Office of State Personnel for removal of employees working in those areas from the state system to their own

---

28. The North Carolina Division of Emergency Management requires all counties to designate an emergency management coordinator for operational purposes, and under federal regulations, that emergency management coordinator must be certified in the Incident Command System training requirements prescribed under the National Incident Management System (NIMS). Failure to comply with NIMS can subject a local government to loss of Emergency Management Preparedness Grant funds. In addition, G.S. 166A-7(e) ties the allocation of federal and state preparedness grant funding to whether local emergency management plans meet state and federal standards and to the professional competency of the local emergency management personnel. So, from a practical, operational, and grant funding standpoint, each county must appoint a qualified emergency management coordinator, but the way in which the county administratively organizes its emergency management functions is discretionary at the local level.

29. "Emergency management" is defined in G.S. 166A-4.

30. *See* Letter from Thomas H. Wright, State Personnel Director, to Weldon Freeman, Department of Crime Control and Public Safety, dated November 21, 2006, on file with the author.

system.[31] These county personnel systems are referred to as substantially equivalent systems, and the counties are referred to as substantially equivalent counties. The most important factor that the Office of State Personnel considers in deciding whether to grant a county substantially equivalent status is whether or not the proposed system is similar enough to the standards established by the State Personnel Commission as set forth in the North Carolina Administrative Code.[32]

When a county is granted substantial equivalency status, all of the human services agencies falling under the county's jurisdiction become subject to the county's policy. It is not possible for the county health department, for example, to be governed by the county's substantially equivalent policy while the county social services department remains under the State Personnel Act regulations. Counties may, however, petition for and be granted substantial equivalency in only a limited number of substantive areas of human resources administration. There are currently six areas for which counties may petition for substantial equivalency status: (1) recruitment, selection, and advancement; (2) classification and compensation; (3) training; (4) employee relations (discipline and dismissal); (5) equal employment opportunity/affirmative action; and (6) political activity.[33] County human services departments therefore may be subject to State Personnel Act rules in all areas; to county personnel rules in all areas (substantial equivalency); to county recruitment, selection, and promotion rules (substantial equivalency in recruitment, selection, and advancement) but to State Personnel Act rules with respect to other areas; or to State Personnel Act recruitment, selection, and promotion rules but to county rules with respect to other areas.

---

31. *See* G.S. 126-11.

32. The State Personnel Commission's rules governing local government employer departments subject to the State Personnel Act may be found at 25 N.C. ADMIN. CODE (hereinafter N.C.A.C.) 01I .1701–01I .2401.

33. *See* 25 N.C.A.C. 01I .2401–01I .2406.

1.2.2.4 Consolidated Human Services Agencies

G.S. 153A-77 authorizes counties to consolidate their health, social services, mental health, developmental disabilities, and substance abuse agencies into one county department of human services.[34] A consolidated human services agency is managed by a single human services director, who is appointed and supervised by the county manager with the advice and consent of a human services board appointed by the county commissioners.[35] The human services director then appoints all human services agency employees, subject to the approval of the county manager.[36] When a county consolidates its human services agencies pursuant to G.S. 153A-77, employees of the consolidated agency lose the protections of the State Personnel Act and become subject to county personnel policies.[37] To the extent that federal funds administered by consolidated human services agencies require the use of competitive recruitment and selection procedures, the board of commissioners will have to adopt such policies for human services employees, if not for all county employees.

1.2.3 Hiring Authority in Mental Health Area Authorities/Local Management Entities

Employees of a mental health, developmental disabilities, and substance abuse authority constitute another category of competitive service employees at the county level. An area authority, also referred to as a local management entity, is a multi-county entity that organizes and monitors the delivery of mental health, development disability, and substance abuse services. It is considered a local political subdivision of the state, although it depends upon the boards of commissioners of its constituent counties for funding.[38] The governing unit of the area authority is the area board,

34. As a practical matter, the current structure of mental health service delivery through multi-county area authorities will preclude the consolidation of mental health services into a single-county consolidated human services agency, except in Mecklenburg County, where mental health was consolidated into a single agency with health and social services in the past. *See* G.S. 153A-76(6) and G.S. 153A-77(c)(1a).

35. *See* G.S. 153A-77(b)(1), (e).

36. *See* G.S. 153A-77(e)(1).

37. *See* G.S. 153A-77(d).

38. However, a single-county area authority is considered a department of the county in which it is located for purposes of G.S. Chapter 159. *See* G.S. 122C-116.

composed of eleven to twenty-five members.[39] The area board appoints the director of the area mental health, developmental disabilities, and substance abuse authority.[40] The area director then appoints employees of the area authority.[41] In contrast to local health and social services directors, the area director is not covered by the State Personnel Act.[42] Other employees of the area authority, however, are subject to the State Personnel Act.

1.2.4 Hiring Authority in Other Kinds of Local Government Entities

North Carolina has a number of other forms of local government entities, including single-county or multi-jurisdiction water and sewer authorities, regional councils of government, and local alcohol and beverage control (ABC) boards. Appointed governing boards have ultimate responsibility for these agencies. The General Statutes grant each type of governing board authority to hire employees but do not impose any further structure on personnel administration and management within the organization.[43] In the absence of any provision in the General Statutes to the contrary, employees of water and sewer authorities, councils of government, and local ABC boards are employees at will.

1.3 Hiring Authority in North Carolina's Community Colleges

North Carolina's community colleges are entities of neither state nor local government. Instead, the operating authority and decision-making power of each community college is shared by the state (through the State Board of Community Colleges) and the county government or governments of the area in which the college is located. Authority to hire community college employees rests with the local community college board of trustees.[44] The trustees may, and most often do, delegate to the community college

---

39. *See* G.S. 122C-118.1(a).
40. *See* G.S. 122C-117(a)(7); G.S. 122C-121.
41. *See* G.S. 122C-121(c)(1); G.S. 122C-154; G.S. 126-5(a)(2).
42. *See* G.S. 122C-121(a).
43. *See* G.S. 162A-6(a)(11) (water and sewer authorities); G.S. 160A-475(2) (councils of government); G.S. 18B-701(c) (local ABC boards).
44. *See* G.S. 115D-20(1) and (2).

president (who is hired by the board) authority to hire the college's faculty, administrators, and staff.[45] The trustees are appointed by four different groups of stakeholders: the local board of education of the local public school administrative unit, the county commissioners of the county or counties in which the community college is located, the governor, and the student government of the community college.[46] Community college employees, both faculty and staff, are employees at will as there is no state statute granting them a legitimate expectation of continued employment along the lines of the tenure granted to public school teachers or University of North Carolina faculty members or along the lines of the State Personnel Act as it applies to employees of county health, social services, mental health, and emergency management personnel. Most community colleges do, however, employ faculty and staff under a contract for a definite term, usually one-year.

1.4 Laws Affecting the Process of Recruitment and Selection

Throughout both the United States Code (the compilation of federal laws passed by Congress) and the North Carolina General Statutes are a number of provisions that are important for the hiring process. Many of these provisions will be discussed elsewhere in this book, but a brief overview is appropriate here.

1.4.1 The Fair Credit Reporting Act

Although it is not obvious from its name, the federal Fair Credit Reporting Act (FCRA) imposes a number of duties on employers who do background checks on their applicants and employees. The FCRA limits the use of commercially prepared reports about individuals in order to protect people's privacy. It governs the use of any kind of report, whether about a person's credit history, criminal background, or general reputation in the community, when it is sold by a person or company in the business of assembling such information for a third party, such as an employer. The FCRA requires

45. *See* G.S. 115D-20(2).
46. *See* G.S. 115D-12.

both public and private employers using third parties to conduct any type of background check to obtain written permission from the applicant or employee before the investigation is done and to provide notice when someone's application for employment or promotion is rejected on the basis of information discovered through the background investigation.[47] Employer obligations under the FCRA are discussed in greater detail in Section 8.3 of Chapter 8, which covers background checks.

1.4.2 The Immigration Reform and Control Act

The federal Immigration Reform and Control Act (IRCA) governs the last step in the hiring process; namely, checking that the person selected for an open position is authorized to work in the United States. The IRCA subjects both public and private employers to civil and criminal liability for knowingly employing an individual who is not authorized to work in the United States. The act requires employers to verify employment eligibility and identity documents for each employee and to record the document information on the Eligibility Verification Form, also known as the I-9 form, within three days of each employee's date of employment.[48] Employers must complete and retain the I-9 form for all employees, including those who are U.S. citizens, for three years after the date of hire or one year after the date of employment ends, whichever is later.[49]

1.4.3 North Carolina's E-Verify Requirement

In 2006, the North Carolina General Assembly enacted legislation requiring the state's community colleges to use the federal E-Verify program to verify the work authorization of new employees.[50] In 2011, it extended that requirement to all North Carolina cities and counties.[51] Other forms of local government employers, however, are not required to use E-Verify.

E-Verify is a free, web-based system operated by the Department of Homeland Security in partnership with the Social Security Administration that allows employers to electronically check the information in an

47. The Fair Credit Reporting Act is codified at 15 U.S.C. §§ 1681–1681x.

48. *See* 8 C.F.R. §§ 274a.2(b)(1)(i), (ii) (2008).

49. *See* 8 U.S.C. § 1324a(h)(3) (2000).

50. *See* G.S. 126-7.1(i).

51. *See* G.S. 160A-169.1 and G.S. 153A-99.1, respectively.

employee's I-9 form against federal databases to verify that newly hired employees are authorized to work. This book does not contain an in-depth discussion of the requirements of the IRCA and the requirement to use E-Verify, as that information may be found in other School of Government publications.[52]

1.4.4 The Law Protecting the Lawful Use of Lawful Products

The General Statutes prohibit discrimination in employment against persons who engage in "the lawful use of lawful products . . . off the premises of the employer during nonworking hours," provided that the use of such a product does not interfere with the employee's job performance.[53] Although it does not identify a product by name, the focus of the statute appears to be tobacco use. A North Carolina employer, whether public or private, cannot refuse to hire or discriminate against a person who smokes tobacco.

Given that employers may prohibit the use of tobacco during working hours spent on the employer's premises, why would an employer want to reject applicants who smoke? The primary reason an employer might want to implement a policy of hiring only nonsmokers is that smokers tend to have higher rates of illness and may increase an employer's health care claims experience rating. That employers may have legitimate concerns about absenteeism and about the health insurance costs they may incur on behalf of smokers does not provide a defense to a discrimination claim under the lawful use of lawful products statute. Instead, the statute expressly allows an employer to offer health, disability, and life insurance policies with differing contribution costs for smokers and nonsmokers (or, as the statute puts it, "based on the use or nonuse of lawful products") if each of three requirements is met; namely, that the differential contribution rates charged employees reflect actuarially justified difference in the cost of employee benefits, that the employer provide employees with written notice

52. *See* Sejal Zota, *Immigration Enforcement in the Workplace: Form I-9, E-Verify and Social Security No-Match Letters: A Brief Guide for North Carolina Public Employers*, Public Employment Law Bulletin No. 36, March 2009, http://sogpubs.unc.edu/electronicversions/pdfs/pelb36.pdf; Sejal Zota, *What Does the 2011 E-Verify Legislation Mean for Local Governments and Employers?*, Immigration Law Bulletin No. 3, July 2011, http://sogpubs.unc.edu/electronicversions/pdfs/ilb03.pdf.

53. *See* G.S. 95-28.2(b).

of the differential rates, and that the employer contribute an equal amount for smokers and nonsmokers as its share of the premium contribution.[54]

1.4.5 North Carolina's Requirement of United States Selective Service Registration

G.S. 143B-421.1 requires all North Carolina public employers to inquire of each applicant for employment whether the applicant is required to and has registered with the United States Selective Service (otherwise known as registering for the draft).[55] Those who are required to register but have not done so are ineligible for public employment at either the state or local government level.

1.4.6 North Carolina's Defense against Civil Liability for Truthful Job References

Many employers, both public and private, will not provide substantive job references because they fear that a former employee may sue them for defamation if they say anything that is other than laudatory. G.S. 1-539.12 was enacted to give employers a safe harbor when giving job references and to encourage the exchange of honest information about employee performance. To this end, G.S. 1-539.12 limits the liability of an employer for defamation when it discloses information to a prospective employer about a current or former employee's job history or job performance unless the employer knows or reasonably should have known that the information it has disclosed is false. The term "job performance" includes the suitability of the employee for re-employment; the employee's skills, abilities, and traits as they relate to suitability for future employment; and in the case of former employees, the reason for separation.

1.4.7 North Carolina's Prohibition against Requiring Applicants to Pay the Cost of Exams or Records

Many employers would like to charge applicants for the cost of the medical examinations and records that they require, as those charges add up quickly when the employer is filling multiple positions. G.S. 14-357.1, however, expressly prohibits employers with twenty-five or more employees from doing so.

---

54. *See* G.S. 95-28.2(d).

55. *See* 50 U.S.C. App. § 453 (Military Selective Service Act).

It is unclear whether G.S. 14-357.1 applies to public employers. In subsection (a), the statute says that

> It shall be unlawful for any employer, as defined in subsection (b) of this section, to require any applicant for employment, as defined in subsection (c), to pay the cost of a medical examination or the cost of furnishing any records required by the employer as a condition of the initial act of hiring.

Subsection (b) defines "employer" in a fairly limited way that does not expressly include the state or its political subdivisions. Subsection (b) says that "employer"

> shall mean and include an individual, a partnership, an association, a corporation, a legal representative, trustee, receiver, trustee in bankruptcy, and any common carrier by rail, motor, water, air, or express company, doing business in or operating within the State.

Violation of the statute carries a penalty of $100 for each violation. Given that medical examinations are likely to cost in excess of $100, public employers should consult their attorneys for advice on whether or not they must comply with the statute.

Chapter 2

Discrimination Law in the Recruitment and Selection Context

Chapter 2

Discrimination Law in the Recruitment and Selection Context

Federal antidiscrimination laws put the most significant limitations on the way in which North Carolina public employers may seek and choose new employees. Indeed, from a legal perspective, much of the process of recruitment and selection revolves around ensuring that those involved in the hiring decision do not engage in unlawful discrimination—either intentionally or unintentionally—and in defending against the possibility that job applicants will perceive discrimination where there is none. Five federal statutes prohibit discrimination in public and private employment on nine different bases. Four state statutes prohibit discrimination in public and private employment on those same nine bases. For public employers, the Equal Protection Clause of the Fourteenth Amendment to the U.S. Constitution also prohibits them, as government entities, from treating different classes of people differently.

This second chapter is a comprehensive look at the laws that protect applicants from discrimination during the hiring process. The law is extensive and sometimes complex. Because many of the specific issues in recruitment and selection discussed later in this book require a basic understanding of these statutes and of the Equal Protection Clause, readers should familiarize themselves with the principles of antidiscrimination law before proceeding further. Because not everyone will need to understand this area of the law in the same depth, the treatment of each of the federal statutes is divided into introductory and more in-depth discussions of the law.

2.1 Title VII of the Civil Rights Act of 1964: Prohibition against Hiring Decisions Made on the Basis of Race, Color, Gender, Religion, or National Origin

2.1.1 Disparate Treatment or Intentional Discrimination in Hiring: The Basic Theory

Title VII of the Civil Rights Act of 1964 prohibits discrimination on the basis of race, color, gender, religion, and national origin. Codified at 42 U.S.C. § 2000e-2, it provides:

> It shall be an unlawful employment practice for an employer—(1) to fail or refuse to hire or to discharge any individual, or otherwise to discriminate against any individual with respect to his compensation, terms, conditions, or privileges of employment, because of such individual's race, color, religion, sex, or national origin.[1]

The categories of race, color, religion, gender, and national origin are referred to as protected classes. When an employer fails to hire or discharges someone because of their race, for example, employment lawyers say that the employer is discriminating against them because of their membership in a protected class or in the protected class of African Americans, Caucasians, or Asians, as the case may be. The law refers to this as disparate treatment discrimination. Disparate treatment discrimination is the *intentional* decision not to hire (or to fire) a person because of membership in a particular protected class.

How does an applicant or employee prove that an employer intentionally discriminated against him or her because of race, color, gender, or other protected characteristic? These days it is the rare employer who states frankly, "I did not hire Susan Sullivan because she is a woman," or "We didn't even bother to read the applications from African American candidates." In the absence of direct and indisputable evidence such as this, plaintiffs must prove intent through circumstantial evidence—that is, evidence from which a fact finder may infer discrimination. In a series of cases, the United States Supreme Court developed a structure of proof for use in disparate treatment cases dependent on circumstantial rather than

---

1. *See* 42 U.S.C. § 2000e-2(a)(1). Title VII applies to employers with 15 or more employees.

direct evidence. A plaintiff establishes a prima facie case[2] of discrimination in hiring when he or she demonstrates that

1. he or she belongs to a protected class;
2. he or she applied and was qualified for a job for which the employer was seeking applicants;
3. despite his or her qualifications, he or she was rejected; and
4. after the rejection, the position remained open and the employer continued to seek applicants from persons with similar qualifications.[3]

This structure of proof is usually referred to by the name of the case which gave rise to it, *McDonnell Douglas Corp. v. Green*. A plaintiff who has made this very limited showing is said to have established a *McDonnell Douglas* prima facie case, and the burden of introducing evidence then shifts to the employer.

If the employer does nothing in response to the plaintiff's prima facie case, the court will presume intentional discrimination and a violation of law on the part of the employer. To avoid such a result, the employer must put forward a legitimate, nondiscriminatory reason why this plaintiff was rejected.[4] Legitimate nondiscriminatory reasons include failure to meet the minimum qualifications for the position,[5] lack of experience or required certifications,[6] poor professional and personal references,[7] or a lackluster

---

2. "Prima facie" may be translated as "at first blush," so in this context, a prima facie case is a case in which it appears that discrimination has occurred absent evidence to the contrary.

3. *See* McDonnell Douglas Corp. v. Green, 411 U.S. 792, 802 (1973); Price v. Thompson, 380 F.3d 209, 212 (4th Cir. 2004); EEOC v. Sears Roebuck & Co., 243 F.3d 846, 851–52 (4th Cir. 2001).

4. Tex. Dep't of Cmty. Affairs v. Burdine, 450 U.S. 248, 254 (1981); *Sears Roebuck*, 243 F.3d at 851–52.

5. *See, e.g.*, Dixon v. Pulaski Cnty. Special Sch. Dist., 578 F.3d 862, 868 (8th Cir. 2009) (applicant for position of buyer did not meet minimum qualifications), *abrogated by* Torgerson v. City of Rochester, 643 F.3d 1031 (8th Cir. 2011); Ramirez v. Kroonen, 44 F. App'x 212, 215 (9th Cir. 2002) (applicant's lack of high school diploma or GED was a legitimate, nondiscriminatory reason for rejecting his application).

6. *See, e.g.*, *Price*, 380 F.3d at 215–17.

7. *See, e.g.*, Grier v. Injured Workers' Ins. Fund, 2 F. App'x 386, 387 (4th Cir. 2001) (concern about applicant's prior employment history was legitimate, nondiscriminatory reason for rejecting applicant); Terrell v. Contra Costa Cnty., 232 F. App'x 626

performance in a personal interview.[8] Sometimes the legitimate, nondiscriminatory reason is simply that the employer preferred the package of experience, qualifications, and self-presentation that another candidate offered.[9] This list is not meant to be exclusive; it merely illustrates the types

---

(9th Cir. 2007) (legitimate, nondiscriminatory reason for promoting white applicant to fire inspector over African American firefighter was that white firefighter had law enforcement certification); Strong v. Paulson, 249 F. App'x 470, 472–73 (7th Cir. 2007) (applicant's falsehoods about prior experience provided legitimate, nondiscriminatory reason for not hiring him).

8. *See, e.g.*, Conner v. Lafarge N. Am., Inc., 343 F. App'x 537, 541 (11th Cir. 2009) (applicant's poor performance in those portions of the interview dealing with leadership, decision making, safety, and computer skills was a legitimate, nondiscriminatory reason for his rejection); Johnson v. City of Mobile, Ala., 321 F. App'x 826, 833 (11th Cir. 2009) (applicant rejected because she was tentative and lacked self-confidence during interview); Joseph v. City of Dallas, 277 F. App'x 436, 440 (5th Cir. 2008) (applicant rejected because he gave poor answers to the hypothetical police scenarios and seemed unable to logically process information during interview); *Strong*, 249 F. App'x at 471 (applicant's responses in interview lacked substance, were not responsive, were rambling, and appeared inconsistent with the experience listed on his resume); Chapman v. AI Transp., 229 F.3d 1012, 1028 (11th Cir. 2000) (plaintiff's poor interview performance was subjective, but legitimate, nondiscriminatory reason for rejection).

9. *See, e.g.*, *Price*, 380 F.3d 209, 215 (4th Cir. 2004) (selecting official's proffered reasons for not hiring one of the most qualified applicants for Biomedical Engineering Technician position—that he was less experienced, especially with laboratory equipment; that he was not certified; that he was not currently working in field; that he had experienced break in service and might require extra training; and that he wanted to redefine position—were legitimate); Davis v. NPC Pizza Hut, 226 F. App'x 890, 891 (11th Cir. 2007) (employer articulated a legitimate, nondiscriminatory reason for promoting successful applicant rather than plaintiff where plaintiff had more years of experience with the company but the successful applicant met the internal minimum qualifications, had years of experience managing multiple restaurants for another company, and had owned and managed several of her own restaurants); Waris v. Heartland Home Healthcare Servs., Inc., 365 F. App'x 402, 405 (3d Cir. 2010) (where candidates both met minimum qualifications, but one had longer work experience and the other had more current work experience, differences were not so disparate that a fact finder could not find that selected candidate was better choice for the job). Courts are emphatic that it is not their role to judge the wisdom of the decisions ultimately made; their role is to ensure that discrimination was not the reason: "We do not sit as a 'super-personnel department weighing the prudence of employment decisions.'" *See* Anderson v. Westinghouse Savannah River Co., 406 F.3d 248, 272 (4th Cir. 2005); Holdcraft v. Cnty. of Fairfax, Va., 31 F. App'x 97, 99 (4th Cir. 2002) (candidate's failure to rank among top three candidates in scores compiled by using objective and subjective criteria was legitimate, nondiscriminatory reason for not hiring him); Bius v.

of reasons that the courts have found legitimate and nondiscriminatory. Legitimate and nondiscriminatory reasons are as varied and nuanced as the positions and the workplaces in which they are found.

Once an employer does offer a legitimate, nondiscriminatory explanation for failing to hire the plaintiff, the case ends unless the plaintiff brings forth evidence that the reasons offered by the employer were not its true reasons but a pretext for discrimination.[10] This evidence is almost always circumstantial. Mere evidence of pretext does not require a verdict for the applicant. Not only must the judge or jury believe that the employer is not being straightforward or truthful about its reasons for rejecting the plaintiff's application, they must also believe the plaintiff's explanation—that the reason for the employer's lack of forthrightness and for its failure to hire the plaintiff is intentional discrimination on the basis of membership in a protected class.[11] Examples of circumstantial evidence of discrimination include an employer requiring the plaintiff to complete certain application steps not required of other applicants, making but then withdrawing a job offer without explanation, and unevenly applying employment criteria to the disadvantage of the applicant.[12]

Thompson, 2003 WL 1348221 at *5 (M.D.N.C. June 14, 2004) (court would not second-guess employer's conclusion that plaintiff's teaching skills were less effective than her competitor's for the position); Duffy v. Belk Inc., 2011 WL 2489931 at **5 (W.D.N.C. June 21, 2011) (plaintiff's disagreement with wisdom of management's business judgment and his belief that he was better qualified to assume new, combined position after reorganization is not evidence of discrimination).

10. *See* Tex. Dep't of Cmty. Affairs v. Burdine, 450 U.S. 248, 253 (1981); EEOC v. Sears Roebuck & Co., 243 F.3d 846, 851–52 (4th Cir. 2001).

11. *See* Reeves v. Sanderson Plumbing Prods., Inc., 530 U.S. 133 (2000); St. Mary's Honor Ctr. v. Hicks, 509 U.S. 502, 519 (1993); Price v. Thompson, 380 F.3d 209, 215–17 (4th Cir. 2004) (unsuccessful applicant for position with National Institutes of Health failed to show that selecting official's proffered legitimate, nonretaliatory reasons for refusal to hire him for Biomedical Engineering Technician position were pretext to retaliate against him for filing Equal Employment Opportunity (EEO) complaint; inconsistencies in selecting official's positions were explained by his nervousness at deposition and fact it was his first time dealing with an EEO complaint, and at most applicant could demonstrate that selecting official was wrong about applicant's lack of certification and was misled by application as to applicant's level of experience).

12. *See, e.g.*, Raad v. Fairbanks N. Star Borough Sch. Dist., 323 F.3d 1185, 1195 (9th Cir. 2003), *opinion amended on denial of reh'g*, 2003 WL 21027351 (9th Cir. 2003) (different treatment than other candidates); Widoe v. Dist. No. 111 Otoe Cnty. Sch., 147 F.3d 726 (8th Cir. 1998) (same). *See also* Kobrin v. Univ. of Minn., 34 F.3d 698, 703

Title VII requires that all complaints of employment discrimination be filed with the United States Equal Employment Opportunity Commission (EEOC) before applicants or employees may bring suit in federal court.[13] The EEOC investigates claims of employment discrimination and issues a nonbinding finding to the effect that it is reasonably likely that discrimination did—or did not—occur.[14] Once the EEOC has issued that finding, or where the EEOC has not issued a finding within 180 days, the applicant or employee receives a so-called right-to-sue letter that allows him or her to proceed with a lawsuit in federal court.[15] The EEOC also attempts to mediate the dispute between the parties where possible.[16] Sometimes the EEOC itself will bring suit against an employer on behalf of the rejected applicant or discharged employee.[17]

Title VII applies to all local government entities and community colleges with 15 or more employees.[18]

2.1.2 Disparate Treatment or Intentional Discrimination in Making Promotions

Employees who believe that they have been denied a promotion on the basis of race, color, gender, religion, or national origin may also bring Title VII disparate treatment claims. In the absence of direct evidence of discrimination—for example, a statement by a supervisor that she did not consider Lucy for the promotional position because Lucy is a Muslim—the same *McDonnell Douglas* burden-shifting framework applies as would in a failure-to-hire case.[19] To establish her prima facie case, Lucy would have to show that (1) she was a Muslim, a protected class; (2) that she was qualified for the promotional position; (3) that she was denied the promotional posi-

---

(8th Cir. 1994) (substantial changes over time in the employer's proffered reason for its employment decision support a finding of pretext).

13. *See* 42 U.S.C. §§ 2000e-4 and 2000e-5; 29 C.F.R. §§ 1601.6(a) and 1601.7(a).

14. *See* 29 C.F.R. §§ 1601.15, 1601.19, and 1601.21.

15. *See* 29 C.F.R. § 1601.28.

16. *See* 42 U.S.C. § 2000e-4(g)(4); 29 C.F.R. §§ 1601.20 and 1601.24.

17. *See* 42 U.S.C. § 2000e-5(f); 29 C.F.R. § 1601.27.

18. *See* 42 U.S.C. § 2000e(b). Strictly speaking, Title VII only covers government employers who have 15 or more employees "for each working day in each of twenty or more calendar weeks in the current or preceding calendar year."

19. *See* Dennis v. Columbia Colleton Med. Ctr., Inc., 290 F.3d 639, 646 (4th Cir. 2002).

tion; and (4) that the employer either continued to seek persons with the same qualifications for the position or that the employer placed someone into the promotional position who had the same qualifications and was not a Muslim.

Once Lucy established her prima facie case, her employer would have the burden of showing that it had a legitimate nondiscriminatory reason for not promoting her. If her employer met that burden, Lucy would have to prove that the nondiscriminatory reason was a pretext and that the real reason that she was not promoted was religious discrimination.

2.1.3 Mixed Motives: When Discrimination Is Only One Factor in a Decision Not to Hire or Promote

Sometimes consideration of race, color, gender, religion, or national origin is only one factor in a decision not to hire an applicant—or only one reason why an applicant believes she or he was not hired. Title VII provides that even if consideration of protected class status is only one part of a negative hiring decision, the employer is liable for discrimination:

> Except as otherwise provided in this subchapter, an unlawful employment practice is established when the complaining party demonstrates that race, color, religion, sex, or national origin was *a motivating factor* for any employment practice, *even though other factors also motivated the practice* (emphasis added).[20]

A mixed-motive case may be proved through either direct or circumstantial evidence.[21] Employers may defend themselves against mixed-motive claims of discrimination by showing that they would have rejected the applicant even in the absence of the unlawful discrimination. This absolves the employer from liability for monetary damages for lost wages, front pay, and emotional distress and punitive damages, as well as from orders to hire the employee. The employer may still be liable for declaratory or

20. See 42 U.S.C. § 2000e-2(m), which codifies the Civil Rights Act of 1991 modifications of the U.S. Supreme Court's holding on mixed-motive cases in *Price-Waterhouse v. Hopkins*, 490 U.S. 228, 258 (1989).

21. *See* Desert Palace, Inc. v. Costa, 539 U.S. 90, 101-102 (2003).

injunctive relief (such as an order not to consider an impermissible factor in the future) and for the plaintiff's attorney fees.[22]

2.1.4 The Bona Fide Occupational Qualification Defense to a Charge of Disparate Treatment or Intentional Discrimination

Employers sometimes require that applicants be male or female, or of a certain religion or national origin, in order to be considered for particular positions. For example, a sheriff might prefer male jailers for positions involving supervision of male prisoners and female jailers for positions involving supervision of female prisoners. A public works director might want to hire men for sanitation and roadwork crews because the director does not think women are capable of lifting the weight necessary to do these jobs. A county social services or health department might want only caseworkers or nurses of Latino background to work in outreach programs directed toward Mexican immigrants. Restaurants such as Hooters and Playboy clubs are known to prefer an all-female wait staff because those businesses use sexual allure as a theme to attract their predominantly male clientele.[23]

With a few exceptions, preferences like those in the examples above are unlawful. For an employer to make hiring decisions based on preferences like these would violate Title VII. But where it is *necessary* for a particular business or organization to hire employees based on religion, sex, or national origin, an employer may defend itself against a disparate treatment claim by asserting what is known as the bona fide occupational qualification, or BFOQ, defense. The BFOQ defense gets its name from the text of the Title VII provision in which it is recognized. Title VII provides that

> it shall not be an unlawful employment practice for an employer to hire and employ employees . . . on the basis of his religion, sex, or national origin in those certain instances where *religion, sex, or national origin is a bona fide occupational qualification* reasonably necessary to the normal operation of that particular business or enterprise . . . .[24] (emphasis added)

---

22. *See* 42 U.S.C. § 2000e-5(g)(2)(b).

23. On Hooters' justification for its hiring policies, see the corporate statement on its website: www.hooters.com/About.aspx. Several employment discrimination lawsuits brought by male applicants against Hooters have settled out of court.

24. *See* 42 U.S.C. § 2000e-2(e)(1).

Title VII does *not* make the BFOQ defense available as a defense to charges of race or color discrimination. In practice, the BFOQ defense is rarely used in the context of religious discrimination because those entities that discriminate on the basis of an applicant's religion tend to be religiously affiliated employers, who are entitled to an independent exemption from Title VII's nondiscrimination mandate as it applies to religion.[25]

The employer bears the burden of proof when it asserts a BFOQ defense. It must prove by a preponderance of the evidence that (1) the job qualification justifying the discrimination is reasonably necessary to the existence of its business; (2) gender or national origin is a legitimate proxy for qualification because either (a) it has a substantial basis for believing that all or nearly all members of the protected class lack the qualification, or (b) it is impossible or highly impractical to ensure by individual testing that its employees will have the necessary qualifications for the job.[26]

The use of the BFOQ defense in response to a claim of age discrimination is discussed below in Section 2.2.1.

2.1.5 A Closer Look at Title VII Disparate Treatment or Intentional Discrimination

2.1.5.1 Equal Employment Opportunity Commission v. Sears Roebuck and Co.: *A Successful Disparate Treatment Failure-to-Hire Case*

Although the employer in the case *Equal Employment Opportunity Commission v. Sears Roebuck and Co.*[27] is a private employer, the case is a good example of one in which the plaintiff both makes his prima facie case and convinces the jury that the employer's proffered nondiscriminatory reason for its failure to hire him is pretext and that the real reason he was rejected for the position was unlawful discrimination.

The *Sears Roebuck* case was a Title VII national origin discrimination case. Francisco Santana, the plaintiff, was a naturalized U.S. citizen who had been born in Mexico. Although he had graduated from high school in the United States and was a member of the Marine Corps, Santana retained

25. *See* 42 U.S.C. §§ 2000e-1(a) and 2000e-2(e)(2).

26. *See* Burwell v. Eastern Air Lines, Inc., 633 F.2d 36, 369 n.10 (4th Cir. 1980) (gender discrimination); Arritt v. Grisell, 567 F.2d 1267, 1271 (4th Cir. 1977) (in context of age discrimination); Brenier v. Nev. Dep't of Corr., 610 F.3d 1202, 1210 (9th Cir. 2010) (gender BFOQ in prison context).

27. EEOC v. Sears Roebuck & Co., 243 F.3d 846 (4th Cir. 2001).

a Mexican accent. Santana had worked as a part-time loss prevention agent at Sears for the entire length of a ten-year posting at a Marine Corps base in California. When he was transferred to the Marine Corps Air Station at Cherry Point, North Carolina, Santana applied for work as a part-time loss prevention agent at the Sears store in Morehead City. Although he received a transfer form from Sears in California and was assured by the Morehead City store that they were interested in hiring him as a part-time loss prevention agent, and despite his repeated calls to the Morehead City store, it was 10 months before the store called Santana for an interview.

During Santana's interview, the human resources specialist commented on his accent, which was also noted by the store's operations manager. The Morehead City store nonetheless offered him a loss-prevention position and told him that he could start as soon as he took his pre-employment drug test. Santana took the drug test the next day and passed. Santana heard nothing for more than a month, despite making repeated inquiries. Finally, he was told that Sears had hired someone else and that the store could not afford a second loss-prevention position. The person hired in Santana's stead was a Caucasian woman without any loss-prevention experience. Santana filed a charge of national origin discrimination with the EEOC.[28]

The EEOC ultimately filed suit against Sears in federal district court. Before the case proceeded to trial, Sears filed a motion for summary judgment, which the district court judge granted. Summary judgment is a pretrial motion that may be brought by either the plaintiff or the defendant or both and asserts that the parties do not disagree on or dispute any of the relevant or material facts in the case. When there are no material facts in dispute, the case does not need to go before a jury for fact-finding and the case can be resolved by having the judge apply the law to the undisputed facts.

Here, the judge found that the EEOC had established a case of national origin discrimination on behalf of Santana.[29] In other words, the court found that Santana had shown that he was Mexican American, that he had applied for a loss-prevention position with the Sears Morehead City store for which there was an opening, that he was qualified for the position by virtue of his ten years of loss-prevention experience with Sears in

---

28. For the underlying facts of the case, see *Sears Roebuck*, 243 F.3d at 847–49.
29. *See Sears Roebuck*, 243 F.3d at 851.

California, and that he was rejected and a white person had been hired instead. In response, Sears had offered as its legitimate, nondiscriminatory reason for not hiring Santana the fact that a Sears regional manager had heard that a loss-prevention agent in California had had sexual harassment issues and that the Morehead City store manager had mistakenly assumed that the loss-prevention agent in question was Santana. Note that while the regional manager's behavior was both callous and careless in that he did not check to see whether the agent with harassment issues was indeed Santana (and California is a big state with a lot of Sears stores), it was not, on its face, discriminatory.

In granting Sears' motion for summary judgment, the judge found that the parties did not disagree on the material facts in the case. He further found that the EEOC had not proven that Sears' stated reason was pretextual and that the most likely reason for its failure to hire Santana was unlawful discrimination.[30] The judge so held despite the fact that Sears' stated reason was not the only reason it had offered. Between the time that Santana filed his EEOC charge and the time the case came before the district court judge, Sears had also proffered as explanation that the Morehead City store had been unable to contact Santana about his application, that the operations manager was not aware of Santana's earlier inquiries and application, that Sears had simply chosen someone else, and that there was a lack of available hours in the loss-prevention department—before settling on the explanation that store managers had misidentified Santana as the person involved with sexual harassment accusations in one of the California stores.[31]

On appeal, the Fourth Circuit Court of Appeals reversed the grant of summary judgment to Sears. The court found that there were material facts in dispute—in particular, whether the Sears manager's claim about thinking Santana was the agent who had engaged in sexual harassment was the real reason for its rejection of him. The court found that there was "ample evidence" from which a jury could find that Sears' asserted legitimate, nondiscriminatory reason for not hiring Santana was false.[32] There was also evidence from which a jury could conclude, as a disparate

30. *See Sears Roebuck*, 243 F.3d at 851.
31. *See Sears Roebuck*, 243 F.3d at 849–51, 852.
32. *See Sears Roebuck*, 243 F.3d at 852–53.

treatment or intentional discrimination case requires, that national origin discrimination was the real reason that Sears rejected him.[33] As the court noted, the *McDonnell Douglas* framework for proving intentional discrimination did not require direct evidence of anti-Latino feeling. Nor did the fact that Sears had hired Latinos into other positions require a finding that Sears had not engaged in national origin discrimination.[34]

2.1.5.2 Wesley v. Arlington County: *A Successful Failure-to-Promote Case*

The Fourth Circuit case *Wesley v. Arlington County* is an example of an intentional discrimination claim based on the employer's failure to promote the plaintiff.[35] This case provides an example in the public employment context. The plaintiff in this case, Tiffanye Wesley, was a female African American firefighter. She was employed by the Arlington County (Virginia) Fire Department, where she rode a fire truck, served as a training center instructor, and held various administrative roles, including community relations and building inspection. When Wesley applied for promotion to the position of captain, she met all of the minimum objective criteria for appointment to that rank.

The Arlington County Fire Department had a three-step promotional process. First, applicants meeting the minimum qualifications with respect to years of experience and education took a written examination. Those scoring highest on the written examination proceeded to an assessment center that tested applicants' practical job-related skills. The human resources department then certified those scoring highest on the assessment center tests as qualified for promotion and forwarded a list of finalists to the fire chief. The relative strengths and weaknesses of these finalists were then discussed by the chief and a panel of senior fire department officers. The chief made the final decision about whom to promote.

Wesley twice scored highly on both the written examinations and the assessment center tests and was twice certified to the list of those eligible for promotion to captain. During the four years that she was on the certified list, she was never promoted. Wesley filed a claim of race and gender discrimination against Arlington County.[36]

---

33. *See* EEOC v. Sears Roebuck Co., 243 F.3d at 854.
34. *See Sears Roebuck*, 243 F.3d at 855.
35. *See* Wesley v. Arlington Cnty., 354 F. App'x 775 (4th Cir. 2009).
36. For the underlying facts of the case, see *Wesley*, 354 F. App'x at 776–78.

The federal district court granted summary judgment to Arlington County, finding that Wesley had failed to make a prima facie case of discrimination in that she had failed to show that she was qualified for the position of captain. Wesley argued that her placement on the certified list of those eligible for promotion to captain satisfied her burden of showing that she was qualified for promotion for the purposes of establishing a prima facie case of discrimination. The county argued and the court agreed that certification to the eligibility list was merely a preliminary step and that to be truly qualified the applicant had to have considerable experience in the fire department, considerable knowledge of fire department practices, interpersonal skills, and problem-solving skills.[37] But even if Wesley had made a prima facie case, the court found, she had failed to show that the county's legitimate, nondiscriminatory reasons for not promoting her—that those promoted had more experience and better skills and that senior fire officers found fault with her performance—were false.[38]

On appeal, the Fourth Circuit disagreed with the district court and reversed the grant of summary judgment. The Fourth Circuit noted that some of the additional factors cited by the county as necessary for "true" qualification were duplicative of the threshold requirements for taking the captain's exam:

> "Considerable experience," for example, is reflected in the minimum years of service required to sit for the test, while "considerable knowledge" and "problem solving skills" are indicated by an applicant's success on the written and assessment center portions of the promotional process. "Interpersonal skills" is a vague and subjective criterion, perhaps best measured by an applicant's standing in the eyes of her peers, supervisors and subordinates; the record includes multiple instances of Wesley's superiors praising her interactions with both coworkers and the public.[39]

In addition to her success in the testing stages, Wesley gained generally positive performance reviews. She also served as an acting captain on

37. *See Wesley*, 354 F. App'x at 779.
38. *See Wesley*, 354 F. App'x at 778, 780–81.
39. *See Wesley*, 354 F. App'x at 779.

numerous occasions, apparently without incident, thus demonstrating she could in fact perform the duties required of the position.[40]

In the Fourth Circuit's judgment, Wesley had clearly established that she was qualified for the position of captain for the purposes of her prima facie case. Whether she was the best qualified person for the position was up to her to prove after the county met its burden of putting forth a legitimate, nondiscriminatory reason for its failure to promote her. Here, the Fourth Circuit found that although the county's reasons—that Wesley was not as experienced and capable as the candidates chosen for promotion and that there were problems with her performance—were plausible enough to meet its burden under the *McDonnell Douglas* framework, Wesley had raised enough question of fact about whether these reasons were pretexts for discrimination for summary judgment to be inappropriate and for the decision to be made by a jury.[41] The court noted that Wesley had as much real firefighting experience as the white males who were promoted. The evidence also showed that her training academy experience was traditionally considered operations experience and had in the past been a steppingstone for white males who were promoted to captain. The department had destroyed records relating to the chief's roundtable discussions about the candidates eligible for promotion, but the testimony of those who had attended was divided about whether the chief actually discussed any of the qualifications and certifications that the county now held forth as being important to the decision to promote.[42]

As for the county's second nondiscriminatory reason for its failure to promote Wesley, the Fourth Circuit found "suspect" inconsistent testimony about whether minor motor vehicle accidents Wesley had in the past or the uncorroborated and uninvestigated allegation of a recruit that Wesley slept on the job entered into the chief's decision. For these reasons, the court concluded that there were genuine reasons of material fact as to whether the county's proffered nondiscriminatory reasons were true or were a pretext for discrimination and that summary judgment was therefore inappropriate.[43]

---

40. *See* Wesley v. Arlington Cnty., 354 F. App'x 775, 779–80 (4th Cir. 2009).
41. *See Wesley* at 354 F. App'x at 781.
42. *See Wesley*, 354 F. App'x at 781–82.
43. *See Wesley*, 354 F. App'x at 782–83.

2.1.5.3 Weaks v. North Carolina Department of Transportation: *An Unsuccessful Disparate Treatment Case*

The facts of the aforementioned cases are not unusual, but cases in which applicants or employees feel that they have been treated unfairly but fail to show that the treatment violated antidiscrimination laws are much more numerous. To understand fully the way in which claims of intentional discrimination work, therefore, it may be useful to consider a failure-to-promote case in which the plaintiff was unsuccessful in maintaining his case. *Weaks v. North Carolina Department of Transportation* is one such case.[44]

In *Weaks*, Michael Weaks, who is African American, was employed by the North Carolina Department of Transportation (DOT) Division of Motor Vehicles (DMV) beginning in 1994. During the period from 1994 to 2008, Weaks was promoted a number of times. In September 2008, Weaks applied for two promotional positions: Assistant Director for Emissions, his first choice, and Law Enforcement Manager of Emissions, his second choice.

Candidates for the position of Assistant Director for Emissions had to fill out an application and questionnaire, both of which were reviewed by a committee that interviewed each applicant. The interview committee had three members, one African American male and two Caucasian males. Weaks and candidate William Keel, who was Caucasian, were the only two candidates rated "most qualified" by the committee. The panel unanimously recommended Keel for the position. Keel had been a sworn law enforcement officer for 27 years, had supervised other agency employees for 17 years, and had been the designated manager for entire programs or districts for the DMV agency for 12 years. Weaks had considerably less experience. Weaks was promoted to his second choice position, Law Enforcement Manager of Emissions.

Weaks then filed a charge with the EEOC alleging that the DMV had failed to promote him to the position of Assistant Director for Emissions because of his race in violation of Title VII. The thrust of his claim was that he was more qualified for the position than Keel and that the interview committee was improperly impaneled, relied on subjective criteria to make

44. *See* Weaks v. N.C. Dep't of Transp., 761 F. Supp. 2d 289 (M.D.N.C. 2011).

the decision in favor of Keel, and ultimately discriminated against Weaks on account of his race.[45]

Weaks easily established his prima facie case. He was a member of a protected class as an African American. He applied for a job for which there was an opening, Assistant Director of Emissions. That he was qualified for the job is evidenced by the fact that only he and one other person, Keel, were rated as "most qualified." He was rejected for the position and the employer hired someone outside Weaks's protected class, the Caucasian Keel.[46]

But the DMV easily established the existence of a legitimate nondiscriminatory reason for its action. Keel was the better qualified of the two, with more extensive and broader supervisory experience over a greater period of time. Weaks could not, in the end, persuade the court (1) that he was the more qualified candidate or (2) that the choice of Keel was a pretext for discrimination. Weaks based his argument on certain factors that he "artificially severed from the employer's focus on multiple factors in combination."[47] The court affirmed that "the crucial issue in a Title VII action is an unlawfully discriminatory motive for a defendant's conduct, not the wisdom or folly of its business judgment."[48] Weaks also claimed that the manner in which the panel was chosen was discriminatory in that two of the panel members did not have sufficient technical expertise in emissions. The court rejected this argument, noting that a policy that designates one member of a selection panel as the technical expert who will provide necessary information to other panel members is not evidence of a policy designed to disadvantage candidates based on race.[49]

Finally, Weaks's other supposed evidence of pretext was his claim that Keel was preselected and that the interview process was a sham. Rumors that decision makers have this person or that person in mind for a promotion are commonplace in the workplace. But, as the court noted, rumors are not evidence. More importantly, even if it were true that Keel had been

45. *See Weaks*, 761 F. Supp. 2d at 298.

46. *See Weaks*, 761 F. Supp. 2d at 298.

47. *See Weaks*, 761 F. Supp. 2d at 302.

48. *See Weaks*, 761 F. Supp. 2d at 303–304, *quoting* Hux v. City of Newport News, 451 F.3d 311, 315 (4th Cir. 2006), *quoting* Jiminez v. Mary Washington Coll., 57 F.3d 369 (4th Cir. 1995).

49. *See* Weaks v. N.C. Dep't of Transp., 761 F. Supp. 2d 289, 305 (M.D.N.C. 2011).

preselected for the position, that fact would not violate Title VII, even if it violated the employer's own procedures. In other cases, the Fourth Circuit has ruled that the fact that a supervisor preselected an employee for a promotion is not sufficient evidence to conclude that the defendant's explanation for hiring the candidate and rejecting the plaintiff is a pretext for unlawful discrimination.[50] In *Mackey v. Shalala*, for example, the defendant, National Institutes of Health (NIH), hired for the position of program director a male with a PhD in a relevant field, who had been working as a university faculty member, instead of the female plaintiff, Mackey, who had a master's degree in educational psychology and had worked as a high school teacher. In rejecting Mackey's claim that the employer's stated preference for the male applicant's credentials was pretext for discrimination, the court said:

> The record in this case, however, essentially is without evidence that HHS's explanation is pretext or that Mrs. Mackey suffered from intentional sex discrimination. In the end, her argument in this case is that her superiors at NIH violated standard hiring procedures by preselecting Bain and placing him into a position that took over many of Mrs. Mackey's duties, and then her superiors falsified records to cover their violations of hiring procedures. Even if Mrs. Mackey's allegations are true, Bain's preselection is not sufficient evidence for jurors reasonably to conclude that HHS's explanation for Bain's hiring was pretext.[51]

In *Kennedy v. Landon*, another Fourth Circuit case, a hiring committee preselected a candidate and invited him to apply for an open position because the committee perceived him to be better qualified than anyone else in the applicant pool. The court held that while the committee may have violated employer guidelines, its invitation to and subsequent preference for the selected candidate was not a pretext for gender discrimination.[52]

In Michael Weaks's case, there was little more than Weaks's own assertions that he was the better qualified candidate. Despite his claim that the committee had preselected Keel, he did not introduce any evidence of preselection, which by itself would not constitute proof of pretext anyway. The

50. *See Weaks*, 761 F. Supp. 2d at 306.
51. *See* Mackey v. Shalala, 360 F.3d 463, 468–69 (4th Cir. 2004).
52. *See* Kennedy v. Landon, 598 F.2d 337, 341 (4th Cir. 1979).

trial court therefore granted the Department of Transportation's motion for summary judgment.

2.1.5.4 Gender as a Bona Fide Occupational Qualification: Protecting a Female Employee versus Protecting the Safety of Others

The BFOQ defense is most often used in response to claims of gender discrimination, but even there it has been construed very narrowly. The U.S. Supreme Court outlined the parameters of the BFOQ defense in 1991 in what is still the leading case on this question, *International Union, United Automobile, Aerospace and Agricultural Implement Workers of America, UAW, v. Johnson Controls, Inc.*[53] In the *Johnson Controls* case, a class of workers at the Johnson Controls battery manufacturing facility challenged its policy that barred fertile women ("women who are pregnant or who are capable of bearing children . . . except those whose inability to bear children is medically documented") from positions that involved exposure to lead. Johnson Controls never denied that the policy treated women differently than it did men (disparate treatment), but it claimed that the danger to a woman's reproductive health posed by lead exposure made this one of Title VII's "certain instances" where gender was a bona fide occupation qualification for the necessary operation of its business.[54] That is to say, Johnson Controls claimed that being male was a bona fide occupational qualification for jobs involving exposure to lead. The Supreme Court disagreed. The Court held that the BFOQ exception only applies where gender actually *interferes* with the employee's *ability to perform* the essential duties of the job.[55] As the Court noted, Johnson Controls showed "no 'factual basis for

53. *See* Int'l Union, United Auto., Aerospace and Agric. Implement Workers of America, UAW v. Johnson Controls, Inc., 499 U.S. 187, 206–207 (1991) (employer may not discriminate against a woman because of her capacity to become pregnant unless her reproductive potential prevents her from performing the duties of her job; BFOQ defense does not apply to fetal protection policies; concerns about the welfare of future children are the business of parents, not employers). *See also* EEOC v. Catholic Healthcare W., 530 F. Supp. 2d 1096, 1105–1107 (fetal safety concerns were not BFOQs mandating that hospital radiology technician and fluoroscopy room nurse not be pregnant).

54. *See Johnson Controls*, 499 U.S. at 202.

55. *See Johnson Controls*, 499 U.S. at 204.

believing that all or substantially all women would be unable to perform safely and efficiently the duties of the job involved.'"[56]

That an employer's underlying purpose might be well-meaning does not change the BFOQ analysis. Discrimination based on gender, the Court held, is permissible when safety is involved only in a very narrow range of circumstances. The safety concern must be a concern for the safety of others present in the workplace, whether they are coworkers or members of the public. The safety concern cannot be one for the safety of the employees affected by the discriminatory policy. The third parties whose safety might be compromised without the imposition of a BFOQ defense must be persons who are in some way "indispensable to the particular business at issue." The Court compared its holding in the *Johnson Controls* case with its conclusions in an earlier case addressing the BFOQ defense, *Dothard v. Rawlinson*.[57] In the *Dothard* case, the Court found that the state employer's "males-only" policy for the position of correctional officer within the contact areas of a maximum-security male prison satisfied the BFOQ exception. There, the purpose of the males-only policy was not to protect female guards, but to reduce the increased risk of violence that the state showed might result if guards were female. The safety of inmates was therefore implicated as well.[58]

Drawing on its holding in the *Dothard* case and in *Western Airlines, Inc. v. Criswell*,[59] an age discrimination case involving the BFOQ defense, the *Johnson Controls* Court held that the job duty in question must relate to the essence or central mission of the employer's business.[60] In the *Dothard* case, the Court noted that the "essence of a correctional counselor's job is

56. *See Johnson Controls*, 499 U.S. at 207, *quoting* Weeks v. S. Bell Tel. & Tel. Co., 408 F.2d 228, 235 (5th Cir. 1969).

57. *See* Dothard v. Rawlinson, 433 U.S. 321 (1977). *But see* United States v. Gregory, 818 F.2d 1114, 1117–18 (4th Cir. 1887) (applying *Dothard* to reverse trial court's dismissal of gender discrimination complaint on behalf of female applicants for correctional officer position because sheriff offered no evidence demonstrating why it could not organize all-male facility so as to accommodate female officers).

58. *See* Int'l Union, United Auto., Aerospace and Agric. Implement Workers of America, UAW v. Johnson Controls, Inc., 499 U.S. 187, 202 (1991), *citing Dothard*, 433 U.S. at 335.

59. *See* Western Airlines, Inc. v. Criswell, 472 U.S. 400 (1985).

60. *See Johnson Controls*, 499 U.S. at 203.

to maintain prison security."[61] In the *Western Airlines* case, it found that the central mission of an airline is safe transportation of passengers and that a maximum age requirement of 60 for flight safety engineers was designed to protect third party passengers.[62] Here, the essence of the business of Johnson Controls was the manufacture of batteries. As one of the lower court judges had observed, the job at Johnson Controls was not to make batteries without risk to fetuses in the same way that the job at Western Airlines was to fly planes without crashing and killing the airline's passengers.[63]

To judge from reported cases, facially discriminatory policies that the employer believes are justified by a bona fide occupational qualification are less and less common. In the public sector, employers tend to adopt policies that expressly discriminate on the basis of gender in a custodial or caregiving context: in prisons and jails, in hospitals, and with social service and home health workers. In several cases involving correctional facilities for female inmates, policies that excluded men from consideration for positions have been upheld as BFOQ justified because of a previous history of sexual abuse of female inmates by male guards at the institution in question.[64] But this is not always the case. In a 2010 Ninth Circuit case, the Nevada Department of Corrections justified its policy of restricting shift supervisors in its women's prison to female correctional officers by asserting that (1) male correctional lieutenants are likely to condone sexual abuse by their male subordinates, (2) male correctional lieutenants are themselves likely to engage in sexual abuse of female inmates, and (3) female correctional lieutenants possess an "instinct" that renders them less susceptible

---

61. *See Johnson Controls*, 499 U.S. at 203, *citing Dothard*, 433 U.S. at 335.

62. *See Western Airlines*, 472 U.S. at 413.

63. *See Johnson Controls*, 499 U.S. at 207.

64. *See* Everson v. Mich. Dep't of Corr., 391 F.3d 737 (6th Cir. 2005) (exclusion of males from certain positions in female correctional institutions was BFOQ where civil rights lawsuits brought by female prisoners against the state showed prevalence of sexual abuse of female prisoners by male guards); Ambat v. City and Cnty. of San Francisco, 693 F. Supp. 2d 1130, 1135–37 (policy of only assigning female deputies to female prisoner housing units was BFOQ where policy was implemented to prevent sexual misconduct); Reese v. Mich. Dep't of Corr., 2009 WL 799173 (E.D. Mich. 2009) at *3–*4 (denying defendants' motion for summary judgment because whether being female was a BFOQ for third-shift control and inmate work transportation positions depended on whether particular positions at all-female correctional facility involved situations where prisoners were most vulnerable to sexual abuse).

to manipulation by female inmates and better equipped for the correctional lieutenant position. The Ninth Circuit found that the department could not meet its BFOQ defense burden because it did not show that "all or nearly all" men would tolerate sexual abuse of female inmates by male guards or that it would be "impossible or highly impractical" to assess applicants for the position of correctional lieutenant individually with respect to their tolerance for or likelihood to engage in sexual abuse. The court held that the department's assumptions about the behavior of both male and female correctional lieutenants were precisely the kind of stereotyping that Title VII was meant to prevent.[65]

Interestingly, female law enforcement or correctional officers are often the ones challenging a sheriff's or department of corrections' policy limiting certain positions in a women's facility to female officers. The result of such requirements is not only to restrict men from these positions but necessarily to force women into them instead of allowing them to fill other positions in other facilities that might be more desirable from a professional standpoint.[66]

2.1.6 Disparate Impact or Unintentional Discrimination in Hiring: The Basic Theory

A Title VII disparate treatment claim requires an applicant to prove that the employer intentionally discriminated on the basis of race, color, gender, religion, or national origin. Employers can unintentionally violate Title VII, as well. If an employer adopts a hiring or promotional practice that causes

---

65. *See* Brenier v. Nev. Dep't of Corr., 610 F.3d 1202, 1211 (9th Cir. 2010).

66. *See, e.g.,* Henry v. Milwaukee Cnty., 539 F.3d 573 (7th Cir. 2008) (court finds for female correctional officers' challenge to policy of requiring each unit of juvenile correctional facility to be staffed by at least one officer of the same sex as detainees because policy did not meet Title VII's BFOQ standard where no staff-on-inmate sexual assaults had occurred, county had not investigated alternatives to same-sex staffing, county allowed officers of the opposite sex to patrol units during shower and clothing changing times, and role-model programs did not require presence of same-sex staff at all times of day). *But cf.* Tipler v. Douglas Cnty., Neb., 482 F.3d 1023, 1025–27 (8th Cir. 2007) (rejecting female officer's challenge to county's gender-based staffing policy where state law required female officers to provide round-the-clock supervision of female inmates and effect on officer's employment opportunities was minimal); Reed v. Cnty. of Casey, 184 F.3d 597, 600 (6th Cir. 1999) (county jailer's decision to assign female deputy to third shift was BFOQ where state required the presence of one female jailer when there were female prisoners lodged in jail).

a disparate impact on members of a protected class, it has engaged in unintentional discrimination, also known as disparate impact discrimination. Imagine the following situation:

> *Paradise County, North Carolina, decides that it will consider only county residents for county jobs. The county hopes that it will engender greater employee commitment and loyalty because employees will have a personal stake in the success of county government. The population of Paradise County is, and has been historically, predominantly white. Because the city of Paradise, where Paradise County government is based, is in the northeast corner of the county, there is a large pool of potential applicants for Paradise County jobs in Heavenly County, which adjoins Paradise County a mere ten miles from the city of Paradise. Heavenly County is predominantly African American. By adopting a residency requirement, Paradise County will have a disparate impact on African Americans. They will necessarily be hired disproportionately to the available labor market, which is measured by commuting distance, not by county lines. Without meaning to do so, Paradise County will have violated Title VII.*

Under Title VII, disparate impact cases can be brought on the basis of race, color, gender, religion, and national origin. Like the example above, a 1981 case involving the North Carolina Highway Patrol illustrates how a job requirement that is neutral on its face can nevertheless have an adverse impact on a protected class. Prior to 1981, the North Carolina Highway Patrol had a minimum height requirement of 5'6" for a state trooper. In a case brought by the United States Department of Justice, the district court found that this requirement had a substantial adverse impact on women: it automatically eliminated 77.3 percent of women between the ages of 18 and 34 from the pool of women who could apply for a position as a state trooper, while eliminating only 9.4 percent of men. In December 1980, there were 1,131 members of the highway patrol, and only one trooper was female. The court further found that the state had never validated the height requirement—that is, it had never shown statistically valid evidence that people taller than 5'6" were more likely to perform well in the position of state trooper than shorter people—and that the evidence the highway patrol did produce in support of its claim that the height requirement was job related lacked factual foundation. Thus, the court concluded that the challenged height requirement discriminated against women in violation of Title VII. The state did not appeal.[67]

Plaintiffs do not have to prove intent in a disparate impact case as they must do in a disparate treatment case. Plaintiffs do, however, have to demonstrate that a particular employment policy or practice that on its face appears to be neutral has in fact caused a significant statistical disparity in the proportionate numbers of protected class members who were hired when this policy or practice was in effect.[68] A rejected applicant who has identified a practice—such as a residency requirement or a height requirement—that has produced evidence of a statistical disparity in the numbers of African Americans hired or the number of women hired, for example, *and* who can show, in addition, that the identified policy or practice actually caused the statistical disparity has established a prima facie case of disparate impact or unintentional discrimination.[69]

---

67. *See* United States v. State of North Carolina, 512 F. Supp. 968 (E.D.N.C. 1981).

68. *See* 42 U.S.C. § 2000e-2(k)(1)(A)(i). *See also* Lewis v. City of Chicago, ___ U.S. ___, 130 S. Ct. 2191, 2197–98 (2010); Ricci v. DeStefano, 557 U.S. 557, 578 (2009); Connecticut v. Teal, 457 U.S. 440, 446–47 (1982); Chapman v. Lorillard Tobacco Co., 342 F. Supp. 2d 383, 394 (M.D.N.C. 2004) (mere absence of minority employees in upper level positions does not demonstrate discrimination without a comparison to the relevant labor pool); United States v. State of North Carolina, 914 F. Supp. 1257, 1264 (E.D.N.C. 1996) (holding that the court had no jurisdiction over the U.S. Attorney General's allegation that North Carolina engaged in unlawful discrimination against women in its hiring practices for correctional institutions).

69. Where the plaintiff shows that a specific employment policy or practice cannot be identified because the employer's recruitment and selection process cannot be broken down for analysis in this way, the hiring process as a whole may be treated as the identified employment practice. *See* 42 U.S.C. § 2000e-2(k)(1)(B)(i). *See, e.g.*, United States v. City of Warren, Mich., 138 F.3d 1083, 1091–94 (6th Cir. 1998) (reversing trial court's finding that United States had failed to meet is burden of providing statistical proof of disparate impact of city's residency requirement and recruiting practices where city failed to employ a single black person, limited its applicant pool to residents of the almost entirely white city, and refused to publicize jobs outside the almost entirely white county in the majority black city which it abutted). *But see* Reshard v. Peters, 579 F. Supp. 2d 57, 76 (D.D.C 2008) (defendant's motion for summary judgment granted where plaintiff did not identify particular practice leading to disparate impact but only alleged disparities in the number of blacks, women, and persons over 55 holding high-level positions compared to whites).

Once a rejected applicant establishes a prima facie case, the burden shifts to the employer to show either that the challenged employment practice does not cause a disparate impact or that even though it causes a disparate impact, it is job related and consistent with business *necessity.*[70] Employers generally demonstrate job relatedness and business necessity by showing that the practice in question has been validated, although sometimes job relatedness and business necessity may be apparent and a formal analysis will not be needed.[71] In the case of a residency requirement, the employer would establish its validity by showing that employees who lived within the employer's jurisdictional boundaries were likely to be better employees than those who lived elsewhere. Without actually doing a validity study, it seems reasonable to assume that persons who live in Buncombe County will make better employees for the city of Asheville than will persons living in Wake County. But it is less easy to see how, in the hypothetical above, residents of Paradise County will make better employees for Paradise County than residents of Heavenly County. Because the residency requirement disproportionately screens out African Americans from consideration for employment with Paradise County, the county will have to show evidence of the relationship between residency and job performance in county positions. Where the practices in question are written examinations or physical abilities tests, validity may be established by demonstrating that applicants with high scores are more likely to perform well on the job than those with low scores.

If the employer demonstrates that the practice is required by business necessity, the burden shifts to the plaintiff to prove that an alternative practice exists that (1) does not result in disparate impact and (2) would serve the defendant's stated objective equally well. Liability for disparate impact discrimination in violation of Title VII is established only if the applicant can prove the existence of such an alternative process.[72]

The disparate impact theory of discrimination was not initially recognized by trial courts. It took a decision by the U.S. Supreme Court and an

---

70. *See* 42 U.S.C. § 2000e-2(k)(1)(A)(i). *See also* Griggs v. Duke Power Co., 401 U.S. 424, 431 (1971); EEOC v. Dial Corp., 469 F.3d 735, 742 (8th Cir. 2006).

71. *See* Albemarle Paper Co. v. Moody, 422 U.S. 405, 425 (1975).

72. *See* 42 U.S.C. § 2000e-2(k)(1)(A)(ii). *See also Dial Corp.*, 469 F.3d at 742; EEOC v. Joe's Stone Crab, Inc., 220 F.3d 1263, 1276 (11th Cir. 2000), Ogletree v. City of Auburn, 619 F. Supp. 2d 1152, 1175 (M.D. Ala. 2009).

amendment to Title VII to anchor disparate impact in antidiscrimination law. The sidebar on page 63 traces the history of disparate impact.

What kinds of applicant selection procedures and employment tests have been shown to result in adverse impact on a protected class? The EEOC's list includes (but is not limited to):

- background checks that provide information on arrest and conviction history;
- background checks that provide information on credit and financial history;
- English proficiency tests that determine English fluency;
- cognitive tests that assess reasoning, memory, perceptual speed and accuracy, and skills in arithmetic and reading comprehension;
- tests that assess knowledge of a particular function or job;
- physical ability tests that measure the physical ability to perform a particular task or the strength of specific muscle groups as well as strength and stamina in general;
- tests that ask applicants to perform sample job tasks and assess performance and aptitude on particular tasks (for example, an assessment center);
- medical inquiries and physical examinations, including psychological tests, that assess physical or mental health;
- personality tests and integrity tests that assess the degree to which a person has certain traits or dispositions (for example dependability or cooperativeness) or aim to predict the likelihood that a person will engage in certain conduct (for example, theft or absenteeism).[73]

In the promotion context, performance appraisals that reflect a supervisor's assessment of an individual's performance could also function as a selection process that produces disparate impact. These types of selection devices will be discussed in greater detail in later chapters.

73. *See* U.S. Equal Employment Opportunity Commission (EEOC), www.eeoc.gov/policy/docs/factemployment_procedures.html.

2.1.7 A Closer Look at Title VII Disparate Impact or Unintentional Discrimination

2.1.7.1 EEOC v. Dial Corp: *A Successful Disparate Impact Failure-to-Hire Case*

In the case *EEOC v. Dial Corp.*, the employer, Dial Corporation, operated a sausage factory at which women and men had worked together in the packing department for a number of years.[74] The packing job required employees be able to lift 35 pounds of sausage at one time to a height of 30 to 60 inches above the floor and to be able to do this continuously throughout the workday. When Dial instituted a strength test to evaluate applicants for this position, the number of women hired decreased rapidly. The EEOC brought a Title VII disparate impact gender discrimination claim on behalf of rejected women applicants for positions in the packing department. Dial defended its use of the strength test on the grounds that the test was one of business necessity as the plant had had an unacceptably high level of worker injuries in the sausage packing area.

The jury found, however—and the court of appeals affirmed—that Dial had not shown that the test was a business necessity. Evidence showed that the injury rate had begun declining before the institution of the test due to greater safety measures and that in the two to three years before Dial began requiring the test, the rate of injury among women was lower than that among men. Furthermore, Dial had not demonstrated the validity of the strength test—that is, that individuals who are able to lift 35 pounds of sausage to a height of 30 to 60 inches above the floor continuously throughout a workday are less likely to suffer on-the-job injuries when working in a packing department position. In addition, Dial had not controlled for other variables that might have caused the decline in injuries.[75] The court also found that Dial had ignored evidence that the strength test was adversely impacting women applicants: statistical disparities are significant if the difference between the expected number and the observed number is greater than two or three standard deviations,[76] and in this case the

74. *Dial Corp.*, 469 F.3d at 735.

75. *See Dial Corp.*, 469 F.3d at 740.

76. *See* Hazelwood Sch. Dist. v. United States, 433 U.S. 299, 308 n.14 (1977); Brown v. Nucor Corp., 576 F.3d 149, 156–57 (4th Cir. 2009) (plaintiffs alleged that company's promotion procedure, which allowed managers and supervisors to use subjective

History of Disparate Impact

As originally enacted in 1964, Title VII's principal nondiscrimination provision held employers liable only for disparate treatment and did not include an express prohibition on policies or practices that produce a disparate impact. But in the 1971 case *Griggs v. Duke Power Co.*, the United States Supreme Court interpreted Title VII to prohibit employers' facially neutral practices that are "discriminatory in operation."[a] The *Griggs* Court held that disparate impact liability is triggered by the absence of "business necessity": "If an employment practice which operates to exclude [minorities] cannot be shown to be related to job performance, the practice is prohibited."[b] The Court reaffirmed its holding four years later in *Albemarle Paper Co. v. Moody*.[c] In 1989, in the case *Wards Cove Packing Company v. Atonio*, the Supreme Court modified its previous disparate-impact decisions by imposing additional requirements on plaintiffs.[d] The Court required plaintiffs to go beyond a showing of statistical disparities in the employer's applicant pool or workforce and to identify the specific practices that caused the statistical disparities. Under the *Wards Cove* decision, employers would no longer have to show business necessity for the practice, just business legitimacy.

The United States Congress, however, disagreed with the Court's interpretation and enacted the Civil Rights Act of 1991 to codify into Title VII the *Griggs* standards for proving disparate impact discrimination. Today, Title VII, as amended, still asks plaintiffs to identify the specific practices that caused each statistical disparity. But where it is impossible to do so, applicants may instead treat the employer's decision-making process as one employment practice. Employers, on the other hand, must again show that a practice is one of business necessity, not just business legitimacy, to avoid liability for disparate impact.

a. Griggs v. Duke Power Co., 401 U.S. 424 (1971).
b. *See Griggs*, 401 U.S. at 431.
c. Albemarle Paper Co. v. Moody, 422 U.S. 405 (1975).
d. Wards Cove Packing Co. v. Atonio, 490 U.S. 642 (1989).

disparity between the hiring of men and women after the adoption of the strength test was almost ten standard deviations. Dial knew of the statistics but continued to use the test nonetheless.[77]

2.1.7.2 Anderson v. Westinghouse Savannah River: *An Unsuccessful Disparate Impact Failure-to-Promote Case*

A Fourth Circuit case involving a failure-to-promote claim, *Anderson v. Westinghouse Savannah River Co.*, illustrates well the difficulty of proving a disparate impact case.[78] The plaintiff, an African American woman, brought both disparate impact and disparate treatment claims based on race. The court rejected the evidence of the plaintiff's expert witness, who had found that disproportionately fewer African Americans received promotions under the employer's competency-based rating system than would be expected given the number of African Americans in the employer's workforce. The court found that the plaintiff's expert failed to prove that the competency-based rating system caused the disparate impact claim because he did not take variables such as education and experience into account.[79] The court explained that in a disparate impact case, causation is not proven merely by showing that the percentage of black applicants who actually succeeded at each step of an interview process was much lower than expected. Anderson's expert should have quantified each of the factors that went into the assessment made by each of three decision makers. These factors included presentation in the interview before the assessors, answers to interview questions, demeanor, and substantive knowledge demonstrated in the interview. The expert should have also taken into account two factors that were important in determining who was granted an interview; namely, education and experience. There are some cases in which an employee challenging a promotion procedure has proven causation through statistics alone, and Anderson relied on them in presenting a case based on

---

criteria to promote employees, had a disparate impact on African American employees who applied for promotion; the court found that the plaintiff's statistical showing of two standard deviations met the Supreme Court's threshold for showing disparate impact for the purposes of showing commonality for Rule 23 certification of a class action). *See also* 1 Barbara Lindemann & Paul Grossman, Employment Discrimination Law 90–91 (3d ed.1996) and cases cited therein.

77. *See* EEOC v. Dial Corp., 469 F.3d 735, 741 (8th Cir. 2006).

78. *See* Anderson v. Westinghouse Savannah River Co., 406 F.3d 248 (4th Cir. 2005), *cert. denied*, 126 S. Ct. 1431 (2006).

79. *See Anderson*, 406 F.3d at 248.

statistical disparities and nothing more. The court said that the only cases in which it was not necessary to prove causation and a plaintiff could prove disparate impact based on statistics alone were those in which supervisors had unfettered discretion to make employment decisions.[80] Here, however, the decision makers did not have unfettered discretion because they had to analyze core competencies and functional competencies specifically identified as relevant for the position in question.[81]

2.1.7.3 An Equally Valid but Less Discriminatory Alternative

Even where an employer shows that the challenged practice is job related and a matter of business necessity, a plaintiff can still prevail if she or he can show that an alternative selection method exists that would both satisfy the employer's needs and result in no, or at least less adverse, impact. A case involving written testing of firefighter candidates shows how a plaintiff might successfully make the case for an alternative procedure. In the 2006 case *Bradley v. City of Lynn, Massachusetts*, the plaintiffs claimed that the cognitive abilities test used by the city had a disparate impact on African American and Latino firefighters.[82] The city claimed that the test was job related and consistent with business necessity. The court found that the test did indeed provide the city with relevant information about the candidates' prospects for success as firefighters but that there were other equally valid but less discriminatory ways to obtain such information. One alternative the court addressed was the possibility of treating applicants whose scores on the written cognitive examination fell within a delineated range of scores as having the same score. In other words, all applicants scoring

---

80. *See Anderson*, 406 F.3d at 266. The plaintiff cited the following cases: Watson v. Fort Worth Bank & Trust, 487 U.S. 977, 990 (1988) (noting that Title VII should apply to "an employer's undisciplined system of subjective decisionmaking"); Caridad v. Metro-North Commuter R.R., 191 F.3d 283, 287 (2d Cir. 1999) (noting that challenged promotion policy directed managers "to hire the most qualified candidate, but no other instructions are given" and that managers have unfettered discretion over hiring for certain positions); Mozee v. Am. Commercial Marine Serv. Co., 940 F.2d 1036, 1042 n.6 (7th Cir. 1991) (explaining that promotion to the position of leadman, which was a prerequisite to a promotion to management, "was left entirely to management's discretion, since it fell outside the seniority bidding system applicable to most hourly employment positions"); Rose v. Wells Fargo & Co., 902 F.2d 1417, 1424 (9th Cir. 1990) (noting that "Wells Fargo admits that the process of job elimination and restaffing was otherwise discretionary and subjective").

81. *See Anderson*, 406 F.3d at 266.

82. Bradley v. City of Lynn, Mass., 443 F. Supp. 2d 145 (D. Mass. 2006).

between 90 percent and 100 percent on the written test would be treated as having scored in the "A" range and would not be ranked within that range; all applicants scoring between 80 percent and 89 percent would be treated as having scored a "B" and would not be ranked within the range, and so on. The city also could have used a combination of physical abilities tests, work style considerations, and life experiences in combination with the cognitive abilities test to rank candidates, as the evidence showed that the addition of these other noncognitive considerations tended to reduce the adverse impact. The evidence also showed that the addition of these other factors would increase the value of the assessment process as a predictor of performance in the job and make the rank ordering of the candidates by score a better predictor of entry-level performance.[83]

Penalties for disparate impact violations include injunctive relief, reinstatement, front pay (until or in lieu of reinstatement), back pay, and attorneys' fees and costs.[84]

2.1.7.4 Measuring Adverse Impact: The EEOC's Four-Fifths Rule

Plaintiffs typically make their prima facie case through the introduction of statistical evidence.[85] There are several different methods that may be used to measure adverse impact. The best known is the EEOC's so-called four-fifths rule, which finds adverse impact when members of a protected class are selected for positions at a rate less than four-fifths (80 percent) of that of another group. The EEOC gives the following example of how the rule works: if 50 percent of white applicants receive a passing score on a test, but only 30 percent of African American applicants pass, the ratio of protected class applicants (African Americans) to that of white applicants (the other group) would be 30/50, which is equal to 60 percent, which violates the four-fifths rule.[86] But courts frequently find a disparate impact

---

83. *See Bradley*, 443 F. Supp. 2d at 174–75.

84. *See* 42 U.S.C. §§ 2000e-5(g)(1) and (k). Note that 42 U.S.C. § 1981a(a)(1) provides that compensatory damages and punitive damages are not available in disparate impact cases.

85. *See, e.g.*, Watson v. Fort Worth Bank & Trust, 487 U.S. 977, 987 (1988).

86. See U.S. Equal Employment Opportunity Commission, Uniform Guidelines on Employee Selection Procedures, 29 C.F.R. § 1607 *et seq.* generally and 29 C.F.R. §§ 1607.4(D) and 1607.16(R) for examples. In *Ricci v. DeStefano*, the Supreme Court assumed the validity of the Uniform Guidelines. *See* Ricci v. DeStefano, 557 U.S. 557, 663 n.11, 634 n.13 (2009) (Ginsburg, J., dissenting).

if the difference between the number of members of the protected class selected and the number that would be anticipated in a random selection system is more than two or three standard deviations.[87] That standard is considered by both social scientists and the courts to indicate a disparity that is too great to have occurred by chance.[88]

2.1.7.5 Proving Disparate Impact without Statistics

Frequently an applicant who believes that a particular employment practice is having an adverse impact on a protected group cannot make a statistical case because the number of applicants is too small to be considered statistically significant.[89] For this reason, the courts do not consider satisfaction of the four-fifths rule to be a requirement for a prima facie case of disparate impact. The United States Supreme Court has called the four-fifths rule a "rule of thumb for the courts."[90] The EEOC rule itself explicitly recognizes the rule's limitations when the statistics are based on small numbers, providing as follows:

> Greater differences in selection rate may not constitute adverse impact where the differences are based on small numbers and are not statistically significant, or where special recruiting or other programs cause the pool of minority or female candidates to be atypical of the normal pool of applicants from that group. Where the user's evidence concerning the impact of a

87. *See* 1 Barbara Lindemann & Paul Grossman 125–26 (3d ed.1996) and cases cited therein.

88. *See* 1 Barbara Lindemann & Paul Grossman 125 and n.81, n.83 (3d ed. 1996), *citing* Hazelwood Sch. Dist. v. United States, 433 U.S. 299, 309 (1977); Castaneda v. Partida, 430 U.S. 482, 496 n.17 (1977).

89. *See, e.g., Watson*, 487 U.S. at 996–97 (statistical deviation also may be unreliable if it is based upon "small or incomplete data sets"). *See also* Stout v. Potter, 276 F.3d 1118, 1123 (9th Cir. 2002) (affirming district court's dismissal of disparate impact claim because "[a] sample involving 6 female applicants in a pool of 38 applicants is likely too small to produce statistically significant results"); Price v. City of Chicago, 2000 WL 1468318 at *4, n.2 (N.D. Ill. 2000), *aff'd*, 251 F.3d 656 (7th Cir. 2001) (sample size of 22 was "too small" for purposes of applying the four-fifths rule); Ogletree v. City of Auburn, 619 F. Supp. 2d 1152, 1175 (M.D. Ala. 2009) (application of four-fifths rule to 12 applicants for fire department position produced statistical results too small to prove disparate impact), *citing* Cooper v. S. Co., 390 F.3d 695, 724 (11th Cir. 2004); *accord* EEOC v. Joe's Stone Crab, Inc., 220 F.3d 1263, 1274 (11th Cir. 2000).

90. *See* Watson v. Fort Worth Bank & Trust, 487 U.S. 977, 995 n.3 (1988).

> selection procedure indicates adverse impact but is based upon numbers which are too small to be reliable, evidence concerning the impact of the procedure over a longer period of time and/or evidence concerning the impact which the selection procedure had when used in the same manner in similar circumstances elsewhere may be considered in determining adverse impact.[91]

Statistics are not the only way of proving a disparate impact case. In a case alleging that nepotism and a word-of-mouth hiring practice maintained an almost exclusively all-white workforce and had a disparate impact on African American applicants, the district court hearing the case found that the plaintiff's statistical evidence was insufficient to make her case. The plaintiff, an African American applicant who wanted a job with the school board in the county in which she had been born and raised, alleged that she had kept her application current but the school board had failed to notify her of openings on three occasions in two years. The plaintiff heard of the openings only after the positions had been filled because the school board did not advertise vacancies but filled them through word of mouth and by posting within schools in the system.[92] On appeal, however, the Fourth Circuit found that the plaintiff had produced evidence that in one seven-year period, at least 46 relatives of school employees had been hired. In addition, the school board itself stipulated that it rarely advertised openings. The plaintiff also offered evidence about other African American applicants who did not apply for jobs because they were not aware of them until after they were filled. All of this evidence taken together, the Fourth Circuit said, showed disparate impact.[93]

2.1.7.6 Validating an Employment Selection Practice to Avoid Disparate Impact

As mentioned above, employers may demonstrate that a challenged practice is job related and consistent with business necessity by showing that the practice, test, or process used has been validated. Typically, employers use formal validation studies, but the use of a formal study is not required. There are three kinds of validation studies: studies that show the challenged

---

91. *See* 29 C.F.R. § 1607.4(D).

92. *See* Thomas v. Washington Cnty. Sch. Bd., 915 F.2d 922, 925 (4th Cir. 1990).

93. *See Thomas*, 915 F.2d at 926.

practice is criterion related, studies that show the challenged practice has content validity, and studies that show the challenged practice has construct validity.[94] Validation is discussed in greater detail in Appendix 3.

2.2 The Age Discrimination in Employment Act of 1967: Prohibition against Hiring Decisions Made on the Basis of Age over 40

Passed three years after Title VII and amended several times since, the Age Discrimination in Employment Act (ADEA) prohibits employers from refusing to hire, from discharging, and from otherwise discriminating against a person in the terms and conditions of employment on the basis of age. The statute currently protects persons 40 years of age and older.[95] Sometimes, more than one applicant may be over 40, and the ADEA does not prohibit an employer from favoring an older individual over a younger individual, even if the younger individual is 40 or over.[96] The ADEA specifically prohibits employers from expressing preferences or limitations related to applicant age in job postings or vacancy notices[97] and from denying or discriminating in the provision of benefits to older employees.[98] With respect to the hiring process, the EEOC's ADEA regulations make clear what the prohibition on expressing age preferences in job advertisements means:

> Help wanted notices or advertisements may not contain terms and phrases that limit or deter the employment of older individuals. Notices or advertisements that contain terms such as age 25 to 35, young, college student, recent college graduate,

94. *See* U.S. Equal Employment Opportunity Commission, Uniform Guidelines on Employee Selection Procedures, 29 C.F.R. § 1607.5(B). *See also* Watson v. Fort Worth Bank & Trust Co., 487 U.S. 977, 998 (1988); Albemarle Paper Co. v. Moody, 422 U.S. 405, 431 (1975); Banos v. City of Chicago, 398 F.3d 889, 892 (7th Cir. 2005).

95. *See* 29 U.S.C. §§ 623(a), 631(a).

96. *See* Gen. Dynamics Land Sys., Inc. v. Cline, 540 U.S. 581, 599–600 (2004). *See also* 29 C.F.R. § 1625.2.

97. *See* 29 U.S.C. § 623(e).

98. *See* 29 U.S.C. § 623(f).

> boy, girl, or others of a similar nature violate the Act unless one of the statutory exceptions applies. Employers may post help wanted notices or advertisements expressing a preference for older individuals with terms such as over age 60, retirees, or supplement your pension.[99]

The ADEA applies to all local government entities and community colleges.[100] The ADEA covers both intentional discrimination on the basis of age (disparate treatment) and unintentional discrimination on the basis of age (disparate impact).

2.2.1 Disparate Treatment or Intentional Discrimination under the ADEA

Like Title VII, on which it was based, the ADEA allows rejected applicants to use either direct or circumstantial evidence to prove that an employer intentionally rejected them because of their age. ADEA claims based on circumstantial evidence employ the *McDonnell Douglas* burden-shifting framework.[101] To establish a prima facie case of age discrimination, the plaintiff must show (1) that he or she is over 40 years of age; (2) that he or she applied for a position; (3) that he or she was qualified for the position; and (4) that he or she was rejected under circumstances that create

---

99. *See* 29 C.F.R. § 1625.4(a). *See also* Boyd v. City of Wilmington, N.C., 943 F. Supp. 585, 590–92 (E.D.N.C. 1996) (preference for candidates with MPA or MSIR degrees did not indicate preference based on age and did not violate the ADEA).

100. *See* 29 U.S.C. § 630(b)(2).

101. *See* Reeves v. Sanderson Plumbing Prods., Inc., 530 U.S. 133, 142 (2000) (assuming without deciding that *McDonnell Douglas* applies to ADEA disparate treatment cases); O'Connor v. Consol. Coin Caterers Corp., 517 U.S. 308, 310 (1996) (same); Hill v. Lockheed Martin Logistics Mgmt., Inc., 354 F.3d 277, 285 (4th Cir. 2004); Berez v. Prudential Ins. Co. of Am., 991 F.2d 787 (4th Cir. 1993). Note, however, that a footnote to the Supreme Court's 1999 decision in *Gross v. FBL Financial Services, Inc.* states that . . . "the Court has not definitively decided whether the evidentiary framework of *McDonnell Douglas* . . . is appropriate in the ADEA context." *See* Gross v. FBL Fin. Servs., Inc., 557 U.S. 167, 175 n.2 (2009). Nevertheless, the federal courts in North Carolina have continued to apply the *McDonnell Douglas* framework to ADEA cases. *See* EEOC v. City of Greensboro, 2010 WL 5169080 *5 at n.15 (slip copy) (M.D.N.C. 2010) and cases cited therein.

an inference of unlawful discrimination.[102] As is the case under Title VII, once an applicant or employee makes a prima facie case, the employer must produce, but need not prove, a legitimate nondiscriminatory reason for the employment action. The burden then moves back to the applicant or employee to prove that the employer's nondiscriminatory reason is false and no more than a pretext.[103]

One way in which the protected class of age differs from Title VII protected classes is that age is relative. It is clear that a rejected applicant can make his or her prima facie case where the applicant is older than age 40 and the person selected for the position is younger than 40. But what if the plaintiff is 50 years old and the person selected is 48 years old? The United States Supreme Court has made clear that under the ADEA, the fact that a plaintiff in the protected class has lost out to another person in the protected class does not matter. It is unlawful discrimination if the decision was based on the plaintiff's age:

> The discrimination prohibited by the ADEA is discrimination "because of [an] individual's age," . . . though the prohibition is "limited to individuals who are at least 40 years of age" . . . . This language does not ban discrimination against employees because they are aged 40 or older; it bans discrimination against employees because of their age, but limits the protected class to those who are 40 or older . . . . to put the point more concretely, there can be no greater inference of age discrimination (as opposed to "40 or over" discrimination) when a 40-year-old is replaced by a 39-year-old than when a 56-year-old is replaced by a 40-year-old.[104]

---

102. *See O'Connor,* 517 U.S. at 310–11; Laber v. Harvey, 438 F.3d 404, 430 (4th Cir. 2006) (discharge); Causey v. Balog, 162 F.3d 795, 800 (4th Cir. 1998); Colin v. Guilford Cnty. Bd. of Educ., 2010 WL 3911426 at *4 (M.D.N.C. 2010) (failure to hire).

103. *See* EEOC v. Allstate Ins. Co., 458 F. Supp. 2d 980, 987 (E.D. Mo. 2006) (". . . as the Supreme Court noted, the provision is unnecessary for disparate-treatment claims under § 623(a)(1) . . . . because . . . an employer can legally reject an applicant for a legitimate nondiscriminatory reason without reference to the RFOA provision, because the decision would not be "because of such individual's age."), *citing* Smith v. City of Jackson, Miss., 544 U.S. 228, 238 (2005).

104. *See O'Connor,* 517 U.S. at 312.

As the Court further noted, in a case relying on circumstantial evidence of discrimination, the evidence must be sufficient to create an inference that the discrimination was based on age. Where the person chosen instead of the plaintiff is only marginally younger than the plaintiff, that inference is not easily made. Neither the choice of a 65-year-old over a 68-year-old, for example, nor the choice of a 37-year-old over a 40-year-old in and of itself suggests that age was the basis of the decision.[105]

2.2.1.1 Minimum Hiring Ages under the ADEA

North Carolina local government employers may want to set minimum age requirements for certain positions for which they believe maturity is necessary. Some positions, such as those of police officer or sheriff's deputy, have minimum ages set by state agencies.[106] Where a state agency or licensing board has not set a minimum age, local governments are free to do so themselves. Where the minimum age is younger than 40, the ADEA is not implicated. The author is not aware of any North Carolina local government positions that have a minimum age over 40.

2.2.1.2 Maximum Hiring Ages and the BFOQ Defense under the ADEA

Local government employers may also want maximum age requirements for certain positions for which they believe that youthfulness is necessary. Setting a maximum age requirement that is under age 40 would appear to constitute a violation of the ADEA on its face. But like Title VII, the ADEA recognizes the bona fide occupational qualification (BFOQ) defense.[107] In the hiring context, this means that it will *not* be a violation of the ADEA to reject an applicant *because of his or her age* when the employer can show

---

105. *See O'Connor*, 517 U.S. at 312–13. *See also* Gibbard v. Potter, 2009 WL 159418 at *6–*7 (W.D.N.C. 2009) (replacement of 41-year-old plaintiff with men in their late thirties did not give rise to inference of age discrimination).

106. The North Carolina Criminal Justice Education and Training Standards Commission and the North Carolina Sheriffs' Education and Training Standards Commission set the minimum age for employment as police officers and sheriff's deputies, respectively, at 20 years of age. *See* 12 N.C. ADMIN. CODE (hereinafter N.C.A.C.) 09B .0101(2) and 12 N.C.A.C. 10B .0301(a)(2), respectively. Neither commission has established a maximum age for law enforcement officers.

107. *See* 29 U.S.C. § 623(f)(1). The requirement that the bona fide occupational qualification be reasonably necessary to the normal operation of the particular business has been uniformly interpreted to refer to the particular job from which the applicant is being excluded. *See* Trans World Airlines, Inc., v. Thurston, 469 U.S. 111, 122 (1985).

that "age is a bona fide occupational qualification reasonably necessary to the normal operation of the particular business." Most ADEA cases that involve the BFOQ defense involve mandatory retirement ages, but the same principles apply equally to hiring cases. The BFOQ defense has been primarily used to justify age limits on positions that affect public safety.

In the case *Western Airlines v. Criswell*, the U.S. Supreme Court approved the criteria developed by the lower courts and the EEOC for analyzing whether an employer has proved that an age limitation is a bona fide occupational qualification.[108] An age limitation is only a BFOQ where it is reasonably *necessary* to the *essence* of the business. The Court made clear that the reasonably necessary standard is a much higher standard than a "reasonable" or a "reasonable basis for believing" standard.[109] It is one that requires an employer to show that there are no alternative means for safe operation of its business. In evaluating what is reasonably necessary, an employer must focus on the core mission of its business, not on peripheral job tasks and qualifications.[110] The employer must also be able to show that either (1) all or substantially all individuals excluded from the position involved could not safely and efficiently perform its job duties,[111] or (2) some of the individuals so excluded possess a trait precluding safe and efficient job performance that it is impossible or highly impractical to identify on an individualized basis or that cannot be ascertained except by reference to age.[112]

2.2.1.3 The ADEA's Exception Allowing Maximum Hiring and Mandatory Retirement for Law Enforcement Officers and Firefighters

Under Section 623(j), the ADEA allows state and local governments to set age restrictions on law enforcement officers and firefighters *without* establishing that age is a BFOQ for those positions:

> It shall not be unlawful for an employer which is a State [or] a political subdivision of a State . . . to fail or refuse to hire or to discharge any individual because of such individual's age if such action is taken-

---

108. *See* Western Airlines v. Criswell, 472 U.S. 400, 416–17 and n.24 (1985).
109. *See Western Airlines*, 472 U.S. at 417–23.
110. *See Western Airlines*, 472 U.S. at 413. *See also* 29 C.F.R. § 1625.6(b).
111. *See Western Airlines*, 472 U.S. at 414, 422–23. *See also* 29 C.F.R. § 1625.6(b).
112. *See Western Airlines*, 472 U.S. at 414–15, 421–22. *See also* 29 C.F.R. § 1625.6(b).

> (1) with respect to the employment of an individual as a firefighter or as a law enforcement officer . . . and the individual has attained- . . . .
>
> (A) the age of hiring or retirement, respectively, in effect under applicable State or local law on March 3, 1983; or
>
> (B) (i) if the individual was not hired, the age of hiring in effect on the date of such failure or refusal to hire under applicable State or local law enacted after September 30, 1996; . . . and
>
> (2) pursuant to a bona fide hiring . . . plan that is not a subterfuge to evade the purposes of this chapter.[113]

Public employers may therefore set maximum ages above which they will not consider an applicant for employment in law enforcement or firefighting. They may reject any applicant who has reached that maximum age at the time of his or her application. Public employers may not, however, reject a law enforcement or firefighting applicant because he or she is over age 40 *unless they have adopted an ordinance setting forth an age restriction*, and they may not reject an applicant because the applicant is only a year or two away from reaching the maximum age restriction.[114]

Note that public employers may also adopt mandatory retirement provisions, provided that one of the following conditions applies: (1) the retirement age was set forth in a law that was in effect on March 3, 1983, or (2) the retirement age was set forth in a law enacted after September 30, 1996, in which case the mandatory retirement age cannot be lower than age 55.[115]

---

113. *See* 29 U.S.C. § 623(j). *See also* Correa-Ruiz v. Fortuno, 573 F.3d 1, 9 n.12 (1st Cir. 2009); Kannady v. City of Kiowa, 590 F.3d 1161, 1166 (10th Cir. 2010); Feldman v. Nassau Cnty., 434 F.3d 177, 184 (2d Cir. 2006).

114. For a clear and concise history of the ADEA's exemption for public safety, including the act's unfulfilled directive to the federal Secretary of Health and Human Services to develop fitness tests to be administered before someone could be rejected or discharged from some positions because of age, see *Correa-Ruiz*, 573 F.3d at 5–6.

115. The requirement that a public safety age restriction be enacted as part of a bona fide hiring plan that is not a subterfuge to avoid compliance with the ADEA is not clear on its face, since the exemption gives government employers permission to discriminate on the basis of age in this limited circumstance. Courts have interpreted this provision to mean that the employer must not use the exemption to evade another substantive provision of the ADEA, and they have identified two instances in

2.2.1.4 Maximum Age Restrictions and the Public Employer: A Hypothetical

Maximum age requirements for positions other than public safety are likely to raise issues under the ADEA, as the following hypothetical shows:

> *The city of Paradise, North Carolina, is reviewing its job descriptions for three positions: police officer, driver for the city's transit authority, and accountant. It is the firm opinion of the county manager that a person's cognitive and physical abilities begin to decline once he or she reaches age 55 and that a mandatory retirement age of 55 is therefore appropriate for some positions. In the case of law enforcement personnel, the manager believes that officers over the age of 55 can neither run as fast as they must to apprehend suspects nor respond to threats as quickly as they once did, because their reflexes have slowed. He also thinks that bus drivers need the quicker reflexes of the young to avoid dangerous traffic situations. As for accountants, last year the county suffered an embarrassing financial loss directly traceable to the fact that the previous accountant, a woman of 60, disliked wearing the reading glasses her age-related vision problems required and misread and incorrectly entered financial data into the county's financial system. In the meantime, the city's human resources director has received an inquiry about a transit driver position from a 57-year-old woman who recently relocated from Chicago, where she had 25 years' experience driving buses for that city. What should the human*

---

which adoption of a mandatory retirement age might be construed to be a subterfuge: (1) where the employer adopts a mandatory age limit to retaliate against an employee who had previously protested practices in violation of the ADEA, or (2) where the employer adopted age limits for law enforcement and firefighters at the same time that it created new, lower-paying positions and allowed the newly retired officers to apply for them, giving rise to the inference that it was seeking a way around age-based pay discrimination. *See Correa-Ruiz*, 573 F.2d at 14; *Kannady*, 590 F.3d at 1173 (rejecting argument that law enforcement retirement system is subterfuge because it was enacted to increase revenues in state pension fund and finding that plaintiff failed to identify a non-hiring substantive provision of the ADEA that the retirement system was designed to evade); *Feldman*, 434 F.3d at 183–84 (rejecting argument that age restrictions in law enforcement that are based on economic rationales are subterfuges to evade the ADEA); Minch v. City of Chicago, 363 F.3d 615, 624–25, 628–29, 630 (7th Cir. 2004) (plaintiffs offered no proof of subterfuge, only proof that city's officials thought that persons over age 63 were too old to be effective in public safety).

resources director tell the manager when he proposes making age 55 the maximum age for employment in these three positions?

In this hypothetical, the human resources director is comfortable with the manager's desire to set a maximum age for service as a police officer at 55. She knows that the ADEA contains an express exemption to maximum hiring and mandatory retirement ages in the case of law enforcement and firefighting personnel. Happily, at the time the Paradise city manager proposes the age 55 limitation for police officers, the city does not have any applications from applicants age 55 or older under consideration. The human resources director can tell the manager that the city may go ahead and amend its personnel ordinance to include such a restriction. With the positions of transit driver and accountant, however, the human resources director will have to disappoint the manager and explain to him why applicants for those positions must be considered without reference to their age.

2.2.1.5 Maximum Age Restrictions for Safety-Sensitive Positions Other Than Law Enforcement

While law enforcement and firefighting positions are among the most visible of a public employer's safety-sensitive positions, there are other positions where an employer might be concerned about an applicant or employee's age. There are, however, no other exemptions that allow a government employer to set a maximum age restriction without showing that age is a BFOQ. The transit system driver in the Paradise hypothetical above is a good example of a position that cannot be subject to an age restriction without evidence that age below 55 is a bona fide qualification.

Suppose, however, that the city's insurance carrier will not cover transit drivers over 55. Wouldn't that turn the age restriction into a BFOQ? The answer to this question is no. The EEOC's ADEA regulations say clearly that "differentiation based on the average cost of employing older employees as a group is unlawful. . . ."[116] That this prohibition includes making distinctions on the basis of liability insurance costs is made clear by two cases, *Enlow v. Salem-Keizer Yellow Cab Co., Inc.,*[117] and *Tullis v. Lear*

---

116. *See* 29 C.F.R. § 1627(f). The regulation makes an exception for seniority provisions in employee benefits plans and equal-cost measures in health insurance. *See* 29 U.S.C. § 623(f)(2).

117. *See* 389 F.3d 802 (9th Cir. 2004).

School, Inc.[118] In the *Enlow* case, the plaintiff was a 73-year-old driver for the Yellow Cab Company when the company changed insurance liability carriers after receiving a quote that was $10,000 less than its current carrier's premium. Unbeknownst to the cab company at the time it entered into the new contract, the new policy did not cover drivers older than age 70. The company therefore terminated Enlow's employment as a driver once the insurance company called Enlow's age to its attention.[119] At trial, the company argued that Enlow had failed to produce any evidence that it had intended to discriminate against him, and the court granted summary judgment in its favor.

The Ninth Circuit, however, reversed, holding that Enlow was not required to show intent in a direct evidence case and that the company's admission that they had terminated him because of the new insurance carrier's restriction constituted direct evidence that the company terminated him on account of his age.[120]

The burden of proof in an age discrimination case is discussed in the sidebar on page 79.

In the *Tullis* case, the plaintiff was a school bus driver for a private school that terminated him when he turned 65 because its liability insurance carrier would not insure school bus drivers who were over 65. The school argued that drivers needed to be alert and capable of acting quickly in an emergency and that at age 65, Tullis had impaired reaction times.[121] The Eleventh Circuit, however, found that there was no evidence in the record about either Tullis's individual reaction times or about the reaction times of persons over 65. Citing the Supreme Court's decision in *Western Airlines, Inc. v. Criswell*, the court said that the standard applicable in this case was that

1. the job qualifications which the employer invokes to justify his discrimination must be reasonably *necessary* to the *essence* of his business; and

---

118. *See* 874 F.2d 1489 (11th Cir. 1989).

119. At issue in the case was whether the termination was permanent or temporary. The Ninth Circuit therefore affirmed the trial court's denial of summary judgment to Enlow because this presented a disputed issue of material fact. *See Enlow*, 389 F.3d at 809, 812–13.

120. *See Enlow*, 389 F.3d at 813.

121. *See Tullis*, 874 F.2d at 1490.

2. the employer be "*compelled* to rely on age as a proxy for the safety-related job qualifications validated in the first inquiry," by showing that either
   a) it had a factual basis for believing that *all or substantially all* persons over the age in question would be unable to perform safely and efficiently the duties of the job, or
   b) it would be "*impossible* or highly impractical" to deal with the older employees on an individualized basis."[122]

To return to the issue raised by the Paradise city manager, the city could surely show that passenger safety is reasonably necessary to the essence of a transit service and thus satisfy the first requirement set forth by the *Tullis* and *Western Airlines* cases. But to maintain an age restriction of 55, the city would have to be able to show that all or almost all persons age 55 or over could not safely drive a bus or other transit vehicle. This would require finding a scientifically rigorous study that investigated the issue and found that to be the case. Alternatively, the city could show that it would be impossible or very impractical to test its driver applicants and employees individually.[123] Earlier ADEA cases in which employers raised a BFOQ defense in response to a claim that the employer discriminated on the basis of age in the hiring of bus drivers tended to deny summary judgment and leave the question of whether or not it is possible to test applicants and drivers individually to the jury, primarily because the parties offered conflicting expert testimony.[124] The issue has not arisen in the more recent transit driver age restriction cases.

---

122. Western Airlines, Inc. v. Criswell, 472 U.S. 400, 413–14 *quoting* Usery v. Tamiami Trail Tours, Inc., 531 F.2d 224, 235–36; *Contra* Maki v. Comm'r of Educ. of State of N. Y., 568 F. Supp. 252 (N.D.N.Y. 1983) (finding that the overwhelming importance of the safe transportation of schoolchildren lowered the standard for proving the need for showing age was proxy for safe driving abilities).

123. In 1976, however, the Fifth Circuit found that available tests could not distinguish those drivers not yet affected by the more crucial age-related, accident-causing impairments with sufficient reliability to ensure passenger safety and found that the bus company's policy of not hiring drivers older than 40 was a BFOQ. *See Usery*, 531 F.2d 224, 238 (5th Cir. 1976).

124. *See* Childers v. Morgan Cnty. Bd. of Educ., 817 F.2d 1556, 1558–59 (11th Cir. 1987); Tuohy v. Ford Motor Co., 675 F.2d 842, 843, 845 (6th Cir. 1982) (pilot for corporate jet); Hodgson v. Greyhound Lines, Inc., 499 F.2d 859, 864, 865 (7th Cir. 1974) (noting conflicting medical testimony as to functional capabilities of older drivers

Claims Involving Age Restrictions Are "Direct Evidence" Cases and Do Not Use the *McDonnell Douglas* Burden-Shifting Framework

As the *Enlow* and *Western Airlines* cases show, the *McDonnell Douglas* burden-shifting analysis—in which the employee produces circumstantial evidence that he or she was at least 40 years old, met the minimum stated qualifications for the job, and was rejected while younger applicants continued to be considered or hired—does not apply where the applicant has direct evidence of discrimination.[a] A maximum age limitation is a decision not to hire (or to fire) someone because of their age and is, as such, direct evidence of discrimination.[b]

a. *See* Trans World Airlines, Inc., v. Thurston, 469 U.S. 111, 121 (1985); Hardin v. Belmont Textile Mach. Co., 355 F. App'x 717, 721 (4th Cir. 2009); Laber v. Harvey, 438 F.3d 404, 430 (4th Cir. 2006).

b. *See* Enlow v. Salem-Keizer Yellow Cab Co., Inc. 389 F.3d, 802, 812–13.

2.2.1.6 Maximum Age Restrictions for Positions That Are Not Safety Sensitive

The Paradise city manager's desire to put an age restriction on the position of accountant is just plain silly. It is an observable fact that people tend to develop trouble with close reading as they grow older. But there is no need to try to generalize about the age at which they can no longer read, because they can correct the situation with reading glasses. There is no evidence that at any particular age presbyopia cannot be corrected with reading glasses and no evidence that at any particular age people will refuse to wear reading glasses. If the manager feared a repeat of the situation with the accountant, the human resources department could develop a transcription/data entry test to weed out any applicant too vain to put on glasses when needed.[125]

but finding that bus company demonstrated that its maximum hiring age policy was based on good-faith judgment concerning the safety needs of its passengers and did not violate ADEA).

125. Note that normal vision impairments that can be corrected by the use of eyeglasses or contact lenses are not disabilities under the ADA. 42 U.S.C. § 12102(4)(e)(ii).

2.2.2 A Closer Look at Disparate Treatment under the ADEA: Mixed-Motive Cases

Unlike Title VII, the ADEA does not allow a rejected applicant for employment to establish discrimination by showing that age was one of a number of motivating factors. An ADEA plaintiff must show that age was the sole reason for the applicant's rejection. In other words, an applicant must prove that but for his or her age, the applicant might have been hired. Thus, when defending against an age discrimination claim in the hiring context, an employer does not have to show that even in the absence of age discrimination it would have rejected the applicant. Instead, the applicant bears the burden of proof in showing that age was *the* motivating factor in his or her rejection.[126]

2.2.3 Unintentional or Disparate Impact Discrimination under the ADEA

Like Title VII, the ADEA prohibits employers from engaging in practices that have an adverse impact on persons protected by the statute.[127] The scope of disparate impact liability under the ADEA, however, is more limited than under Title VII. Why is that so? First, age, more so than the classifications protected from discrimination under Title VII, sometimes *does* have some relevance to a person's ability to perform certain types of job duties. The ADEA allows employers to differentiate among applicants or employees "where the differentiation is based on reasonable factors other than age."[128] The reasonable factors other than age (RFOA) defense is an affirmative defense, which means that the employer must prove it by a preponderance of the evidence.[129] Thus, some employment criteria may be reasonable and may allow an employer to escape liability using the RFOA defense even where there is an adverse impact on older workers.

The second way in which disparate impact under the ADEA differs from the treatment of disparate impact under Title VII is in the absolute

---

126. *See* Gross v. FBL Fin. Servs., Inc., 557 U.S. 167, 173–80 (2009).

127. *See* Smith v. City of Jackson, Miss., 544 U.S. 228, 232 (2005).

128. *See* 29 U.S.C. § 623(f)(1); 29 C.F.R. § 1627.7.

129. *See* Meacham v. Knolls Atomic Power Lab., 554 U.S. 84, 87 (2008). See also the EEOC's regulation on the use of the RFOA defense in ADEA disparate impact cases at 29 C.F.R. § 1625.7. Note that the RFOA defense applies only to disparate impact claims and does not apply to disparate treatment claims. *See* 29 C.F.R. § 1625.7(d).

requirement that an ADEA plaintiff prove which specific practices cause the statistical disparity. Under Title VII, an applicant bringing a discrimination claim does not have to identify the particular practice that causes the disparate impact if the decision-making process cannot be broken down in this way. In contrast, under the ADEA as the U.S. Supreme Court interpreted it in the 2005 case *Smith v. City of Jackson*, applicants and employees must do more than allege adverse impact or put forth statistical imbalances. They are instead "responsible for isolating and identifying the specific employment practices that are allegedly responsible for any observed statistical disparities."[130]

Third, the RFOA defense to a claim of adverse impact remains somewhat easier for an employer to prove than is the business necessity defense required by Title VII. The business necessity defense requires employers to show that there are no other ways for it to achieve its goals that do not result in a disparate impact on a protected class. The RFOA defense has no such requirement. It only requires that the way an employer chooses to achieve its goals be reasonable:

> A reasonable factor other than age is a non-age factor that is objectively reasonable when viewed from the position of a prudent employer mindful of its responsibilities under the ADEA under like circumstances. Whether a differentiation is based on reasonable factors other than age must be decided on the basis of all the particular facts and circumstances surrounding each individual situation. To establish the RFOA defense, an employer must show that the employment practice was both reasonably designed to further or achieve a legitimate business purpose and administered in a way that reasonably achieves that purpose in light of the particular facts and circumstances that were known, or should have been known, to the employer.[131]

---

130. *See City of Jackson*, 544 U.S. at 241. In *City of Jackson*, the Supreme Court held that because the Civil Rights Act of 1991 only amended Title VII and did not amend the ADEA, the Court's disparate impact holdings in the *Wards Cove* case (discussed in the sidebar on page 63) continue to apply to the ADEA.

131. *See* 29 C.F.R. § 1625.7(e)(1). Subsection (e)(2) sets forth some of the considerations relevant to whether a practice is based on a reasonable factor other than age.

Thus, in the *City of Jackson* case, the city's decision to give larger raises to lower-level law enforcement employees than to those with more seniority was reasonable given its stated goal of bringing salaries into line with those of surrounding police departments and improving its retention rate. Despite the fact that it resulted in a statistical imbalance in the number and dollar amount of raises awarded to older employees as compared to younger employees, the city was not liable for disparate impact.[132]

2.3 North Carolina Law Prohibiting Discrimination on the Basis of Race, Color, Gender, Religion, National Origin, or Age

The North Carolina Equal Employment Practices Act, found in Sections 143-422.1 through 143-422.3 of the North Carolina General Statutes (hereinafter G.S.), declares that it is the public policy of the state to "protect and safeguard the right and opportunity of all persons to see, obtain and hold employment without discrimination or abridgement on account of race, religion, color, national origin, age, sex or handicap by employers which regularly employ 15 or more persons."[133] The act, however, has no independent enforcement mechanism and does not authorize a private right of action.[134] Instead, the courts treat claims brought under the Equal Employment Practices Act as claims of wrongful discharge in violation of public policy.[135]

---

132. *See City of Jackson*, 544 U.S. at 242–43.

133. *See* N.C. Gen. Stat. (hereinafter G.S.) § 143-422.2.

134. *See* Smith v. First Union Nat. Bank, 202 F.3d 234, 247 (4th Cir. 2000) (absent a clear indication from the courts or the legislature of North Carolina that a private right of action does exist under the North Carolina Equal Employment Practices Act, it would be inappropriate for a federal court to create one);

135. *See, e.g.*, Bendross v. Town of Huntersville, 159 N.C. App. 228 (2003); Gibbs v. Guilford Tech. Cmty. Coll., 149 N.C. App. 972 (2002).

2.4 The Americans with Disabilities Act

The Americans with Disabilities Act (ADA) prohibits employers from discriminating on the basis of disability against a qualified individual with respect to job application procedures; the hiring, advancement, and/or discharge of employees; employee compensation; job training; and other terms, conditions, and privileges of employment.[136] The ADA may be the most complex of the federal antidiscrimination statutes in that it is the only statute that requires employers to take certain actions in addition to abstaining from other actions: the ADA requires employers to provide a reasonable accommodation to the *known* physical or mental limitations of applicants and employees, unless doing so would impose an undue hardship on the employer's operations. *The obligation to make reasonable accommodation is a form of nondiscrimination.*[137] Each situation is based on an individual assessment of the applicant's or employee's disability with respect to the position in question. The ADA also prohibits employers from asking any questions of job applicants that are likely to reveal the existence of a disability until it has extended a conditional offer of employment. This prohibition effectively means that an employer cannot ask any questions about the applicant's medical history or conditions, nor may it require a medical examination, before offering the applicant a job.[138]

While Title VII protects everyone who might experience discrimination on the basis of race, color, gender, religion, or national origin, and the ADEA protects anyone age 40 or above, whom the ADA protects is less clear. Analyzing whether an individual falls within the ADA-protected class requires applying a series of definitions. In order to understand what it means to say that the ADA prohibits employers from discriminating on the basis of disability against a qualified individual, we must define the term "disability," as well as the phrase "qualified individual." The ADA defines a disability as a physical or mental impairment that substantially limits a person in performing one or more major life activities.[139] This definition, in turn, requires definition of the phrase "major life activities." Major

---

136. The employment provisions of the ADA are codified at 42 U.S.C. §§ 12111–12213. The EEOC's ADA regulations may be found at 29 C.F.R. Part 1630.

137. *See* 29 C.F.R. Part 1630, App. § 1630.9.

138. *See* 42 U.S.C. § 12112(d); 29 C.F.R. §§ 1630.14(a) and (b).

139. See 42 U.S.C. § 12102(1)(A).

life activities are defined by the statute and EEOC regulations through examples. Major life activities include

- caring for oneself
- performing manual tasks
- walking
- seeing, hearing, speaking
- breathing
- learning
- eating
- bending
- reading
- working
- sitting
- standing
- sifting
- reaching
- thinking
- interacting with others
- sleeping
- speaking
- concentrating
- communicating.[140]

Major life activities also include major bodily functions, such as

- functions of the immune system
- neurological and brain functions
- normal cellular growth
- respiratory and circulatory function
- digestive and bowel functions
- reproductive functions
- endocrine functions.[141]

Persons who have a record of such an impairment or are regarded as having such an impairment are covered by the ADA.[142] The ADA provides that the definition of disability is to be construed in favor of broad coverage of individuals.[143]

Once it has been established that an individual has a disability within the meaning of the law, employers and applicants must consider the meaning of the phrase "qualified individual." A qualified individual means one who has the prerequisite skills, experience, education, and other job-related requirements of the position and who, *with or without reasonable accommodation,* can perform the "essential functions" of the job.[144] The essential

---

140. *See* 42 U.S.C. § 12102(2)(A); 29 C.F.R. § 1630.2(i)(1)(i).
141. *See* 42 U.S.C. § 12102(2)(B); 29 C.F.R. § 1630.2(i)(1)(ii).
142. *See* 42 U.S.C. § 12102(1)(B) and (C), (3)(A).
143. *See* ADA Amendments Act, Pub. L. No. 110-325, § 3(4)(A)(2008).
144. *See* 29 C.F.R. § 1630.2(m).

functions of the job are the basic, fundamental duties that the employee must perform. The term essential functions does not include the marginal functions of the position.[145] A job function may be considered essential for any of several reasons, including but not limited to the following:

- the reason the position exists is to perform that function;
- there is a limited number of employees available among whom the performance of that job function can be distributed;
- the function is highly specialized so that the person in the position is hired for his or her expertise or ability to perform the particular function.[146]

Evidence of whether a particular function is essential includes, but is not limited to, the employer's own judgment as to which functions are essential, written job descriptions prepared before advertising or interviewing applicants, the amount of time spent on the job performing the function, the consequences of not requiring the person in the position to perform the function, the work experience of past incumbents in the job, and the current work experience of persons in the same or similar positions.[147]

The ADA applies to all local government entities and community colleges with 15 or more employees.[148]

2.4.1 Disparate Treatment or Intentional Discrimination under the ADA

Under the ADA, individual applicants who have been denied employment because they have a disability may bring a claim of disparate treatment or intentional discrimination against the offending employer. As is the case with Title VII and ADEA disparate treatment claims, the burden-shifting framework of *McDonnell Douglas Corp. v. Green* applies where there is no

---

145. *See* 29 C.F.R. § 1630.2(n).

146. *See* 29 C.F.R. § 1630.2(n)(2).

147. *See* 29 C.F.R. § 1630.2(n)(3) and 29 C.F.R. Part 1630, App. § 1630.2(n).

148. *See* 42 U.S.C. § 12111(5)(A). Strictly speaking, the ADA only covers government employers who have 15 or more employees "for each working day in each of twenty or more calendar weeks in the current or preceding calendar year." The State of North Carolina may not be sued for money damages under the ADA, although it is subject to a suit for injunctive relief under *Board of Trustees of the University of Alabama v. Garrett*, 531 U.S. 356, 374 (2001). Local governments may be sued both for money damages and for injunctive relief as remedies for violations of the ADA.

direct evidence of discrimination and proof must be circumstantial.[149] Take Marcus, for example, who believes that his application for the position of budget analyst has been rejected because he suffers from epilepsy but has no direct evidence of disability discrimination. To establish a prima facie case, Marcus would have to show that (1) he has epilepsy and that it is a disability within the meaning of the ADA; (2) he is qualified to perform the essential functions of the position of budget analyst; and (3) the employer rejected his application because of his disability[150] or was unreasonably unwilling to accommodate his needs for accommodation, namely, that another person drive to meetings outside of the office.[151] Once Marcus has established his prima facie case of discrimination, the burden shifts to the employer to articulate a legitimate, nondiscriminatory reason for rejecting Marcus's application. If the employer meets this burden, the presumption of intentional discrimination disappears, but Marcus can still prove disparate treatment by offering evidence demonstrating that employer's explanation is merely a pretext for discrimination.

2.4.2 Disparate Impact or Unintentional Discrimination under the ADA

The disparate impact or unintentional discrimination theory of discrimination is available under the ADA as it is under Title VII and the ADEA. The standard of proof that a rejected applicant must meet under the ADA, however, is lighter than that under Title VII and the ADEA. As noted above, the general rule against discriminating on the basis of disability in set forth in 42 U.S. § 12112(a):

---

149. *See* Raytheon Co. v. Hernandez, 540 U.S. 44, 49 (2003) (presuming but not holding that the *McDonnell Douglas* burden of proof applies); Wilson v. Phoenix Specialty Mfg. Co., Inc., 513 F.3d 378, 387 (4th Cir. 2008), *citing* St. Mary's Honor Ctr. v. Hicks, 509 U.S. 502, 511 (1993).

150. *See* Rhoads v. FDIC, 257 F.3d 373, 387 n.11 (4th Cir. 2001); Huppenbauer v. May Dep't Stores Co., 99 F.3d 1130 (4th Cir. 1996); Tyndall v. Nat'l Educ. Ctrs., 31 F.3d 209, 212 (4th Cir. 1994).

151. Implicit in the fourth element is the ADA requirement that the employer and employee engage in an interactive process to identify a reasonable accommodation. *See* Haneke v. Mid-Atl. Capital Mgmt., 131 F. App'x 399, 400 (4th Cir. 2005) (finding disputed issue of material fact as to whether both parties met their respective burdens of engaging in the interactive process in good faith, and whether that caused a failure to accommodate).

> No covered entity shall discriminate against a qualified individual on the basis of disability in regard to job application procedures, the hiring, advancement, or discharge of employees, employee compensation, job training, and other terms, conditions, and privileges of employment.

The statute gives very specific definitions of what the phrase "discriminate against a qualified individual on the basis of disability" means in subsection (b). In subsections (b)(6) and (7), it addresses the use of qualification standards and testing, which are the areas in which disparate impact on the basis of disability is most likely to occur:

> (b) As used in subsection (a) of this section, the term "discriminate against a qualified individual on the basis of disability" includes—
>
>> (6) using qualification standards, employment tests or other selection criteria that *screen out or tend to screen out an individual with a disability* ***or*** *a class of individuals with disabilities* unless the standard, test or other selection criteria, as used by the covered entity, is shown to be *job-related for the position in question and is consistent with business necessity*; and
>>
>> (7) failing to select and administer tests concerning employment in the most effective manner to ensure that, when such test is administered to a job applicant or employee who has a disability that impairs sensory, manual, or speaking skills, such test results accurately reflect the skills, aptitude, or whatever other factor of such applicant or employee that such test purports to measure, rather than reflecting the impaired sensory, manual, or speaking skills of such employee or applicant (except where such skills are the factors that the test purports to measure) (emphases added).[152]

Like Title VII and the ADEA, the ADA allows rejected applicants to show that a facially neutral employment practice—here, the use of qualifications

152. *See* 42 U.S.C. §§ 12112(b)(6) and (7).

or tests to screen and evaluate applicants—has had the effect of removing applicants with given disabilities from further consideration for employment. Where the ADA differs from Title VII and the ADEA is in the fact that a plaintiff does not need to show that the qualification standard or test has had a disparate impact on a group or class of applicants with disabilities—the plaintiff need only show that the employer used a selection device that screened him or her out. Under the ADA, the plaintiff does not need to prove that others were similarly screened out or to make a statistical showing comparing the number of persons with the disability that one would find in the demographic pool compared to the number considered for the position.[153] Another way of saying this is that under the ADA, a recruitment or hiring practice can have a disparate impact against a single person.

The ADA expressly says, however, that an employer may use a qualification standard, test, or other selection device that screens out persons with particular disabilities if that selection device is "job-related and consistent with business necessity" and satisfaction of the standard or performance of the test or selection process cannot be accomplished through reasonable accommodation.[154] The burden is on the employer to prove job relatedness and business necessity. Determining whether a selection device is job related involves analyzing the questions or subject matter contained in the test or criteria used by an employer in making hiring or promotional decisions. In other words, to show job relatedness, an employer must

---

153. *See* Gonzales v. City of New Braunfels, Tex., 176 F.3d 834, 839 (5th Cir. 1999), *citing* 1 Barbara Lindemann & Paul Grossman, Employment Discrimination Law 333–34 (3d ed. 1996). *See also* Prewitt v. U.S. Postal Serv., 662 F.2d 292, 307 (5th Cir. 1981) (Rehabilitation Act case) ("In our opinion, in the disparate impact context, there should be only minor differences in the application of the Griggs principles to handicap discrimination claims. One difference, however, is that, when assessing the disparate impact of a facially-neutral criterion, courts must be careful not to group all handicapped persons into one class, or even into broad subclasses. This is because 'the fact that an employer employs fifteen epileptics is not necessarily probative of whether he or she has discriminated against a blind person.'"). *See also* Jeffrey v. Ashcroft, 285 F. Supp. 2d 583, 588 (M.D. Pa. 2003) (analyzing testing criteria under a hybrid disparate treatment-disparate impact approach). *Contra* Spivey v. Beverly Enters., Inc., 196 F.3d 1309, 1314 (11th Cir. 1999) (plaintiff failed to present statistical evidence to demonstrate that this policy in practice has a disproportionate impact on pregnant employees).

154. *See* 42 U.S.C. § 12113(a). *See also* Bates v. United Parcel Serv., Inc., 511 F.3d 974, 995 (9th Cir. 2007).

demonstrate that the qualification standard or selection device fairly and accurately measures the individual's actual ability to perform the essential functions of the job.[155] When every person excluded by the qualification standard is a member of a protected class—that is, persons with particular disabilities—an employer must demonstrate a predictive or significant correlation between the qualification and performance of the job's essential functions.[156] The employer's burden is high, but it is generally lower when "the job clearly requires a high degree of skill and the economic and human risks involved in hiring an unqualified applicant are great . . . .," as in the case of public safety positions. For example, in one recent case from the Eleventh Circuit, the court found that a minimum hearing standard was job related where U.S. Marshals Service officers needed to possess a certain level of unaided hearing to perform the job's essential functions adequately at all times.[157] In contrast, in a recent Ninth Circuit decision, the court held that an employer's use of a U.S. Department of Transportation hearing standard applicable only to drivers of heavier weight trucks for drivers of lighter weight vehicles was not job related.[158]

Business necessity, in contrast, analyzes whether there is a business reason that makes the employer's use of a test or criteria in hiring or promotions necessary.[159] Under the ADA, to show that a disputed qualification standard is "consistent with business necessity," the employer must show that it "substantially promotes" the business's needs. For a safety-based qualification standard, "[i]n evaluating whether the risks addressed by . . . [the] qualification standard constitute a business necessity, the court should take into account the magnitude of possible harm as well as the probability of occurrence." Finally, to show that "performance cannot be accomplished by reasonable accommodation," the employer must demonstrate either that no reasonable accommodation currently available would cure the performance deficiency or that such reasonable accommodation poses an "undue hardship" on the employer.[160]

---

155. *See Bates*, 511 F.3d at 996.

156. *See* Allmond v. Akal Sec., Inc., 558 F.3d 1312, 1316–17 (11th Cir. 2009), *cert. denied*, 130 S. Ct. 1139 (2010); *Bates*, 511 F.3d at 996, *citing* Albemarle Paper Co. v. Moody, 422 U.S. 405, 431 (1975).

157. *See Allmond*, 558 F.3d at 1316–17.

158. *See Bates*, 511 F.3d at 996–97.

159. *See Allmond*, 558 F.3d at 1316–17.

160. *See* Bates v. United Parcel Serv., Inc., 511 F.3d 974, 996–97 (9th Cir. 2007).

Once an employer demonstrates that the pertinent qualification standard is job related and consistent with business necessity, the burden shifts to the plaintiff to offer a reasonable accommodation that would seem to allow him or her to satisfy that standard. The employer would then have to show that performance of the job could not be accomplished through the proposed accommodation or that it would pose an undue hardship.[161] But as noted in the section on disparate treatment under the ADA, reasonable accommodation may include acquiring or modifying equipment or devices, job restructuring, providing readers and/or interpreters, or making physical changes to the workplace.[162] Particularly relevant to the qualification standards is the observation found in the ADA's legislative history that "accommodation may entail adopting an alternative, less discriminatory criterion."[163]

2.4.3 Three Things That Make the ADA Different from Title VII and the ADEA

2.4.3.1 Difference Number One: The ADA Prohibits Pre-Offer Medical Inquiries

Under Title VII and the ADEA, application questions pertaining to the applicant's race, date of birth, age, and so forth are not unlawful on their face. But the fact that an employer has asked those questions will certainly be used as evidence of discriminatory intent in a failure-to-hire case. The ADA is different in that it expressly prohibits employers from directly asking a job applicant about a disability or asking any other questions that are likely to reveal the existence of a disability.[164] Title 42, Section 12112(d), of the U.S. Code provides:

> (1) In general. The prohibition against discrimination as referred to in [§ 12112(a)] shall include medical examinations and inquiries.

---

161. *See Bates*, 511 F.3d at 996–97; *Allmond*, 558 F.3d at 1317. *See also* Peter Susser, Disability Discrimination and the Workplace 1005 and cases cited at n.203 (2005).

162. *See* 42 U.S.C. § 12111(A); 29 C.F.R. § 1630.2(a).

163. *See Bates*, 511 F.3d at 997.

164. Note that the ADA has separate rules for pre-offer medical inquiries and examinations and post-offer medical inquiries and examinations, and for inquiries and examinations of current employees.

(2) Preemployment.
   (A) Prohibited examination or inquiry. Except as provided in paragraph (3), a covered entity shall not conduct a medical examination or make inquiries of a job applicant as to whether such applicant is an individual with a disability or as to the nature or severity of such disability.
   (B) Acceptable inquiry. A covered entity may make pre-employment inquiries into the ability of an applicant to perform job-related functions.

(3) Employment entrance examination. A covered entity may require a medical examination after an offer of employment has been made to a job applicant and prior to the commencement of employment duties of such applicant, and may condition an offer of employment on the results of such examination, if—
   (A) all entering employees are subjected to such an examination regardless of disability;
   (B) information obtained [is kept confidential, with limited exceptions]; and
   (C) the results of such examination are used only in accordance with this subchapter.

An employer therefore may not ask, "Do you need a reasonable accommodation to perform this job?" or "Do you have any medical conditions that would prevent you from performing this job?" or even "Have you ever filed a workers' compensation claim?"[165] An employer may ask, however, about the applicant's ability to perform specific job functions, such as his or her ability to lift a certain amount of weight, and about the applicant's nonmedical qualifications and skills, such as work history, education, and required licenses and certifications. An employer may also ask applicants to describe or demonstrate how they perform job tasks.[166]

165. *See* 29 C.F.R. Part 1630, App. § 1630.13(a).

166. See 29 C.F.R. §§ 1630.13 and 1630.14 and 29 C.F.R. Part 1630 App. §§ 1630.13(a) and 1630.14(a), which address pre-employment medical inquiries and examinations. *See also* U.S. Equal Employment Opportunity Commission, *ADA Enforcement Guidance: Preemployment Disability-Related Questions and Medical Examinations* (October 10, 1995), www.eeoc.gov/policy/docs/preemp.html.

Once an offer has been extended, the employer may require the successful applicant to take a medical examination, provided that it requires medical exams of all new employees in the same job category. Once an offer has been extended, the employer may also ask disability-related questions, including questions about an applicant's workers' compensation history, attendance record at previous jobs, and health.[167] If a conditional offer is withdrawn after a post-offer medical examination or discussion of the applicant's medical history, the reasons for withdrawal of the offer must be job related and consistent with business necessity.[168] The prohibition against making pre-offer medical inquiries is discussed in more detail in Chapter 5.

Once an applicant becomes an employee, an employer is prohibited from requiring a medical examination or making inquiries of an employee as to whether the employee is disabled and about the nature or severity of the disability unless the examination or inquiry is shown to be job related and consistent with business necessity.[169]

2.4.3.2 Difference Number Two: Employers Must Make the Recruitment and Selection Process ADA Compliant

What affirmative obligations does the ADA place on employers in the hiring process? First, an employer must ensure that the job application process itself is accessible to persons with disabilities. For example, although an employer need not have its job postings or standard form application preprinted in Braille, it should be prepared either to do so if requested or to provide vision-impaired applicants with readers or transcribers to assist them in completing the application. Employers should also make job postings available in TDD form for those with visual impairments.

In addition, the human resources office should be easy to reach for persons with disabilities. There should be clearly marked and ample parking for applicants who arrive using wheelchairs or who cannot walk for long distances. The entrance to the building where the human resources office is located should be wheelchair accessible. If the human resources office is not located on the ground floor, there should be a wheelchair-accessible eleva-

---

167. *See* 29 C.F.R. § 1630.14(b).

168. *See* 29 C.F.R. § 1630.14(b)(3).

169. *See* 42 U.S.C. § 12112(d)(4). See also 29 C.F.R. §§ 1630.13 and 1630.14, which address pre-employment medical inquiries and examinations.

tor. Similarly, if managers, department heads, and hiring committees will interview candidates somewhere other than the human resources office, the employer must either schedule interviewing and testing in another handicap-accessible location or have an accessible contingency location set aside in case a candidate arrives and needs wheelchair or elevator accessibility without that need having been apparent earlier.[170]

Job applicants with disabilities sometimes ask for changes or modifications to some of the evaluative processes that the employer uses, such as tests or assessment centers.[171] An applicant may request additional time to complete an examination, a written test in lieu of an oral examination if he or she is hearing-impaired, or the use of an oral examination in place of a written test if the applicant's vision is impaired.[172] Other types of accommodations could include giving an examination in an individual rather than a group setting. Sometimes an applicant's disability is obvious, as is the need for a modification of the application process. But sometimes it is not. The ADA requires an employer to provide a reasonable accommodation to the *known* physical or mental limitations of a qualified individual with a disability.[173] Where an applicant's disability is not obvious, an employer may ask him or her to document it.

---

170. *See, e.g.,* Adeyemi v. Dist. of Columbia, 525 F.3d 1222, 1224 (D.C. Cir. 2008) (where deaf applicant showed up for interview without giving enough notice that hearing interpreter would be needed, city accommodated applicant by typing questions on a computer screen and allowing employee to type responses).

171. *See* 29 C.F.R. § 1630.11; U.S. Equal Employment Opportunity Commission, *Technical Assistance Manual on the Employment Provisions (Title I) of the Americans with Disabilities Act* (January 1992), at V-18–V-21.

172. *See, e.g.,* Digianni v. Bloomberg, 311 F. App'x 492, 494 (2d Cir. 2009), *cert. denied,* 129 S. Ct. 2880 (2009) (affirming grant of summary judgment to employer who had reasonably accommodated applicant with learning disability who requested and received extra time to complete timed writing sample and still failed to meet minimum competency requirements); Fink v. New York City Dep't of Pers., 53 F.3d 565, 567 (2d Cir. 1995) (city reasonably accommodated visually impaired candidates for promotion with a tape recording of the examination, a tape recorder, permission to use their own tape recorders if they preferred, a reader-assistant to help with the operation of the recorder and to read them questions and answers, a private room, and double the time afforded to other test-takers).

173. Vague or conclusory statements revealing an unspecified incapacity are not sufficient to put an employer on notice of its obligations under the ADA. *See* Huppenbauer v. May Dep't Stores Co., 99 F.3d 1130 at *6 (4th Cir. 1996) (employee's attestations to his ability to do job at time of hire and subsequent requests for transfers to

An employer may ask an applicant for medical documentation that establishes the existence of a disability entitling that applicant to a reasonable accommodation in the application process or in the job itself, should the applicant be successful. However, an employer cannot ask for more information than is necessary to establish the existence of a disability. For example, an employer is not entitled to the complete psychiatric history of an applicant suffering from post-traumatic stress disorder—the employer is entitled only to documentation of the disorder, its current effects, and the long-term outlook for the applicant's recovery.[174]

2.4.3.3 Difference Number Three: An Employer Has a Duty to Reasonably Accommodate a Disability

A reasonable accommodation may be needed by an applicant or a current employee. The definition of "reasonable accommodation" is the same in either situation: a reasonable accommodation is any change or adjustment to a job or work environment that allows a qualified applicant or employee with a disability to enjoy equal employment opportunities. There are three major kinds of reasonable accommodations:

1. changes to a job application process (for example, modifying examinations);
2. changes to the work environment or to the way a job is usually done to enable a qualified person with a disability to perform a position's essential functions; or
3. changes that allow an employee with a disability to enjoy equal benefits and privileges of employment enjoyed by other similarly situated employees (for example, access to training).[175]

---

another department with similar duties undermined claim that he had put employer on notice of his disability), *citing* Morisky v. Broward Cnty., 80 F.3d 445, 448 (11th Cir. 1996) (knowledge that applicant for custodial position could not read and had taken special education courses was not sufficient to put county on notice of applicant's developmental disorder because it does not always follow that someone who is illiterate is necessarily suffering from a physical or mental impairment).

174. *See* U.S. Equal Employment Opportunity Commission, *Enforcement Guidance: Disability-Related Inquiries and Medical Examinations of Employees under the Americans with Disabilities Act*, No. 915.002 (July 27, 2000), at 12.

175. *See* 29 C.F.R. § 1630.2(o).

Most accommodations fall into the second category and may include changes or modifications to training materials or policies or acquiring or modifying equipment or devices. In the case of an applicant who has been offered the position or a current employee, reasonable accommodations may include job restructuring, modified work schedules, reassignment to a vacant position, provision of readers and/or interpreters, leave without pay, or physical changes that make the workplace more readily accessible to persons with disabilities.[176]

The ADA requires the employer and the applicant or employee to work together to identify appropriate accommodations by using an informal, interactive process. In other words, the burden of finding a reasonable accommodation, if one exists, is on neither the individual with the disability nor the employer. The burden is on both. A reasonable accommodation is an effective accommodation—one that removes the workplace barrier at issue. But if there are two possible reasonable accommodations, the employer may choose which one to implement; it does not have to choose the accommodation that the applicant or employee prefers.[177]

2.4.4 A Closer Look at the ADA

2.4.4.1 Mixed-Motive Cases

The U.S. Supreme Court has not ruled on whether a mixed-motive theory of liability is available in an ADA disparate treatment case, but the Fourth Circuit appears to recognize the mixed-motive theory, even if it has not expressly so held. To establish a prima facie case of disability discrimination based on the theory that the applicant's disability was one of a number of reasons that the applicant was rejected, the Fourth Circuit has held that a plaintiff must show (1) that he or she had a disability; (2) that he or she was qualified for the job; and (3) that his or her disability played *a motivating role*, but not necessarily the only role, in the decision not to hire the plaintiff.[178] A plaintiff who makes this demonstration is entitled to relief.[179]

---

176. *See* 42 U.S.C. § 12111(9); 29 C.F.R. § 1630.2(o)(2).

177. *See* 29 C.FR Part 1630, App. § 1630.9.

178. *See* Daye v. Sch. Bd. of City of Norfolk, 18 F. App'x 125, 127 (4th Cir. 2001).

179. *See* Baird *ex rel.* Baird v. Rose, 192 F.3d 462, 470 (4th Cir. 1999) (middle school student public accommodations case holding that causation standards applicable in Title VII actions, and not the "solely because of" disability standard applicable under the Rehabilitation Act, are applicable to violations of the ADA).

2.4.4.2 The ADA and Section 504 of the Rehabilitation Act of 1973

Section 504 of the Rehabilitation Act of 1973 (amended and reauthorized in 1992) was the first federal civil rights bill to protect the right of persons with disabilities to equal employment. Section 504 prohibits discrimination on the basis of disability by the federal government, by federal contractors, and by recipients of federal financial assistance. By the act's terms, those groups include state and local governments and public colleges and universities.[180] The scope of the Rehabilitation Act is more limited than that of the ADA because it applies only to programs or businesses that receive federal funds, but the regulations and case law that arose under the Rehabilitation Act provided a model for the ADA. Today, however, it is Title I of the ADA that is the standard against which complaints of employment discrimination brought under the Rehabilitation Act are judged.

2.4.4.3 The ADA and Small Public Employers

As noted above, Title I of the ADA and the ADA regulations issued by the Equal Employment Opportunity Commission[181] cover all state and local government employers with 15 or more employees.[182] But that doesn't mean that smaller government employers are not required to accommodate persons with disabilities. Local government employers with fewer than 15 employees are covered by regulations issued under the Rehabilitation Act of 1973,[183] which also prohibits discrimination in employment against handicapped persons. The substance of the law that governs the treatment of disabled persons by local government employers is not measurably different for those small jurisdictions with fewer than 15 employees than it is for jurisdictions with 15 or more employees, because the ADA is based on the earlier Rehabilitation Act and later Rehabilitation Act cases have looked to ADA cases for precedent and guidance.

---

180. *See* 29 U.S.C. §§ 794(b)(1) and (2).
181. 29 C.F.R. Part 1630.
182. *See* 42 U.S.C. § 12111(5)(A).
183. 29 U.S.C. § 701. *See also* 42 U.S.C. § 12132 (2002); 28 C.F.R. § 35.140(a).

2.5 North Carolina Law Prohibiting Disability Discrimination

In 1985, prior to the passage of the federal Americans with Disabilities Act, the North Carolina General Assembly enacted the North Carolina Persons with Disabilities Protection Act.[184] The Persons with Disabilities Protection Act applies to any employer with 15 or more full-time employees. The act makes it a discriminatory practice to

> fail to hire or consider for employment or promotion, to discharge, or otherwise to discriminate against a qualified person with a disability on the basis of a disabling condition with respect to compensation or the terms, conditions, or privileges of employment.[185]

Like the ADA and the federal Rehabilitation Act on which that statute was based, the Persons with Disabilities Act requires employers to investigate and make any possible reasonable accommodations to the hiring process or to the job that would enable a disabled applicant or employee to complete the application process or perform the job.[186] Courts usually look to analogous ADA and Rehabilitation Act cases to assist in interpreting this statute.[187]

2.6 Genetic Information Nondiscrimination Act

Title II of the Genetic Information Nondiscrimination Act of 2008 (GINA) prohibits employers from discriminating on the basis of genetic information and medical history.[188] An employer may never use genetic information to make an employment decision because genetic information is not relevant to an individual's current ability to work. Although the two statutes are related, GINA is distinct from the ADA in that the ADA prohibits

---

184. *See* G.S. 168A-1–168A-11.

185. *See* G.S. 168A-5(a)(1).

186. *See* G.S. 168A-4.

187. *See, e.g.,* Johnson v. Bd. of Trs. of Durham Tech. Cmty. Coll., 157 N.C. App. 38, 46 (2003) (applying U.S. Supreme Court's decision in *McKennon v. Nashville Banner Publishing Co.,* 513 U.S. 325 (1995), to facts at bar).

188. GINA is codified at 42 U.S.C. §§ 2000ff–2000ff-11. The EEOC's GINA regulations are at 29 C.F.R. Part 1635.

discrimination on the basis of manifested conditions that meet the ADA's definition of disability, while GINA prohibits discrimination based on genetic information that may indicate that a condition may manifest itself in the future. GINA applies to employers with 15 or more employees.[189]

GINA prohibits the use of genetic information to discriminate in employment. This is an absolute prohibition. Unlike other nondiscrimination statutes, GINA provides no defenses for an employer: it recognizes no business necessity that would allow for the use of genetic information in making employment decisions. In addition to its prohibition against discrimination, GINA expressly prohibits employers from requesting, requiring, or purchasing genetic information. It also requires employers to keep any genetic information that they accidentally acquire confidential.

Genetic information for the purposes of GINA includes

- an applicant's or employee's genetic tests;[190]
- an applicant's or employee's family member's genetic tests;[191]
- the manifestation of any disease or disorder in any of the applicant's or employee's family members (with disease or disorder not limited to inheritable conditions);[192]
- a request for or receipt of genetic services by an applicant or employee; or
- genetic information concerning a fetus or embryo of an applicant, employee, or family member.

Genetic information does not include information about an applicant's, employee's, or family member's race, gender, ethnic background, or age or the fact that a person currently has a disease or disorder (if, of course, the disease or disorder met the ADA's definition of disability, the person would be covered under that statute).

Some examples of genetic tests include

- the test for the BRCA1 or BRCA2 gene, which indicates that the person has a greater risk of breast or ovarian cancer;
- the test for Huntington's Disease;

---

189. *See* 42 U.S.C. § 2000ff(B)(i); 29 C.F.R. § 1635.2(d).
190. *See* 29 C.F.R. § 1635.3(f).
191. *See* 29 C.F.R. § 1635.3(a).
192. *See* 29 C.F.R. § 1635.3(b).

- carrier screening to determine whether a person is at risk of transmitting a disease-causing gene to his or her children (for example, screening for the cystic fibrosis gene, sickle cell anemia, spinal muscular dystrophy, or fragile X syndrome); and
- DNA information about paternity.[193]

Standard medical tests such as cholesterol tests, blood glucose tests, or tests for drug or alcohol use are not genetic tests.

2.6.1 GINA's Impact on the Hiring Process

There are two primary ways in which GINA affects the hiring process. First, an employer may not directly ask an employee about genetic information during the hiring process, nor may it ask others, such as professional or personal references of the applicant, about the applicant's genetic information. The EEOC's GINA regulations specifically prohibit employers from searching the Internet for genetic information about an applicant.[194] In addition, when an employer has an applicant fill out a post-offer medical questionnaire or undergo a post-offer medical examination consistent with the ADA, it must direct the applicant and the physician performing the examination not to collect genetic information—that is, not to collect medical history.[195]

Second, during the hiring process employers sometimes inadvertently acquire information about an applicant's family medical history. Suppose, for example, that an employer asks an applicant about a gap in his or her job history and the applicant replies that he or she withdrew from the workforce for six months in order to care for a parent or child with cancer. Under GINA's definition of genetic information, the employer will have acquired family medical history that qualifies as genetic information. In this case, however, there are many different answers that an applicant might have given to explain the six-month period during which he or she did not work—the previous employer may have gone out of business, for example—so the employer cannot be said to have asked a question that

193. *See* 29 C.F.R. § 1635.3(f)(2).
194. *See* 29 C.F.R. § 1635.8(a).
195. *See* 29 C.F.R. § 1635.8(d).

was likely to reveal genetic information. In this case, the employer is not liable for violating GINA.[196]

2.7 North Carolina Law Prohibiting Discrimination Based on Genetic Information

Like GINA, G.S. 95-28.1A prohibits employers from denying employment to or refusing to hire someone on the basis of genetic information that concerns that person or a member of their family. G.S. 95-28.1A applies to all state agencies and to all local government employers, regardless of size. Although the North Carolina statute predates GINA by more than 10 years, no reported cases have as yet arisen under it.[197]

2.8 The Uniformed Services Employment and Reemployment Rights Act

The Uniformed Services Employment and Reemployment Rights Act of 1994 (USERRA) is the successor statute to the Vietnam-era Veterans' Reemployment Rights Act of 1968. It was enacted to prohibit employment discrimination against those who serve in the United States armed forces and to make it easier for people to perform non-career service in the armed forces by minimizing the disruption to their civilian careers.[198] USERRA protects any person serving in the United States Army, Navy, Air Force, Marine Corps, and Coast Guard and their reserve units, as well as persons serving in the Army National Guard and Air National Guard, the commissioned corps of the Public Health Service, and "any other category of persons designated by the President in time of war or national emergency."[199]

---

196. *See* 29 C.F.R. §§ 1635.8(b)(i) and (b)(ii)(B).

197. Even before the General Assembly enacted the general prohibition against discrimination based on genetic information, it had prohibited discrimination against anyone possessing the sickle cell trait or hemoglobin C trait in G.S. 95-28.1.

198. USERRA is codified at 39 U.S.C. § 4301–4333. The U.S. Department of Labor's administrative rules implementing USERRA may be found at 20 C.F.R. §§ 1002.1–1002.314.

199. *See* 38 U.S.C. §§ 4303(13), (16).

USERRA affects the recruitment and selection process in two ways. First, USERRA prohibits discrimination in hiring (and in all aspects of the employment relationship) against someone who is or *shall be* performing, has performed, or *intends to perform* military service. Thus, a person's initial employment application cannot be rejected on the ground that he or she is a member of the military reserves and is therefore likely to be absent when called up for duty. Similarly, if an employer were to learn that an applicant is not currently a member of the reserves, National Guard, or other branch of the uniformed services but intends to enlist, it could not reject the applicant on that basis.

Nor could an employer reject an applicant merely because his or her military service would make the applicant unavailable to start employment on a particular day. A Massachusetts case involving an application to become a municipal police officer by a person on active service in the Army illustrates this principle.[200] Thomas McClain was an enlisted member of the U.S. Army. Before joining the Army, he took and passed the Massachusetts civil service examination required of all new police officers. Near the end of his term of service with the Army, the city of Somerville offered him a position as a police officer contingent on his availability to attend a previously scheduled police academy training session. McLain could not, however, obtain a release from the Army to attend the training session. Although the city considered McLain an "outstanding candidate" and freely admitted that it would have hired him if he had been available to start the training session, it withdrew its offer because of his unavailability. McLain sued the city of Somerville, alleging that it had violated his rights under USERRA by refusing to hire him because his military service prevented him from beginning his police training on a particular date. The court granted summary judgment in the case for McLain, finding that an employer may not discriminate in hiring based on a prospective employee's unavailability due to his obligation to perform military service.[201]

---

200. *See* McLain v. City of Somerville, 424 F. Supp. 2d 329 (D. Mass. 2006).

201. *See McLain*, 424 F. Supp .2d at 336–38. *See also* Beattie v. Trump Shuttle, Inc., 758 F. Supp. 30 (D.D.C. 1991) (decided under predecessor Veteran's Reemployment Rights Act).

2.8.1 Disparate Treatment or Intentional Discrimination under USERRA

State and local government employees alleging violations of USERRA may seek to enforce their rights by filing a complaint with the Secretary of Labor or by bringing suit against the government employer in either state court or the United States District Court.[202] As with other federal antidiscrimination statutes, rejected applicants may bring disparate treatment or intentional discrimination claims under USERRA. A plaintiff establishes a prima facie case of discrimination based on military status by showing that (1) he or she is a member of the U.S. armed forces or intends to become a member of the U.S. armed forces; (2) he or she is qualified for the job for which his or her application was rejected; and (3) his or her military status or intended military status was a motivating factor or a substantial motivating factor in the decision not to hire the plaintiff.[203] At this point, the burden shifts to the employer to show that the plaintiff would not have been hired, even if he or she had had no military obligations.[204] If the employer cannot prove that and the applicant wins the case, the court may require the employer to employ the person, pay the person back wages and the amount of lost benefits, or both, and if the court finds the violation to be willful, it may award the plaintiff an amount equal to his or her back wages and/or benefits as liquidated damages.[205]

2.8.2 Disparate Impact or Unintentional Discrimination under USERRA

It is unclear whether disparate impact claims are available under USERRA. To date, none have been decided.[206]

---

202. *See* 38 U.S.C. §§ 4322; 4323(a), (b).

203. Brandsasse v. City of Suffolk, Va., 72 F. Supp. 2d 608, 617 (E.D. Va. 1999).

204. *See* Petty v. Metro. Gov't of Nashville-Davidson Cnty., 538 F.3d 431, 446 (6th Cir. 2008).

205. *See* 38 U.S.C. § 4323(d)(1).

206. *See* Fink v. City of New York, 129 F. Supp. 2d 511, 522 (E.D.N.Y. 2001) (observing in dicta that a policy that requires all persons, regardless of veteran status, to take their promotional exam on a given date and gives no opportunity for a makeup examination systematically discriminates against veterans and has a disparate impact). *But see* Miller v. City of Indianapolis, 281 F.3d 648, 651 (7th Cir. 2002) ("whether a disparate impact claim can be prosecuted under USERRA will wait for another day").

2.8.3 USERRA and the Promotional Process

Employees cannot be denied consideration for newly available promotions simply because they are on military leave and are not present to apply for them.[207] Where the promotional process involves sitting for an examination, as law enforcement and firefighting frequently require, failure promptly to offer an employee performing military service a makeup promotional exam may constitute discrimination.[208] USERRA is not, however, an affirmative action hiring statute. An employer need not hire a member of the armed forces if that person is not the best person for the job.[209]

2.8.4 Filling Vacancies Caused by Military Leave

The second way that USERRA affects the hiring process is that it requires employers to grant employees job-protected leave to serve in the armed forces, whether they are called to duty voluntarily or volunteer for service. Employees are entitled to take military leave for cumulative periods as long as five years, and in some cases, for even longer periods.[210] Thus, USERRA creates temporary vacancies (and in some cases, long-term temporary vacancies) for which employers must hire new workers. When hiring an employee into a USERRA-created vacancy, the employer must make clear to applicants that they may be dismissed when the person who regularly holds the position returns from duty. This is especially important where an

---

207. *See* Haskins v. Dep't of Navy, 86 MSPB 357 (2000) (allegation that agency failed to consider employee for promotion while he was serving in Operation Desert Storm states a claim for which relief may be granted under USERRA); *Brandsasse*, 72 F. Supp. 2d at 619 (city's initial refusal to allow plaintiff to sit for a promotional exam that conflicted with his active duty orders, followed by retaliatory investigation when he insisted on enforcing his right to take the exam, constitutes discrimination under USERRA).

208. *See Fink*, 129 F. Supp. 2d at 520 (reasonable jury could find that plaintiff's military status was a motivating factor in denying his request for a promptly administered promotional exam upon his return from duty).

209. *See* Gambrill v. Cullman Cnty. Bd. of Educ., 395 F. App'x 543, 544 (11th Cir. 2010) (district court did not err in concluding that regardless of plaintiff's military involvement, the defendants would have hired the successful applicant because he was the most qualified candidate to be assistant principal). *See also* Madden v. Rolls Royce Corp., 563 F.3d 636, 638 (7th Cir. 2009) (reason for not hiring temporary employee permanently was not his military status but his dangerously incompetent work as an engineer).

210. *See* 38 U.S.C. §§ 4312 (a)(2), (c)(1)–(4), (f)(1).

ordinance gives employees who have completed a probationary period the right to continued employment absent performance or conduct issues (a so-called property right in employment). A temporary employee whose performance is outstanding—perhaps even better than that of the employee on military leave—generally cannot displace the serviceperson from that position.[211] If the employer wishes to keep the temporary employee on as a permanent employee, it will have to make room for both the returning serviceperson and the temporary employee.

2.9 North Carolina Law Protecting Those Who Serve in the Military from Discrimination

G.S. 127B-12 and 127B-14 also prohibit discrimination in employment against military personnel by public entities. Specifically, the General Statutes enjoin an "officer or employee of the State, or of any county, city and county, municipal corporation, school district, water district, or other district" from discriminating against members of the Armed Forces "with respect to their employment, appointment, position or status" and from denying, disqualifying, or discharging them "from their employment or position by virtue of their membership or service in the military forces of this State or of the United States."[212] These provisions do not, however, provide persons serving in the armed forces or reserves any greater rights in employment than does USERRA. Violations of these provisions of the General Statutes constitute Class 2 misdemeanors. In addition, G.S. 127A-202.1 prohibits discrimination in employment on the basis that an applicant is a member of the North Carolina National Guard or has performed, applied to perform, or has an obligation to perform service in the National Guard.

---

211. If the leave has been for 90 days or fewer, employers must reemploy employees returning from a military absence in the position that the employee would have held on the date of reemployment had he or she actually been working during the period of military service. If the leave exceeded 90 days, the employer has the option of placing the returning employee in a position of "similar seniority, status and pay." *See* 38 U.S.C. § 4313(a). *See also* Davis v. Halifax City Sch. Sys., 508 F. Supp. 966, 968 (E.D.N.D. 1981) (under predecessor Veterans Reemployment Rights Act statute); Cole v. Swint, 961 F.2d 58, 60 (5th Cir. 1992) (Veterans Reemployment Rights Act); Kay v. Gen. Cable Corp., 144 F.2d 653, 655 (3d Cir. 1944) (Selective Training and Service Act of 1940).

212. See G.S. 127B-12, and more generally, G.S. 127B-10–127B-15.

While the General Statutes require state agencies and institutions to observe a veteran preference in employment, they do not require local government employers to do so.[213] Local government employers and community colleges are, however, free to adopt such a policy.[214]

2.10 The Equal Protection Clause of the United States Constitution

What happens when applicants for public employment feel they are being treated unfairly because the employer has a residency requirement? Or when applicants for law enforcement positions with a city are rejected because they sport tattoos? Can a county prohibit its employees from cohabiting with convicted felons? Government employers have been challenged over policies like these by applicants and employees through lawsuits alleging that the employers' actions violate the Equal Protection Clause of the Fourteenth Amendment to the U.S. Constitution.[215] The Equal Protection Clause provides that no state shall "deny to any person within its jurisdiction the equal protection of the laws." This means that neither the federal government, nor a state or political subdivision of a state, shall intentionally and arbitrarily discriminate against anyone through the terms of a statute or other legislative enactment or through the application of the terms of the statute by an officer or employee of the government.[216] Most

213. *See* G.S. 126-82 and 128-15.

214. 23 N.C.A.C. 02C .0210(a)(30) makes clear that community colleges are not considered state institutions for the purposes of the veterans' preference and that each community college has the authority to adopt its own policy on veterans.

215. Public employees are entitled to bring lawsuits alleging that the action of a government employer has violated the Equal Protection Clause. *See* Booth v. Maryland, 327 F.3d 377, 382–83 (4th Cir. 2003); Adams v. Trs. of the Univ. of N.C. Wilmington, 640 F.3d 550, 566 (4th Cir. 2011). For instances of equal protection challenges similar to the above hypotheticals, see *Lewis v. City of Kinston*, 127 N.C. App. 274 (1997) (residency requirement); *Inturri v. City of Hartford, Conn.*, 365 F. Supp. 2d 240 (D. Conn. 2005), *aff'd sub nom. Inturri v. City of Hartford*, 165 F. App'x 66 (2d Cir. 2006) (tattoos); *Via v. Taylor*, 224 F. Supp. 2d 753, 761–62 (D. Del. 2002) (cohabiting with felon).

216. *See* Vill. of Willowbrook v. Olech, 528 U.S. 562, 564 (2000); Yan-Min Wang v. UNC-CH Sch. of Med., 2011 WL 4552300 (N.C. App. 2011) (finding that plaintiff did not identify any classification upon which she was denied equal protection).

laws do, in fact, differentiate in some way between groups of persons. The Equal Protection Clause does not prohibit this. What the Equal Protection Clause requires is that government not treat any differently persons who are in all relevant respects alike and that it refrain from using invidious classification schemes like those based on race or gender.[217] In the hypotheticals set forth at the beginning of the above paragraph, a plaintiff's claims would be that

- the government employer created a classification based on residency that violated the Equal Protection Clause by treating residents of one place as eligible for government employment, while treating residents of other places as ineligible;
- the government employer violated the Equal Protection Clause by treating people with tattoos differently than people without them;
- the government employer burdened its employees' fundamental First Amendment right to free association in violation of the Equal Protection Clause by prohibiting them from residing with convicted felons, while other citizens who do not work for the government employer are free to do so.

The reality is that laws do make distinctions among people. The Supreme Court has held that it will uphold the legislative classification so long as it bears a rational relation to some legitimate end, provided that the law making the classification neither burdens a fundamental right, such as voting or marrying, nor targets a protected or "suspect" class such as race or gender.[218] There is no fundamental right to public employment, so applicant and employee equal protection claims must be based on their employer's burdening of some other right (like the right of free association) or on the employer's classifying them in an impermissible manner.[219] The rational relation test, more commonly referred to as the rational basis test, gives great deference "to legislative determinations as to the desirability of par-

217. *See* Romer v. Evans, 517 U.S. 620, 631 (1996); Nordlinger v. Hahn, 505 U.S. 1, 10 (1992).

218. *See* Clark v. Jeter, 486 U.S. 456, 461 (1988).

219. *See* United Bldg. & Constr. Trades Council v. Mayor of Camden, 465 U.S. 208, 219 (1984) (holding that there is no fundamental right to government employment for purposes of the Equal Protection Clause); Mass. Bd. of Retirement v. Murgia, 427 U.S. 307, 313 (1976) (holding that governmental employment is not per se a fundamental right requiring strict scrutiny on an equal protection challenge).

ticular statutory discriminations."[220] Under rational basis review, it is not the court's role to second-guess the government or to determine whether the desired goal is actually served by the challenged statute or regulation. Rather, the court need only determine whether the legislature "rationally might have believed . . . that the desired end might be served."[221]

In contrast to rational basis review, which is referred to as regular scrutiny, any classification that does burden a fundamental right or creates a classification along the lines of race or national origin lines (race and national origin being deemed suspect classes) will be subject to strict scrutiny, passing constitutional muster only if it is narrowly tailored to serve a compelling state interest.[222] Classifications that are created along gender lines are considered "quasi-suspect" and are subject to intermediate scrutiny by the courts. To withstand intermediate scrutiny, a statutory classification must be substantially related to an important governmental objective.[223]

Equal protection challenges to particular recruitment and selection practices will be discussed in more detail in later chapters.

2.11 Affirmative Action and Local Government Hiring

The law of affirmative action has undergone major changes since the first challenge to its use was considered by the U.S. Supreme Court in 1976. Today, the status of affirmative action in local government employment is unclear. This much is clear, however. Affirmative action is almost always lawful when it is undertaken to remedy past, identifiable discrimination by the government unit that has lingering effects in the present. An affirmative action plan must be limited in scope and duration. Remedying general societal discrimination or providing minority role models is not a lawful basis on which a local government may adopt an affirmative action plan, although operational needs, particularly in public safety departments, may

---

220. *See* McCool v. City of Philadelphia, 494 F. Supp. 2d 307, 317 (E.D. Pa. 2007), *quoting* City of New Orleans v. Dukes, 427 U.S. 297, 303 (1976).

221. *See McCool*, 494 F. Supp. 2d at 321.

222. *See* Dunn v. Blumstein, 405 U.S. 330, 335 (1972); *Clark*, 486 U.S. at 461.

223. *See Clark*, 486 U.S. at 461; Mississippi Univ. for Women v. Hogan, 458 U.S. 718, 723–24, and n.9 (1982).

sometimes justify a race-conscious approach to recruitment and selection. Court-ordered affirmative action is always lawful.

Because affirmative action plays a more limited role in hiring than it once did, and because the law of affirmative action is complex, a comprehensive treatment of the history and current status of affirmative action in local government hiring may found in Appendix 2 at the back of this book.

Chapter 3

Defining and Advertising the Job

Chapter 3

Defining and Advertising the Job

The first step in the recruitment process is simply stated, although perhaps less simply done: the employer must review and revise the job description for any position it seeks to fill. There is no legal definition or required format for a job description. Generally speaking, it includes identifying information (such as job title); the main purpose and scope of the job; a list of the job's primary or essential duties; whether or not the job has supervisory responsibility; the end results or accountabilities that the employee is expected to achieve or meet; and the minimum qualifications and/or minimum knowledge, skills, and abilities and minimum experience that a person must have to be able to perform the job's essential duties. The job description may also contain one or more qualifications and experiences that the employer prefers but will not require the successful applicant to have.

A job description fulfills a number of different purposes. From a practical standpoint, a job description contains the information needed for assigning the position to an appropriate pay grade and for classifying it as exempt or nonexempt for Fair Labor Standards Act purposes. It provides applicants and employees with an understanding of the specific tasks they are to perform and the expected results of that performance and sets the job in context within the structure and goals of the larger organization. For recruiting and selecting a person to fill the job, the job description provides a blueprint for advertising the position, screening applicants, and questioning and testing those applicants who seem most promising. Once someone fills the position, the job description forms the basis for a supervisor's evaluation of the employee's performance.

Once the job description has been drafted or updated, the employer's next step is to draft and place a job advertisement. As is the case with the job description, there is no legally required format or legally required content for a job posting or job advertisement. On one level, a job posting or advertisement is nothing more than a notice to the public that an employer has a vacancy that it is seeking to fill. Considered from this perspective, a bare-bones notice may well suffice, leaving it up to interested parties to seek out further details from the employer. At another level, however, a job posting or advertisement is an opportunity for an employer to market its opening as a special one and its organization as a desirable place to work. Properly framed, the job posting or advertisement can help an employer attract the kind of applicants it wants.

The skill of drafting a job description that accurately reflects a job as it is performed by an incumbent employee and the art of crafting a job advertisement go beyond the scope of this book. There are, however, a few legal rules that employers should be aware of as they try to put together these two key components of the recruitment and selection process.

3.1 Legal Issues Raised by Job Descriptions

Although there is no legal requirement that an employer have a job description for any particular job or for all jobs, job descriptions fulfill an important function in litigating claims of unlawful discrimination. This is especially true with respect to claims brought under the Americans with Disabilities Act (ADA), but it is also true of Title VII and age discrimination claims.

3.1.1 Job Descriptions and ADA Discrimination Claims

The ADA defines a "qualified individual" as "an individual who, with or without reasonable accommodation, can perform the essential functions of the employment position that such individual holds or desires."[1] Persons who cannot perform the job's essential functions are not qualified and are

1. *See* 42 U.S.C. § 12111(8).

not protected by the ADA, even if they have a disability. The ADA does not require employers to modify the essential functions of a job in order to make an accommodation for individuals who are not physically capable of performing them.

Before an employer can assess whether an applicant can perform the essential functions of a position, it must have defined the functions and identified those that are essential and those that are marginal. If an applicant is rejected and claims that he or she was qualified but was rejected on account of a disability, the essential functions of the position will play a central role in the case. In defining a qualified individual, the ADA continues:

> For the purposes of this subchapter, consideration shall be given to the employer's judgment as to what functions of a job are essential, and if an employer has prepared a written description before advertising or interviewing applicants for the job, this description shall be considered evidence of the essential functions of the job.[2]

While the job description is *evidence* of the essential functions of the job, courts also consider whether the requirements stated in the job description measure the essential functions of the job as it is *actually performed*. In one ADA case, the plaintiff, who had been injured in a workplace accident and was no longer able to perform the duties of his original position, was permitted to apply for other positions within the company. The plaintiff had been a courier for FedEx but could no longer perform the position because it required that an employee be able to lift up to 75 pounds and the plaintiff had a 57 pound lifting restriction. Among other jobs the plaintiff applied for was that of customer service agent. That position also required the ability to lift up to 75 pounds. When the plaintiff was not chosen for that position, he brought an ADA and Title VII race discrimination lawsuit against FedEx.

The plaintiff argued that the customer service agent position's lifting requirement was arbitrary and not bona fide, based on the fact that agents do not often have to pick up packages heavier than 50 pounds. He did not argue and could not show that they *never* lifted such packages. FedEx, on

---

2. *See* 42 U.S.C. § 12111(8).

the other hand, offered a validation study for the positions of both courier and customer service agent that showed that the ability to lift 75 pounds was an essential job function as described in the position description. The district court hearing the case granted FedEx's motion for summary judgment in part on the basis that the plaintiff could not perform one of the essential functions of the job.[3]

In another case, the question of whether driving was an essential function of a pharmacy supervisor position was a material issue of disputed fact. The employee, a regional pharmacy manager, had requested reassignment to a position as a pharmacy supervisor as a reasonable accommodation of his diabetic neuropathy, which made driving difficult for him, but his employer had denied the request. The employer contended that driving was an essential function of the pharmacy supervisor position to which the plaintiff requested a transfer, but the plaintiff argued that the job posting did not include driving as one of the job duties/functions and did not mention driving under the preferred qualifications. The employer argued in response that under the section entitled "Physical Demand Analysis," the job description said that the position required "many hours in a car (approximately 30,000 miles yearly)."[4] The court did not ultimately decide the issue of whether driving was in fact an essential function, finding that the reassignment would not be a reasonable accommodation because it would require the displacement of another employee. But the case is another example of the central role the job description plays in resolving issues of whether an employee with a disability is qualified for a particular position. Thus, it is not only important that the employer have a job description but also that it be accurate and up-to-date and reflect the standard of knowledge, skills, and abilities against which the employer will be measuring job applicants.

---

3. *See* Williams v. Fed. Exp. Corp., 1999 WL 1940039 (W.D.N.C. 1999), *aff'd sub nom.* Williams v. Fed. Exp. Corp., 202 F.3d 262 (4th Cir. 1999). *See also* Pandazides v. Va. Bd. of Educ., 946 F.2d 345, 349 (4th Cir. 1991) (determination of whether a teacher with learning disabilities was qualified within the meaning of the federal Rehabilitation Act involved determination of whether requirement imposed by board of education actually measured the essential functions of the job).

4. *See* Schneider v. Giant of Maryland, LLC, 389 F. App'x 263, 268 (4th Cir. 2010).

3.1.2 Job Descriptions and Title VII Discrimination Claims

In a Title VII discrimination case analyzed under the *McDonnell Douglas* burden shifting standard, once the plaintiff has made a prima facie case and the employer has offered a legitimate, nondiscriminatory reason for rejecting the applicant, the plaintiff must then prove that the proffered nondiscriminatory reason was merely a pretext and that the employer's real reason was unlawful discrimination.[5] One way in which a plaintiff may prove pretext is by demonstrating that the employer's nondiscriminatory reasons are not reflective of essential functions of the job as set out in the job description. This is precisely why the Fourth Circuit overturned grants of summary judgment to the employer in the case *Ham v. Washington Suburban Sanitary Commission*.[6] In the *Ham* case, the defendant, a Maryland water and sewer authority, underwent a reorganization. As part of the reorganization, it created the new position of "lead electrical/mechanical technician" and prepared a new job description for it. The essential functions included in the job description were to direct and assign subordinate technicians to install, repair, or modify various types of equipment systems or devices and to oversee and take the lead in the more difficult electrical and mechanical maintenance activities set forth in the job description. The position description specified that a minimum number of years of experience in electrical or mechanical work or an equivalent combination of skills and experience were required. The description did not mention a need for administrative skills, writing abilities, or the ability to advocate the commission's new productions initiative.

One of the African American plaintiffs in the *Ham* case was rejected in spite of his superior technical skills and long experience in favor of a white candidate who had strong communication skills and involvement in the productions initiative but did not meet the minimum experience requirement set forth in the job description. The Fourth Circuit overturned the district court's grant of summary judgment for the employer, finding that a reasonable jury could have inferred from the employer's own job description that its legitimate, nondiscriminatory reason for the white

---

5. For a full discussion of how a typical Title VII intentional discrimination case proceeds, see Chapter 2, Sections 2.1.1 and 2.1.5.

6. *See* Ham v. Washington Suburban Sanitary Comm'n, 158 F. App'x 457, 466 (4th Cir. 2005).

candidate's selection—his written communication skills—was a pretext for discrimination.[7]

3.1.3 Preferred versus Required Qualifications

Employers frequently wrestle over whether to characterize certain qualifications that they seek as preferred or required. Could a decision to list qualifications as either preferred or required limit the employer's options when it comes time to choose among real individuals, each with his or her own unique set of qualifications and experiences? What should an employer do where it very much desires the person it hires to have a given credential but does not want to require it as it is unsure whether it will be able to identify an otherwise desirable candidate who meets the qualification standard?

To some extent, the decision as to whether a given credential should be denoted as preferred or required will be a function of the particular job duties as they are actually performed with a particular employer, the employer's analysis of the demographics of its labor market, and the culture of the employer itself. Nevertheless, an understanding of the legal issues that may arise when one or the other term is used can assist employers in making the preferred versus required determination.

Where an employer hires someone who does not meet any of a position's *required* qualifications, it cannot defend itself against a discrimination claim by saying that it has hired the better-qualified person. If

---

7. *See Ham*, 158 F. App'x at 459–60, 464–69. *See also* Dennis v. Columbia Colleton Med. Ctr., Inc., 290 F.3d 639, 646 (4th Cir. 2002) (hiring manager's assertion that it was both managerial experience and computer knowledge that set the successful candidate apart from the plaintiff had flavor of post hoc rationalizations where neither was emphasized in the written job description); Rutschman v. Univ. of N.C. at Greensboro, 1993 WL 264542 (M.D.N.C. 1993) (plaintiff failed to make a prima facie case of disability discrimination where he did not meet the job requirements of having one year of work experience handling money or previous experience as a postal window clerk, bank teller, or food store cashier); Goico v. Boeing Co., 347 F. Supp. 2d 955, 981 (D. Kan. 2004) (where employer suddenly places critical importance upon a factor not listed in the job requisition as a required or preferred qualification there were genuine issues of material fact as to whether employer's proffered reasons for not selecting older aeronautical engineer of Cuban origin for test pilot position were pretextual); Jimenez v. City of New York, 605 F. Supp. 2d 485, 526 (S.D.N.Y. 2009) (genuine issue of material fact precluding summary judgment where selected applicant's experiences were all in fields that were not relevant to the fields listed in the job posting).

the rejected candidate did have the required qualifications, the disparity between what the job description clearly stated and the employer's rationalization for why it chose the candidate without those qualifications leaves the employer open to the inference that those reasons were a pretext for unlawful discrimination.

Where an employer hires someone who does not meet some or all of a position's *preferred* requirements, on the other hand, there is generally no inference of unlawful discrimination to be drawn. In a Title VII claim, it is the employer's motivation and intent, not its business judgment, that is at issue.[8] Unless the rejected candidate's qualifications are so superior that they "jump off the page and slap [you] in the face," the fact that a rejected candidate had better qualifications is not sufficient to prove pretext and infer discrimination.[9]

A community college hiring case from Alabama makes this clear. The college was seeking a speech instructor. The job description listed both required and preferred qualifications. The required qualifications were a specified number of graduate credit hours in speech and the preferred qualifications were an additional number of graduate credit hours in English, reading, or another closely related subject, as well as teaching experience in a community college and experience with technological innovation in the classroom. One candidate, a white male, had both the required and

---

8. *See* Keaton v. Cobb Cnty., Ga., 2009 WL 212097, at *4 (11th Cir. Jan. 30, 2009) (plaintiff introduced no evidence supporting her contention that employer's legitimate, nondiscriminatory explanation was pretext). *See also* Wrenn v. Gould, 808 F.2d 493, 502 (6th Cir. 1987) (finding that plaintiff had established prima facie case of retaliatory failure to hire but that employer's reasons for hiring first job applicant were not pretextual even though plaintiff was involved in civil rights litigation with previous employer).

9. *See Dennis*, 290 F.3d at 648, *quoting* Deines v. Tex. Dep't of Protective Servs., 164 F.3d 277, 280–81 (5th Cir. 1999), and *citing* Lee v. GTE Fla., Inc., 226 F.3d 1249, 1254 (11 Cir. 2000). *See also Keaton*, 2009 WL 212097, at *4. (". . . a plaintiff must show that the disparities between the successful applicant's and [her] own qualifications were of such weight and significance that no reasonable person, in the exercise of impartial judgment, could have chosen the candidate selected over the plaintiff"), *quoting* Springer v. Convergys Customer Mgmt. Grp., Inc., 509 F.3d 1344, 1349 (11th Cir. 2007). *But see* Ash v. Tyson Foods, Inc., 546 U.S. 454, 457 (2006) ("The visual image of words jumping off the page to slap you (presumably a court) in the face is unhelpful and imprecise as an elaboration of the standard for inferring pretext from superior qualifications.").

the preferred qualifications. He had a PhD in communication theory and research and had taught at a number of four-year colleges, as well as at community colleges. The selected candidate was an African American woman. She met the required qualifications for the position, but she had only a master's degree in communication studies and had taught only at a community college. The rejected candidate sued for reverse race and gender discrimination. After the rejected applicant made his prima facie case,[10] the college gave as its legitimate, nondiscriminatory reason for selecting the other candidate her enthusiasm for the position, her familiarity with the institution and with the type of students at the institution, and the fact that she would command a smaller salary. The plaintiff challenged those reasons as pretextual. The court, however, found that a reasonable fact-finder could conclude that the college was not motivated by discriminatory intent but had chosen a candidate that better fit the institution, impressed the president more, and cost less than the rejected candidate.[11]

Employers should therefore identify as required only those qualifications that are necessary and for which the employer cannot make an exception. If the employer could conceivably make an exception, then it should probably describe the qualification as preferred. Such a designation will not tie the employer's hands, nor will it leave the employer open to an inference of discrimination if it chooses someone without the preferred qualification over someone with it. But note that an employer who lists a qualification as preferred but not required cannot then later claim that it rejected an applicant merely because he or she did not have the qualification. The employer has already said in that case that the qualification was not necessary.[12]

---

10. Because Title VII prohibits discrimination based on a person's race and gender, rather than on the fact that a person is a member of a group underrepresented in the workforce, such as African Americans or women, a white male is covered by Title VII to the same extent as is an African American man, an African American woman, or a white woman. To establish the first element of a prima facie case, the plaintiff here would have only to show that he was white and was male.

11. *See* Emanuel v. George C. Wallace Cmty. Coll., 2008 WL 4767727 (M.D. Ala. Oct. 27, 2008).

12. *See* EEOC v. City of Greensboro, 2010 WL 5169080 (M.D.N.C. 2010) (rejecting employer's motion for summary judgment on grounds that plaintiff did not have the necessary qualifications).

3.2 Legal Issues Raised by Job Advertisements

As noted above, there is no legally required format or legally required content for a job advertisement. While some advertisements are brief and provide only the position's title or perhaps bullet points of the position's primary duties, others are quite lengthy. The author surveyed a number of advertisements for jobs with public employers in newspapers and on government employer websites and observed that many advertisements fall into the latter, lengthy category. In fact, many of these advertisements are actually the job descriptions themselves. One explanation for this may be a preference on the part of employers to make easily accessible everything that an applicant might want to know about the job. Another explanation might be a misplaced fear on the part of employers that failure to list all job duties and all prerequisites in detail may somehow lead to liability for employment discrimination.

A job description and a job advertisement, however, have two entirely different functions. The job description exists to inform employees and supervisors of the specific tasks the employee is to perform and what results the organization expects from the employee. It also places the job within the larger structure and goals of the organization. The job advertisement exists to catch the attention of those qualified for the position and to induce them to apply for it. *There is no legal reason why employers need to list every essential and marginal function of a position when advertising a job opening.*

An analysis of necessary knowledge, skills, and abilities need not be included in a job advertisement. Human resources professionals consider an analysis of the knowledge, skills, and abilities necessary to perform each job (KSA analysis) a best practice. A KSA analysis is drawn from the job description itself, as well as from interviews with those who currently hold the job, and it underlies the entire recruitment process. A KSA analysis can help human resources managers and hiring supervisors structure the interview and testing process and prepare a development plan for the employee in the position. It can also help human resources managers group the position with other positions with similar requirements for the purposes of classification and compensation. A formal KSA analysis may be shared with an applicant for a position, although it does not have to be. But a job advertisement, which is intended to elicit interest in the position and the employer, does not need to include a KSA analysis unless the analysis would contribute to that end.

3.2.1 Accountant Wanted: A Hypothetical Job Advertisement

In the following hypothetical, Chris Reed is a new hire in Paradise County's human resources department. One of his first assignments is to take the job description for the entry-level accountant position and draft a job advertisement for it. Chris's first draft reads as follows:

Paradise County seeks accountant.

Duties:

- Performs general accounting duties such as maintaining a general ledger, making journal entries, advising supervisors in regard to appropriate balances and fund transfers, and reconciling trial balances, bank statements, and accounts.
- Assists in the development and implementation of new accounting procedures and systems in order to provide a clear audit trail of financial transactions.
- Prepares a variety of tax, financial, and statistical reports and analyses to comply with state, federal, and local requirements and to provide pertinent information for decision making.
- Assists in the organization and preparation of the annual budget, including estimation of revenues and appropriations.
- Keeps informed of economic trends and advises responsible officials regarding financial planning and investments.
- May coordinate the introduction and maintenance of data processing operations, including the preparation of schedules, in relation to accounting functions.
- Assists in the implementation of new accounting pronouncements.
- Participates in meetings concerning equipment purchases, capital construction, and other expenditures that have an impact on county finances.
- Work is performed under general direction of a Senior Accountant or other higher-level employee with leeway allowed for the exercise of independent judgment in planning and carrying out assignments.
- Supervision may be exercised over clerical support staff. Does related work as required.

Qualifications include:

- Working knowledge of trends and current developments in the field of accounting.
- Ability to review reports, find and define problems, and propose solutions.
- Ability to cope with stringent deadlines.
- Ability to devise and maintain accounting systems.

- Ability to prepare and analyze complex financial and statistical records, reports, and statements.
- Ability to prepare and present complex oral and written reports clearly and concisely.
- Ability to plan and supervise the work of others.
- Ability to operate a computer terminal.
- Ability to perform close, detailed work involving considerable visual effort and strain.
- Good judgment.
- Accuracy.

Requirements:

- Graduation from an accredited college or university with a bachelor's degree or higher in accounting, business administration, or closely related field.
- Four years relevant experience.
- Advanced certification of CPA or CMA strongly preferred.
- SAP financial software experience preferred.
- Advanced Excel spreadsheets skills.
- Strong written, analytical, and communication skills, as well as a working. knowledge of accounting principles and concepts.

The successful candidate should be young and energetic. He should be of neat appearance and good character. Equal Employment Opportunity/Affirmative Action Employer.

Chris sits down with Sandy Aubrey, the Paradise County human resources director, to review Chris's draft. Sandy begins by looking over the duties and qualifications sections.

Sandy: *Whoa! I think we need to take this one step at a time, Chris. First of all, we do not need to list every essential and marginal function in the job description in the ad. We have limited space in an outside advertisement. And even internal postings should be concise in order to keep people's attention focused. The first three job duties you have listed are the most important and the ones on which the person will spend the bulk of their time. This is an entry-level position, and the person we ultimately hire may not initially perform all of the other job functions you have included but may grow into them over time.*

Chris: *I'm not sure I understand. Shouldn't we mention those additional duties that the person may take on over time? Couldn't we be sued if we don't mention them?*

Sandy: *I'm glad you're thinking about that, but no, Chris, we couldn't be sued. First of all, the additional job duties are in our job description and we will share them and discuss them with anyone we hire. Second, an employer can always add or take away job duties as the needs of the organization change. We are not locking the county and the employee into an immutable contract. But maybe you are right and we should mention some of those other duties. Something along the lines of "may also assist in the preparation of the annual budget and in the maintenance and preparation of accounting-related data processing operations.*

Chris: *I see what you mean about not listing all the additional job duties in the ad. But we should still list all the qualifications the person should have, right?*

Sandy: *I don't think we need to include such a detailed list of qualifications in the advertisement or posting. It is true that a person will need the knowledge and skills you've listed to be able to perform the primary duties of the job, but I think the list is more useful to us in thinking about how to structure the interview and assessment process than it is for capturing people's attention and making them interested in applying for the position.*

Chris: *So, do you mean that a job posting is more like—well, more like an ad that you would see on a website or TV for a product?*

Sandy: *Yes, it is. That's a good way of thinking about it, Chris.*

Next, Sandy looks over Chris's section on requirements.

Sandy: *For the purposes of this ad, I'd rather not list anything as being a qualification or requirement. In fact, I'd prefer something like this: Paradise County seeks a person for this entry-level position with a BS in accounting, preferably with some internship or work experience in accounting. The person should also have Excel spreadsheet skills and strong analytical and communication skills. SAP financial software experience would be a plus.*

Chris: *But why don't we want to say that we prefer someone with a master's degree or who is a CPA?*

Sandy: *This is an entry-level position for which we will pay an entry-level salary. We do not want someone whose qualifications are such that they will be unhappy doing basic work and will expect promotions and a higher salary more quickly than usual. In a tough economy, we will probably get applications from over-qualified people. But I don't want to position ourselves in such a way that folks with higher degrees and more experience can use the ad to argue that since they were better qualified and were not hired, we must have discriminated against them. I've spoken with our attorneys on this and I am confident that we are on solid ground here.*

Sandy is correct in her assessment. While it is true that rejecting someone because they are "over-qualified" can be a pretext for discrimination,[13] courts have found for the employer when it can show that the job did not require the applicant's superior qualifications and that the employer did indeed hire someone with lesser qualifications.[14]

---

13. *See Taggart v. Time Inc.*, 924 F.2d 43, 47–48 (2d Cir. 1991) (age discrimination case) for an extreme statement of this position ("Denying employment to an older job applicant because he or she has too much experience, training or education is simply to employ a euphemism to mask the real reason for refusal, namely, in the eyes of the employer the applicant is too old. . . . An employer might reasonably believe that an overqualified candidate—where that term is applied to a younger person—will continue to seek employment more in keeping with his or her background and training. . . . for [older applicants] loss of employment late in life ordinarily is devastating economically as well as emotionally. . . . an older applicant that is hired is quite unlikely to continue to seek other mostly non-existent employment opportunities").

14. *See* Robinson v. Potter, 453 F.3d 990, 994 (8th Cir. 2006) (Rehabilitation Act case) (applicant could not show that postal service's claim that she was overqualified by virtue of possessing a college degree and having specialized knowledge in statistical research not necessary for an entry-level position involving secretarial and scheduling duties was pretextual); Coleman v. Quaker Oats Co., 232 F.3d 1271, 1290

Sandy moves on to the last paragraph of Chris's draft and is disturbed by what she reads.

Sandy: *Chris, saying that the successful candidate should be "young and energetic" is an absolute no-no! That sentence has got to go.*

Sandy is correct when she says that the county cannot use the terms "young" and "energetic" in its job advertisement because they are likely to discourage workers over the age of 40 from applying. The Age Discrimination in Employment Act (ADEA) explicitly prohibits the use of such language in advertising job openings:

> Help wanted notices or advertisements may not contain terms and phrases that limit or deter the employment of older individuals. Notices or advertisements that contain terms such as age 25 to 35, young, college student, recent college graduate, boy, girl, or others of a similar nature violate the Act . . . .[15]

(9th Cir. 2000) (age discrimination case) ("[A]n employer may choose not to hire an employee because he is overqualified for a position without violating ADEA . . . where the criteria that make the employee overqualified and the reasons for the employer's concern are defined . . . placing [Coleman] in this position would have meant a large pay cut and a two-step demotion. Coleman's previous position as an account executive is an objective criterion and Quaker defined its concern that a demotion would have meant a loss of morale. Thus explained, Quaker's rejection of Coleman as overqualified is a legitimate nondiscriminatory reason . . . ."); EEOC v. Ins. Co. of N. Am., 49 F.3d 1418 (9th Cir. 1995) (age discrimination case) (insurance company's refusal to interview or hire job applicant who was over the age of 40 as loss control representative on the basis that he was overqualified for position did not violate the ADEA given manager's explanation that he feared someone with applicant's extensive background in loss control would delve too deeply into accounts to which he would be assigned and impose upon insureds' time to an inappropriate degree). *See also* Jordan v. City of New London, 225 F.3d 645 (2d Cir. 2000) (summary judgment for employer affirmed in 1983 case where policy of removing from consideration for employment as police officer those who scored too highly on examination was rational way to reduce job turnover caused by hiring overqualified applicants and thereby lessen the economic cost involved in hiring and training police officers who did not remain long enough to justify the expense). *See also* Phillips v. TXU Corp., 2006 WL 3900112 (N.D. Tex. Dec. 29, 2006) (race discrimination case) (while "overqualified" is a euphemism for "too old" in age discrimination context, such reasoning does not necessarily extend to the context of race discrimination, and defendant's explanation that the plaintiff was overqualified for the position was a legitimate, nondiscriminatory reason for her non-selection).

15. *See* 29 C.F.R. § 1625.4(a).

Sandy: *And Chris, what were you thinking when you said "he should be of neat appearance and good character"? Do you really think that only men can be accountants?*

Chris: *What do you mean? I was just trying to say that this is a position that a lot of people will want but that they have to understand that this is a professional workplace.*

Sandy: *I think we can address our expectation that the person hired will act and dress like a professional at the interview stage. But why did you say "he"?*

Chris: *Did I phrase it that way? I didn't mean to. I've got a buddy who might be interested in this position and I suppose I had a mental picture of him as I drafted this section. We should change that.*

Sandy: *You bet we should!*

Once again, Sandy is correct. Just as the ADEA prohibits employers from using language like "young" or "youthful," Title VII prohibits us from printing or publishing

> any notice or advertisement relating to employment . . . indicating any preference, limitation, specification, or discrimination, based on race, color, religion, sex, or national origin, except . . . when religion, sex, or national origin is a bona fide occupational qualification . . . .[16]

Sandy: *This is the sort of thing that could easily be missed before the ad gets posted and could come back to haunt us as supposedly direct evidence of a discriminatory motive. You have to be more careful, Chris.*

Chris: *Well, at least I didn't forget to put in the ad that we are an affirmative action, equal employment opportunity employer.*

Sandy: *We are an equal opportunity employer, but we are not an affirmative action employer. So let's change that statement, too.*

---

16. *See* 42 U.S.C. § 2000e-3(b).

Sandy is also correct on this point. As discussed in detail in Appendix 2, local government and community college employers will likely violate the Equal Protection Act of the U.S. Constitution if they adopt affirmative action[17] plans without a strong basis in evidence showing that the employer engaged in discrimination in the past and that there are present and continuing effects of that past discrimination.[18] In most cases, public employers should not advertise themselves as "affirmative action" or "AA" employers. Employers may advertise themselves as "equal employment opportunity" or "EEO" workplaces as a way of signaling that they do not discriminate and that they seek applications from persons of different race, color, gender, religion, national origin, and age and with and without disabilities.[19] However, there is no requirement that employers include the "equal employment opportunity" designation on their job postings, nor does any legal liability flow from not including it.[20]

After Sandy's edits, the advertisement for Paradise County's accountant opening reads as follows:

Paradise County seeks accountant.

Duties:

- Performs general accounting duties such as maintaining a general ledger, making journal entries, advising supervisors in regard to appropriate balances and fund transfers, and reconciling trial balances, bank statements, and accounts.
- Assists in the development and implementation of new accounting procedures and systems in order to provide a clear audit trail of financial transactions.

---

17. See Appendix 2, Section App. 2.1.

18. See Appendix 2, Section App. 2.3.

19. *See, e.g.*, Equal Employment Opportunity Commission, *Technical Assistance Manual on the Employment Provisions (Title I) of the Americans with Disabilities Act* (January 1992), at V-2 ("Employers may wish to indicate in job advertisements and notices that they do not discriminate on the basis of disability or other legally prohibited bases. An employer may want to include a statement such as: "We are an Equal Opportunity Employer. We do not discriminate on the basis of race, religion, color, sex, age, national origin, or disability.").

20. *See* Lewis v. Tobacco Workers' Int'l Union, 577 F.2d 1135, 1143 (4th Cir. 1978) (about a union's failure actively to promote its image as an equal opportunity employer, the court said, "[w]e do not think a failure of the company to announce innocence is a violation of Title VII"); EEOC v. Sheet Metal Workers Int'l Ass'n, Local No. 122, 463 F. Supp. 388, 425 (D. Md. 1978) (union's failure to publicize its nondiscrimination is not a basis for imposing Title VII liability).

- Prepares a variety of tax, financial, and statistical reports and analyses to comply with state, federal, and local requirements and to provide pertinent information for decision making.

This position may also assist in the preparation of the annual budget and in the maintenance and preparation of accounting-related data processing operations.

This is an entry-level position. The County seeks a person with

- A BS in accounting, preferably with some internship or work experience in accounting.
- Excel spreadsheets skills.
- Strong written, analytical, and communication skills.
- SAP financial software experience would be a plus.

Paradise County is an Equal Employment Opportunity employer.

3.2.2 Advertising a Position

There is no federal or state law or regulation requiring public or private employers to advertise an open position. With only one exception, there is no federal or state law or regulation directing employers how or where to advertise, should they decide to do so. That exception may be found in the North Carolina Administrative Code, which requires local government employers covered by the State Personnel Act—county social services departments, local health departments or districts, some consolidated human services agencies, area mental health authorities, and certain emergency management agencies—to list with the North Carolina Employment Security Commission any positions for which they seek applicants from outside the agency and to post prominently in an area known to employees any positions for which they seek internal applicants.[21] But even an agency governed by the State Personnel Act has the freedom to choose with respect to an individual vacancy whether to seek candidates from within first or whether to advertise outside immediately.

Human resources professionals advocate and employers generally follow a policy of advertising positions broadly. Advertising positions widely is the most likely way for an employer to get the best possible applicant pool from which to select a new employee. In today's labor economy, that generally means using some combination of posting—internal posting, posting on

---

21. *See* 25 N.C. Admin. Code 1I .1902(b) and (c).

community bulletin boards, and listing the vacancy with the Employment Security Commission and with the career centers of local community colleges and nearby four-year colleges—and using multiple media sources, including local newspapers; a local government's own website; community access TV; Internet job sites such as Monster.com; professional publications relevant to the position at hand; publications directed toward government employees, such as the North Carolina League of Municipalities newsletter or *Southern City*; and, depending on the position, newspapers with statewide circulation, such as the *Raleigh News and Observer* or the *Charlotte Observer*. To increase the likelihood of receiving applications from outstanding female and minority candidates, employers may also target places such as the career centers of all-female or historically black colleges; media published by or for women, African Americans, or Latinos; or women's or minority professional associations.

3.2.3 Choosing Not to Advertise a Position

Sometimes employers do not want to advertise so broadly. Advertising is expensive, and to be effective, the advertisement usually has to remain accessible for a period of time. As a legal matter, not every vacancy and no vacancy in particular must be advertised. There are three ways in which employers may lawfully fill a position without publicly advertising for applicants: by promoting a current employee to the vacant position, by offering a position to a previously identified person outside the organization, or through so-called word-of-mouth recruiting. Let us consider each practice in turn.

3.2.3.1 Promotion of a Current Employee to a Vacant Position without Advertising

The city of Paradise, North Carolina, has decided to reorganize the way it delivers water services and has created a new position, that of director of water and wastewater utilities. The city's policy is to advertise vacant positions except where a position could be filled by promoting a qualified current employee. The city has just such an internal candidate, John Barnett. He meets all of the newly defined position's minimum and preferred qualifications and is well regarded by both city management and his coworkers. While there may be other employees who would apply should the posi-

tion be posted internally, the city manager would like to promote John Barnett without considering anyone else for the position. She is confident Barnett can do the job and would like to get the director in place and the reorganization under way as soon as possible. Can the manager appoint Barnett to the position without soliciting applications either internally or externally?

The manager may appoint Barnett to the position of director of water and wastewater utilities without posting the job internally or advertising it externally. In the absence of a law requiring her to solicit applications, the manager is free to identify a candidate, approach him or her, and offer the position. It is not uncommon for employees who would have liked to have been chosen for a position to claim that the employer has not advertised or opened up the process of selection for discriminatory reasons. The courts, however, have made quite clear that in the absence of other evidence, no inference of discrimination may be drawn from the fact that a supervisor or manager has preselected someone to fill an open position.[22] As the Fourth Circuit noted, "If one employee was unfairly preselected for the position, the preselection would work to the detriment of all applicants for the job, black and white alike." While preselection may establish that an employee was treated unfairly, the court continued, it does not by itself prove racial discrimination."[23] In choosing Barnett, the manager in the hypothetical has not done so on the basis of race, color, gender, religion, national origin, age, disability, genetic information, or military status, nor has she dismissed the idea of considering other possible applicants on those grounds.

---

22. *See* Anderson v. Westinghouse Savannah River Co., 406 F.3d 248, 271 (4th Cir. 2005) (where employer's legitimate, nondiscriminatory reason for not hiring plaintiff was plaintiff's lower ratings, plaintiff could not show that reason was pretextual merely by showing that employer had preselected the successful candidate). *See also* Goostree v. Tennessee, 796 F.2d 854, 861 (6th Cir. 1986) (although evidence suggested that male applicant was preselected and that fact cast serious doubt on credibility of employer's proffered reasons for selecting him, there was no evidence that his gender was the basis for preferential treatment); Fields v. Vilsack, 798 F. Supp. 2d 82, 90 (D.D.C. 2011) (no evidence of preselection of successful applicants).

23. *See* Blue v. U.S. Dep't of the Army, 914 F.2d 525, 541 (4th Cir. 1990). *See also* Jackson v. Winter, 497 F. Supp. 2d 759, 770 (E.D. Va. 2007) (while demonstrating that successful candidate was preselected would show that the selection process was unfair, it did not by itself prove discrimination).

But what if the city of Paradise had a personnel policy that required every position to be either posted internally or advertised externally? Couldn't the manager's decision to promote Barnett without considering other candidates be evidence of discriminatory motive in those circumstances? Again, the courts have said no.[24] This is especially true where a supervisor has firsthand knowledge of some of the possible candidates and makes an employment decision based on that knowledge.[25] Indeed, courts have not found discriminatory motive even where managers have falsified records to cover their violations of hiring procedures.[26] Failure to follow employer policies may raise a number of questions about the judgment of the hiring manager or supervisor, but it is not sufficient evidence to conclude that the hiring decision was discriminatory.

---

24. *See* Moore v. Mukasey, 305 F. App'x 111, 117 (4th Cir. 2008) ("even if McCrary preselected Roberts by promoting her in violation of governing regulations—a question we do not decide—this type of preselection would be insufficient in this case to establish pretext"); Kennedy v. Landon, 598 F.2d 337, 341 (4th Cir. 1979) (although "the pre-selection of Hardy may have violated the rules and regulations of the Department of Corrections, it does not evidence the type of discrimination that is prohibited by Title VII . . . . [where the] parties to this litigation concede that Hardy was the best qualified candidate for the position"); Randle v. City of Aurora, 69 F.3d 441, 454–55 (10th Cir. 1995) ("The City apparently promoted Gilmore because she was the most qualified candidate for the position and Randle has offered no evidence suggesting that this reason was pretextual—i.e., that she was more qualified for the position. Thus, Randle has failed to show how the City discriminated against her by allegedly failing to follow its own posting procedures"); Foster v. Dalton, 71 F.3d 52, 56 (1st Cir. 1995) ("Title VII does not outlaw cronyism"). *See also* Autry v. N.C. Dep't of Human Res., 820 F.2d 1384, 1385–86 (4th Cir. 1987) (fact that candidate selected for promotion was a friend of the hiring manager and daughter of politically influential woman did not give rise to inference that plaintiff suffered disparate treatment discrimination).

25. *See* Springer v. Convergys Customer Mgmt. Grp. Inc., 509 F.3d 1344, 1350 (11th Cir. 2007).

26. *See* Mackey v. Shalala, 360 F.3d 463, 468–69 (4th Cir. 2004) (even if plaintiff's superiors violated standard hiring procedures by preselecting successful applicant and then falsifying records to cover their violations of hiring procedures, that was not sufficient evidence to conclude that employer's explanation for hiring successful applicant was pretext).

3.2.3.2 Offering a Position to an Outside Candidate without Advertising

> *Suppose that the city manager knows of someone outside the organization that she thinks has the scientific and technical expertise necessary to do an effective job. To that end, she calls her friend Bruce Byrne, a former classmate at UNC-Paradise who went through the environmental engineering program in its School of Public Health, and tells him about the position. They discuss the position several times over the next week, both by phone and in person. Byrne is interested, and nothing in their discussions causes the manager to think that Byrne would be anything other than an excellent director of water and wastewater utilities and an asset to city government. Can the manager offer Byrne the position without advertising the position either internally or externally?*

The answer to this question is identical to the answer to the first hypothetical situation. The only difference between the first and the second hypothetical is that in the first hypothetical, the manager identifies an internal candidate and offers him the job without posting and advertising the position, while in the second hypothetical, the manager identifies an external candidate and offers him the job without posting or advertising the position. In the absence of any statutory or regulatory requirement that the position be advertised, the employer may target an individual and offer the job to him or her.[27] If there were a personnel policy or ordinance requiring that the position be advertised, the manager might face questions from the city council, but there can be no inference of discrimination without other evidence.[28]

---

27. *See, e.g.*, *Goostree*, 796 F.2d at 861 ("[p]reselection . . . does not violate Title VII when such preselection is based on the qualifications of the party and not on some basis prohibited by Title VII."); Nyunt v. Tomlinson, 543 F. Supp. 2d 25, 39 (D.D.C. 2008), *aff'd sub nom.* Nyunt v. Chairman, Broad. Bd. of Governors, 589 F.3d 445 (D.C. Cir. 2009).

28. There are some earlier cases from other jurisdictions where employers have sought other applicants but ultimately offered the job to a candidate whom others perceived to be preselected and where the courts tended to see "preselection" as calling into question the employer's proferred legitimate, nondiscriminatory reason for rejection. That has not been the trend in the Fourth Circuit, however. *See* Coble v. Hot Springs Sch. Dist. No. 6, 682 F.2d 721, 728–29 (8th Cir. 1982) (evidence of preselection operates to discredit the employer's proffered explanation for its employment

3.2.3.3 Word of Mouth Recruiting in Lieu of Advertising

> *Imagine that the city of Paradise is a small municipality of about 5,000 residents and 75 employees. Although the city has grown in recent years, it has retained the practice of recruiting new employees through word-of-mouth and has advertised vacant positions only when it has otherwise been unable to find someone through its informal process. Although the city has adopted the manager–council form of government, the manager knows that the city council feels strongly that advertising vacant positions widely and interviewing multiple candidates for every position is too expensive for a city of this size. "That's fine for a big city," says one of the council members. "But for a small town like Paradise, we just do fine talking to folks we know." With the creation of the new director of water and wastewater utilities position, which requires scientific and technical expertise, the manager had hoped to bring about a formal change in the city's recruiting policy, but that is not to be. Can the city fill this and all of its positions through word-of-mouth recruiting?*

This is a more complicated question than whether a local government or community college employer may fill a particular job vacancy with a targeted promotion or outside hire. A policy or practice of word-of-mouth recruiting is not per se unlawful. Indeed, even courts have recognized that there may be very attractive reasons for an employer to favor word-of-mouth recruiting:

> . . . the passive stance is the cheapest method of recruitment. It may also be highly effective in producing a good work force. There are two reasons. The first is that an applicant referred by an existing employee is likely to get a franker, more accurate, more relevant picture of working conditions than if he learns about the job from an employment agency, a newspaper ad, or a hiring supervisor. The employee can give him the real low-down about the job. The result is a higher probability of a good match,

---

decision); EEOC v. Safeway Stores, Inc., 634 F.2d 1273, 1281 (10th Cir.1980) (same), *cert. denied*, 451 U.S. 986 (1981); United States v. Wattsburg Area Sch. Dist., 429 F. Supp. 1370, 1378 (W.D. Pa. 1977) (same); Abrams v. Johnson, 534 F.2d 1226, 1229–30 (6th Cir. 1976) (same); Hartman v. Wick, 600 F. Supp. 361, 364 (D.D.C. 1984) (same).

> and a lower probability that the new hire will be disappointed or disgruntled, perform badly, and quit. Second, an employee who refers someone for employment may get in trouble with his employer if the person he refers is a dud; so word of mouth recruitment in effect enlists existing employees to help screen new applicants conscientiously.[29]

The legal issue raised by word-of-mouth-recruiting is that historically, when used in conjunction with an all-white or predominantly white workforce, it has tended to exclude African American and other minority groups as effectively as policies or practices that are intentionally discriminatory. As one early decision explained,

> [T]he Company's recruitment policy, . . . which depended primarily upon existing employees to refer new prospects for employment, operated to discriminate against blacks. . . . With an almost completely white work force, it is hardly surprising that such a system of recruitment produced few, if any, black applicants. As might be expected, existing white employees tended to recommend their own relatives, friends and neighbors, who would likely be of the same race.[30]

Word-of-mouth recruiting is a textbook example of a hiring practice with the potential to cause disparate impact. The leading Fourth Circuit case in this area is the 1990 case *Thomas v. Washington County School Board*.[31] The plaintiff in this case was an African American woman who applied for a job in the county in which she had been born and raised. Patricia Thomas kept her application current, but the school board failed to notify her of openings on three occasions in two years, and she only heard of the openings after the positions had been filled. The county school board did not have a practice of advertising vacant positions but instead filled them through word-of-mouth and by posting within schools in the

---

29. *See* EEOC v. Consol. Serv. Sys., 989 F.2d 233, 236 (7th Cir. 1993) (use of word-of-mouth recruiting did not give rise to inference of intentional, disparate treatment discrimination in absence of evidence that employer was biased).

30. *See* Parham v. Sw. Bell Tel. Co., 433 F.2d 421, 426–27 (8th Cir. 1970) (employer's practice of recruiting new employees by using recommendations of current employees had effect of excluding African American applicants in violation of Title VII).

31. Thomas v. Washington Cnty. Sch. Bd., 915 F.2d 922 (4th Cir. 1990).

system. The district court hearing the case found that Thomas did not offer sufficient statistical evidence to prove disparate impact discrimination. The number of positions involved in her claim was too small to produce statistically significant results. The Fourth Circuit, however, held that statistics are not the only way of proving a disparate impact case. Here, Thomas showed that between 1981 and 1988, at least 46 relatives of school employees were hired. Among them, one relative of the one black high school teacher was hired. The rest were white. Thomas also produced a stipulation by the school board that they rarely publicly advertised openings, as well as evidence from other African American applicants who did not apply for jobs because they did not become aware of them until after they were filled. The court found that this indeed showed that the school system's use of word-of-mouth recruiting and internal posting had a disparate impact.[32]

Word-of-mouth recruiting is especially suspect when an employer has an open application and advertising practice for some positions but fills other positions—especially managerial or higher-paying positions—through employee referrals. In one Fourth Circuit case, for example, a retail company used word-of-mouth hiring to fill vacancies among its long-distance drivers, who were all white, while using a general advertising and open recruitment policy for its warehouse and terminal operations, which had a racially mixed workforce. The long-distance driving positions were better paid and considered more desirable.[33] Similarly, in a gender discrimination case, the company did not post or announce vacancies in salaried jobs and posted vacancy announcements in its higher-paying factory jobs only in

---

32. *See Thomas*, 915 F.2d at 926. This case was decided before Congress amended Title VII through the Civil Rights Act of 1991 to clarify the burden of proof in a disparate impact case. For the elements necessary to make a prima facie case of disparate impact discrimination and for the burden of proof in a disparate impact case, see Chapter 2, Sections 2.1.6 and 2.1.7. Even where the plaintiff's statistics show an imbalance in the workforce relative to the relevant labor market, that alone is not sufficient to establish a prima facie case of disparate impact or unintentional discrimination. The plaintiff must show a causal relationship between an identified practice, such as word-of-mouth recruiting, and the statistical disparity. *See* 42 U.S.C. § 2000e-2(k)(1)(A)(i). *See also* Lewis v. City of Chicago, ___ U.S. ___, 130 S. Ct. 2191, 2197 (2010); Bennett v. Nucor Corp., 656 F.3d 802, 818 (8th Cir. 2011) (employees' statistical evidence was inadequate to demonstrate employer's promotion practices had a disparate impact on them).

33. *See* Barnett v. W.T. Grant Co., 519 F.2d 543, 549 (4th Cir. 1975).

the plant itself, where there weren't any women employees. Instead, for its higher-level jobs and higher-paying jobs, the company relied on word-of-mouth recruiting. The court found that the employer's practice of using word-of-mouth recruiting for its better jobs constituted gender discrimination in violation of Title VII.[34]

Word-of-mouth recruiting practices do not, however, always result in or perpetuate workforces segregated by race or gender. An employer with a diverse workforce may well be able to use word-of-mouth recruiting and maintain that diversity. There is no question that where word-of-mouth recruiting results in a workforce that has substantially the same proportion of African Americans, women, or other protected classes as are present in the local labor market, there will be no finding of unlawful discrimination in the absence of other evidence.[35] *Clark v. Chrysler Corp.*, a Seventh Circuit case from Indiana involving a discrimination claim against an automobile manufacturing company, is a good illustration of this principle.[36] In this case, the court found that Chrysler used two primary recruiting tools, obtaining referrals through the county employment security agency and posting notices of available positions at the gate of its local automobile manufacturing plant. The plaintiff, an African American woman, claimed that these practices had a disparate impact on African Americans because (1) the use of word-of-mouth to publicize available positions through Chrysler's predominantly white workforce tended to exclude blacks, (2) the practice of limiting referrals to those coming through the county employment security agency tended to exclude unemployed African Americans from other counties which had larger black populations within the relevant labor market, and (3) the eventual termination of referrals from the county employment security office restricted the African Americans within the county from being apprised of job openings at the plant.

---

34. *See* Cox v. Am. Cast Iron Pipe Co., 784 F.2d 1546, 1551–52 (11th Cir. 1986). *See also* EEOC v. Metal Serv. Co., 892 F.2d 341, 350 (3d Cir. 1990) (fact that black applicants were required to undergo burdensome application process while white applicants were hired through word-of-mouth through an all-white workforce was sufficient to establish a prima facie case of discrimination).

35. *See, e.g.*, Diggs v. W. Elec. Co., 587 F.2d 1070, 1072 (10th Cir. 1978) (because statistical evidence indicated that employer's employment of minority group members exceeded their percentage in the local workforce, the employer was not liable for discriminatory hiring practices).

36. *See* Clark v. Chrysler Corp., 673 F.2d 921 (7th Cir. 1982).

The plaintiff's allegations represented the very sort of discriminatory impact that word-of-mouth recruiting has traditionally had in historically segregated places and occupations. The court nevertheless found that none of Chrysler's practices had a disparate impact on African Americans because (1) a comparison of applicants to persons hired indicated that African Americans were hired for production and office jobs in a proportion greater than their representation in the applicant pool, and (2) a comparison of the persons hired for office and production jobs with the relevant labor market indicated that blacks were hired in a proportion greater than their representation within the relevant labor markets.[37]

Employers should note, however, that the mere fact of advertising may not insulate them from charges of disparate impact discrimination. In 1986, the United States Department of Justice brought a disparate impact discrimination lawsuit against the city of Warren, Michigan, after a lengthy investigation into that city's hiring practices.[38] The city of Warren is located in Macomb County, Michigan. It shares a border with the city of Detroit and neighboring Wayne County. According to the 1980 census, Warren's resident civilian labor force was 0.2 percent African American. Macomb County's resident civilian labor force outside of the city of Warren was 1.3 percent African American. Detroit's resident civilian labor force at this time was 59.7 percent African American. Before the Department of Justice filed suit, Warren's regular recruiting practice was to advertise in three newspapers with circulation primarily in Macomb County and to post notices of municipal employment opportunities in municipal buildings. Warren did not advertise opportunities for municipal work in the *Detroit Free Press*, the *Detroit News*, or any other periodicals of general circulation in the Detroit metropolitan area. In addition to these recruiting methods, Warren limited its applicant pool by requiring all applicants for municipal positions other than police and firefighter positions to have been Warren residents for a specified duration.

At the trial, the United States presented evidence that Warren's refusal to advertise police and firefighter job openings outside of predominantly white Macomb County resulted in a practically all-white applicant pool for those positions. Warren did begin to advertise municipal positions in

---

37. *See Clark*, 673 F.2d at 927–29.

38. United States v. City of Warren, Mich., 138 F.3d 1083 (6th Cir. 1998).

periodicals with a circulation in the Detroit metropolitan area once the government had brought suit against it, and the racial composition of the applicant pool for city jobs generally changed as a result: the number of African American applicants increased by six standard deviations. The Sixth Circuit held that Warren's pre-1986 recruiting methods had a disparate impact on African Americans and violated Title VII.[39]

3.2.4 Using the North Carolina Employment Security Commission to Advertise Positions and Screen Applicants

An increasing number of local government employers use the North Carolina Employment Security Commission (ESC) and the North Carolina Job Link program to advertise openings and, where the employer so requests, to do initial screening of applications and administration of skill tests.[40] Among the recruitment and selection services offered by the ESC are assistance with job analysis and job specifications and publication of job advertisements statewide on the ESC website, in its offices, and through Job Link. Whether they limit advertisement to the ESC or use additional resources such as their own websites or newspaper advertisements, employers may refer all applicants to the ESC for application itself and, if the employer chooses, for a specified level of screening. In addition, if an employee hired through use of the ESC's services is terminated within the first 100 days of employment due to his or her inability to do the work, the employer's unemployment insurance account will not be charged. Employers do not

---

39. *See* United States v. City of Warren, Mich., 138 F.3d 1083, 1088–94 (6th Cir. 1998). *Cf. EEOC v. Joe's Stone Crab, Inc.*, 220 F.3d 1263 (11th Cir. 2000), where the court rejected the EEOC's disparate impact claim because there was no identifiable facially neutral practice causing the restaurant's wait staff to be almost entirely male. The restaurant had a publicly noticed hiring call once a year, but the evidence showed that extremely few women applied because the restaurant's reputation was that it only hired men. In remanding the case for further proceedings on the EEOC intentional discrimination charge, the Eleventh Circuit suggested that reputation may be more probative of intentional discrimination than of disparate impact discrimination.

40. The Employment Security Commission was formerly a free-standing state agency, but is now a part of the North Carolina Department of Commerce. The Job Link program itself is a part of the Department of Commerce's Division of Workforce Solutions.

have to go to the ESC's main offices in Raleigh but may visit their local ESC offices to arrange for ESC assistance in filling a position.[41]

There is no legal downside to using the ESC's services. Employers should consider, however, whether limiting their advertisements to publication through the ESC's offices and Job Link website will narrow the pool of applicants to their detriment. While there does not appear to be any significant possibility of unlawful disparate impact—that is, a screening of minority or female candidates—employer advertisements that are limited to the ESC may be less likely to be seen by those who have exhausted their unemployment benefits or by those who are currently employed but seeking a better position. Posting through the ESC as a supplement or complement to other forms of advertising, on the other hand, can enlarge the pool of a public employer's applicants, and using the ESC to perform initial screening of applicants and administration of basic skill tests can free an employer's human resources staff to focus on fine-tuning interview, advanced testing, and background check processes.

41. For more information, visit the ESC's websites at www.ncjobconnector.com/Forms/JCHome.aspx; www.ncesc1.com/business/findemployees/findemploymain.asp?init=true; www.ncesc1.com/business/downloads/downloadmain.asp#employeeForms.

Chapter 4

Personnel Policies Related to Recruitment and Selection

Chapter 4

Personnel Policies Related to Recruitment and Selection

Most employers adopt general guidelines or policies about who they will consider for employment and how they will go about doing so. This chapter analyzes the legal issues raised by three preliminary policies that public employers sometimes adopt: residency requirements restricting employment to residents of the hiring jurisdiction or its surrounding area, antinepotism policies restricting the employment of members of the same family or household, and policies limiting consideration of former employees for rehire.

4.1 Residency Requirements

Sometimes, local governments and community colleges prefer their employees to reside within their city or county limits. Among the reasons for this preference are

- a feeling that the organization's employees should contribute to the tax base;
- a desire that the organization's employees have a vested interest in the success of the community and its government;
- a perception that by residing in the community, the organization's employees will better understand its conditions and problems;
- a desire to reduce tardiness and absenteeism that might be caused by a lengthier commute;

- a need to have employees, particularly public safety employees, able to respond to emergencies in as brief a time as possible; or
- a combination of the above.

The North Carolina General Statutes (hereinafter G.S.) give cities and counties express authority to make local residency a required qualification for employment. The statutes make no mention of the lawfulness of residency requirements one way or another with respect to area authorities, water and sewer authorities, and other local government entities or with respect to community colleges.

The statutory sections authorizing cities and counties to impose residency requirements differ, although not for any apparent reason:

> **G.S. 160A-60. Qualifications for appointive office.**
> Residence within a city shall not be a qualification for or prerequisite to appointment to any city office not filled by election of the people, unless the charter or an ordinance provides otherwise. City councils shall have authority to fix qualifications for appointive offices, but shall have no authority to waive qualifications for appointive offices fixed by charters or general laws.[1]
>
> **G.S. 153A-25. Qualifications for appointive office.**
> The board of commissioners may fix qualifications for any appointive office, including a requirement that a person serving in such an office reside within the county. The board may not waive qualifications fixed by law for an appointive office but may fix additional qualifications for that office.

Thus, a municipality that wishes to adopt a residency requirement for employment must do so by adopting a policy to that effect by ordinance, while a county need not incorporate such a policy into its ordinance book but may merely adopt it by resolution for it to be effective and lawful. For whatever reason, the General Assembly has not given other local government employers and community colleges explicit authority to impose residency requirements. Such authority may be presumed, however, by more

---

1. Note also N.C. Gen. Stat. (hereinafter G.S.) § 160A-281, which authorizes a city "to appoint a chief of police and to employ other police officers who may reside outside the corporate limits of the city unless the council provides otherwise."

general grants of power to hire employees and set the terms and conditions of their employment.[2]

4.1.1 Three Types of Legal Challenges to Residency Requirements

Local government residency requirements have been considered by North Carolina's appellate courts only twice. In both cases, the plaintiffs claimed that the residency requirement was unconstitutional under the Equal Protection Clause of the U.S. Constitution.[3] In one case, *Maines v. City of Greensboro*, the North Carolina Supreme Court found the city's residency ordinance to be constitutional.[4] In the second case, *Lewis v. City of Kinston*, the North Carolina Court of Appeals found the residency ordinance invalid under the Equal Protection Clause.[5] Elsewhere, however, local government residency requirements have been challenged on two additional grounds. One might be considered a variation on the Equal Protection Clause challenge: applicants and employees in other states have claimed that residency requirements violate their constitutional right to interstate travel. Title VII has provided the other basis for challenging residency requirements: where housing patterns are segregated by race or national origin, a residency requirement can have a disparate impact on a minority group. Consideration of these three types of challenges to residency requirements will make clearer the limits that a local government must observe in drafting a residency requirement.

4.1.1.1 Equal Protection Challenges to Residency Requirements

The Equal Protection Clause of the Fourteenth Amendment to the U.S. Constitution says that no state shall "deny to any person within its jurisdiction the equal protection of the laws." In deciding whether a statute or

---

2. For water and sewer authorities, see G.S. 162A-6(a)(11); for public health authorities, see G.S. 130A-35.3(a)(7); for local ABC boards, see G.S. 18B-701(a)(3) and (8); for regional councils of government, see G.S. 160A-475(2). For community colleges, see G.S. 115D-20(1) and (2), 115D-25, and 115D-25.2.

3. On the Equal Protection Clause, see also Chapter 2, Section 2.10, and the discussion of affirmative action and equal protection in Appendix 2.

4. *See* Maines v. City of Greensboro, 300 N.C. 126 (1980). An earlier residency requirement case heard by the North Carolina Supreme Court involved a declaratory judgment interpreting two statutes, now repealed, that conflicted. *See* Bland v. City of Wilmington, 278 N.C. 657 (1971).

5. *See* Lewis v. City of Kinston, 127 N.C. App. 150 (1997).

ordinance violates the Equal Protection Clause, courts first look to whether they burden a fundamental right, such as the right to vote, or target a suspect class, such as race or national origin. If the law neither burdens a fundamental right nor targets a suspect class, then courts generally apply what is known as "the rational relationship test."[6] The rational relationship test looks to see whether a law or requirement bears a rational relationship to one or more legitimate state purposes. In other words, when a statute, ordinance, or policy of government creates or defines a group of people subject to that legislation or policy, the distinctions between groups of people must have some relevance to the purpose for which the group is being distinguished from others in the first place.[7] A challenge to the explicit distinctions made by a statute or ordinance is known as a facial challenge: the plaintiff is claiming that on its very face, without looking to see how it works in action, the law violates the Equal Protection Clause.

Another kind of Equal Protection Clause–based challenge is known as an as-applied challenge. In an as-applied challenge, the claim is not that the law as it is written treats people dissimilarly based on their membership in a particular group of people or a protected class, but that the law is being applied in a purposefully discriminatory manner. As-applied challenges may be brought by a group of people similarly affected or by a single plaintiff, in which case the claim is referred to as a class-of-one challenge. Historically, this was the vehicle for a number of public employee challenges to employment-related laws and policies, but since the U.S. Supreme Court's decision in 2008 in *Engquist v. Oregon Department of Agriculture*, the use of the as-applied equal protection challenge has been severely curtailed.[8] In the *Engquist* case, the Court held that equal protection claims

---

6. *See* Bd. of Trs. of Univ. of Ala. v. Garrett, 531 U.S. 356, 366–67 (2001) (failure of state governments, which have sovereign immunity against suits brought under the ADA, to make special accommodations for the disabled is not a violation of equal protection so long as their actions toward persons with disabilities are rational); Romer v. Evans, 517 U.S. 620, 631 (1996) (amendment to Colorado Constitution prohibiting any state action designed to protect gays and lesbians from discrimination bore no rational relationship to any legitimate government interest); Tri-Cnty. Paving, Inc. v. Ashe Cnty., 281 F.3d 430, 438–39 (4th Cir. 2002) (county's moratorium on asphalt plants and ordinance governing the development of polluting industries rationally related to government purpose to protect the health, safety, and welfare of its citizens);

7. *See Lewis*, 127 N.C. App. at 153.

8. *See* Engquist v. Or. Dep't of Agric., 553 U.S. 591 (2008).

could not be brought by a single individual (a class of one) in the context of public employment. Before the *Engquist* case, an applicant for a government position or a current public employee could claim, for example, that a residency requirement might be rationally related to a local government objective but that it was being applied to the applicant or employee in a different way than it was applied to others. After the *Engquist* decision, only a group of applicants or employees can bring such a claim—for example, if a residency requirement were arbitrarily enforced against some applicants but not against others.

The *Maines* case, which was decided in 1980, included facially unconstitutional, as well as class-of-one, as-applied equal protection claims—the latter claim of the kind invalidated by the Supreme Court's *Engquist* decision. The *Maines* case involved a Greensboro city ordinance that required employees to be permanent residents of the city and gave the city manager authority to adopt rules to enforce the residency requirement. The plaintiff was a firefighter who had been terminated for moving his residence outside the city limits in violation of the ordinance. The court rejected the firefighter's as-applied equal protection claim, that the manager had made exceptions to the ordinance and had enforced it only as to him, thus violating the equal protection clause by applying the ordinance unequally to persons similarly situated. The court found that the employees to whom the manager had granted exceptions had already entered into leases or purchase agreements but had not yet moved at the time the ordinance was enacted, which brought them within the spirit of the ordinance's grandfather clause allowing those already living outside the city limits to remain there until they moved for any reason. The plaintiff, in contrast, had not entered into any sort of commitment to live outside the city and was not similarly situated to those who had been granted exemptions.[9]

The *Lewis* case, in contrast to the *Maines* case, involved a claim that the residency requirement violated the Equal Protection Clause on its face. At issue in the *Lewis* case was a Kinston city ordinance requiring city employees to live within Lenoir County, the county in which Kinston is located. An administrative policy adopted in accordance with the ordinance allowed the city manager to grant extensions or waivers to employees who could show extreme hardship. The plaintiff in this case was a

9. *See Maines*, 300 N.C. at 159–60.

police officer who lived in Lenoir County at the time he became employed with the city but subsequently moved to Duplin County. Told to move back to Lenoir County or lose his job, the police officer instead brought an action for a declaratory judgment. He asked the court to declare the ordinance and administrative policy unconstitutional and enjoin the city from enforcing them.

In deciding whether the ordinance violated the Equal Protection Clause, the court of appeals applied the rational relationship test and considered whether it bore a rational relationship to one or more legitimate state purposes.[10] The Kinston city manager testified at trial that the city enacted the ordinance because it wanted city employees to contribute to the city's tax base, vote in city elections, participate in the community, and be quickly available in the event of a disturbance or disaster.

While the court did not question that the city's stated purposes in passing the ordinance were legitimate government concerns, it found that because the ordinance required residents to live within Lenoir County, rather than in the city itself, it did not bear a rational relationship to those purposes: Lenoir County residents could not contribute to the city's tax base or vote in its elections, and residents of neighboring counties could participate in community life as much as those living in Lenoir County. Also fatal to the city's argument was the fact that the city's call-back response time for emergency personnel, including the plaintiff police officer, was one hour. The court noted that many locations in neighboring counties, including the police officer's residence in Duplin County, were within the one-hour response time and as close or closer to Kinston than some locations within Lenoir County. The ordinance, therefore, violated the Equal Protection Clauses of both the U.S. Constitution and the North Carolina Constitution.[11] The plaintiff had also challenged the administrative policy's provision giving the city manager discretion to grant waivers to the residency requirement. The court of appeals said that because there

---

10. *See Lewis*, 127 N.C. App. at 153.

11. *See* Lewis v. City of Kinston, 127 N.C. App. 150, 153–54 (1997). The courts have consistently interpreted the Equal Protection Clause of the North Carolina Constitution as synonymous with that of the U.S. Constitution. See *Tri-Cnty. Paving*, 281 F.3d at 436 n.6 (4th Cir. 2002); Simeon v. Hardin, 339 N.C. 358, 377 (1994).

were no standards or guidance in the ordinance to restrict or limit the manager's discretion, the policy was void.[12]

A majority of cases from other jurisdictions, however, have found residency requirements constitutional, including one case from Wisconsin whose facts parallel those in the *Lewis v. City of Kinston* case. In *Kiel v. City of Kenosha,* the federal Seventh Circuit Court of Appeals held that the city could require its employees to live in the county in which the city was located, even though there were residences in a neighboring county that were closer to the city than some in the county.[13] In this case, the city framed its rationale in much the same way as did the city of Kinston, except that the city of Kenosha emphasized the services and benefits that city and county residents shared.[14]

In a rational basis equal protection case, the burden rests with the plaintiff challenging the statute or ordinance to show no "reasonably conceivable state of facts that could provide a rational basis for the classification."[15] In one case from Illinois, a municipal golf course mechanic challenged the city's residency requirement. Although neither the city council nor the city manager could articulate a reason for having a residency requirement for a golf course mechanic, the Seventh Circuit found the residency requirement rationally related to the government interest in having employees who are available for work emergencies on short notice. "Granted," the court said, "there are probably not too many middle-of-the-night emergencies where a golf course mechanic would be needed, but it is not outside the realm of possibility."[16] All a court needs to find a rational relationship is a possible set of facts that would justify the requirement. In a New Jersey case, the court found that the preamble to a challenged residency requirement ordinance provided the rational basis for its enactment; namely, to "provide unto the City economic benefits."[17]

---

12. *See Lewis,* 127 N.C. App. at 155.

13. Kiel v. City of Kenosha, 236 F.3d 814 (7th Cir. 2000).

14. *See Kiel,* 236 F.3d at 816.

15. Gusewelle v. City of Wood River, 374 F.3d 569, 578 (7th Cir. 2004), *citing* Bd. of Trs. of the Univ. of Ala. v. Garrett, 531 U.S. 356, 367 (2001), and cases cited therein.

16. *See Gusewelle,* 374 F.3d at 578.

17. *See* Salem Blue Collar Workers Ass'n v. City of Salem, 33 F.3d 265, 272 (3d Cir. 1994).

4.1.1.2 A Variation of the Equal Protection Challenge: Residency Requirements as Violating the Constitutional Right to Interstate Travel

Some equal protection challenges to residency requirements have been framed somewhat differently than the challenges discussed above. In these variants of the typical equal protection claim, the plaintiffs have alleged that the residency requirement has burdened their fundamental right to interstate travel, which the Supreme Court has long recognized as a basic right under the Constitution.[18] But in a 1972 case, *McCarthy v. Philadelphia Civil Service Commission*, the Supreme Court rejected the claim that a local government residency requirement violates on its face an applicant or employee's fundamental right to travel.[19] Applicants and employees nevertheless continued to bring claims alleging an equal protection violation of the fundamental right to travel on an as-applied basis.[20] That avenue is now foreclosed by the Supreme Court's decision in the *Engquist* case.

4.1.1.3 Disparate Impact Challenges to Residency Requirements

In some circumstances, residency requirements may have a disparate impact on underrepresented groups in a local government's workforce. Disparate impact, which is discussed in greater detail in Chapter 2, occurs where an employment practice that is neutral on its face and adopted without a discriminatory motive results in a hiring pattern that is functionally equivalent to that produced by intentional discrimination. It is unlawful under Title VII.[21] Residency requirements may result in disparate impact where the residents of the city or county in question are predominantly of one race or national origin (generally, white and/or English-speaking) and the available labor pool includes adjacent cities or counties whose populations are more racially and ethnically diverse. In a disparate impact case,

---

18. *See* Dunn v. Blumstein, 405 U.S. 330, 338 (1972), and cases cited therein.

19. *See* McCarthy v. Philadelphia Civil Serv. Comm'n, 424 U.S. 645, 647 (1976); Andre v. Bd. of Trs. of Vill. of Maywood, 561 F.2d 48, 53 (7th Cir. 1977) (appropriately defined and uniformly applied bona fide residence requirements do not impermissibly violate the right to interstate travel).

20. *See, e.g.*, Campbell v. City of Allen Park, 829 F.2d 576, 580–81 (6th Cir. 1987); McCool v. City of Philadelphia, 494 F. Supp. 2d 307, 317 (E.D. Pa. 2007); Ass'n of Cleveland Fire Fighters v. City of Cleveland, Ohio, 502 F.3d 545, 548–50 (6th Cir. 2007). *But cf.* Walsh v. City and Cnty. of Honolulu, 460 F. Supp. 2d 1207 (D. Hawaii 2006) (permanently enjoining enforcement of Hawaii's pre-employment residency requirement).

21. *See* 42 U.S.C. § 2000e-2(k)(1)(A)(i).

the initial burden is on the employee to show—usually by demonstrating statistical disparities—the disparate impact caused by the practice. The burden then shifts to the employer to show either that the challenged employment practice does not cause a disparate impact or that it is job related and consistent with business necessity.[22] If the employer demonstrates that the practice is required by business necessity, the burden shifts to the plaintiff to prove that an alternative practice exists that does not result in disparate impact and that would have served the defendant's stated objective equally well.[23]

Employers defending against claims of disparate impact resulting from residency requirements must go beyond merely articulating a rational basis for the challenged practice. They must present objective evidence demonstrating a nexus between the residency requirement and a particular employment goal. Employers have made the following claims of business necessity: (1) residency requirements increase the likelihood that firefighters will live in the area, which means that they will be more familiar with the buildings and the streets and also that they will be able to respond more quickly in the case of an emergency;[24] (2) local workers are more likely to be loyal in the performance of their work and would be less likely to be tardy or absent;[25] and (3) residency requirements foster pride in the community.[26] In addition, to defend themselves successfully against claims of disparate impact, employers must show that a requirement is job related and that it was not "an artificial, arbitrary, or unnecessary barrier, because it measure[s] skills related to effective performance of [the job]."[27] If an

---

22. *See* 42 U.S.C. § 2000e-2(k)(1)(A)(i). *See also* Griggs v. Duke Power Co., 401 U.S. 424, 431 (1971); EEOC v. Dial Corp., 469 F.3d 735, 742 (8th Cir. 2006).

23. *See* 42 U.S.C. § 2000e-2(k)(1)(A)(ii). *See also Dial*, 469 F.3d at 742; EEOC v. Joe's Stone Crab, Inc., 220 F.3d 1263, 1276 (11th Cir. 2000), Ogletree v. City of Auburn, 619 F. Supp. 2d 1152, 1175 (M.D. Ala. 2009).

24. *See* Nat'l Ass'n for the Advancement of Colored People v. N. Hudson Reg'l Fire & Rescue, 742 F. Supp. 2d 501, 522 (D.N.J. 2010).

25. *See* Newark Branch, Nat'l Ass'n for the Advancement of Colored People v. Town of Harrison, N.J., 940 F.2d 792, 805 (3d Cir. 1991). *See also* Meditz v. City of Newark, 658 F.3d 364 (3d Cir. 2011) (noting similarities of business justifications to those in the *Harrison* case and lack of evidence offered by city and instructing district court to analyze evidence produced by city, if any, on remand).

26. *See N. Hudson Reg'l Fire & Rescue*, 742 F. Supp. 2d at 522.

27. *See* Connecticut v. Teal, 457 U.S. 440, 451 (1982); Lanning v. Se. Pa. Transp. Auth., 308 F.3d 286, 286 (3d Cir. 2002).

employment practice that operates to exclude minorities cannot be shown to be related to job performance, the practice is prohibited.[28]

It is hard for residency requirements to meet the job-related standard. Courts have rejected the claim that living within the city or county will mean that employees are more familiar with the area and will respond more quickly. In one case, the court acknowledged that there were good business reasons to require police officers and firefighters to live in or close to the community they served, but it found that there were other means in ensure the availability of uniformed personnel in an emergency that would have a less discriminatory impact, such as a reasonable response time or distance requirement.[29] In another case, the court found that living in a particular area before becoming a firefighter was not a minimum requirement necessary for the successful performance of the job because candidates could easily study the area and learn its geography.[30] The court also rejected the defendant employer's alternative argument that the residency requirement promoted swift emergency response time by increasing the probability that its firefighters would live nearby because the defendant had not produced any evidence demonstrating how often—if ever—off-duty firefighters are required to respond to an emergency.[31] With respect to the argument that workers living in the city or county would be more loyal, would be absent less frequently, and would foster a sense of community among the workers and the people they served, courts have found them "too nebulous" to justify practices that have a discriminatory effect.[32]

---

28. *See* Ricci v. DeStefano, 557 U.S. 557, ___ (2009) (quoting Griggs v. Duke Power Co., 401 U.S. 424, 431 (1971) (alteration in original).

29. *See Town of Harrison*, 940 F.2d at 804–05 (3d Cir. 1991). *See also Meditz*, 658 F.3d at 364.

30. *See Town of Harrison*, 940 F.2d at 805; Nat'l Ass'n for the Advancement of Colored People v. N. Hudson Reg'l Fire & Rescue, 742 F. Supp. 2d 501, 522–23.

31. *See* Newark Branch, Nat'l Ass'n for the Advancement of Colored People v. Town of Harrison, N.J., 940 F.2d 792, 805 (3d Cir. 1991); *N. Hudson Reg'l Fire & Rescue*, 742 F. Supp. 2d at 522–23.

32. *See* Nat'l Ass'n for the Advancement of Colored People v. N. Hudson Reg'l Fire & Rescue, 665 F.3d 464, 482 (3d Cir. 2011); *Town of Harrison*, 940 F.2d at 805.

4.2 Anti-Nepotism Policies

Many North Carolina local governments and community colleges have adopted anti-nepotism policies that either prohibit the organization from employing two members of the same family or prohibit one family member from being employed in a position that supervises or manages another family member. The primary reasons that employers adopt anti-nepotism policies are (1) to avoid conflicts of interest, favoritism, or the appearance of favoritism; and (2) to avoid the negative effect on workplace morale that employing two members of the same family might generate either because of their special bond or because family conflict may sometimes carry over into the workplace. Anti-nepotism policies of both types have been challenged under both the Equal Protection Clause and Title VII. The courts have generally found anti-nepotism policies lawful except where they have been applied in a discriminatory manner.

The situations that seem to give rise most frequently to applicant and employee complaints and result in legal challenges involve the marriage relationship. *Woodard v. County of Wilson*, a 2010 case from the Fourth Circuit, is typical of such challenges. The plaintiff in the case was a social worker with Wilson County, North Carolina. The county's anti-nepotism policy prohibited "two members of an immediate family" from being employed within the same department; the policy defined "immediate family" to include sons-in-law and daughters-in-law and mothers-in-law and fathers-in-law. Several years after she was hired, the plaintiff began to date a man whose mother also worked at the Wilson County Department of Social Services, albeit in a custodial rather than a social services position. After the plaintiff's marriage, the county terminated her employment (but not that of her mother-in-law, who had worked there longer and who had not, as the county explained, taken the action that initiated the policy conflict). The plaintiff filed suit, claiming that the county's policy violated the Equal Protection Clause by burdening her fundamental right to marriage. The plaintiff argued that the burdening of a fundamental right required analysis under the strict scrutiny standard.[33]

The Fourth Circuit held that government may legitimately impose reasonable regulations that do not significantly interfere with decisions to marry, in which case the regulation is entitled only to rational basis

---

33. *See* Woodard v. Cnty. of Wilson, 393 F. App'x 125, 126–28 (4th Cir. 2010).

review.[34] It found that Wilson County's anti-nepotism policy did not significantly interfere with the right to marry as the plaintiff had indeed gotten married—the policy merely required her to find another job within the county or to leave county employment. Applying rational basis review, the court further found that the policy was rationally related to the county's goals of reducing actual or apparent favoritism and avoiding intrafamilial workplace conflict.[35] In its decision, the Fourth Circuit made frequent reference to an earlier case, *Waters v. Gaston County*, where it made similar findings. That case was almost factually identical to the *Woodard* case except for the fact that the plaintiffs were both employed as paramedics by the same emergency medical services department.[36]

Applicants and employees have also challenged no-spouse policies as violating their First Amendment right to freedom of association. Although this type of challenge has not been heard in either a North Carolina appellate court or in the Fourth Circuit, these claims have generally not been successful where they have been raised. In *Montgomery v. Carr*, a 1996 case, the Sixth Circuit held that First Amendment associational right to marry cases were subject to the same level of scrutiny, namely rational basis scrutiny, as Fourteenth Amendment fundamental right to marry cases. In the *Montgomery* case, two teachers at a vocational school married and, in accordance with an anti-nepotism policy, one was transferred to another school in the same district. In finding the policy constitutional, the court noted that none of the justifications for the no-spouse policy were "overwhelming" but added that "they do not have to be. The justifications merely

34. *See Woodard*, 393 F. App'x at 127, *citing* Zablocki v. Redhail, 434 U.S. 374 (1978); Waters v. Gaston Cnty., 57 F.3d 422, 425 (4th Cir. 1995).

35. *See Woodard*, 393 F. App'x at 128.

36. *See Waters*, 57 F.3d 422 (4th Cir. 1995). *See also* Wright v. Metrohealth Med. Ctr., 58 F.3d 1130 (6th Cir. 1995) (public hospital's anti-nepotism policy did not burden fundamental right to marriage or fundamental right to work and was rationally related to government interest in avoiding conflicts of interest and negative effects on other workers' morale); Parks v. City of Warner Robins, Ga., 43 F.3d 609, 614–16 (11th Cir. 1995) (same), *citing* Parsons v. Cnty. of Del Norte, 728 F.2d 1234, 1237 (9th Cir.) (per curiam) (same), *cert. denied*, 469 U.S. 846 (1984); Espinoza v. Thoma, 580 F.2d 346, 349 (8th Cir. 1978) (same).

have to be rational in their tendency to further a legitimate government aim."[37] Other courts have found similarly.[38]

Clearly, then, a local government or community college could adopt an anti-nepotism policy that prohibits relatives—married couples, blood relatives, and in-laws—from working in the same department or in supervisory roles over one another. But can a public employer prohibit relatives from both working anywhere within the organization, even if they are in different departments and neither one has supervisory or management authority over the other? The author has not found any cases from any jurisdiction, within North Carolina or without, directly addressing this question. All of the cases cited in this section have involved anti-nepotism clauses that prohibit family members or spouses from working in the same department or having supervisory authority over one another. This may very well turn out to be a fact-specific inquiry should it ever reach the courts. If an anti-nepotism policy reasonably serves a public employer's concerns about favoritism, discipline, and morale when applied to a department, it is likely to be reasonable when applied to a small public employer. Many North Carolina municipalities have fewer than 50 employees, and a number of them have fewer than 25 employees. The same logic that applies to analysis of a police or fire department's need for an anti-nepotism policy should apply to a small employer. Conversely, it is hard to see a rational relationship for an anti-nepotism policy prohibiting any two family members from employment anywhere within the city of Charlotte, for example, or within Wake County. Public employers who wish to implement anti-nepotism policies should carefully consider the reasons they are proposing the policy and how those reasons relate to the organization as a whole and to different departments and divisions.[39]

Must—or may—an employer include persons who are living together but not married within the boundaries of an anti-nepotism policy? A public

37. *See* Montgomery v. Carr, 101 F.3d 1117, 1124–29, 1131 (6th Cir. 1996). *See also* Vaughn v. Lawrenceburg Power Sys., 269 F.3d 703, 710–13 (6th Cir. 2001) (anti-nepotism policy did not violate First Amendment right to "marital" association).

38. *See, e.g.*, Sioux City Police Officers Ass'n v. City of Sioux City, 495 N.W.2d 687, 696–98 (Iowa 1993).

39. Note that some states have statutory prohibitions against marital status discrimination, which have served as another basis for challenging anti-nepotism policies. North Carolina, however, does not have such a law.

employer who adopts an anti-nepotism policy may define the boundaries of the relationships it seeks to regulate however it chooses so long as the policy as a whole satisfies the requirements of the rational relationship test. An employer may choose to include same-sex and opposite-sex couples living together in a romantic or committed relationship within the group of those it will not allow to work together. In a 1978 case, the Eighth Circuit affirmed a public employer's interpretation that an anti-nepotism employment policy that on its face was limited to spouses and immediate family members included those who were "not legally married" but were living together "with all the attendant responsibilities and commitments of marriage."[40] In a Michigan case, the Michigan Supreme Court, acting as an employer, made an ad hoc decision to prohibit the plaintiff, a deputy court administrator, from receiving any further promotions once she began living with one of the court's justices. The court issued this directive precisely because the plaintiff's relationship with the justice did not fit within the four corners of its anti-nepotism policy. The federal district court hearing the case found that the plaintiff could bring a claim that her court employer had interfered with her right to intimate association under the First and Fourteenth Amendments, noting that

> [t]he right to "intimate association" is not limited to familial relationships but includes relationships characterized by "relative smallness, a high degree of selectivity in decisions to begin and maintain the affiliation, and seclusion from others in critical aspects of the relationship."[41]

But as with cases claiming interference with the right to marry, the federal court found that the state court's decision did not directly interfere with her right to intimate association as she was not prevented from living with the justice. Only her opportunity for promotion was affected. Under the circumstances, rational basis review applied. The court's policy, motivated as it was by a desire that couples in a committed, romantic relationship not

---

40. *See Espinoza*, 580 F.2d at 349 (unmarried couple living in "espoused" relationship falls within the meaning of public transit company's anti-nepotism policy).

41. *See* Pucci v. Michigan Supreme Court, 601 F. Supp. 2d 886, 903 (E.D. Mich. 2009), *quoting* Beecham v. Henderson Cnty., Tenn., 422 F.3d 372, 375 (6th Cir. 2005), which cites Roberts v. U.S. Jaycees, 468 U.S. 609, 620 (1984).

both hold leadership positions in the court at the same time, passed muster under that standard.[42]

Thus, an employer may prohibit employees from sharing an apartment or otherwise cohabiting as the courts have recognized such prohibitions as rationally related to an orderly workforce.[43] Alternatively, it may choose to limit the policy's application to those who are in relationships that are defined by law—such as marriage, and by extension, the in-law relationship—and to blood relations of a specified degree. As one court observed of a county anti-nepotism policy that was limited to immediate family members:

> A rule which included unmarried cohabitants would be difficult to apply. Cohabitation does not always involve marital and familial relationships, and the County could reasonably decline to bar all cohabitants from permanent employment. Inquiry into non-familial relationships might easily invite a host of interpersonal conflicts disruptive of morale. Instead the County has reasonably drawn the line at the immediate family.[44]

Each local government and community college employer differs. No one approach is right for all.

An employer who adopts an anti-nepotism policy must be prepared to apply it to all employees. Because anti-nepotism policies by definition involve one employee's close relationship with an applicant or another employee, employer attempts to apply the policy sometimes meet with emotionally charged resistance. Where an employer has not applied the policy across-the-board, an employee who is denied an exception may well think that the employer's motivation is discriminatory. In a case involving General Motors, for example, a shift supervisor became engaged to and ultimately married a woman who worked on his shift. The company gave the employee a choice between being transferred or being demoted to avoid being the supervisor of his own wife, which was prohibited by the company's anti-nepotism policy. The company denied the employee's

---

42. *See Pucci*, 601 F. Supp. at 904.

43. *See* Shawgo v. Spradlin, 701 F.2d 470, 482–83 (5th Cir. 1983) (no first amendment right of association violated by no-cohabitation policy of police department).

44. *See* Parsons v. Cnty. of Del Norte, 728 F.2d 1234, 1238 (9th Cir.) (per curiam), *cert. denied*, 469 U.S. 846 (1984).

request that he be accommodated by being moved to a different shift than his wife because as a supervisor, he had to be able to work all shifts and because the company feared that other supervisors might feel hesitant to discipline the wife of a colleague. The employee alleged that the company had either ignored the anti-nepotism policy or accommodated employees affected by it in numerous other instances and charged that the reason it was enforcing the policy against him was race discrimination in violation of Title VII. Although the case was ultimately decided in the employer's favor (because the plaintiff failed to introduce any evidence other than conjecture that race was the motivating factor in the employer's decision to demote him), the employer's inconsistency in its application of the anti-nepotism policy (if true) could be responsible for its very need to defend against this lawsuit.[45] Similarly, not enforcing the anti-nepotism policy when a family relationship first becomes apparent can lead to suspicion that it is discrimination rather than policy that drives an employer's decision to terminate or transfer one or both family members. In the case *Yancey v. Weyerhaeuser Co.*, for example, a jury found in favor of the plaintiff on his age discrimination claim and rejected as pretextual the employer's proffered reason for terminating him—namely, that he and his son both worked in the same area of the railroad's yard operation—because the employer had allowed them to work in the same area for five years before taking any action.[46]

Although this issue arises primarily when two employees marry after beginning to date while on the job, employers should note that female employees who are terminated under anti-nepotism policies have sometimes challenged those policies as having a discriminatory impact on women. Such claims have not generally been successful as there have not been enough terminations, transfers, or demotions under an employer's anti-nepotism policy to make the case that the policy is the cause of a dis-

45. *See* Anderson v. Gen. Motors Corp., 991 F.2d 794 (unpublished disposition) at *1 (1993). *See also* Trent v. Valley Elec. Ass'n, 195 F.3d 534 (9th Cir. 1999) (fact-finder entitled to believe that sole reason for termination was employee's live-in relationship with an independent contractor of employer and that reason was not pretext for gender discrimination); Roche v. Town of Wareham, 24 F. Supp. 2d 146, 153 (D. Mass. 1998) (inconsistently applied policy that results in the hiring of women cannot support gender discrimination claim).

46. *See* Yancey v. Weyerhaeuser Co., 277 F.3d 1021, 1024–25 (8th Cir. 2002).

criminatory impact.[47] Nor have claims that the policies disproportionately affect women sufficed to prove discriminatory intent in a disparate treatment case.[48] Nevertheless, employers with anti-nepotism policies should periodically do a self-audit to ensure that it is not always the female or older employee of a family pair against whom action is taken.

4.3 Policies Prohibiting the Rehiring of Former Employees

Consider the following personnel policy provisions:

1. An employee who resigns in good standing or who is separated because of a reduction in force may be reinstated within three (3) years of the date of separation with the approval of the department head and the city manager.
2. The city will not consider for reemployment any person previously employed by the city and terminated for cause.
3. Former employees will not be considered for rehire.

These three statements all appear in North Carolina public employer personnel policies, sometimes singly, sometimes the first in conjunction with the second. All are lawful. North Carolina local government and community college employers may adopt any rehire policies they choose (or they

47. *See, e.g.*, *Roche*, 24 F. Supp. 2d at 152–53 ("use of proportional statistics as an analytic tool in a sample universe of only 62 is an inexact science"); Thomas v. Metroflights, Inc., 814 F.2d 1506, 1509 (10th Cir. 1987) (application of anti-nepotism policy in two instances with adverse employment decisions affecting two women does not prove discrimination even though impact rate is 100 percent); Adamson v. Multi Cmty. Diversified Servs., Inc., 514 F.3d 1136, 1152 (10th Cir. 2008) (application of anti-nepotism policy to fire one man and his wife and daughter does not establish any sort of significant or statistically supported inference of age discrimination); Houck v. City of Prairie Vill., Kan., 166 F.3d 1221 (10th Cir. 1998) (plaintiff submitted no evidence to support theory that because women have been historically discriminated against in the workplace, they have less seniority than men and that therefore anti-nepotism policy had disparate impact).

48. *See, e.g.*, Parks v. City of Warner Robins, Ga., 43 F.3d 609, 617 (11th Cir. 1995) (plaintiff's assertion that 84 percent of city's supervisory employees were men was not enough to prove that a disproportionate number of employees forced to transfer to another department or to leave the city's employ will be women and to prove discriminatory intent).

may choose not to adopt one at all), provided that the policy (1) does not discriminate on its face on the basis of race, color, gender, religion, national origin, age, disability, genetic information, or military status and (2) does not have a disparate impact on any protected class. In the absence of a policy prohibiting the rehiring of former employees, employers are free to reject an application from a former employee for the same reasons and under the same conditions that govern their consideration of new applicants for employment. Former employees have challenged policies that prohibit rehiring, but the author has not found a single case in which the courts have found such policies unlawful per se.

Chapter 5

Lawful and Unlawful Questions: Applications and Interviewing

Chapter 5

Lawful and Unlawful Questions: Applications and Interviewing

Questions are at the heart of the hiring process. They are found at the outset, in written form on the application form. Later, when initial applications have been sorted, the most promising candidates face questions at an oral interview with the employer's representatives. Framing questions that both elicit the information employers need to know to evaluate a candidate and give each candidate an opportunity to highlight his or her own unique set of knowledge and skills is an art. Managers, directors, and supervisors who have spent time perfecting their interviewing techniques sometimes resent the intrusion of legal concerns into the application and interview process. The law, some have complained, seems designed to prevent them from learning anything about job applicants. It is the job of human resources professionals and city, county, and community college attorneys to ensure that their managers' carefully crafted questions do not violate antidiscrimination or privacy laws. While it is sometimes difficult to strike the right balance, it is possible to learn all the information relevant to making a decision about an applicant without asking a single unlawful question.

An Initial Matter: Application versus Interview

Whether or not an inquiry is lawful does not depend upon whether it is asked on an application or in an interview. The same questions will be lawful or unlawful regardless of where they are asked.

Expressly Unlawful Questions versus Questions Better Left Unasked

Only two statutes, the Americans with Disabilities Act (ADA) and the Genetic Information Nondisclosure Act (GINA), expressly prohibit the asking of certain types of questions. Under the ADA, employers may *not* directly ask a job applicant about a disability, nor may they ask any other questions that are likely to reveal the existence of a disability. The ADA has separate rules for pre-offer inquiries and examinations and post-offer medical inquiries and examinations, and for inquiries and examinations of current employees. GINA prohibits employers from acquiring *genetic information* about applicants or employees except in certain very limited circumstances. Although the ADA allows employers to make unlimited medical inquiries after a conditional offer of employment has been made, GINA limits this right with respect to genetic information. Employers may not ask for genetic information as part of a routine medical history even after an offer has been made.

Neither Title VII nor the Age Discrimination in Employment Act contains any express prohibitions against the asking of any particular questions. Nevertheless, absent an actual need to know in order to evaluate a candidate, employers should avoid making inquiries into an applicant's race, color, gender, religion, national origin, or age. If a rejected applicant challenges a hiring decision, the Equal Employment Opportunity Commission (EEOC) and, should it come to that, a jury—may consider the very asking of a question related to protected class status as evidence that the applicant's membership in that class influenced the decision to reject him or her:

> Generally, making pre-employment inquiries which directly or indirectly disclose the applicant's race, color, religion, sex, or national origin does not constitute an automatic violation of Title VII, as long as the inquiries are made of all applicants. However, unless justified, such inquiries may be important evidence of discriminatory selection, since it is reasonable to assume that all questions on an application form or in a pre-employment interview are asked for some purpose and that hiring decisions are made on the basis of the answers given.[1]

---

1. *See* Equal Employment Opportunity Commission (EEOC) Informal Discussion Letter dated August 5, 2002, from Dianna B. Johnston, Assistant Legal Counsel,

Interviewers sometimes ask questions that are unlawful as phrased, but not in intent. For example, in an interview for a night-shift public safety position, a supervisor might ask applicants, "Do you have any problems staying awake?" If the supervisor is asking whether the applicant has narcolepsy, a sleep disorder characterized by excessive sleepiness and sleep attacks at inappropriate times, then the question is one prohibited by the ADA. If, on the other hand, the supervisor wants to make sure that applicants are not working two or more jobs and have enough time to sleep, the proper way to pose the question might be, "Will you be working any other jobs while you are employed here?" Or, imagine that an employer asks applicants where they were born. There are three possible reasons for such an inquiry. First, the employer might really want to know whether any of the applicants were born in a town called Podunk, because he has bet his brother-in-law that such a town actually exists. This is the least likely alternative. Second, the employer may want to make sure that it is only hiring Americans of Anglo heritage, and not, for example, Latinos, be they immigrants themselves or children of immigrants. Such an intention would violate Title VII's ban against national origin discrimination. Asking where an applicant was born would not be an unlawful question per se, but in the case of a complaint, the EEOC or a jury would be entitled to assume that place of birth was taken into account in the hiring decision. Third, and most likely, the employer may want to know whether the applicant is legally authorized to work in the United States and equates being born in the United States with authorization to work, either because the interviewer does not know better or because he or she is simply being sloppy in their expression. What the employer wants to know is a legitimate area of inquiry, but rather than asking applicants where they were born, the motives for which question can be open to interpretation, the interviewer should ask directly, "Are you authorized to work in the United States?"

The remainder of this chapter is divided into two sections. The first part discusses the explicit prohibitions against asking for medical information and examinations under the ADA and GINA. The second part discusses questions that are not unlawful on their face but that could lead applicants,

---

www.eeoc.gov/eeoc/foia/letters/2002/titlevii_ada_ inquiries.html. *See also* EEOC Informal Discussion Letter dated May 9, 2006 from Dianna B. Johnston, Assistant Legal Counsel, www.eeoc.gov/eeoc/foia/letters/2006/titlevii_adea_preemployment_inquiries.html.

the EEOC, and juries to question whether the employer had discriminatory intent in asking them. Both sections will discuss possible ways to rephrase a question that looks unlawful or improper but is actually seeking relevant and lawful information.

5.1 Expressly Unlawful Questions: The Americans with Disabilities Act

There is no question that prolonged or frequent absences by a single employee or by a group of employees leads to decreased productivity and a delay and decline in the quality of a local government's services. Seen from this perspective, a public employer's interest in an applicant's attendance history and health conditions is reasonable, and the following hypothetical may not seem far-fetched:

> *Paradise, North Carolina, is searching for a new utilities director. After advertising the opening and screening the 56 applications that have been submitted, the city manager identifies six candidates that she would like to interview. She asks the assistant manager and department heads from the public works and engineering departments, as well as the current director of the water treatment plant, to participate in the interviewing process. Before they meet with the first candidate, she asks each member of the interview committee to draft a list of questions to be asked of the various candidates.*
>
> *The heads of the engineering and public works departments have developed some fairly technical questions, and the director of the water treatment plant has a number of questions about how candidates would handle employee discipline. The assistant manager's questions, on the other hand, reflect his recently completed study of employee productivity. Not surprisingly, employee productivity in certain departments with high absenteeism is poor, and the assistant manager has become obsessed with winnowing out "malingerers" and "the lazy," as he refers to certain employees. Department*

heads, he says, have to set the standard for the employees they supervise. His list of questions therefore includes the following:

1. *What medical problems might limit your ability to do a job?*
2. *Have you ever been treated by a psychiatrist?*
3. *Are you taking any prescription drugs?*
4. *Have you ever filed a workers' comp claim?*

The assistant manager also proposes giving an EKG and testing applicants' susceptibility to stress at the same time that the interview takes place.

The manager is uneasy and asks the city attorney whether the assistant manager's questions are permissible.

The Paradise city manager is right to be uneasy. The ADA prohibits the asking of each of these questions. It also prohibits administering the proposed tests. Imagine that one of the six applicants chosen for an interview was under the care of a psychiatrist for six months following the death of a close family member. The applicant has come to terms with his loss and is no longer under the care of a psychiatrist. When the assistant manager learns that the applicant has seen a psychiatrist, however, he stereotypes this applicant as unstable and lobbies against his hiring. Another applicant answers the question about prescription drug use by disclosing that she suffers from hypothyroidism and takes a synthetic thyroid supplement. The assistant manager jumps to the conclusion that this candidate will lack energy and initiative, based on his recollection that one of the symptoms of hypothyroidism is excessive tiredness. In both cases the assistant manager makes assumptions about the ways in which these applicants' medical conditions would affect their ability to perform the job of utilities director. His opinions may affect whether these two candidates continue to be considered strong contenders for the position. The relevant questions might never be asked; namely, how depression and hypothyroidism has affected these individuals in the past and how their conditions affect them now, as depression and hypothyroidism manifest themselves in different ways in different people. It is to protect applicants against precisely these sorts of stereotypes about what it means to have certain medical conditions that the ADA prohibits employers from making any medical inquiries of an applicant until he or she has been extended a conditional offer of employment.

5.1.1 The ADA's Prohibition on Pre-Offer Medical Inquiries and Examinations

The ADA has separate rules for pre-offer inquiries and examinations and post-offer medical inquiries and examinations, and for inquiries and examinations of current employees. Title 42, Section 12112(d), of the U.S. Code provides:

(1) In general. The prohibition against discrimination as referred to in [§ 12112(a)] shall include medical examinations and inquiries.

(2) Preemployment.

 (A) Prohibited examination or inquiry. Except as provided in paragraph (3), a covered entity shall not conduct a medical examination or make inquiries of a job applicant as to whether such applicant is an individual with a disability or as to the nature or severity of such disability.

 (B) Acceptable inquiry. A covered entity may make preemployment inquiries into the ability of an applicant to perform job-related functions.

(3) Employment entrance examination. A covered entity may require a medical examination after an offer of employment has been made to a job applicant and prior to the commencement of employment duties of such applicant, and may condition an offer of employment on the results of such examination, if—

 (A) all entering employees are subjected to such an examination regardless of disability;

 (B) information obtained [is kept confidential, with limited exceptions]; and

 (C) the results of such examination are used only in accordance with this subchapter.

Once an applicant becomes an employee, an employer is prohibited from requiring a medical examination or making inquiries of an employee as to whether the employee is disabled and about the nature or severity of the disability unless the examination or inquiry is shown to be job related and consistent with business necessity.[2]

---

2. *See* 42 U.S.C. § 12112(d)(4).

The regulations promulgated by the EEOC pursuant to its authority to enforce the ADA outline what constitutes a permissible pre-employment inquiry and an acceptable medical examination with only slightly more detail than the statute itself. Title 29 of the Code of Federal Regulations, Section 1630.14, says:

> (a) Acceptable pre-employment inquiry. A covered entity may make pre-employment inquiries into the ability of an applicant to perform job-related functions, and/or may ask an applicant to describe or to demonstrate how, with or without reasonable accommodation, the applicant will be able to perform job-related functions.
>
> (b) Employment entrance examination. A covered entity may require a medical examination (and/or inquiry) after making an offer of employment to a job applicant and before the applicant begins his or her employment duties, and may condition an offer of employment on the results of such examination (and/or inquiry), if all entering employees in the same job category are subjected to such an examination (and/or inquiry) regardless of disability.[3]

What this means in practical terms is that an employer may ask an applicant questions to which there are many possible non–disability related answers.[4] Imagine that a county health department is concerned about proper dosing of medications dispensed in its clinics. May it ask applicants for a clinical nursing position what measures they would take to double-check that they are dosing correctly? The question is directly related to a job function and does not require an answer that is likely to reveal the existence of a disability. Possible answers might include taking a second look at the prescription and the amount dispensed before administering the drug to the patient or using only newer vials, needles, or measuring spoons that have legible notations rather than older equipment where the markings

---

3. *See* 29 C.F.R. §§ 1630.14(a) and (b).

4. *See* U.S. Equal Employment Opportunity Commission, *ADA Enforcement Guidance: Preemployment Disability-Related Questions and Medical Examinations* (hereinafter *ADA Enforcement Guidance: Preemployment Disability-Related Questions and Medical Examinations*), No. 915.002 (October 10, 1995), at 4, www.eeoc.gov/policy/docs/preemp.html.

have worn away. A possible answer might even include an affirmation that the nurse always wears his or her reading glasses before dispensing medication. While uncorrected vision deficiencies may qualify as a disability, the use of reading glasses is not likely to raise a disability issue. Contrast this with the question, "Do you have any kind of vision problem or dyslexia that might cause you to misread a doctor's prescription or a dosage measurement?" The first question had many possible answers that were not related to medical conditions. An inquiry into a vision problem or dyslexia, on the other hand, can only elicit an answer that relates to a medical condition, whether it is to confirm or deny the existence of the condition.

5.1.2 Areas That Employers Typically Want to Explore with Applicants

5.1.2.1 Ability to Perform Job Functions

Employers almost always want to ask questions about an applicant's ability to perform relevant job functions, and the ADA does not prohibit an employer from doing so. After providing an applicant with an explanation or description of the position's job duties, an employer may directly ask the applicant, "Can you perform all functions of the job?" This question is not more likely to elicit medical or disability-related information than other types of information. For example, an applicant may not be able to perform all of the functions of the job because he or she does not have the requisite training or experience or because some functions are time-specific and the applicant cannot be at work at those times.

The question, "What current or past medical problems might limit your ability to do a job?," on the other hand, is unlawful under the ADA. By its own terms, the question asks for medical information. Surprisingly, this very question appeared on a Wal-Mart corporate interview comments sheet and was asked by two Wal-Mart hiring managers of a New Mexico job applicant with a partially amputated arm.[5] The applicant was rejected for a retail position with Wal-Mart and filed a complaint with the EEOC, which in turn filed suit against Wal-Mart. A jury found that Wal-Mart had acted with reckless indifference by failing to remove the question from its

5. *See* EEOC v. Wal-Mart Stores, Inc., 11 F. Supp. 2d 1313 (D.N.M. 1998), *aff'd*, 202 F.3d 281 (10th Cir. 1999).

interview sheet and by failing to educate or train its managers about the ADA. It awarded the plaintiff $100,000 in punitive damages. The Tenth Circuit Court of Appeals upheld the verdict and the award.

Also unlawful is the inquiry into whether an applicant will need a reasonable accommodation to perform any of the job functions. "Reasonable accommodation" is a legal term of art that derives from the ADA.[6] Its clear implication is that a person needing an accommodation has a disability. It is not, however, unlawful to ask whether an applicant can perform all of the job functions "with or without a reasonable accommodation." That is because both a person without a disability and a person with a disability can answer in the affirmative without revealing the existence of the disability.[7]

An employer may also ask applicants to demonstrate how they would perform one or more job functions.[8] For example, if a position in the facilities division of a local government or community college required an employee to be able to move objects and boxes weighing up to 50 pounds, the facilities director could ask all applicants for the position whether they were able to move 50-pound objects. Applicants might answer, "Yes, I can," or they might answer, "No, I cannot, because I haven't seen the inside of a gym in 20 years and spend most of my time sitting on the couch watching singing competitions," or they might answer, "No, I cannot, because I have a condition that limits my lifting ability to 25 lbs." There are many possible answers to the question, and the question is neither designed to nor particularly likely to elicit information about a disability. Similarly, an employer might ask all applicants for the position to demonstrate that they can indeed move a 50-pound object. One applicant might hoist the object on a shoulder and walk it across the room. Another might, depending on the object, push it across the room. Still another might have a limitation that prevents him or her from hoisting or pushing the object and instead might grab a dolly, wedge the object on it, and wheel it across the room. Asking an applicant to demonstrate a physical ability is permissible under

6. *See* 42 U.S.C. § 12111(9).

7. *See ADA Enforcement Guidance: Preemployment Disability-Related Questions and Medical Examinations*, at 4.

8. *See ADA Enforcement Guidance: Preemployment Disability-Related Questions and Medical Examinations*, at 4.

the ADA so long as the employer asks all applicants for the position to do so.[9]

An employer may initiate a conversation about the need for a reasonable accommodation only when the employee has disclosed the existence of a disability or is obviously disabled. A person who appears at an interview with an assistance dog, for example, may have a visual impairment and be using a seeing eye dog, or the person may have an impairment that affects balance and needs the dog to walk properly. In such a case, the employer may not ask about the impairment itself ("Are you blind or are you off-balance?"). The employer may, however, note the presence of the dog and ask the applicant whether he or she needs an accommodation during the interview process or in order to perform job functions. In one case, in trying to determine whether and how a reasonable accommodation might be made for a deaf applicant for a position as a public school system information technology specialist, it was permissible to ask how the applicant communicated in offices where no one knew sign language. The court held this to be a pre-employment inquiry into the ability of the applicant to perform job-related functions and entirely appropriate.[10] In contrast, when an applicant for a position of addiction therapist at a healthcare facility appeared at the interview in a motorized chair, the EEOC found that the interviewers' questions about whether the applicant could perform the essential functions of the position were lawful but that the inquiry into whether he had "any mental or physical disabilities that would restrict" him from carrying out his duties was not lawful, even though this question was asked of all interviewees and not just the complainant.[11]

What happens if an employer suspects that an applicant cannot perform all of the position's duties due to a disability, but the existence of a disability is not obvious and the applicant has not directly said that he or she has a disability? The employer does not have any real options in this case. If the employer has not been asking all applicants to demonstrate their ability to perform a job requirement, it cannot ask one applicant about whose ability

---

9. *See ADA Enforcement Guidance: Preemployment Disability-Related Questions and Medical Examinations*, at 4.

10. *See* Adeyemi v. Dist. of Columbia, 525 F.3d 1222, 1229 (D.C. Cir. 2008) (finding no evidence of disability discrimination).

11. *See* Adair v. Principi, EEOC DOC 01A24528, 2004 WL 73642 (EEOC) (January 7, 2004).

it has questions. While an employer may ask any applicant whether or not he or she will be able to do the job, with or without a reasonable accommodation, it may not question an applicant's response that he or she will be able to do the job. In one matter before the EEOC, an applicant for a temporary filing clerk position who suffered from diabetes and two herniated discs was asked by an employer whether he could "really do the job" given that he was currently receiving disability benefits for those conditions. The EEOC found that this question was an improper and prohibited disability-related inquiry, ordered the employer to take corrective action, and awarded the complainant compensatory damages.[12]

5.1.2.2 Physical Ability or Agility

Neither a physical ability or physical fitness test nor a test of physical agility is a medical examination for the purposes of the ADA. The EEOC describes a physical fitness test as one "in which an applicant's performance of physical tasks—such as running or lifting—is measured."[13] Physical ability or physical fitness tests may be given at any time in the hiring process. Department heads or outside consultants who work on the design of these tests sometimes include a blood pressure or heart rate reading at the start and at the end of the test. This simple act of measurement of the applicant's physiological response to exertion turns the physical ability or physical fitness test into a prohibited medical examination. Neither blood pressure nor heart rate response may be taken in connection with a physical abilities test.[14]

Employers are justifiably concerned that applicants who are not in good physical shape may take a fitness assessment and not only fail but possibly collapse in the course of the test. An applicant who has led a sedentary lifestyle and not done any running, for example, might well have difficulty—even serious difficulty—completing a timed one-mile run, for example. Although an employer may have no choice but to provide applicants with medical assistance if they find themselves in trouble during a fitness test,

---

12. *See* Edwards v. Principi, EEOC DOC 01A30010, 2004 WL 321121 (EEOC) (February 11, 2004).

13. *See ADA Enforcement Guidance: Preemployment Disability-Related Questions and Medical Examinations*, at 14.

14. *See ADA Enforcement Guidance: Preemployment Disability-Related Questions and Medical Examinations*, at 14.

that does not justify the regular use of blood pressure, heart rate, or other measurements of physiological or biological functions during or after a physical fitness assessment. The most an employer can do to screen out applicants who should not be subjecting themselves to the stresses of fitness testing is to give applicants a description of the fitness or agility test and, before allowing them to take the test, require a certification from their personal physician that they may safely take the test.[15]

5.1.2.3 Attendance

Employers justifiably want to be able to count on their employees showing up for work every day, and the courts have recognized that reliable attendance is an essential job function for most positions.[16] As such, questions about attendance are job related. But employers cannot ask a job applicant how many days during the previous year they were out sick, because such a question would "relate directly to the severity of an individual's impairments" and is "likely to elicit information about a disability."[17] Employers may, however, ask the question, "How many Mondays or Fridays were you absent last year on leave other than approved vacation leave?" as a way of determining whether an applicant has abused a previous employer's leave policies by taking long weekends without approval.[18] That is because questions about how many days an applicant was absent from his or her last job that do not reference sick leave are not likely to elicit information about a

---

15. *See ADA Enforcement Guidance: Preemployment Disability-Related Questions and Medical Examinations*, at 14.

16. *See, e.g.*, Tyndall v. Nat'l Educ. Ctrs., Inc. of Cal., 31 F.3d 209, 213 (4th Cir. 1994) ("a regular and reliable level of attendance is a necessary element of most jobs"); Vandenbroek v. PSEG Power Conn. L.L.C., 2009 WL 4730427 (2d Cir. 2009) (unpublished) (same); Rios-Jimenez v. Principi, 520 F.3d 31 (1st Cir. 2008) (same); Brannon v. Luco Mop Co., 521 F.3d 843 (8th Cir.) (same), *cert. denied*, 129 S. Ct. 725 (2008); Carr v. Reno, 23 F.3d 525, 529 (D.C. Cir. 1994 (same); Ridenhour v. Fieldcrest Cannon, Inc., 1996 WL 578510 (M.D.N.C. 1996) (same).

17. *See ADA Enforcement Guidance: Preemployment Disability-Related Questions and Medical Examinations*, at 8.

18. Note that in EEOC Informal Discussion Letter dated May 31, 2000, from Peggy Mastroianni, Associate Legal Counsel, the EEOC staff advises amending that question to "How many Mondays or Fridays were you absent last year on leave other than approved vacation or leave for religious observances?" in order to avoid excluding applicants who observe the Sabbath, because the question as originally framed would seem to ask them to include religious observances.

disability. There are many reasons for employee absences, ranging from car trouble to child care issues to "spring fever."[19]

5.1.2.4 Psychological and Psychiatric Treatment and Testing

The Americans with Disabilities Act defines "disability" as including both physical and mental impairments that substantially limit one or more major life activities.[20] A "mental impairment" is further defined to mean "any mental or psychological disorder, such as an intellectual disability (formerly termed "mental retardation"), organic brain syndrome, emotional or mental illness, and specific learning disabilities."[21] As with medical examinations that are designed or likely to elicit information about a physical disability, so too any question or examination that is likely to elicit information about a mental disability may not be asked or administered before an offer of employment is extended. Clearly, the question, "Have you ever been treated by a psychiatrist or clinical psychologist?" is one that cannot be asked before an offer is made. But what about the question "Have you ever received counseling?" Counseling can occur in many different guises. In addition to psychiatrists and psychologists, pastors and others trained through religious ministries offer counseling. There are also career counselors, guidance counselors in the schools, and so-called personal coaches, many of whom themselves administer tests that seek to illuminate aspects of a person's psychological, emotional, and intellectual makeup. To the author's knowledge, neither the EEOC nor the courts have ever addressed the issue of whether the question "Have you ever received counseling?" is a permissible inquiry before the applicant receives an offer. The close association of the term "counseling" with psychology, however, suggests that this is a question that should be avoided.

As for psychological testing, precisely which tests are prohibited pre-offer by the ADA and which are permissible can be confusing. The EEOC considers any test that would provide evidence and result in identification of a mental disorder or impairment such as those recognized in the American Psychiatric Association's *Diagnostic and Statistical Manual of Mental Disorders* to be a medical examination that may not be administered before

---

19. *See ADA Enforcement Guidance: Preemployment Disability-Related Questions and Medical Examinations*, at 8.

20. *See* 42 U.S.C. § 12102(1)(A); 29 C.F.R. § 1630.2(g)(1).

21. *See* 29 C.F.R. § 1630.2(h)(2).

a conditional offer of employment is made, as would be any other examination that is interpreted by a mental health professional.[22] It does not matter if an employer does not intend to use a psychological test to identify mental disabilities but has a more limited aim of learning about an applicant's personality traits. In its Enforcement Guidance on pre-employment disability-related questions, the EEOC gives the following example of a test that is unlawful during the pre-offer period:

> A psychological test is designed to reveal mental illness, but a particular employer says it does not give the test to disclose mental illness (for example, the employer says it uses the test to disclose just tastes and habits). But, the test also is interpreted by a psychologist, and is routinely used in a clinical setting to provide evidence that can be used to diagnose mental health (for example, whether an applicant has paranoid tendencies, or is depressed). Under these facts, this test is a medical examination.[23]

Cases can to some extent help delineate the boundaries of psychological versus non-psychological testing. One well-known test, the Minnesota Multiphasic Personality Inventory (MMPI), was the subject of a 2005 case from the Seventh Circuit, *Karraker v. Rent-A-Center, Inc.*[24] In that case, the MMPI test was part of a series of exams given to candidates for promotion from the entry-level salesman position in a furniture rental store. Candidates were asked 502 questions from the MMPI test. The employer claimed that it used the test to measure personality traits. The problem identified by the court was that the MMPI does not simply measure such potentially relevant traits as whether someone works well in groups or is comfortable in a fast-paced office. Instead, the MMPI considers where an applicant falls on scales measuring traits such as depression, hypochondriasis, hysteria, paranoia, and mania. Scores on certain parts of the MMPI are sometimes used in diagnoses of certain psychiatric disorders. Candidates

---

22. *See ADA Enforcement Guidance: Preemployment Disability-Related Questions and Medical Examinations*, at 13, 15.

23. *See ADA Enforcement Guidance: Preemployment Disability-Related Questions and Medical Examinations*, at 14.

24. 411 F.3d 831 (7th Cir. 2005)

for promotion who scored at or above a certain level in such areas were not considered for promotion.[25]

The company introduced evidence that there were two scoring protocols for use with the MMPI test, one a medical protocol used for identifying traits consist with mental disorders and the other a vocational protocol used for assessing a candidate's suitability for different positions within an organization. The company used the vocational scoring protocol and did not use a psychologist to interpret the results. The Seventh Circuit nevertheless found that (1) because the MMPI test was designed, at least in part, to reveal mental illness (when used with the medical scoring protocol) and (2) because persons with certain scores on the vocation scoring protocol would likely be identified as having traits symptomatic of mental illness if the medical protocol were used, the test was best categorized as a medical examination.[26]

Now consider a test that was required of all applicants for a security guard position with a national security and protection corporation. The test, called the PASS-III D.A.T.A. Survey, consisted of 100 statements to which applicants had to respond by marking boxes labeled "yes," "?," or "no." For scoring purposes, responses were broken down into three sections: an "alienation index," a "trustworthiness attitudes index," and a "drug attitudes index."[27] The test did not ask direct questions about mental or psychological health, but its administration and evaluation materials promoted the test as a way of identifying "the more alienated, poor trust risk candidates, that are most likely to become behavior problems if hired" and elsewhere explained that "people with alienated attitudes also show some emotional

---

25. *See Karraker*, 411 F.3d at 833–34. *See also* Barnes v. Cochran, 944 F. Supp. 897, 904–05 (S.D. Fla. 1996), where the sheriff required an applicant for employment as a corrections deputy to undergo a clinical examination by a licensed psychologist that covered a wide range of incidents in the plaintiff's life and also probed areas tending to disclose specific psychological disabilities such as PTSS, included a review of the plaintiff's medical records, and included evaluation of the plaintiff's performance on the Minnesota Multiphasic Personality Inventory, the Inwald Personality Inventory, the Otis Lennon School Ability Test, the Hilson Profile/Success Quotient Test, and the California Psychological Inventory. The court said, "Such an extensive examination constitutes a prohibited pre-employment medical examination.

26. *See Karraker*, 411 F.3d at 837.

27. *See* Thompson v. Borg-Warner Protective Servs. Corp., 1996 WL 162990 at *1 (N.D. Cal. 1996).

instability," and that "when the candidate demonstrates a lenient attitude toward abusive behavior and the score is high, he or she has a higher than average potential for current substance abuse."[28]

The plaintiff, who had been rejected because of his responses to the test, claimed that the use of the PASS-III D.A.T.A. test was an impermissible use of a medical examination designed to identify behaviors symptomatic of mental impairment. The court disagreed, noting that no medical or mental health professional interpreted the results of the test and saying:

> Plaintiffs submit no evidence showing that the PASS-III survey is designed or used to elicit information about a mental impairment, as opposed to merely revealing mental or personality characteristics which may be disfavored. Evidence that the test is designed to reveal "behavioral problems" and "emotional instability" is insufficient; there is no evidence in the record that "behavioral problems" and "emotional instability," as those are revealed in the PASS-III survey, are either themselves disabilities or are characteristics that can lead to identifying whether an applicant has an impairment, whether defined by the DSM or by some other parameter.[29]

The test in the PASS-III D.A.T.A. case and the use to which it was put are similar to one in a fictional example provided by the EEOC in its Enforcement Guidance:

> An employer gives the IFIB Test . . . an examination designed and used to reflect only whether applicants have characteristics that lead to identifying whether an applicant is likely to lie. This test, as used by the employer, is not a medical examination.[30]

---

28. *See Thompson*, 1996 WL 162990 at *5.

29. *See Thompson*, 1996 WL 162990 at *7. This analysis would not change in light of the changes to the ADA made by the ADA Amendments Act of 2008.

30. *See ADA Enforcement Guidance: Preemployment Disability-Related Questions and Medical Examinations*, at 15–16.

5.1.2.5 Drug and Alcohol Use

Drug and alcohol addiction are treated differently under the ADA, so different rules apply to pre-offer questions about drug and alcohol use and to pre-employment drug and alcohol testing.

Drug use. Employers may not ask applicants about their lawful use of prescription or over-the-counter drugs before making a conditional offer of employment. Questions about the use of medications are likely to elicit information about a disability, unless, of course, interviewer and applicant are discussing their favorite medications for seasonal flu or allergies—conditions that are not disabilities.[31] But employers *may* ask applicants whether they use *illegal* drugs before making a conditional offer of employment. They *may not,* however, ask about use of *prescription* drugs until they have extended an offer. Nor may they ask whether the applicant has been addicted to or abused drugs in the past, although they may ask if the applicant ever used illegal drugs in the past.

At first glance, these rules may seem inconsistent, but the statutory text is clear on how drug use is to be treated. Title 42, section 12114(a), of the U.S. Code excludes employees and applicants who are "currently engaging in the illegal use of drugs" from the protection of the ADA.[32] This means that whether an applicant is a current recreational user of illegal drugs or currently addicted to an illegal drug, his or her use of drugs is a lawful area of inquiry in the pre-offer stage of the hiring process. That being said, persons with a *history* of drug *addiction* or drug *treatment* who are no longer using drugs illegally or who are still in a rehabilitation program but no longer using drugs are considered persons with a disability under the ADA. Title 42, Section 12114(b), of the U.S. Code says:

> Nothing in subsection (a) of this section shall be construed to exclude as a qualified individual with a disability an individual who—
>
> (1) has successfully completed a supervised drug rehabilitation program and is no longer engaging in the illegal use of drugs,

---

31. *See ADA Enforcement Guidance: Preemployment Disability-Related Questions and Medical Examinations*, at 9.

32. *See also* 29 C.F.R. § 1630.3(a), which defines the terms "drug" and "illegal use of drugs." *See also* Dovenmuehler v. St. Cloud Hosp., 509 F.3d 435, 439 (8th Cir. 2007); Thompson v. Davis, 295 F.3d 890, 896 (9th Cir. 2002).

or has otherwise been rehabilitated successfully and is no longer engaging in such use;

(2) is participating in a supervised rehabilitation program and is no longer engaging in such use; or

(3) is erroneously regarded as engaging in such use, but is not engaging in such use . . .[33]

Thus, a question such as "Have you ever been addicted to or abused drugs in the past?" is likely to elicit information about an ADA-recognized disability. Merely asking whether the employee ever tried or used an illegal drug in the past, on the other hand, does not address the issues of addiction and rehabilitation. A person may have tried once or occasionally taken an illegal drug without having been addicted to that drug.[34]

Pre-employment drug testing. Of course, asking applicants whether they are currently using illegal drugs is only likely to get an honest response when the applicant does not use drugs. For this reason, many employers in both the public and private sectors require job applicants to undergo a pre-employment drug test. The ADA does permit employers to administer pre-employment drug tests before an offer is made. "A test to determine the illegal use of drugs," the statute declares, "shall not be considered a medical examination."[35] Applicants may be rejected based on their use of illegal drugs.

The lawful use of prescription drugs not infrequently causes an applicant's drug test to register as positive. Imagine the following scenario:

John Meyer applies for a job with the information technology department of Paradise County. He is sent for the county's standard pre-employment drug test, which is positive for the use of amphet-

---

33. *See* 42 U.S.C. § 12114(b); 29 C.F.R. § 1630.3(b). *See also* Hernandez v. Hughes Missile Sys. Co., 362 F.3d 564, 568 (9th Cir. 2004); Collings v. Longview Fibre Co., 63 F.3d 828, 831–32 (9th Cir. 1995).

34. *See ADA Enforcement Guidance: Preemployment Disability-Related Questions and Medical Examinations*, at 10.

35. *See* 42 U.S.C. § 12114(d)(1); 29 C.F.R. § 1630.16(c). Section 12114(b) also says that employers may adopt "reasonable policies or procedures, including but not limited to drug testing, designed to ensure that an individual described in paragraph (1) or (2) [i.e., who has undergone rehabilitation] is no longer engaging in the illegal use of drugs." *See also* 29 C.F.R. § 1630.3(c).

amines. The employer's designated medical review officer reports the result to the county's human resources director, who in turn informs Meyer that he will no longer be considered for employment and instructs him to contact the medical review officer if he wishes to discuss the test results. Meyer takes a number of prescription drugs, of which he now informs the medical review officer. One of the drugs is likely responsible for the positive result, and the medical review officer reports to the human resources department that the positive result was an error and that Meyer has passed the drug test. Meyer is reinstated into the applicant pool.

A medical review officer (MRO) is a licensed physician who is responsible for receiving and reviewing laboratory results generated by an employer's drug testing program and determining if there is a legitimate medical explanation for laboratory-confirmed results and for protecting the confidentiality of the drug testing information. The ADA itself does not require employers to use a medical review officer, nor do North Carolina Administrative Code regulations governing the conduct of employer drug testing impose such a requirement.[36] However, public employers who hire people into positions that require the employee to hold a valid commercial driver's license (CDL) or to operate public transit vehicles are required by the U.S. Department of Transportation (DOT) to conduct both pre-employment drug testing and random drug testing on these employees and to use a medical review officer when drug testing employees in accordance with its regulations.[37]

Public employers would be wise to use a medical review officer for non-DOT drug testing as well. The use of an MRO ensures both that there is someone with the appropriate training to determine whether prescription medications are the cause of a positive result and that there is a buffer between the applicant and the employer, who is not entitled to know anything about the existence of a medical condition or disability at the pre-offer stage, even where there has been a positive drug test result. The

---

36. *See* 13 N.C. Admin. Code 20 .0304.

37. *See* 49 C.F.R. Part 40 on U.S. Department of Transportation drug testing requirements generally and Subpart G (49 C.F.R. §§ 40.121–40.169) on medical review officers.

most an employer can ask of an applicant with a positive test result is what medications they are taking that could cause the positive result and whether he or she is taking the medication under a lawful prescription.[38] The employer may not ask about the underlying condition for which the medication is prescribed.

A recent case from the Tenth Circuit, *Harrison v. Benchmark Electronics Huntsville, Inc.*, illustrates the way in which employment-based drug testing may go astray.[39] John Harrison had a temporary job with Benchmark Electronics testing and repairing electronic boards. Harrison applied for a permanent position with the company at the urging of his supervisor, Don Anthony. As part of the application process, Harrison took a pre-employment drug test, which he failed. The medical review officer reported the result to the human resources department, which in turn asked Anthony to ask Harrison to come by. The policy of the human resources department was not to tell supervisors or anyone else if an applicant had failed a drug test, but whether someone slipped or Anthony guessed, Anthony told Harrison that he had tested positive for barbiturates. Anthony called the medical review officer from his office and had Harrison talk to him from there, while Anthony remained in the office. As it turned out, Harrison suffered from epilepsy and took legally prescribed barbiturates to control his condition. The medical review officer cleared Harrison, but Anthony no longer wished to hire him. Not only had the company apparently decided not to hire him because of his disability, it had also violated the prohibition against pre-offer medical inquiries when Anthony remained in the room during the course of Harrison's discussion with the medical review officer. Harrison sued the company for disability discrimination and the Tenth Circuit held that the hiring supervisor's interference with the MRO's communication with Harrison provided him with grounds for recovery under the ADA.[40]

Many employers wait until a conditional offer of employment has been made before they give a pre-employment drug test in order to save money by testing only those applicants the employer wants to hire. Employers who

---

38. *See ADA Enforcement Guidance: Preemployment Disability-Related Questions and Medical Examinations*, at 10.

39. *See* Harrison v. Benchmark Elects. Huntsville, Inc., 593 F.3d 1206 (10th Cir. 2010).

40. *See Harrison*, 593 F.3d at 1214–17.

do not wish to use the services of an MRO for non-CDL employees should also wait until a conditional offer has been extended. At this point, if the drug test is positive, managers, supervisors, and human resources may inquire into and discuss an applicant's lawful use of prescription drugs. Further discussion into the nature of the underlying condition and the expectation about long-term use of the medication may be appropriate where the drug could have a sedative effect that could impact the employee's performance. For those employers who have applicants undergo drug testing earlier in the hiring process, before a conditional offer is made, extra caution is called for when a drug test result is positive in order to avoid liability for a pre-offer inquiry into a disability.

Alcohol use. Unlike its treatment of drug addiction, the ADA does not make a distinction between past and present addiction to alcohol. Current alcoholism, as well as alcoholism for which a person may have successfully completed a rehabilitation program, are both disabilities covered by the ADA.[41] An employer may ask an applicant whether or not he or she drinks alcohol, because that is not likely to reveal that the employee is an alcoholic.[42] Many people enjoy a glass of beer or wine over dinner or after work, and an employer might want to point out that a position that requires on-call time will not allow an employee to indulge in those habits when the employee must be available after hours. An employer cannot, however, ask an employee how much or how often he or she drinks alcohol, because that may well reveal symptoms of alcoholism.[43]

Unlike a pre-employment drug test, which may be administered before an offer of employment has been extended, a pre-employment alcohol test may only be given post-offer. The statutory exemption of pre-employment

---

41. *See* 29 C.F.R. Part 1630, App. § 1630.16(b). *See also* Mararri v. WCI Steel, Inc., 130 F.3d 1180, 1182–83 (6th Cir. 1997) (upholding summary judgment for an employer who discharged an employee for violating last chance agreement; the court noted that while the ADA protects an individual's status as an alcoholic, being an alcoholic does not insulate an employee from the consequences of his own actions); Larson v. Koch Ref. Co., 920 F. Supp. 1000, 1004 (D. Minn. 1996) (while the ADA protects an employee's status as an alcoholic, an employer need not tolerate misconduct caused by alcoholism).

42. *See ADA Enforcement Guidance: Preemployment Disability-Related Questions and Medical Examinations*, at 11.

43. *See ADA Enforcement Guidance: Preemployment Disability-Related Questions and Medical Examinations*, at 11.

drug testing from inclusion as a medical examination does not extend to pre-employment alcohol testing.[44] A positive result on a pre-employment alcohol test may presumably reveal information about the disability of alcoholism and is thus not permitted before the employer makes an offer.

5.1.2.6 Previous Workers' Compensation Claims

Asking whether an applicant has ever received workers' compensation is an impermissible medical inquiry at pre-offer stage because such questions relate directly to the severity of an applicant's impairments.[45]

5.1.2.7 Obtaining Signatures on Medical Release Forms before an Offer Is Made

Some employers ask applicants to sign releases for background checks and for medical records at the time they fill out application forms. The reason human resources professionals cite for this practice is convenience. If an applicant is selected for an interview or ultimately for the position, the human resources department does not have to track the applicant down to obtain a signature because the appropriate releases are already on file. This practice complies with the ADA, so long as the release form does not ask the applicant questions about his or her medical history or to identify a disability and so long as the employer does not, in fact, obtain medical information prior to extending an offer to the applicant.[46] While not required, it is preferable that the release form itself indicate that the records will not be obtained until after an offer is made.[47] There is no regulation or holding to the effect that an employer may only ask for a release for medical records at the time of application if it makes that request of all applicants. Nevertheless, given the requirement that employers may only ask about ability to perform job duties if they ask the question of all applicants for

---

44. *See ADA Enforcement Guidance: Preemployment Disability-Related Questions and Medical Examinations*, at 16.

45. *See ADA Enforcement Guidance: Preemployment Disability-Related Questions and Medical Examinations*, at 9. *See also* Downs v. Mass. Bay Transp. Auth., 13 F. Supp. 2d 130, 138 (D. Mass. 1998).

46. *See, e.g.*, Green v. Joy Cone Co., 278 F. Supp. 2d 526, 540 (W.D. Pa. 2003) (plaintiff suffered no injury by being asked to sign medical release form at time of application).

47. *See Green*, 278 F. Supp. 2d at 541–42 ("although we do find this problematic, it is not a violation of the ADA unless and until an applicant's medical records are requested prematurely").

a position and may only require post-offer medical examinations if they require them of all applicants for similar positions, the prudent employer will only ask for a signature on a medical release upfront if it asks this of all applicants.

5.1.3 When Is an Offer an Offer for ADA Purposes?

What constitutes a "conditional offer" for the purposes of the ADA's exception for post-offer medical examinations? For the purposes of Title 42, Section 12112(d)(3), of the U.S. Code, a job offer is real if the employer has evaluated all relevant nonmedical information that it reasonably could have obtained and analyzed prior to making the offer.[48] In a case involving an application to a South Carolina sheriff's department, the plaintiff was sent for a medical examination at a time when the credit report check, physical abilities test, drug screening test, drug use questions, and polygraph examination all remained to be completed.[49] The plaintiff brought suit, alleging that the sheriff had violated the ADA by requiring him to take a medical examination before he had received a conditional offer of employment and that the sheriff refused to hire him when the medical examination revealed

48. *See ADA Enforcement Guidance: Preemployment Disability-Related Questions and Medical Examinations*, at 17. *See also* O'Neal v. City of New Albany, 293 F.3d 998, 1008–09 (7th Cir. 2002); *Downs*, 13 F. Supp. 2d at 138. If a job offer is conditioned not only on the applicant successfully passing a medical examination but also on a myriad of nonmedical screening tests, the offer is not real. *O'Neal*, 293 F.3d at 1008; Buchanan v. City of San Antonio, 85 F.3d 196, 199 (5th Cir. 1996) (so-called conditional offer made clear that the offer was not conditioned solely on a medical examination but was instead conditioned on successful completion of "the entire screening process," which included "physical and psychological examinations, a polygraph examination, a physical fitness test, an assessment board, and an extensive background investigation."); Garlitz v. Alpena Reg'l Med. Ctr., 2011 WL 6016498 (E.D. Mich. 2011) (question of material fact as to whether plaintiff had received a real offer before medical exam given that defendant used pre-offer behavior, as well as behavior during medical examination questions about sex and birth control, as reasons for rescinding offer); Malone v. Greenville Cnty., 2008 WL 4557498 (D.S.C. 2008), *report and recommendation adopted as modified*, 2008 WL 4458868 (D.S.C. 2008) ("If, therefore, conditions of employment remain at the time the offer is made, to wit, a personal interview or background investigation, then the offer is not 'real' and the employer is prohibited from making any inquiry into the medical condition of the applicant").

49. *Malone*, 2008 WL 4557498 (D.S.C. 2008).

that he was a diabetic.[50] The sheriff's office responded that although the other tests and checks were nonmedical in nature, each of those elements of the hiring process had the potential to implicate medical information concerning the plaintiff and, therefore, could not have been performed before the conditional offer. The court declined to address each component of the hiring process at issue, finding that it was enough that both a credit report and physical abilities test were outstanding at the time of the offer to render that offer not "real" and to make the medical inquiries unlawful.[51]

In another case, this one involving an application for a flight attendant position, the employer airline required applicants to undergo medical examinations before it had completed background checks, including employment verification and criminal history checks. Here, the court found that "the offers were not real" and the medical examinations "premature."[52]

---

50. Although the plaintiff in this case was a person with a disability, employers should take note that the majority of federal courts of appeal have held that an applicant need not be disabled within the meaning of the ADA in order to bring suit alleging a violation of the ADA's prohibition against pre-offer medical questions and examinations. *See, e.g.,* Harrison v. Benchmark Electronics Huntsville, Inc., 593 F.3d 1206, 1213 (11th Cir. 2010) (42 U.S.C. § 12112(d)(2) does not limit coverage to applicants who are also "qualified individuals with disabilities"); Fredenburg v. Contra Costa Cnty. Dep't of Health Servs., 172 F.3d 1176, 1182 (9th Cir. 1999) (plaintiffs need not prove that they are qualified individuals with a disability in order to bring claims challenging the scope of medical examinations under the ADA); Griffin v. Steeltek, Inc., 160 F.3d 591, 594–95 (10th Cir. 1998) (same). *But see* Griffin v. Steeltek, Inc., 261 F.3d 1026, 1028–29 (10th Cir. 2001) (even if employer technically violated ADA's prohibition against asking pre-employment questions regarding medical history by asking prohibited questions, employee was not entitled to nominal or punitive damages absent proof that he suffered injury by intentional discrimination). *See also* Denton v. Chicago Transit Auth., 2010 WL 1922771 (N.D. Ill. 2010) (the job applicant need not be disabled in order to maintain an action for improper pre-offer medical examinations and inquiries), *aff'd,* 400 F. App'x 90 (7th Cir. 2010), *reh'g denied* (Jan. 26, 2011); Mack v. Johnstown Am. Corp., 1999 WL 304276 (W.D. Pa. 1999) (same). *See also* Conroy v. N.Y. State Dep't of Corr. Servs., 333 F.3d 88, 96 (2d Cir. 2003) (employee needs to be a person with a disability to bring suit for employer's improper medical inquiries); *Contra* O'Neal v. City of New Albany, 293 F.3d 998, 1007 (7th Cir. 2002) (to prove a violation of prohibition on pre-offer medical inquiries, a plaintiff must demonstrate that he suffered some tangible injury-in-fact and collecting authority); Armstrong v. Turner Indus., Inc., 141 F.3d 554, 561 (5th Cir. 1998).

51. *See Malone,* 2008 WL 4557498.

52. *See* Leonel v. Am. Airlines, Inc., 400 F.3d 702, 709 (9th Cir. 2005), *opinion amended on denial of reh'g,* 2005 WL 976985 (9th Cir. 2005).

The airline argued that it was trying to expedite the process and prevent the competition from hiring its applicants, but the court held that the airline had not shown why it could not complete the background check process before moving on to the medical examinations:

> . . . . [American Airlines] has not shown why it could not expeditiously have issued two rounds of conditional offers—the first, after the interviews, informing applicants that they had reached the final stages of the application process and would be hired absent problems with their background checks or medical examinations; and the second, after completion of the background checks, ensuring employment if the applicant passed the medical examination.[53]

American argued in the alternative that even if the offers were not real, the company did not violate the ADA because it evaluated the appellants' nonmedical information before it considered their medical information. The court, however, rejected that defense, holding that the statutes regulate the sequence in which employers collect information, not the order in which they evaluate it.[54]

Sometimes, however, an employer simply cannot evaluate all relevant nonmedical information before the offer and subsequent medical questioning and examinations take place. In its Enforcement Guidance, the EEOC gives two examples of situations in which it would allow other parts of the hiring process to be incomplete at the time of the conditional offer and subsequent medical inquiries. One occurs quite commonly: a job applicant asks the employer not to contact his or her current employer for a reference until it extends a conditional job offer.[55] Applicants do not, after all, want to jeopardize their current jobs unless they can be sure that the new position is really in the offing. The other example comes from law enforcement, where the EEOC recognizes that it may be too costly for a law enforcement agency to conduct both pre-offer polygraph examinations that ask nonmedical questions and post-offer polygraph examinations

53. *See Leonel,* 400 F.3d at 710.

54. *See Leonel,* 400 F.3d at 710–11, *citing ADA Enforcement Guidance: Preemployment Disability-Related Questions and Medical Examinations,* at 2.

55. *See ADA Enforcement Guidance: Preemployment Disability-Related Questions and Medical Examinations,* at 18.

that ask medically related questions.[56] So, medical questions and examinations can come before a prospective employer talks with an applicant's current employer and as part of one comprehensive pre-offer polygraph examination.

5.1.4 Post-Offer Medical Examinations

Once a conditional offer of employment has been made, an employer may ask applicants questions about their medical conditions and about any disabilities they may have. It may also require applicants to take a medical examination before they actually begin working. The only limitation on an employer's ability to explore an applicant's medical status is that if the employer does ask medical questions or require an examination, it must ask the same questions and perform the same examination whenever it hires an employee into that same job category.[57] The medical questions and examination do not have to be job related and consistent with business necessity.[58] They may be broader in scope than information that is needed to assess the applicant's ability to do the job and could include, for example, questions about workers' compensation claims filed in the past or psychiatric or psychological counseling that the employee has received. That being said, employers should conduct any inquiries and examinations with care and limit the information sought to that which they truly need. As discussed in several other chapters, the EEOC assumes that any information that an employer acquires about an applicant or employee is used in making current and future decisions about that person's employment.[59]

At this stage, the employer may also directly ask whether applicants will need a reasonable accommodation to perform the job, although as with other medical questions and examinations, this question must be asked of all persons in the same job category. If someone does need a reasonable accommodation and the disability that necessitates the accommodation is not obvious, the employer may ask for documentation from a medical

---

56. *See ADA Enforcement Guidance: Preemployment Disability-Related Questions and Medical Examinations*, at 17–18.

57. *See* 29 C.F.R. § 1630.14(b).

58. *See* 29 C.F.R. § 1630.14(b)(3). *See also* O'Neal v. City of New Albany, 293 F.3d 998, 1008 (7th Cir. 2002) (post-offer examination does not have to be job related); Miller v. City of Springfield, 146 F.3d 612, 615 (8th Cir. 1998) (same); Garlitz v. Alpena Reg'l Med. Ctr., 2011 WL 6016498 (E.D. Mich. 2011) (same).

59. See the discussion of expressly unlawful questions at the beginning of this chapter.

professional of the disability and of the employee's functional limitations.[60] The ADA requires employers to "make reasonable accommodations to the known physical or mental limitations of an otherwise qualified individual with a disability who is an applicant or employee, unless [the employer] can demonstrate that the accommodation would impose an undue hardship on the operation of the business of [the employer]."[61] The process of accommodation requires employers to "initiate an informal, interactive process with [the employee] . . . . This process should identify the precise limitations resulting from the disability and potential reasonable accommodations that could overcome those limitations."[62] How to reasonably accommodate a disability is beyond the scope of this book, but employers may generally find good guidance in the EEOC's Enforcement Guidance, which may be found on the EEOC's website.[63]

5.1.5 Withdrawing an Offer Based on the Results of a Medical Inquiry or Examination

An employer is permitted to withdraw a conditional job offer if a post-offer medical inquiry or examination reveals that the applicant cannot perform an essential job function even with a reasonable accommodation. The standard for rescinding an offer is that the reason be "job-related and consistent with business necessity."[64] If the reason is related to job safety, the employer must be able to show that in the position, the applicant poses a direct threat of substantial harm to himself or herself, to other employees, or to the general public and that the threat cannot be mitigated even with a reasonable accommodation.[65] As the EEOC explains:

> The results of a medical inquiry or examination may not be used to disqualify persons who are currently able to perform the

---

60. *See ADA Enforcement Guidance: Preemployment Disability-Related Questions and Medical Examinations*, at 19.

61. *See* 42 U.S.C. § 12112(b)(5)(A).

62. *See* 29 C.F.R. § 1630.2(o)(3).

63. See the EEOC's webpage entitled "Disability Discrimination," www.eeoc.gov/laws/types/disability.cfm; U.S. Equal Employment Opportunity Commission, *Enforcement Guidance: Reasonable Accommodation and Undue Hardship Under the Americans with Disabilities Act*, No. 915.002, October 17, 2002, www.eeoc.gov/policy/docs/accommodation.html; and the EEOC's webpage entitled "Small Employers and Reasonable Accommodation, www.eeoc.gov/facts/accommodation.html.

64. *See* 42 U.S.C. § 12112(d)(3)(C); 29 C.F.R. § 1630.14(b)(3).

65. *See* 42 U.S.C. § 12113(b); 29 C.F.R. Part 1630, App. § 1630.2(r).

> essential functions of a job, either with or without an accommodation, because of fear or speculation that a disability may indicate a greater risk of future injury, or absenteeism, or may cause future workers' compensation or insurance costs. An employer may use such information to exclude an individual with a disability where there is specific medical documentation, reflecting current medical knowledge, that this individual would pose a significant, current risk of substantial harm to health or safety.[66]

On its face, this is a reasonable standard. Applying the rule to specific situations, however, is more problematic. Consider the following two examples given by the EEOC. In the first, a medical history reveals that a job candidate has re-injured his back seriously on several occasions while doing similar work. This person's back condition has become progressively worse. The EEOC says that in this situation, an employer could withdraw the job offer because "[e]mploying this person in this job would incur significant risk that he would further reinjure himself."[67] A little further on, the EEOC gives a variation on this example. In the second example, an applicant for a position that requires heavy lifting has an abnormal back x-ray. An employer may not withdraw its job offer because it fears—based solely on the back x-ray—that this applicant is more likely to suffer an on-the-job injury while lifting. But if the employer has evidence that the applicant has injured and re-injured his or her back multiple times "in similar jobs," and there is no reasonable accommodation that can reduce the risk of re-injury, then the employer may withdraw the job offer.[68] These examples seem to recognize an employer's right to refuse to hire those individuals whom a reasonable person might think will be likely to injure themselves on the job, but they are misleading. In the first example, the EEOC finds it permissible for an employer to withdraw an offer based on medical history alone, without a current physical examination of the applicant. In the second example, it says it is impermissible to withdraw an offer where there is a current x-ray showing an abnormality in the absence of a history of re-

66. *See* Equal Employment Opportunity Commission, *Technical Assistance Manual on the Employment Provisions (Title I) of the Americans with Disabilities Act* (January 1992) (hereinafter *EEOC Technical Assistance Manual*), at VI-8.

67. *See EEOC Technical Assistance Manual* at VI-7.

68. *See EEOC Technical Assistance Manual* at VI-8.

injury. These examples would seem to suggest that the medical history is more important than the current examination. How this is to be reconciled with the EEOC's warning in the same document that medical information may be used only to exclude an application where there is specific, *current* medical documentation about the applicant is unclear.

Now compare two other EEOC examples with an actual case. In the first EEOC example, an applicant for a job that requires the occasional lifting of more than 50 pounds is rejected because he has a lifting limitation of 50 pounds. This is unlawful, says the EEOC, because the employer "has not considered possible accommodations, such as sharing the occasional heavy weight lifting with another employee or providing a device to assist lifting."[69] However, there is at least one case at the federal trial court level in which a judge found that the mere fact that an offer of employment was subsequently withdrawn because of the candidate's inability to lift up to 45 pounds without assistance—an essential function of the position—did not suggest any inference that the employer regarded him as a person with a disability and discriminated against him on that basis.[70]

The second example posits a different situation entirely. Here, a workers' compensation history record reveals that an applicant made several workers' compensation claims in previous jobs that were all denied. The EEOC says that the employer might have a "legitimate business reason" to think that this applicant submits fraudulent workers' compensation claims. Revoking the job offer for this reason would not involve any possible disability that the applicant has but rather would be because the employer doubts the person's honesty.[71]

All of these issues played a role in a Tenth Circuit case, *Garrison v. Baker Hughes Oilfield Operations, Inc.*[72] The plaintiff, Garrison, applied for a housekeeper position that required the unassisted lifting of up to 45 pounds, usually of trash. After receiving a conditional offer of employment, the employer had Garrison answer a medical questionnaire and undergo a physical examination. On the medical questionnaire, Garrison indicated

---

69. *See EEOC Technical Assistance Manual* at VI-8.

70. *See* Stinson v. W. Suburban Hosp. Med. Ctr., 1998 WL 188938 (N.D. Ill. 1998).

71. *See EEOC Technical Assistance Manual* at VI-7.

72. Garrison v. Baker Hughes Oilfield Operations, Inc., 287 F.3d 955 (10th Cir. 2002).

that he had not had hearing loss; pain in the shoulder, arms, or hands; leg or foot problems; or back pain, strain, or surgery. The employer's physician found no limitations on Garrison's physical abilities and recommended him for the position. As part of the post-offer medical review process, the human resources department then obtained Garrison's past workers' compensation records. Notwithstanding his answers on the questionnaire, Garrison had received workers' compensation benefits for several injuries arising from previous employment. He had suffered injuries to his hearing, neck, shoulder, elbow, hand, back, abdomen, lungs, knee, and feet. After learning of Garrison's previous injuries, the employer withdrew its conditional offer of employment. Garrison then telephoned the human resources manager to ask why the company had withdrawn the job offer. Referring to Garrison's previous workers' compensation claims, the human resources manager said, "So when we look at those kind of histories, we look at those in terms of where we are placing people for possible future injuries. . . . Well, the positions that we were looking at you for are those positions that would put you in a position to likely be injured again and we don't do that."[73]

At trial, the jury found for Garrison on his claim that he had unlawfully been denied employment in violation of the ADA. The appeals court upheld the jury's finding and award, noting that although Garrison had admitted that he falsely represented his medical history and that the employer would be within its rights to reject him for this reason, it was within the jury's discretion to conclude that the job offer was withdrawn because of unsubstantiated speculation about future risks from a perceived disability, not because of the dishonesty. The Tenth Circuit found that there was substantial evidence to support this conclusion.[74]

The *Garrison* case illustrates well the dangers of accessing an applicant's workers' compensation history, despite the EEOC's position that a history of workers' compensation claims in similar positions may form the basis of a decision to reject an applicant that is job related and consistent with business necessity. It is impossible to know either the employer's true motivation or why the jury found as it did, but it is worth considering whether

---

73. *See Garrison*, 287 F.3d at 958.
74. *See Garrison*, 287 F.3d at 960.

the real reason the company rejected Garrison was the claims history, his untruthful answers to the questions about his medical condition, or a combination of the two, and whether the human resources manager, when put on the spot by Garrison's phone call, found it easier to talk about his injuries than to confront him about his dishonesty. Whatever the truth is, the human resources manager's response to Garrison no doubt played an important role in the jury's decision and allowed them to discount any importance that the company may have placed on his false answers, a fact that would likely be the last straw for many employers, regardless of what the medical history and examination actually suggested. Equally speculative is the role that the physician's medical examination played. Without the workers' compensation history, the company likely would have hired Garrison, given that the physician "recommended" him, as the court's decision described it.[75] Did the fact that the company did not seem to put any weight on the doctor's finding that he was fit for the job contribute to the jury's conclusion that discrimination was the real reason for the withdrawal of the offer? Should an employer seek to learn an applicant's workers' compensation history at all?

The author has found relatively few reported cases addressing issues raised by a withdrawal of a job offer based on the results of a post-offer medical history and examination. But the very lack of clarity in this area suggests that employers would be well advised to follow a conservative approach to post-offer medical examinations. Although the ADA allows employers to obtain unrestricted medical histories and to perform unrestricted medical examinations, they would be wise to avoid seeking any information—through histories, questionnaires, or examinations—that they could not clearly use in determining whether or not a candidate can perform the essential functions of the job. Instead, employers should place significant weight on the results of any current medical examinations that they require candidates to undergo. Obtaining workers' compensation claims history should be done only after careful consideration.

---

75. *See Garrison*, 287 F.3d at 958.

5.2 Expressly Unlawful Questions: The Genetic Information Nondiscrimination Act

The Genetic Information Nondiscrimination Act (GINA) adds a slight wrinkle to the rules on post-offer medical inquiries and examinations. As discussed more fully in Chapter 2, GINA prohibits employers from acquiring *genetic information* about applicants or employees except in certain very limited circumstances. Although the ADA permits employers to make unlimited medical inquiries after a conditional offer of employment has been made, GINA limits this right with respect to genetic information. Employers may *not* ask for genetic information as part of a routine medical history even post-offer. Under GINA, genetic information includes family medical history as well as information obtained through an individual's or family member's genetic tests.[76]

Many physicians have patients and others they examine fill out medical questionnaires. Employers who have some or all of their employees undergo physical medical examinations after the conditional offer of employment must ensure that the physicians performing the examinations do not *ask* for family medical history or the results of any genetic testing that the applicant has had. Employers should not assume that medical professionals have any knowledge of the employment provisions of GINA. It is the employer's responsibility to make sure that the medical professionals that they use do not ask for any information protected by GINA. An employer does not have to intentionally ask for genetic information in order to violate GINA: violation occurs if an employer unintentionally obtains genetic information or family history. But what if the medical provider that an employer uses asks for family medical history or genetic test results even though the employer has told the provider not to do so? On its website page on GINA, the EEOC advises:

> If a covered entity tells its health care provider not to collect genetic information and the health care provider does so anyway, the employer will not be liable for that particular collec-

76. Under GINA, a genetic test is an analysis of human DNA, RNA, chromosomes, proteins, or metabolites that detects genotypes, mutations, and chromosomal changes. A test that does not do these things is not a genetic test. A test to detect the presence of disease that does not involve analysis of genotypes, mutations, or chromosomes is not a genetic test. *See* 29 C.F.R. § 1635.3(f).

> tion of genetic information, but the covered entity must take additional reasonable measures within its control to prevent this behavior in the future. This could include no longer using the services of that health care provider.[77]

The EEOC's GINA regulations give employers a safe harbor by providing that if an employer uses its suggested language or something similar in documents requesting medical information, any genetic information that it receives in response to the request will be deemed an inadvertent, rather than an unlawful, acquisition. The language that the EEOC recommends is as follows:

> The Genetic Information Nondiscrimination Act of 2008 (GINA) prohibits employers and other entities covered by GINA Title II from requesting or requiring genetic information of an individual or family member of the individual, except as specifically allowed by this law. To comply with this law, we are asking that you not provide any genetic information when responding to this request for medical information. 'Genetic information' as defined by GINA, includes an individual's family medical history, the results of an individual's or family member's genetic tests, the fact that an individual or an individual's family member sought or received genetic services, and genetic information of a fetus carried by an individual or an individual's family member or an embryo lawfully held by an individual or family member receiving assistive reproductive services.[78]

---

77. *See* U.S. Equal Employment Opportunity Commission, *Background Information for EEOC Final Rule on Title II of the Genetic Information Nondiscrimination Act of 2008*, www.eeoc.gov/laws/regulations/gina-background.cfm. This follows from 29 C.F.R. § 1635.8(b)(1)(i)(A), which says, "If a covered entity acquires genetic information in response to a lawful request for medical information, the acquisition of genetic information will not generally be considered inadvertent unless the covered entity directs the individual and/or health care provider from whom it requested medical information (in writing, or verbally, where the covered entity does not typically make requests for medical information in writing) not to provide genetic information."

78. *See* 29 C.F.R. § 1635.8(b)(1)(i)(B).

5.2.1 What Happens When an Employer Violates the ADA or GINA's Rules on Medical Questions and Examinations?

Applicants and employees who believe that they have been discriminated against on the basis of either a disability or their genetic information or who believe that an employer has unlawfully obtained medical information or genetic information about them may file charges with the EEOC. They may ultimately bring a lawsuit in federal court, just as applicants and employees may do if claiming race, gender, or another prohibited form of discrimination under Title VII. Employers may be ordered to hire an applicant or to promote or reinstate an employee or to pay back pay or other money damages, including attorneys' fees and costs.[79]

5.3 Bottom Line: Pre-Employment Questions and Medical Examinations under the ADA and GINA

1. Employers may not directly ask job applicants about disabilities and may not ask any other questions that are likely to disclose a disability. Employers should follow one simple rule: ask no medical or health-related question at the application and interview stages of the hiring process.
2. Employers may ask applicants about their ability to perform specific job functions, such as their ability to lift a certain amount of weight, and about their nonmedical qualifications and skills, such as work history, education, required licenses, and certifications.
3. Employers may ask applicants to describe or demonstrate how they perform specific job tasks.
4. If an applicant volunteers information about a disability, the employer may ask whether the applicant will need a reasonable accommodation to perform the job.
5. Employers may not require applicants to take a medical examination before a job offer is extended.
6. Employers may ask applicants to take nonmedical tests before a job offer is extended—for example, physical agility tests, skills tests, personality profile tests, or pre-employment drug tests (but

79. *See* 42 U.S.C. § 12117 (ADA) and 42 U.S.C. § 2000ff-6(a) (GINA).

not a pre-employment alcohol test)—provided that all applicants for the same position are required to take the test.

7. Once an employer extends an offer, it may require the successful applicant to take a medical examination, provided that the employer requires medical examinations of all new employees or all new employees in the same position or department. The physician or other medical professional conducting the physical examination may not ask questions about the applicant's family medical history or about any genetic testing that the applicant or a family member has undergone. The employer is liable for any such questions that medical personnel acting on its behalf may ask.
8. Once an employer extends an offer, it may also ask disability-related questions, including questions about the successful applicant's workers' compensation history and attendance record at previous jobs and about the applicant's health. An employer may not ask questions about the applicant's family medical history or about any genetic testing that the applicant or a family member has undergone.
9. If the employer withdraws a conditional offer of employment after a post-offer medical examination or discussion of the applicant's medical history, the reasons for the withdrawal of the offer must be job related and consistent with business necessity.

5.4 Questions Giving Rise to Inferences of Discrimination Based on Race, Color, Gender, Religion, National Origin, or Age

In contrast to the Americans with Disabilities Act and the Genetic Nondiscrimination Act, there are no expressly prohibited inquiries under Title VII and the Age Discrimination in Employment Act (ADEA). But employers must nonetheless be vigilant that the supervisory and human resources personnel involved with the hiring process do not intentionally or unintentionally ask questions that suggest that an applicant's protected class status has played a role in the decision not to hire him or her. If a question is not job related, it is reasonable to wonder why it is being asked and to assume, as the EEOC does, that the answer is being taken into account in the decision-making process. The following sections discuss some of the most common questions that either appear on applications or are asked in interviews and that are not, on their face, job related. As such, if they are asked, they may suggest that discrimination is at work in the hiring process.

5.4.1 Questions about Family Status

5.4.1.1 Are you single, married, or divorced?

Marital status is not a protected class under either federal or state anti-discrimination law. Nevertheless, the concept of marriage carries with it certain stereotypes, some of which are gender related. Some people think that single employees, male and female alike, are more dependable and more devoted to their careers. Others think that married employees are more stable and more likely to stay in their jobs. Some think this is true of married male employees more than of married female employees. Consider the now-dated stereotype of the "career woman"—a phrase that in its day was rarely used to refer to a married woman.

Why would an employer ask an applicant about marital status? The primary legitimate reasons for asking a job applicant questions about his or her marital status is because the information is necessary for income tax withholding purposes and for insurance benefits purposes. This information, however, may be just as easily obtained after the applicant is actually hired.

There are very few instances in local government and community college employment where an applicant's marital status is relevant to a job's duties. If one assumes, as the EEOC has made clear it does, that the information is being gathered because it will be used in the decision-making process, then two possibilities suggest themselves: (1) that the employer's decision maker has pre-conceived notions about the relative desirability of single and married people as employees, and possibly about the relative desirability of married male applicants and married female applicants; or (2) that the person asking the question is interested in the availability of the applicant for dating or another intimate relationship. No employer should allow its hiring process to leave an applicant with either of those two impressions. Questions about marital status should not be asked except on the IRS W-4 form and on benefits application forms.

5.4.1.2 Do you prefer Miss or Mrs.? What is your maiden name? Did you ever go by another name?

Although questions such as these might be perceived as subterfuges to gain information about a woman's marital status, they can also be poorly phrased questions from which the employer hopes to learn whether the applicant has used other names that need to be cross-referenced in a background check. The better question would be "Is there any additional information, such as different name or nickname, that is needed to check your references?"

5.4.1.3 Are you planning to start a family soon? Do you have any children? Who watches the kids while you are at work? Do you plan to have any (more) children?

This is a more dangerous question than the question about marital status, especially if asked only of women. The stereotype still persists that because of child-raising responsibilities, mothers are not as committed to their careers and will sacrifice work responsibilities in favor of the care of their children. It is the case, as the EEOC noted in a 2007 guidance, that women continue to be the primary caregivers in most families.[80] While such caregiving may be predominantly focused on the woman's own children, women also assume roles in caring for aging parents and parents-in-law. As such, they are disproportionately the victims of stereotyping about the commitment and reliability of persons who care for young children and the elderly.[81]

As is the case with questions about marital status, questions about an applicant's children are rarely related to job functions. Whatever the employer representative's motives really are in asking such questions, they give rise to an inference of what is known as "gender plus" or "sex plus" discrimination. Gender plus discrimination occurs when an employer discriminates not against the class of men or women as a whole but against a subclass of men or women so designated by their gender plus another

---

80. *See* U.S. Equal Employment Opportunity Commission, *Enforcement Guidance: Unlawful Disparate Treatment of Workers with Caregiving Responsibilities,* No. 915.002 (May 23, 2007) (hereinafter *Enforcement Guidance on Workers with Caregiving Responsibilities*), at 2 with citations therein.

81. *See Enforcement Guidance on Workers with Caregiving Responsibilities* at 5–6.

characteristic.[82] Gender plus claims are usually brought by women, and the plus characteristic is typically "married," "mothers," "mothers of young children," or a combination of these characteristics.[83]

It is legitimate for an employer to be concerned about applicants' reliability and availability for work. As the EEOC notes, "Title VII does not prohibit discrimination based solely on parental or other caregiver status, so an employer does not generally violate Title VII's disparate treatment proscription if, for example, it treats working mothers and working fathers in a similar unfavorable (or favorable) manner as compared to childless workers."[84] The mere fact that a female applicant is married or has children and does not get the job does not automatically give rise to an assumption that the employer discriminated against her. But where one of the employer's representatives has made comments that suggest gender-based stereotyping of women with children, that will likely be seen as strong evidence of discrimination and, in some cases, enough to establish liability

---

82. *See* Phillips v. Martin Marietta Corp., 400 U.S. 542, 544 (1971) (Title VII does not permit one hiring policy for women with pre-school-age children and another hiring policy for men with pre-school-age children); Back v. Hastings on Hudson Union Free Sch. Dist., 365 F.3d 107, 118 n.7 (2d Cir. 2004) (female school psychologist with a young child could show that she was denied tenure because of her sex by relying on evidence of gender-based comments about working mothers and other evidence of sex stereotyping and was not required to show that similarly situated male workers were treated more favorably); Gee-Thomas v. Cingular Wireless, 324 F. Supp. 2d 875, 881 (M.D. Tenn. 2004) (recognizing prima facie case of sex plus marital and family status discrimination in promotion decision but finding insufficient evidence to show that employer's proferred reason was pretextual).

83. In addition to *Phillips*, 400 U.S. 542, *Back*, 365 F.3d 107, and *Gee-Thomas*, 324 F. Supp. 2d 875, all cited in note 82, see also *Coleman v. B-G Maintenance Management of Colorado, Inc.*, 108 F.3d 1199, 1203–05 (10th Cir. 1997) (recognizing sex plus discrimination but finding insufficient evidence on which to return a verdict in plaintiff's favor); *Fisher v. Vassar College*, 70 F.3d 1420, 1433–34, 1448 (2d Cir. 1995) (recognizing a sex plus claim of sex plus marital status but finding insufficient evidence to sustain the district court's finding of liability), *aff'd en banc*, 114 F.3d 1332 (1997), *cert. denied*, 522 U.S. 1075 (1998); *Bryant v. International School Services, Inc.*, 675 F.2d 562, 573 n.18 (3d Cir. 1982) (recognizing a claim of sex discrimination premised on marital status but observing that such a claim was not at issue in the case); and *Fuller v. GTE Corp./Contel Cellular, Inc.*, 926 F. Supp. 653, 658 (M.D. Tenn. 1996) (finding that plaintiff had failed to establish a prima facie case of disparate treatment either due to her gender or her status as a mother of young children).

84. *See Enforcement Guidance on Workers with Caregiving Responsibilities*, at 11.

even in the absence of other evidence that the employer has treated married men or men with children differently.[85]

The case *Chadwick v. WellPoint, Inc.,* illustrates this point well.[86] Chadwick was a longtime employee of WellPoint, an insurance company, where her work involved the pursuit of overpayments and reimbursements from third parties and where she had already received promotions. In 2006, her supervisor encouraged her to apply for a promotion to a management position. Chadwick was already performing several of the responsibilities of the position and had received excellent reviews on her most recent performance evaluation. Her competition for the job was another woman who held the same current position with the company. Chadwick, however, had been in the position for seven years, while the other candidate had only one year's experience in the current position. She had not scored as highly as Chadwick on her most recent evaluation, either.

The other candidate got the job. At the time of the decision, Chadwick was the mother of an eleven-year-old son and six-year-old triplets. She was also taking one course per semester at a nearby university. Chadwick filed

---

85. *See Enforcement Guidance on Workers with Caregiving Responsibilities*, at 9, *citing* Plaetzer v. Borton Auto., Inc., 2004 WL 2066770, at *6 n.3 (D. Minn. 2004) (evidence of more favorable treatment of working fathers is not needed to show sex discrimination against working mothers where an "employer's objection to an employee's parental duties is actually a veiled assertion that mothers, because they are women, are insufficiently devoted to work, or that work and motherhood are incompatible"); Lust v. Sealy, Inc., 383 F.3d 580, 583 (7th Cir. 2004) (reasonable jury could have concluded that the plaintiff's supervisor did not recommend her for a promotion because he assumed that, as a working mother, the plaintiff would not accept a promotion that would require her to move because of its disruptive effect on her children); Santiago-Ramos v. Centennial P.R. Wireless Corp., 217 F.3d 46, 55 (1st Cir. 2000) (comments by decision makers reflecting concern that the plaintiff might not be able to balance work and family responsibilities after she had a second child could lead a jury to conclude that the plaintiff was fired because of sex). *But cf.* Weightman v. Bank of N.Y. Mellon Corp., 772 F. Supp. 2d 693, 706–07 (W.D. Pa. 2011) (in case alleging unlawful termination based on gender, manager's comment that "you need to make a decision, either you're going to be a mom or have a career" did not constitute direct evidence of discrimination where it was made outside of the decision-making context); Philipsen v. Univ. of Mich. Bd. of Regents, 2007 WL 907822 (E.D. Mich. 2007) (holding that a plaintiff cannot establish a prima facie case of sex discrimination against women with young children in the absence of comparative evidence that men with young children are treated more favorably).

86. *See* Chadwick v. WellPoint, Inc., 561 F.3d 38 (1st Cir. 2009).

a discrimination claim, alleging that WellPoint denied her the promotion based on the gender-based stereotype that mothers, particularly those with young children, neglect their work duties in favor of their presumed child care obligations. In addition to highlighting her superior qualifications, Chadwick offered evidence of three comments made by those involved in the promotion process (all women), one of which was especially telling. When the manager with final decision-making authority told Chadwick that she did not get the promotion, she said, "It was nothing you did or didn't do. It was just that you're going to school, you have the kids and you just have a lot on your plate right now." Later in the same conversation, she said, "If [the three interviewers] were in your position, they would feel overwhelmed." When she was deposed in the course of the lawsuit, the decision maker said that she decided not to promote Chadwick because she interviewed poorly and that she had only told Chadwick that she had "too much on her plate" in an ill-advised attempt to soften the blow. The district court found that this was not sufficient evidence from which a jury could conclude that WellPoint had engaged in gender plus discrimination and granted summary judgment to the company. On appeal, the First Circuit reversed, finding that a reasonable jury could well have found that the reason Chadwick was denied the promotion was because she was the mother of small children.[87] Thus, Chadwick won her sex discrimination case even though the person who got the promotion was herself a woman and everyone involved in the decision-making was female.

The best practice for employers is to avoid asking any questions about or engaging in any discussion about an applicant's children or interest in having children, regardless of whether the applicant is a man or a woman. Questions about an applicant's ability to meet the position's workload and stated work schedule should be asked directly of all candidates, not just women. After all, there are many reasons why an applicant, male or female, might not be able to meet the employer's expectations. The applicant might have transportation issues because of, for example, an unreliable automobile or unreliable public transportation, or the applicant might have another job without a fixed schedule or with on-call responsibilities. Like Chadwick, the applicant also might be enrolled in a local community college or university. Employers are well within their rights to explore an

87. *See Chadwick,* 561 F.3d at 39–42.

applicant's ability to fulfill the job's requirements in terms of both attendance and ability to show up on time and to work a full day. But this is best addressed by asking, "Will you be able to meet this work schedule on a regular basis?"

5.4.2 Questions about Age or Date of Birth

Applicant age is rarely related to an individual's ability to perform a job's duties. Asking applicants how old they are would be, in most cases, evidence that the employer is taking age into account in the hiring decision. Employers should therefore refrain from making a direct inquiry into age and from asking for an applicant's date of birth. Employers may need a date of birth in order to conduct a criminal background check and for EEO reporting purposes. But this information may be obtained either through the use of a tear-off sheet at the front or back of the application that is retained in the human resources department and not shown to decision makers or it may be obtained later, once the employer has narrowed down the list of applicants into one or two finalists.

Section 1625.5 of the EEOC's ADEA regulations advises employers as follows:

> A request on the part of an employer for information such as Date of Birth or age on an employment application form is not, in itself, a violation of the Act. But because the request that an applicant state his age may tend to deter older applicants or otherwise indicate discrimination against older individuals, employment application forms that request such information will be closely scrutinized to assure that the request is for a permissible purpose and not for purposes proscribed by the Act. That the purpose is not one proscribed by the statute should be made known to the applicant by a reference on the application form to the statutory prohibition in language to the following effect:
>
> The Age Discrimination in Employment Act of 1967 prohibits discrimination on the basis of age with respect to individuals who are at least 40 years of age," or by other means. The term "employment applications," refers to all written inquiries about employment or applications for employment or promotion

> including, but not limited to, résumés or other summaries of the applicant's background. It relates not only to written preemployment inquiries, but to inquiries by employees concerning terms, conditions, or privileges of employment as specified in section 4 of the Act.[88]

5.4.3 Questions about Educational History

5.4.3.1 What year did you graduate from high school? What year did you graduate from college?

If an employer is trying to extrapolate the age of an applicant by asking questions like these, it should not do so—these questions are as unadvisable as the more direct "How old are you?" Indeed, some rejected applicants have brought age discrimination claims with their primary evidence the fact that the employer asked for dates of attendance in order to learn their age, but courts have rejected such inquiries as the basis of liability for age discrimination in the absence of any other evidence.[89] The more likely and perfectly lawful reason for an employer to inquire into dates of attendance or graduation is to assess the state of the applicant's knowledge or to put together a fuller picture of the applicant's job and job-related experiences. An employer should not, therefore, hesitate to ask for dates of high school or college graduation or of licensing or course certifications.

5.4.3.2 Do you have a high school diploma?

An informal survey by the author of job openings with North Carolina local governments in February 2012 showed that a sizeable number of local government employers require a high school degree for manual labor, maintenance, and clerical positions. The reality is, however, that it is not necessary to have finished high school or to have a college degree for every position at the local government or community college level, however desirable an employer may think it is. While requiring a high school diploma

---

88. *See* 29 C.F.R. § 1625.5.

89. *See* Calderwood v. Gen. Mills, 13 F. App'x 787, 789 (10th Cir. 2001) (inclusion of college graduation date on application did not give rise to inference of age discrimination); Norville v. Staten Island Univ. Hosp., 196 F.3d 89, 98 (2d Cir. 1999) (even assuming that interviewer could have inferred each applicant's age based on their respective answers, there is simply no evidence that age discrimination was the purpose of question about when applicants had graduated from nursing school).

is not illegal per se, if the requirement has a disparate impact on African American or Latino applicants or members of any other protected class, the employer would have to show that the diploma is a business necessity.[90] Statewide, the 2010–2011 North Carolina high school graduation rate was 82.6 percent for white students and 86.9 percent for Asian American students. Racial and ethnic minority students other than Asian Americans had lower graduation rates. The 2010–2011 graduation rate for African American students was 71.5 percent and for Latino students it was 68.8 percent. Native American students graduated at a rate of 69.7 percent.[91] The likelihood that a high school diploma requirement will have disparate impact on African American and Latino job applicants will vary from city to city and county to county depending on how great the disparity in the local high school graduation rates is.

The potential for a high school graduation requirement to have a disparate impact, however, is well illustrated by the case *Carpenter v. Stephen F. Austin State University*. In that case, a class of African American and female service, maintenance, and clerical employees brought suit against the university employer, alleging that the university's requirement that those hired into certain positions in these areas have high school diplomas had a disparate impact on African Americans.[92] The district court found that in the relevant labor market, more whites graduated from high school than did African Americans and that more whites and males were college graduates than were African Americans and women. It further found that the university had established job qualifications solely by describing the educational status of the current holder of the position at the time the

---

90. *See* Griggs v. Duke Power Co., 401 U.S. 424, 431–33 (1971); Drake v. City of Fort Collins, 927 F.2d 1156, 1161 (10th Cir. 1991) (plaintiff failed to establish a prima facie case of disparate impact where two-year college requirement operated less harshly on African American applicants than on white applicants and plaintiff was the only African American applicant rejected on this basis); Stevenson v. Int'l Paper Co., Mobile, Ala., 516 F.2d 103, 116 (5th Cir. 1975). For an in-depth discussion of disparate impact, see Chapter 2, Sections 2.1.6 and 2.1.7.

91. *See* N.C. Department of Health & Human Services, N.C. State Center for Health Statistics, *Data for Four-Year High School Graduation Rate by Race/Ethnicity, 2010–2011*, updated January 19, 2012, http://healthstats.publichealth.nc.gov/indicator/view_numbers/HSGradRate.RaceEth.html.

92. *See* Carpenter v. Stephen F. Austin State Univ., 706 F.2d 608, 612, 621 (5th Cir. 1983).

job descriptions were formulated. The university produced no evidence showing that the requirement of a high school diploma was job related, much less a business necessity, except to assert that supervisory employees benefited from formal education. The university had never had a validity study done of the high school diploma requirement.[93] At the conclusion of the trial, the district court ordered the university to validate the job qualifications and provide preferential treatment to those employees who had wrongfully been denied more advanced job assignments. On appeal, the Fifth Circuit affirmed.[94]

Does the possibility that an educational requirement might result in a disparate impact on an underrepresented group mean that an employer cannot impose it? The answer to that question is no. An employer may always have an educational requirement when it is job related and consistent with business necessity. Even where an educational requirement has no clear relationship to the specific job functions and merely reflects an employer's desire for a better-educated workforce, high school diploma and college degree requirements will not be unlawful unless there is a disparity in educational attainments in the geographic area from which the employer draws its workforce. Employers who have educational requirements for any of their positions should examine each position and consider both whether the educational requirement is job related and necessary and whether it is likely to have a disparate impact.

5.4.4 Questions about Religion

5.4.4.1 What church do you attend? What religion are you? What holidays do you celebrate? Can you provide a reference from a minister or pastor?

Inquiries into an applicant's religious beliefs and practices are always inappropriate in the public sector, as there are no instances other than the employment of chaplains by public hospitals or universities where religion

93. On validity studies, see Chapter 2, Section 2.1.7.6, and Appendix 3.

94. *See Carpenter,* 707 F.2d at 622–23. *See also* Payne v. Travenol Labs., Inc., 565 F.2d 895, 899 (5th Cir. 1978) (evidence in employment discrimination action contained ample evidence of disparate impact and lack of business necessity in employer's requirement of 12th-grade education or equivalency for employment in office, clerical, technician, and supervisory positions and of a college degree for positions of systems, traffic, or scheduling analyst).

is directly related to a position's job duties.[95] However, an applicant's religious beliefs and practices can conflict with certain of an employer's workplace practices or policies—for example, when a work schedule involves weekend hours and the applicant is unavailable because he or she observes Saturday or Sunday as the Sabbath, or when the employer has a uniform policy against headwear and an applicant's religion requires him or her to wear a turban or headscarf. Religion is the only Title VII protected category that requires something more than mere nondiscrimination. Like the ADA, Title VII requires employers to reasonably accommodate employees' sincerely held religious beliefs, practices, and observances unless the accommodation would pose an undue hardship.[96] Under Title VII, "undue hardship" is anything more than a minimal cost or burden, in contrast to the ADA's much higher standard.[97] While the topic of Title VII reasonable accommodation of employee religious beliefs and practices is beyond the scope of this book, a few observations about religious discrimination in the context of hiring are in order.[98]

The primary reason employers may have concerns about an applicant's religion is because of the potential for conflict between the position's job duties and work schedule and the applicant's sincerely held religious belief. Here, as always, the employer should ask applicants directly whether they will be able to perform all of the position's duties and whether they will be able to meet the work schedule. The employer should not reference religion since there are many reasons other than religion that an applicant might not be able to meet the job's requirements. It is the responsibility of the applicant to inform the employer of a bona fide religious belief that

---

95. While public hospitals and universities may not have Christian denomination-specific chaplains, they frequently have Christian, Jewish, and, increasingly, Muslim chaplains, for which religious affiliation will be a job requirement, notwithstanding the institution's public status.

96. *See* 42 U.S.C. §§ 2000(j) and 2000e-2(a).

97. *See* U.S. Equal Employment Opportunity Commission, *Compliance Manual, Section 12: Religious Discrimination,* No. 915.003 (July 22, 2008) (hereinafter *Compliance Manual, Section 12: Religious Discrimination),* at 2–3, www.eeoc.gov/policy/docs/religion.html.

98. For a comprehensive discussion of religious discrimination in violation of Title VII and reasonable accommodation of religious beliefs and practices, see 1 BARBARA T. LINDEMANN & PAUL GROSSMAN, EMPLOYMENT DISCRIMINATION LAW Ch. 9 (4th ed. 2007). *See also Compliance Manual, Section 12: Religious Discrimination.*

conflicts with an employment requirement. An applicant cannot maintain a prima facie case of religious discrimination in violation of Title VII unless it can show both the existence of a belief that conflicts with an employment requirement and that the employer knew or had reason to know of this belief.[99] A Title VII reasonable accommodation does not require an employer to eliminate entirely any conflicts between religious practice and employment requirements; the employer is required only to reasonably accommodate the practice.[100] As the courts have recognized, "because of business necessity and the legitimate rights of other employees," Title VII does not "impose a duty on the employer to accommodate at all costs."[101] Thus, if accommodating an applicant's or employee's religious needs means that the employer will have to ignore seniority rights or otherwise make a significant imposition on other employees (by forcing them to work a different shift, for example), the employer need not provide the accommodation.[102] As with the ADA, however, an employer must still show that it has at least considered the possibility of accommodation and engaged in some kind of interactive process with the applicant or employee.[103]

---

99. *See* EEOC v. Firestone Fibers & Textiles Co., 515 F.3d 307, 312 (4th Cir. 2008) (employer reasonably accommodated employee's religious practices through use of its flexible absence policy).

100. *See Firestone Fibers & Textiles,* 515 F.3d at 313.

101. *See Firestone Fibers & Textiles,* 515 F.3d at 313, *quoting* Philbrook v. Ansonia Bd. of Educ., 479 U.S. 60, 70 (1986).

102. *See Firestone Fibers & Textiles,* 515 F.3d at 317, *citing* Trans World Airlines, Inc. v. Hardison, 434 U.S. 63, 78–83 (1977) and Chalmers v. Tulon Co. of Richmond, 101 F.3d 1012, 1021 (4th Cir. 1996). *See also* Aron v. Quest Diagnostics, Inc., 174 F. App'x 82, 83–84 (3rd Cir. 2006) (accommodating request of Orthodox Jew not to work on Saturdays was undue hardship where Saturday work requirement was enforced for all employees and making accommodation would result in unequal treatment of other employees and negatively affect employee morale).

103. *See* Redmond v. GAF Corp., 574 F.2d 897, 903 (7th Cir. 1978) (upholding trial court's finding that employer made no effort to explore accommodation of employee's inability to work on Saturdays due to religious obligations); EEOC v. Abercrombie & Fitch Stores, Inc., 798 F. Supp. 2d 1272, 1287 (N.D. Okla. 2011) (granting summary judgment to plaintiff where employer did not consider application of Muslim woman wearing head scarf because the head scarf conflicted with the store's image policy for salespersons); Hellinger v. Eckerd Corp., 67 F. Supp. 2d 1359, 1366 (S.D. Fla. 1999) (denying defendant's motion for summary judgment where employer rejected application of Orthodox Jew for pharmacist position out of hand because his religious beliefs did not allow him to sell condoms).

As is the case when an applicant has an obvious disability, an applicant's appearance at an interview will sometimes alert an employer to the potential need for an accommodation of religious beliefs. It would be unlawful, for example, for an employer with a policy prohibiting head wear to reject an applicant wearing a headscarf or hajib because the applicant is, or the employer assumes the applicant is, Muslim. What the employer should do is inform the applicant of the policy and ask if that conflicts with any religious practices. It might be the case that the applicant chooses, but is not required, to wear the head scarf.

Where religious practice dictates the wearing of certain articles of clothing or requires men not to shave but to wear a beard, the degree to which it is reasonable for an employer to accommodate that practice will vary with the particular circumstances. In general, courts have not required accommodations of religious clothing and grooming requirements where the requirements are related to public safety. In the case *Webb v. City of Philadelphia*, for example, a female police officer who wore a headscarf in accordance with Muslim practice was disciplined by the police department for violating the directive outlining acceptable dress and presentation for officers. The officer brought a claim of religious discrimination, arguing that the department should allow her to wear the headscarf as a reasonable accommodation of her religious practice. The district court found, and the Third Circuit affirmed, that the importance of the police force's appearance of uniformity, nonpartisanship, and neutrality made such an accommodation an undue hardship.[104] The Fifth Circuit made a similar finding in a case involving a police officer's desire to wear a cross on his uniform as a testament to his evangelical Christianity. In that case, *Daniels v. City of Arlington, Texas*, the police chief had issued a "no pins of any kind" directive and had suggested as an accommodation that the officer wear a cross ring or bracelet, wear the pin under his uniform or transfer to a non-uniformed position where he could wear the pin. The officer rejected each of these proposed accommodations and insisted on wearing the cross on his uniform. The court found that the officer's insistence on wearing his pin was an undue hardship on the department, holding that "[a] police

104. *See* Webb v. City of Philadelphia, 562 F.3d 256, 260–62 (3rd Cir. 2009).

department cannot be forced to let individual officers add religious symbols to their official uniforms."[105]

Courts have held employers to stricter accommodation standards where the clothing or grooming requirements are based on customer preference or image. In *EEOC v. Abercrombie & Fitch Stores, Inc.*, for example, the employer store justified its rejection of a teenage girl who wore a head scarf for religious reasons for a sales position by claiming that the wearing of a head scarf would negatively impact the brand and as such was an undue hardship. The company had a "Look Policy" that required its in-store salespersons to dress in Abercrombie-like clothing and to reflect the image that its clothing was designed to project. The district court granted summary judgment to the EEOC because Abercrombie had commissioned no studies and had no data to support its claim that granting an exemption for the wearing of a head scarf would be an undue hardship.[106]

5.4.5 Questions about National Origin

5.4.5.1 What an unusual name! What kind of name is that? French? Spanish? Where were you born? Where were your parents and grandparents born? Is English your native language? Do you speak any foreign languages? Are you a U.S. citizen?

All of these questions seek information on national origin or ancestry. They and others like them should be avoided. Title VII prohibits discrimination in hiring and all other aspects of employment based on national origin,[107] and the Immigration Reform and Control Act prohibits discrimination against authorized workers based on citizenship and national origin.[108] Persons may be authorized to work in the United States without being citizens, so authorization to work is a job-related inquiry, while citizenship is not. It is permissible to ask an applicant, "Are you legally eligible to work in the United States?"

For some positions, the ability to speak another language may be desirable or even necessary. Employers should not ask indirect questions such

105. *See* Daniels v. City of Arlington, Tex., 246 F.3d 500, 506 (5th Cir. 2001).

106. *See Abercrombie & Fitch Stores, Inc.*, 798 F. Supp. 2d at 1287.

107. *See* 42 U.S.C. § 2000e-2(a).

108. *See* 8 U.S.C. § 1324b(a)(1). *See also* Sejal Zota, *Immigration Enforcement in the Workplace: Form I-9, E-Verify and Social Security No-Match Letters: A Brief Guide for North Carolina Public Employers*, PUBLIC EMPLOYMENT LAW BULLETIN NO. 36, March 2009, http://sogpubs.unc.edu/electronicversions/pdfs/pelb36.pdf.

as "What is your native language?," which suggests that the applicant was not born in this country or "Do you know any foreign languages and, if so, how did you learn them?" If it is relevant to the job, the employer may ask whether the applicant reads or speaks fluently any foreign languages or a particular foreign language. If it is relevant to the job, the question should be asked of all applicants.

5.4.6 Criminal History

5.4.6.1 Have you ever been arrested?

The use of arrest and conviction records in hiring is discussed in detail in Chapter 8, "Background Investigations of Applicants for Employment." In general, employers should not ask whether an applicant has an arrest record. Members of minority groups, especially male members of minority groups, have been arrested in numbers disproportionate to their representation in the population at large, so the use of an arrest record as a screening device will tend to have a disparate impact on minority group members. An employer should not give any consideration to the fact that an employee has been arrested unless it is prepared to go out and do an investigation into whether or not it is likely that the applicant engaged in the behavior forming the basis of the arrest. Unless the employer is prepared to do so, it should avoid asking questions about arrests in the first place.

5.4.6.2 Have you ever been convicted of a felony?

The EEOC has acknowledged that felony convictions, as opposed to arrest records or misdemeanor convictions, may be relevant to the position in question. In order to avoid disparate impact on members of minority groups, employers may not use convictions as an absolute bar to employment. They must instead give individualized consideration to the circumstances of the felony conviction, such as the nature and gravity of the offense and the amount of time that has passed since the conviction or the completion of the sentence. The employer must also consider the relationship of the underlying behavior to the position that the applicant seeks.[109] As with pre-offer inquiries into medical conditions, the EEOC

---

109. *See* U.S. Equal Employment Opportunity Commission, *EEOC Policy Statement on the Issue of Conviction Records under Title VII of the Civil Rights Act of 1964, as amended, 42 U.S.C. § 2000e et seq.* (1982), February 4, 1987, www.eeoc.gov/policy/docs/convict1.html.

will presume that even in the absence of other evidence of discrimination, the employer has asked the question because it intends to use the information in making the hiring decision.[110] An employer may, however, use particularly relevant felony convictions as bars to further consideration of an application. Thus, it would be permissible to bar an applicant with a conviction for embezzlement from further consideration for a position as an accountant or accounts payable administrator or to bar a convicted sex offender from consideration for a position working with children. Asking for information about particular, relevant offenses before doing a criminal background check would therefore be permissible under Title VII.

Note that employers who use third-party for-profit entities to perform criminal background checks are subject to the federal Fair Credit Reporting Act (FCRA). The FCRA requires employers to obtain written permission from an applicant before a background investigation is done and to provide notice when someone's application for employment or promotion is being rejected on the basis of information disclosed in the background investigation. The FCRA's detailed rules about how permission is to be obtained and notice given are discussed in Chapter 8.

5.4.7 Credit History

5.4.7.1 Do you own your own home or do you rent? Have you ever been more than 30 days late on a bill? Have you ever been sued for failure to repay a loan or debt?

The use of credit history in hiring has been found to have an adverse impact on members of minority groups. There are few positions in local government or community colleges where a person's credit score will be related to job duties, unless the position involves financial responsibilities. Employers should avoid questions about credit history. For a full discussion of the limitations that Title VII places on performing credit checks as part of a background check, see Chapter 8.

---

110. *See* U.S. Equal Employment Opportunity Commission, *Policy Guidance on the Consideration of Arrest Records in Employment Decisions under Title VII of the Civil Rights Act of 1964, as amended, 42 U.S.C. §2000e et seq.*, No. 915.061, 9/7/90, www.eeoc.gov/policy/docs/arrest_records.html.

Chapter 6

Testing of Applicants and Candidates for Promotion: Written Examinations

Chapter 6

Testing of Applicants and Candidates for Promotion: Written Examinations

Many employers use scored tests in the selection process. A scored test is one that results in a numerical measurement of an applicant's knowledge, skills, and abilities in a particular area. Examples of scored tests include IQ or cognitive skills tests, tests of knowledge about criminal law and procedure for law enforcement officers, data-entry or typing tests for clerical or administrative positions, and the North Carolina Police Officer Physical Ability test (POPAT). The next two chapters cover the legal issues that employers face when they use scored testing as part of their hiring process. This chapter focuses on written examinations, while Chapter 7 considers physical ability tests and assessment centers.

The primary legal issue raised by the use of scored tests is that of adverse or disparate impact. Both Title VII and the Americans with Disabilities Act (ADA) allow the use of scored tests, Title VII expressly,

> Notwithstanding any other provision of this subchapter, it shall not be an unlawful employment practice . . . for an employer to give and to act upon the results of any professionally developed ability test provided that such test, its administration or action upon the results is not designed, intended or used to discriminate because of race, color, religion, sex or national origin.[1]

and the ADA by implication by prohibiting an employer from

1. *See* 42 U.S.C. § 2000e-2(h).

> using qualification standards, employment tests or other selection criteria that screen out or tend to screen out an individual with a disability or a class of individuals with disabilities unless the standard, test or other selection criteria, as used by the covered entity, is shown to be job-related for the position in question and is consistent with business necessity; and
>
> . . . failing to select and administer tests concerning employment in the most effective manner to ensure that, when such test is administered to a job applicant or employee who has a disability that impairs sensory, manual, or speaking skills, such test results accurately reflect the skills, aptitude, or whatever other factor of such applicant or employee that such test purports to measure, rather than reflecting the impaired sensory, manual, or speaking skills of such employee or applicant (except where such skills are the factors that the test purports to measure).[2]

The Age Discrimination in Employment Act (ADEA) does not mention scored tests, but as with any employment practice, a scored test that results in adverse impact on persons over 40 years of age may not be used to make hiring decisions unless the use of that particular test is job related and consistent with business necessity.[3]

Selection devices like tests should make "reliable and meaningful distinctions between individuals on the basis of their ability to perform particular tasks with competence and/or to function successfully in particular jobs."[4] When the use of a scored test results in a noticeable disparity among protected classes—between African Americans and whites, men and women, Latinos and whites, or any other pairing—an employer should consider itself put on notice that the test may not be accurately distinguishing between those who can do the job and those cannot.

---

2. *See* 42 U.S.C. §§ 12112(b)(6) and (7).

3. See the discussion of disparate impact in Chapter 2, Sections 2.1.6 and 2.1.7.

4. *See* Barbara Lerner, *Employment Discrimination: Adverse Impact, Validity, and Equality*, 1979 Sup. Ct. Rev. 17, 18 (1979).

6.1 Scored Testing and Disparate Impact: A Hypothetical

Consider the following hypothetical:

> *The city of Paradise, North Carolina, decides to use a written examination as part of its hiring process for entry-level firefighters. The test is designed by the fire chief and assistant fire chief. They draft questions and problems based on their own experiences in firefighting and also incorporate questions from the written examinations of other jurisdictions. The test is administered to a large and diverse pool of applicants. After it is scored, 80 percent of white applicants have passed the test, while only 20 percent of African American applicants and 16 percent of Latino applicants have passed.*

These results should set alarms ringing in the Paradise fire and human resources departments. The federal Equal Employment Opportunity Commission's (EEOC) Uniform Guidelines on Employee Selection Practices (Uniform Guidelines), discussed briefly in the section on Title VII disparate impact in Chapter 2 and in the sidebar on pages 216–17,[5] says that a test that results in members of a protected class being chosen for a position or passing a test at a rate less than four-fifths (80 percent) of the passage rate of another group has an adverse impact on that protected class.[6] While the four-fifths rule has come under increasing criticism in recent years, it is still the standard used by most courts.[7] Here, the ratio of the passage rate of African American applicants to that of whites is 20:80 or 25 percent, and the ratio for Latino applicants to that of white applicants is 16:80 or 20 percent, both of which constitute adverse impact under the Uniform Guidelines and make the test unlawful in the absence of evidence that it is job related and consistent with business necessity.[8]

---

5. See Chapter 2, Section 2.1.6.

6. *See* 29 C.F.R. § 1607.4(D).

7. See the sidebar on Uniform Guidelines, below. *See also* 1 Barbara Lindemann & Paul Grossman, Employment Discrimination Law 179–83 (4th ed. 2007) and citations therein.

8. Note that the four-fifths rule is not absolute. Smaller differences in selection rate may constitute adverse impact where they are significant in both statistical and practical terms or where an employer's conduct and practices have discouraged applicants disproportionately on grounds of race, sex, or ethnic group. Greater differences in selection rate may not constitute adverse impact where the differences are based on small numbers and are not statistically significant. *See* 29 C.F.R. § 1607.4(D).

Uniform Guidelines on Employee Selection Procedures

The Uniform Guidelines on Employee Selection Procedures were jointly developed and adopted in 1978 by the Equal Employment Opportunity Commission, the U.S. Civil Service Commission (now Office of Personnel Management), the U.S. Department of Labor, and the U.S. Department of Justice.[a] They were designed to provide a framework for determining how to use tests and other selection procedures consistent with the requirements of federal antidiscrimination law. The Uniform Guidelines were developed in accordance with then-existing court decisions, the practical experience and previously issued guidelines of the issuing agencies, and "the standards of the psychological profession."[b]

The Uniform Guidelines are best known as the source of the "four-fifths rule," which finds adverse impact when members of a protected class are selected for positions at a rate less than four-fifths (80 percent) of that of another group. The four-fifths rule is not absolute: the Uniform Guidelines expressly recognize both that smaller differences in selection rates may, under certain circumstances, constitute adverse impact and that greater differences in selection rates may not constitute adverse impact where the differences are based on small numbers and are not statistically significant or in other atypical circumstances.[c] Accordingly, the courts sometimes look beyond the four-fifths rule and find disparate impact if, for example, the difference between the number of members of the protected class selected and the number that would be anticipated in a random selection system is more than two or three standard deviations.[d]

Because the Uniform Guidelines have not been revised since they were first issued in 1978, they have come under increasing attack over the years as being outdated. The drafters of the Uniform Guidelines used as their reference point the American Psychological Association's 1974 Standards for Educational and Psychological Tests, which have since been updated multiple times, most recently in 1999.[e] In May 2007, the EEOC held a public meeting on employment testing and screening. Among the invited speakers were the chief psychologist in the EEOC's Office of General Counsel, two psychologists whose firms specialize in employment discrimination analyses, and several attorneys experienced in the litigation of adverse impact discrimination cases on behalf of both employers and employees. The speakers emphasized that the Uniform Guidelines do not

---

a. *See* 43 Fed. Reg. 38295, 38312 (Aug. 25, 1978). The Uniform Guidelines may be found in the Code of Federal Regulations at 29 C.F.R. Part 1607.

b. *See* 29 C.F.R. § 1607.1(C).

c. *See* 29 C.F.R. § 1607.4(D).

d. *See* 1 BARBARA LINDEMANN & PAUL GROSSMAN, EMPLOYMENT DISCRIMINATION LAW 90–91 (4th ed. 2007) and cases cited therein.

e. A revision of the 1999 Standards was released for public comment in January 2011, and a final version is projected to be released in late 2012 or 2013. *See* www.apa.org/science/about/psa/2011/01/testing.aspx.

represent the current state of professional research and experience in the field of test development and validation and are not useful in helping employers design tests and validation strategies or in helping courts evaluate the merits of disparate impact cases.[f]

On January 21, 2011, President Obama issued Executive Order 13563, directing all federal agencies to plan for a retrospective analysis of significant regulations. The EEOC developed a proposed plan, which it duly published along with a request for public comment. Critics' objections to the Uniform Guidelines are well summarized in a letter submitted by the Society for Industrial and Organizational Psychology (SIOP), a division of the American Psychological Association that focuses on performance in organizational and work settings. In that letter, the SIOP strongly urged the EEOC to include the Uniform Guidelines in the first group of regulations to be looked at in the retrospective analysis. The letter, dated March 2011, noted that the APA's Standards for Educational and Psychological Testing were at the time of writing undergoing a third revision and that SIOP's own Principles for the Validation and Use of Personnel Selection Procedures had been revised three times since 1978, most recently in 2003. The SIOP president noted:

> Revisions to these technical guidance documents have been made to ensure that contemporary selection is based on current scientific research. Over the last 33 years there have been considerable advances in validation theory, substantial refinements in our understanding of how to best implement traditional validation strategies, and new evidence related to the availability and adequacy of modern alternative validation strategies. Further, the practice of employee assessment has changed dramatically over this time frame as new technologies have emerged. We suggest the Guidelines as a high-priority for revision because we believe the regulatory standards should consider contemporary scientific research and practice."[g]

The EEOC did not include the Uniform Guidelines in its first five sets of regulations for review.[h] For the near future, at least, the Uniform Guidelines will apparently continue to be the touchstone for analyzing selection procedures that cause disparate impact.

---

f. For links to a transcript of the hearing and to the written remarks of the invited speakers, see www.eeoc.gov/eeoc/meetings/archive/5-16-07/index.html.

g. *See* Letter from Eduardo Salas, President, Society for Industrial and Organizational Psychology, to U.S. Equal Employment Opportunity Commission, dated March 22, 2011, www.eeoc.gov/laws/regulations/upload/Link-2-SIOP-UGESP-Response.pdf

h. *See* U.S. Equal Employment Opportunity Commission, *Equal Employment Opportunity Commission Plan for Retrospective Analysis of Existing Rules* (July 29, 2011), www1.eeoc.gov//laws/regulations/retro_review_plan_final.cfm?renderforprint=1.

The fire department, however, should not even have to calculate the passing rate ratios to see that this test does not do what it should: identify those candidates with the ability to perform the job of entry-level firefighter. There is no basis for thinking that African American and Latino applicants have less ability and are less fit to perform the job of firefighter than white applicants.[9] Yet this is what the results of this test suggest. Where in the testing process did the city of Paradise go astray and what should it do in the face of these disparate testing results?

In retrospect, it is easy to say that Paradise should have validated its exam before giving it to applicants. To validate a test—or any selection device—means to establish through objective evidence that the test or criterion accurately predicts who will be successful in the position in question. Validation studies, however, are time-consuming and expensive because they are typically performed by outside consultants with specialized training. Neither Title VII nor the ADA requires employers to validate scored tests before using them.[10] The Uniform Guidelines expressly say, "These guidelines do not require a user to conduct validity studies of selection procedures where no adverse impact results."[11] This makes eminent sense as some selection devices and criteria seem to be valid on their face.[12] The most obvious examples of selection criteria that would be valid on their face are the requirements that law enforcement officers have successfully completed a Basic Law Enforcement Training course as approved by the North Carolina Department of Justice and that public school teachers have a degree from a four-year college and be certified to teach by the North Carolina Department of Public Instruction. Unfortunately for employers, scored tests are almost never valid on their face. However, if a scored test

9. *See* Vulcan Soc'y of the New York City Fire Dep't v. Commission, 490 F.2d 387, 392 (2d Cir. 1973); United States v. City of Chicago, 385 F. Supp. 543, 554–55 (N.D. Ill. 1974) (both noting how illogical such a conclusion would be).

10. *See* 42 U.S.C. § 2000e-2(k). Although the Uniform Guidelines by their own terms are not applicable to adverse impact claims brought under the Age Discrimination in Employment Act (ADEA), the Americans with Disabilities Act (ADA), or the Rehabilitation Act of 1973, *see* 29 C.F.R. § 1607.2(D), courts still treat them as a standard against which to measure disparate impact.

11. *See* 29 C.F.R. §§ 1607.1(B) and 1607.4(C).

12. For a good discussion of face validity, see Barbara Lerner, *Employment Discrimination: Adverse Impact, Validity, and Equality*, 1979 Sup. Ct. Rev. 17, 18–25 (1979).

has not been validated but does not result in adverse impact, there is no legal issue.

The history of scored test disparate impact litigation makes clear that in a perfect world of unlimited resources, the city of Paradise should have taken two steps that it did not at the outset of the process. First, it should have performed a thorough job analysis.[13] Second, it should have had the exam designed—or at least reviewed—by someone with training in test design rather than by its own employees, however knowledgeable and experienced they might be about the substantive field.[14]

6.2 Step One: Conducting a Job Analysis

If the point of a pre-employment test is to identify those applicants who are best able to perform particular tasks or to carry out a specific set of responsibilities, then it is crucial that an employer understand what knowledge, skills, and abilities and what personal characteristics are needed for a person to be successful in that particular job. In other words, an employer must look beneath the job description and identify those specific things that enable persons who are successful in the job to perform the functions set forth in the job description.[15] That process of identifying what is needed for success in performing a position's duties is called a job analysis. The Uniform Guidelines require that a study of the content or construct validity of a scored test include a job analysis.[16]

---

13. *See* Guardians Ass'n of New York City Police Dep't, Inc. v. Civil Serv. Comm'n of City of New York, 630 F.2d 79, 95 (2d Cir. 1980).

14. *See Guardians Ass'n*, 630 F.2d at 96 (2d Cir. 1980), and cases cited therein. *See also* Harless v. Duck, 619 F.2d 611, 616 (6th Cir. 1980) (rejecting test developed by police officers through an "intuitive process"); United States v. City of Erie, Pa., 411 F. Supp. 2d 524, 553 (W.D. Pa. 2005) (city police officers' testimony about the usefulness and validity of a physical abilities screening test is irrelevant "as that is more properly a subject for expert opinion").

15. *See* United States v. Cnty. of Fairfax, Va., 629 F.2d 932, 943 (4th Cir. 1980); Vanguard Justice Soc'y, Inc. v. Hughes, 592 F. Supp. 245, 258 (D. Md. 1984); M.O.C.H.A. Soc'y, Inc. v. City of Buffalo, 2009 WL 604898 (W.D.N.Y. Mar. 9, 2009). *See also* 29 C.F.R. §§ 1607.14(C)(2) and (4).

16. *See* 29 C.F.R. § 1607.14(A).

As discussed in Chapter 3, a job description provides applicants and employees with an understanding of the specific tasks they are to perform and the expected results of that performance; it also forms the basis for a supervisor's evaluation of the employee's performance. The job description sets the particular job in context within the structure and goals of the larger organization. The list of tasks and essential functions is necessary for assigning the position to an appropriate pay grade and for classifying it as exempt or nonexempt for Fair Labor Standards Act purposes. The content of a job description usually includes identifying information (such as job title); the main purpose and scope of the job; a list of the job's primary or essential duties; whether or not the job has supervisory responsibility; the end results or accountabilities that the employee is expected to achieve or meet; and the minimum qualifications and/or minimum knowledge, skills, and abilities and minimum experience that a person must have to be able to perform the job's essential duties. The job description may also contain one or more qualifications and experiences that the employer prefers but will not require the successful applicant to have.

A job analysis, in contrast, looks at the work behaviors and the tasks associated with them and their relative importance. The work behaviors selected for measurement through testing should be the critical or important work behaviors that constitute most of the job.[17] One judge translated the Uniform Guidelines' requirement of a job analysis as a requirement for "a thorough survey of the relative importance of the various skills involved in the job in question and the degree of competency required in regard to each skill."[18] A job analysis may also measure traits or characteristics important for successful performance of the individual components of the job.[19] Examples of the kinds of traits (sometimes called constructs) that might be identified through a job analysis include integrity, adaptability, inductive and deductive reasoning, and spatial orientation.[20]

---

17. *See* 29 C.F.R. § 1607.14(C)(2).

18. *See* Vulcan Soc'y of the City of New York Fire Dep't, Inc. v. Civil Serv. Comm'n of the City of New York, 360 F. Supp. 1265, 1274 (S.D.N.Y. 1973), *aff'd in part, remanded in part*, 490 F.2d 387 (2d Cir. 1973).

19. *See* 29 C.F.R. § 1607.14(D)(2).

20. *See* United States v. City of New York, 731 F. Supp. 2d 291, 303–04 (E.D.N.Y. 2010).

If it is to be the reasonable basis on which to base a pre-employment test, a job analysis must be individualized for the particular position with the particular employer for which the test is selecting out applicants. In the foregoing hypothetical, it would not suffice for the city of Paradise to use a pre-existing job analysis for the generic position of firefighter or for the position as it exists in another city or county.[21]

Job analysis is a technical skill rather than a legal subject, and it is beyond the scope of this chapter, the ability of the author, or the decisions in scored test cases to instruct employers in how to do a job analysis. But consideration of one Maryland case can provide an illustration of the complexity involved in doing a thorough job analysis. In the case *Vanguard Justice Society, Inc. v. Hughes*,[22] Baltimore, Maryland, police officers challenged that city's 1982 use of a written exam to determine eligibility for promotion to sergeant. The exam was one part of a three-step promotional process and was worth 40 percent of a candidate's overall score for eligibility for promotion. A candidate's score on the written exam also helped determine whether that person would advance to the final step in the process, an oral examination. Thus, a poor performance on the written exam effectively ended any chance that a candidate had of being promoted. The plaintiffs challenged only the written exam, based on its adverse impact on African American officers. The challenged exam was a modified version of the city's 1981 sergeant's promotional exam and was based on a modified version of a job analysis performed by outside experts (the consultants) in connection with the 1981 exam. The district court ultimately found that the original 1981 exam had been properly validated but that the 1982 exam that had resulted in disparate impact on African American officers was *not* a properly validated exam despite being based on a modification of the 1981 job analysis and of the 1981 exam. The city had done no studies and could provide no evidence that the 1982 exam itself drew meaningful distinctions between those who could perform the duties of the sergeant position competently and those who could not. It was thus unlawful under Title VII.[23]

---

21. *See* Walston v. Cnty. Sch. Bd. of Nansemond Cnty., 492 F.2d 919, 926 (4th Cir. 1974); Rogers v. Int'l Paper Co., 510 F.2d 1340, 1350–51 (8th Cir. 1975), *vacated*, 423 U.S. 809; Vanguard Justice Soc'y, Inc. v. Hughes, 592 F. Supp. 245, 259–60 (D. Md. 1984).

22. 592 F. Supp. 245 (D. Md. 1984).

23. *See Vanguard Justice Soc'y*, 592 F. Supp. at 248–49.

In reaching its decision the court first looked closely at the 1981 exam and at the job analysis on which it was based. The 1981 job analysis consisted of five steps. First, the consultants developed a list of tasks related to job components that sergeants in the Baltimore police department generally performed based on interviews, observations of full shifts, and questionnaires completed by 73 randomly selected incumbent sergeants. The tasks that the consultants identified included reviewing bulletins on changes to departmental policies and completing quarterly performance reviews on subordinates. Some of the broader job components identified by the consultants included general report review and evaluating subordinates' performance.[24] The consultants then asked those holding the position of sergeant to assign point values to each task and to each job component that the consultants had identified. The sergeants were to assign point values based on the frequency with which the task or component occurred; on the individual importance, complexity, and criticalness of each; and on the amount of time normally spent performing each task or component.[25]Second, the consultants constructed a list of skills, knowledge, abilities, and personal characteristics (which they referred to as SKAPs) for each job component. Examples of the SKAPs that the consultant identified included reading comprehension; memory for facts/ideas/operations; substantive area knowledge; planning/organizing; sensitivity; ability to act under stress/pressure; and report preparation ability, written communication skill, and oral communication.[26] Third, the consultants asked a randomly selected group of sergeants to assign point values to each SKAP based on the importance of each SKAP to each identified job component. Fourth, the consultants used a formula to determine the importance of each SKAP to the job of police sergeant in the Baltimore police department based on the results of this survey. Finally, the consultants determined which of the three parts of the promotional process that the city proposed to use—written test, performance appraisal, or assessment center—would be most effective for testing a given SKAP cluster.[27]

---

24. *See Vanguard Justice Soc'y*, 592 F. Supp. at 249 n.13.
25. *See Vanguard Justice Soc'y*, 592 F. Supp. at 249.
26. *See Vanguard Justice Soc'y*, 592 F. Supp. at 249 n.16.
27. *See* Vanguard Justice Soc'y, Inc. v. Hughes, 592 F. Supp. 245, 249–50 (D. Md. 1984).

The *Vanguard Justice* case illustrates two important ideas about job analysis in the context of scored testing. The first is that doing a thorough job analysis can be a complex and—for a lay person—daunting task. The second is that the adequacy of the job analysis can make or break an employer's defense if it administers a test that has a disparate impact and is challenged on that basis.[28] Consider that the court in the *Vanguard Justice* case found that the job analysis performed for the 1981 promotional examination was in accordance with what was called for by the Uniform Guidelines.[29] The problem was that the city had piggybacked the 1982 job analysis and exam onto the job analysis for the 1981 exam. The court noted that the work on the 1981 job analysis—in particular, the identification of the job tasks and job components—had begun in 1979 and that it was unclear whether all of the tasks and components had the same importance in 1982 as they did in the period 1979–81. In addition, working on its own, the Baltimore civil service commission changed the 1981 job analysis by "randomly" (the court's term) leaving out some SKAPs and keeping others, with the result that some important work behaviors were omitted from the 1982 job analysis while others were overemphasized.[30]

Even in hindsight, it is hard to know what Baltimore should have done. Perhaps it should have used the 1981 job analysis to construct a new test; perhaps it should have used the 1981 job analysis and 1981 test because the 1981 test had not resulted in adverse impact.[31] Hiring outside expert consultants to perform a job analysis is something that only a relatively large jurisdiction with a stable and ample revenue base can afford to do. For most North Carolina cities, a professional job analysis will not be financially feasible except on rare occasions and for special recruitment or promotional processes—if even then. What is more, a professional job analysis is not the end of the story.

---

28. *See* United States v. Cnty. of Fairfax, Va., 629 F.2d at 943; Guardians Ass'n of New York City Police Dep't, Inc. v. Civil Serv. Comm'n of the City of New York, 633 F.2d 232, 242–43 (2d Cir. 1980), *aff'd*, 463 U.S. 582 (1983); United States v. City of New York, 731 F. Supp. 2d 291, 301–02 (E.D.N.Y. 2010); Vulcan Soc'y of the City of New York Fire Dep't, Inc. v. Civil Serv. Comm'n of the City of New York, 360 F. Supp. 1265, 1276 (S.D.N.Y. 1973), *aff'd in part, remanded in part*, 490 F.2d 387 (2d Cir. 1973).

29. *See Vanguard Justice Soc'y*, 592 F. Supp. at 258.

30. *See Vanguard Justice Soc'y*, 592 F. Supp. at 258–60.

31. *See Vanguard Justice Soc'y*, 592 F. Supp. at 252.

6.3 Step Two: Constructing a Written Test of Knowledge, Skills, and Abilities

One of the benefits of using testing professionals in developing a pre-employment or promotional exam is that they can design the test to satisfy the appropriate validation model. When an employer wishes to measure the abilities that an applicant must already possess in order to step into the job and start performing its assigned duties on the first day, the expert will know that a content-valid test is needed—one that tests for knowledge or factual information needed for the particular job, in the case of written tests, or one that tests the applicant's capacity to carry out a physical function, such as running in pursuit of a suspect, in the case of a physical abilities test. Testing professionals will know *not* to test for skills that can easily be learned on the job, as that will invalidate the test. Experts will also more easily identify the kinds of personal qualities and potential, such as leadership or creativity, that are needed based on the job analysis and will know how to design a test that validly tests for these qualities or constructs.[32]

The potential perils of failing to use experts in test design are again illustrated by the *Vanguard Justice* case. There, the consultants designed the original 1981 written examination to test only applicants' relevant "knowledges." Other SKAPs were evaluated through either the performance appraisal (for example, constructs like dependability/responsibility and honesty/truthfulness) or through an assessment center (for example, scheduling/assigning ability, report review ability, planning/organizing, and oral communication skill) or both (ability to size up/evaluate, decisiveness, listening/attentiveness, and report preparation ability, among others).[33] In designing the 1982 exam, the Baltimore civil service commission added the SKAP "reading comprehension" to the job component clusters to be measured by the written exam without any training in how one might measure reading comprehension in this context. It also replaced the assessment center with a more limited oral examination, although there was no evidence showing that this change caused disparate impact. The consultants determined the content of the 1981 written exam and wrote

32. *See* Zamlen v. City of Cleveland, 906 F.2d 209, 218 (6th Cir. 1990); Guardians Ass'n of New York City Police Dep't, Inc. v. Civil Serv. Comm'n of City of New York, 630 F.2d 79, 91–92 (2d Cir. 1980).

33. *See* Vanguard Justice Soc'y, Inc. v. Hughes, 592 F. Supp. 245, 251 (D. Md. 1984).

or chose its test questions. The civil service commission determined the content of the 1982 exam and chose its test questions. There was no pre-testing, as there had been with the 1981 exam; indeed, to maintain the security of the test, even the police department administration did not see the 1982 test before it was administered.[34] After the 1982 test was given, 17.4 percent of the white candidates scored sufficiently well on the test and the performance appraisals to proceed to the oral examination. Only 10.9 percent of African American applicants passed the first two parts of the promotional process. The African American pass rate was thus three-fifths of the white pass rate and violated the Uniform Guidelines' four-fifths rule. The results of the performance appraisal were the same for African American and white candidates—hence, the disparate impact was caused solely by the written exam.[35] For a layperson, it is startling to learn that a test properly constructed and professionally validated cannot be modified by an employer without the possibility that it will lose its validity. But that is exactly what happened in the *Vanguard Justice* case. The 1981 exam did not cause disparate impact and the court found it to have been properly validated. The 1982 exam, although modeled on the 1981 exam, was not validated, caused disparate impact, and was unlawful under Title VII.

It is worth noting that courts have tended to view scored tests that have been constructed in-house without the benefit of a testing professional with suspicion. As one judge opined, " . . . . employment testing is a task of sufficient difficulty to suggest that an employer dispenses with expert assistance at his peril. Certainly, the decision to forgo such assistance should require a Court to give the resulting test careful scrutiny."[36]

For the public employer without the resources to employ testing consultants to construct a pre-employment or promotional test, one strategy might be to "pre-test" the test—whether it is a written test or a physical abilities test—on those employees currently holding the position for which the test has been designed as a selection device. Most tests of knowledge

34. *See Vanguard Justice Soc'y*, 592 F. Supp. at 252.

35. *See Vanguard Justice Soc'y*, 592 F. Supp. at 254.

36. *See* Guardians Ass'n of New York City Police Dep't, Inc. v. Civil Serv. Comm'n of City of New York, 630 F.2d 79, 96 (2d Cir. 1980), *citing* Kirkland v. N.Y. State Dep't of Corr. Servs., 520 F.2d 420, 425–26 (2d Cir. 1975) and Vulcan Soc'y of New York City Fire Dep't, Inc. v. Civil Serv. Comm'n of City of New York, 490 F.2d 387, 395–96 (2d Cir. 1973); United States v. City of New York, 731 F. Supp. 2d 291, 308 (E.D.N.Y. 2010).

and of physical ability are evaluated for content validity. For a test to be content valid, the knowledge, skills, and aptitudes required for successful examination performance must be the knowledge, skills, and aptitudes required for successful job performance. Any test on which successfully performing incumbent employees cannot answer a substantial percentage of the questions or perform a substantial percentage of the skills tested cannot reasonably be considered content valid.[37]

6.4 Responding to a Written Test That Causes Disparate Impact

When the city of Paradise realizes the disparity between the test scores of white and African American candidates for firefighter, on one hand, and between the scores of white and Latino candidates on the other, the city attorney calls a meeting of the manager, human resources director, and fire chief. They discuss their options. "What about setting lower passing scores for African American and Latino applicants? Or giving them bonus points to bring them into the competitive range with the white candidates?" asks the city manager. "Many employers are tempted to do just that when they realize that a selection device has resulted in adverse impact, but Title VII prohibits it," says the city attorney. "At heart, using different scoring techniques for minority and white applicants is just another form of race-based classification and discrimination." The city attorney grabs the United States Code and shows the relevant section of Title VII to the group seated around his conference table:

> It shall be an unlawful employment practice for a respondent, in connection with the selection or referral of applicants or candidates for employment or promotion, to adjust the scores of, use different cutoff scores for, or

37. *See* 29 C.F.R. § 1607.5(A); United States v. City of Chicago, 385 F. Supp. 543, 560 (N.D. Ill. 1974). *See also* United States v. City of New York, 731 F. Supp. 2d 291, 307–08 (E.D.N.Y. 2010).

> otherwise alter the results of, employment related tests on the basis of race, color, religion, sex, or national origin.[38]

"What about banding the scores?" asks the human resources director. "Banding scores is a good practice," says the city attorney, "but I'm not so sure it is wise in this case." "What do you mean by 'banding the scores'?" the manager and fire chief ask simultaneously.

6.4.1 Score Banding and Race Norming

Score banding is the practice of treating people whose test scores fall within a specific range, called the band, as having the same score. Banding is widespread—nowhere more so than in our educational institutions where grades of 90–100 are typically all denoted an "A," grades of 80–89 are a "B," grades of 70–79 are a "C," grades of 60–69 are a "D," and anything below a score of 60 is considered failing, or an "F." Score banding in itself is not discriminatory, and indeed, it makes a great deal of sense when the range of abilities in a group being tested is fairly narrow. The difference between the person who gets 100 questions correct and the person who gets 97 questions correct is not very meaningful, and a decision maker will be better served by considering other factors.[39]

---

38. *See* 42 U.S.C. § 2000e-2(l). *See also* Dean v. City of Shreveport, 438 F.3d 448 (5th Cir. 2006) (city's separation of applicants' civil service exam scores by race in effect used different cutoff scores on the basis of race in violation of Title VII; although city used same cutoff score in determining whether applicants had passed the exam, city then selected the same number of blacks and whites to proceed with application process, starting with the highest exam score on each segregated list).

39. *See* Chicago Firefighters Local 2 v. City of Chicago, 249 F.3d 649, 655–56 (7th Cir. 2001) (city's practice of banding scores on firefighter promotional exam did not constitute race norming in violation of Title VII); Horan v. City of Chicago, 2002 WL 338160 (N.D. Ill. 2002). *See also* Boston Police Superior Officers Fed'n v. City of Boston, 147 F.3d 13 (1st Cir. 1998) (difference between exam performance of African American candidate promoted to police lieutenant over white candidates who scored one point higher was negligible); Officers for Justice v. Civil Serv. Comm'n of City & Cnty. of San Francisco, 979 F.2d 721, 728 (9th Cir. 1992) (banding is at least equally valid to rank order promotions); Bridgeport Guardians, Inc. v. City of Bridgeport, 933 F.2d 1140, 1148 (2d Cir. 1991) (plaintiffs rebutted city's evidence that exam was consistent with business necessity by showing that the City could have chosen to use banding in order to alleviate the disparate racial effect of the examination).

Score banding is, however, discriminatory and violates Title VII when it is adopted *after the fact* in order to make a protected class's test results seem higher.[40] When done for this reason, score banding is just another form of race norming. So while the city of Paradise should consider adopting the policy of using score banding on all of its employment testing generally, it cannot adopt that practice now to change the impact that the testing procedure has had on African American and Latino applicants.

6.4.2 Cutoff Scores and Rank Order Selection

The Paradise management team is feeling stymied. "Bob," the fire chief says to the city attorney, "we put these folks in rank order based on their test scores and we were going to call them in for interviews and the like based on that. If we had a valid test, would there be any problem with placing them in rank order?" The city attorney furrows his brow. "First of all," he says, "if we move forward with banding our test scores on future tests, as I recommend, we won't have rank ordering. Everyone in the same band will have the same rank. But I have a question for you. How far down the rank order do you go in interviewing? Do you interview everyone who passes? How do you set the passing score, anyhow?"

"We do interview everyone who passes," says the chief. "That is because we take the number of positions that we anticipate filling in the next year and add 10 to it. Say that final number is 25. We set the passing score at the score that the 35th person in rank order has earned. That way we have left the top of the applicant pool to explore further."

"Whoa! Stop right there!" exclaims the city attorney. "You will not have a test that will pass muster under Title VII unless you have validated it for both the cutoff score and for use in rank ordering of applicants."

40. *See* Ricci v. DeStefano, 557 U.S. 557, 590 (2009) ("Had the City reviewed the exam results and then adopted banding to make the minority test scores appear higher, it would have violated Title VII's prohibition of adjusting test results on the basis of race"). *See also Chicago Firefighters Local 2*, 249 F.3d at 656 ("We have no doubt that if banding were adopted in order to make lower black scores seem higher, it would indeed be . . . forbidden").

What many local government and community college employers fail to realize about scored testing is that the content of the test is not the only aspect of the process that they must validate. If they are going to hire or promote people based on their rank order in testing results, the employer must have the test validated for that use. The employer must also validate the cutoff score that it proposes to use if there is one score above which applicants will proceed with the interviewing process and below which applicants are automatically rejected. It is possible for a test to be valid for use on a pass/fail basis linked to a particular score but not to be valid for use with rank ordering.[41]

The Uniform Guidelines provide that rank ordering should be used only if it can be shown that "a higher score . . . is likely to result in better job performance. Where a selection procedure supported solely or primarily by content validity is used to rank job candidates, the selection procedure should measure those aspects of performance which differentiate among levels of job performance."[42] This makes sense because if test scores do not vary directly with job performance, ranking the candidates on the basis of their scores will not select better employees. The relationship between higher scores and better job performance may be inferred except where the test scores reveal a disparate racial impact.[43]

The Uniform Guidelines state that a cutoff score "should normally be set so as to be reasonable and consistent with normal expectations of acceptable proficiency within the work force."[44] This also makes sense because a cutoff score unrelated to job performance would lead to the rejection of

---

41. *See* 29 C.F.R. § 1607.5(G). *See also, e.g., Guardians Ass'n*, 630 F.2d at 99–101 (the city used the results of the exam to compile a rank ordering of applicants and then selected a passing score sufficient to generate the required number of potential trainees, neither of which uses was properly validated). *See also* 1 BARBARA LINDEMANN & PAUL GROSSMAN, EMPLOYMENT DISCRIMINATION LAW 213 n.254 (4th ed. 2007) ("Employers wanting to rely exclusively on scored tests as a selection device have a dilemma if test results cannot be used for rank-ordering or as a cutoff. Employers either can continue to use rank-ordering or cutoffs and be prepared to validate such use, or they can alter their practice, using test results as one of several factors in the selection process, for instance, in conjunction with a subjection evaluation.").

42. *See* 29 C.F.R. § 1607.14(C)(9).

43. *See* Guardians Ass'n of New York City Police Dep't, Inc. v. Civil Serv. Comm'n of City of New York, 630 F.2d 79, 99–100 (2d Cir. 1980).

44. *See* 29 C.F.R. § 1607.5(H); Bew v. City of Chicago, 252 F.3d 891, 894–95 (7th Cir. 2001).

applicants who were fully capable of performing the job. When a cutoff score unrelated to job performance produces disparate racial results, Title VII is violated.

There is a Fourth Circuit case that is worth noting. *Walston v. County School Board of Nansemond County, Virginia* considers the issues raised by the use of a test that was not developed locally. In the *Walston* case, the court found that a school district's use of a national teacher examination as the basis for retaining experienced teachers in its employ violated Title VII when it resulted in the dismissal of more African American teachers than white teachers. The use of the test was problematic for a number of reasons. Notwithstanding that the test was developed by the nationally recognized Educational Testing Service, there was no evidence, for example, that the questions on the test bore any relationship to the knowledge needed for teaching in the Nansemond County schools. With respect to cutoff scores, the school district had set a cutoff score of 500 because it was receiving applications from teachers who could not be hired in other states that had a cutoff score of 500. But as the court noted, there was no evidence establishing any correlation between any score whatsoever on the national teaching examination and successful classroom teaching.[45]

To validate a cutoff score, the employer must put forth evidence from which it may be inferred that the cutoff score measures the minimal qualifications needed to successfully perform the job.[46] Employers may demonstrate the correlation between achievement of a particular cutoff score on a test and prediction of successful performance in a job in different ways. First, an employer might retain an expert in the field to assess the minimal level of knowledge or ability needed to perform the job well and correlate that with test answers. Second, an employer might analyze the test results to locate a logical break-point in the distribution of scores.[47] If,

45. *See* Walston v. Cnty. Sch. Bd. of Nansemond Cnty., Va., 492 F.2d 919, 924–25 (4th Cir. 1974).

46. *See* Isabel v. City of Memphis, 404 F.3d 404, 413 (6th Cir. 2005) (city failed to demonstrate that cutoff score was job related and consistent with business necessity); Lanning v. Se. Pa. Transp. Auth., 181 F.3d 478, 489 (3d Cir. 1999); United States v. State of Del., 2004 WL 609331 at *1 and *26 (D. Del. 2004) (while written test for employment as state trooper was both content- and criterion-valid, cutoff score caused disparate impact and was not shown to be valid).

47. *See Guardians Ass'n*, 630 F.2d at 105; M.O.C.H.A. Soc'y, Inc. v. City of Buffalo, 2009 WL 604898 (W.D.N.Y. Mar. 9, 2009).

for example, 70 percent of those taking a test scored a 78 out of a possible 100 points, no one scored between 70 and 78, and the remaining 30 percent of test takers scored below 70 points, a score of 78 might be an appropriate cutoff. Another possibility is to have a sample of persons currently holding the position and performing well in it take the test and use those results to set the cutoff.[48] In one early case involving a claim that a testing program for admittance to an apprenticeship program for skilled craft jobs had a racially disparate impact, the evidence showed that 40 percent of a sample of then-working machinists and mill-wright journeymen would not have been able to achieve admission to their respective crafts using the challenged cutoff score.[49] An employer could not ask for a clearer sign that the cutoff score it set was not job related and consistent with business necessity.

There are no reported cases that have held that setting a lower cutoff score than that chosen initially is a form of race norming in violation of Title VII. In the hypothetical, therefore, the city of Paradise may consider whether setting a different cutoff score would allow more African American and Latino candidates to continue in the hiring process for the entry-level firefighter position such that there would not be a disparate impact. The city must, however, eliminate the use of rank ordering in the selection process because it has not performed an appropriate validation study to show that rank ordering is consistent with business necessity.

6.4.3 Is an Employer Liable for Disparate Impact Where the Bottom Line Is Good?

Suppose the city of Paradise had continued with its firefighter hiring process and ended up with a hiring class whose numbers did not show disparate impact? In other words, imagine that although the written examination resulted in disparate impact, some African American and Latino candidates progressed to a physical abilities test, assessment center, or interview stage and were hired in numbers sufficient that the entire hiring process did not show disparate impact? Would this bottom-line statistic immunize Paradise from liability for disparate impact for the written examination?

---

48. *See, e.g., Bew*, 252 F.3d at 895.

49. *See* Rogers v. Int'l Paper Co., 510 F.2d 1340, 1351 (8th Cir. 1975) (directing defendant to conduct new validation studies conforming to Uniform Guidelines), *vacated on other grounds*, 423 U.S. 809 (1975).

The answer to this question is no. The U.S. Supreme Court has held that individual components of a hiring process may constitute separate and independent employment practices subject to Title VII disparate impact analysis even if the overall decision-making process does not disparately impact a protected group. Even if the bottom line does not show discriminatory impact, the individual employment practices resulting in disparate impact are unlawful.[50] This is especially true where the challenged practice is an examination that is being used as a bright-line barrier to hiring or promotion—that is, where candidates may only be hired or promoted if they pass the test. Title VII was enacted to give *individuals* the opportunity to compete equally on the basis of job-related criteria.[51] A focus on the bottom line ignores the opportunity denied to individuals when an employment selection device is not job related and arbitrarily selects out members of a protected class.

6.5 The Written Test Dilemma: The U.S. Supreme Court's Decision in *Ricci v. DeStefano*

Even when an employer does everything right in the area of written examinations, it may still face liability for discrimination. The 2009 U.S. Supreme Court case *Ricci v. DeStefano* illustrates how despite using a rigorous process to design a scored test for firefighter promotions and despite validating the test before use, the city of New Haven, Connecticut, nonetheless found that administration of the test resulted in disparate impact on African American firefighters.[52] In accordance with the city charter, the city's civil service commission had to certify the test results before they could be used as the basis for promotional decisions. The commission voted not to certify

50. *See* Connecticut v. Teal, 457 U.S. 440, 451 (1982); Stout v. Potter, 276 F.3d 1118, 1122 (9th Cir. 2002); Smith v. Xerox Corp., 196 F.3d 358, 370 (2d Cir. 1999) ("Even if the overall decision-making process did not create an adverse impact on a protected group, that group still has a cause of action if it can show that some component of the decision-making process caused a disparate impact."); Newark Branch, Nat'l Ass'n for the Advancement of Colored People v. City of Bayonne, N.J., 134 F.3d 113, 124 (3d Cir. 1998); Davidson v. Citizens Gas & Coke Util., 470 F. Supp. 2d 934, 940 (S.D. Ind. 2007); Bradley v. City of Lynn, Mass., 443 F. Supp. 2d 145, 158–59 (D. Mass. 2006).

51. *See Teal*, 457 U.S. at 451.

52. *See* Ricci v. DeStefano, 557 U.S. 557 (2009).

the results in light of the disparate impact. A group of white and Latino firefighers who would have been promoted had the test results been certified brought a Title VII lawsuit against New Haven, alleging that the city's decision not to promote them was based on race.[53] The city's defense summarized the conundrum it faced in this situation: had it used the test results to make promotions within the fire department, it would have opened itself up to a Title VII disparate impact lawsuit. Yet not using the test results had left the city facing a Title VII disparate treatment claim. The federal trial court granted summary judgment to the city and its decision was affirmed on appeal by the federal Second Circuit Court of Appeals. The case made its way up to the U.S. Supreme Court, which reversed the Second Circuit's decision, holding that New Haven had violated Title VII when it threw out the results of the test and declined to promote the white firefighters.

6.5.1 The Background

The test at issue in the *Ricci* case was a written examination for promotion to the rank of lieutenant or captain in the New Haven, Connecticut, fire department. Although the Supreme Court decision was issued in 2009, the exam itself was administered in 2003. One hundred eighteen New Haven firefighters took the exam. The written examination accounted for 60 percent of an applicant's promotional application score; an oral examination accounted for the additional 40 percent of the total score. The results of the exams would determine which firefighters would be considered for promotions during the next two years and the order in which they would be considered. For this reason, many firefighters studied for months, and some paid for preparation materials at their own expense.[54] The preparation materials cost about $500.00.[55]

---

53. The actual suit alleged violations of both Title VII and the Equal Protection Clause, but the Supreme Court did not reach the constitutional claim since it found in the white firefighters' favor under the statute. *See Ricci*, 557 U.S. at 576–77, *quoting* Escambia Cnty. v. McMillan, 466 U.S. 48, 51 (1984) ("[N]ormally, the Court will not decide a constitutional question if there is some other ground upon which to dispose of a case.").

54. *See Ricci*, 557 U.S. at 561–65.

55. *See Ricci*, 557 U.S. at 568.

6.5.2 Constructing the Test

The city paid approximately $100,000 to outside testing consultants specializing in public safety to develop and administer the examinations. The consultants began by performing job analyses to identify the tasks, knowledge, skills, and abilities essential for New Haven's lieutenant and captain positions. The consultants interviewed incumbent captains, lieutenants, and their supervisors and rode with and observed other on-duty officers. Using the information they had gathered, the consultants wrote job-analysis questionnaires and administered them to most of the incumbent battalion chiefs, captains, and lieutenants in the city's fire department. At every stage of the job analyses, the consultants deliberately oversampled minority firefighters to ensure that the resulting job analyses would not unintentionally lead to the development of examinations that favored white candidates.

Based on the job analysis, the consultants developed written examinations to measure the candidates' job-related knowledge. For both the lieutenant and captain promotional examinations, the consultants compiled a list of training manuals, department procedures, and other materials to use as sources for the test questions, first getting the approval for their use from the fire chief and assistant fire chief. Then, using these approved sources, the consultants drafted a multiple-choice test for each position. Each test had 100 questions and was written below a 10th-grade reading level. Once the tests were ready, the city opened a three-month test preparation period. The city gave firefighters who intended to take the promotional exams a list that identified the source material for the questions, including the specific chapters from which the questions were taken.[56]

The consultants also developed the oral examinations, again using the job analyses they had developed. The oral exams were structured as assessment centers and put candidates in hypothetical situations to test incident-command skills, firefighting tactics, interpersonal skills, leadership, and management ability, among other things. Each candidate was evaluated by three assessors, drawn from a pool of 30 assessors who were battalion chiefs, assistant chiefs, and chiefs from departments of similar sizes to New Haven's throughout the country. The consultants assembled the pool, but the city approved each assessor based on his or her resume. Sixty-six percent of the panelists were minorities, and each of the nine

---

56. *See Ricci*, 557 U.S. at 564–66.

three-member assessment panels contained two minority members. The consultants trained the panelists for several hours on the day before the city administered the examinations, teaching them how to score the candidates' responses consistently using checklists of desired criteria.[57]

6.5.3 Results of the Tests

Seventy-seven firefighters took the lieutenant examination—43 were white, 19 were African American and 15 were Latino. Thirty-four of the candidates passed—25 whites, 6 African Americans, and 3 Latinos. These results represent a 58.1 percent pass rate for white candidates, a 31.6 percent pass rate for African American candidates, and a 20 percent pass rate for Latinos. Both the African American pass rate and the Latino pass rate fell below the Uniform Guidelines' four-fifths rule. The city's charter provided for a so-called rule of three, whereby the city filled each vacancy by choosing one person from among the top three candidates on the promotions list at any given time. At the time the exam was given, eight lieutenant positions were open. This meant that the top 10 high-scoring candidates were immediately eligible for consideration for promotion to lieutenant. All 10 were white. As it later turned out, subsequent vacancies would have allowed at least three black candidates to be considered for promotion to lieutenant.

Forty-one lieutenants completed the captain examination—25 were white, 8 were African American, and 8 were Latino. Twenty-two of the candidates passed—16 whites, 3 African Americans, and 3 Latinos—in other words, 64 percent of the white candidates passed the exam, while only 37.5 percent of both African American and Latino candidates were successful, a pass-rate that again violated the four-fifths rule. At the time the exam was given, seven captain positions were open. Under the rule of three, the top nine high-scoring candidates would be considered to fill the seven open positions. Of the nine, seven were white and two were Latino. None were African American.[58]

New Haven's civil service commission held a series of five public hearings to hear testimony about whether it should certify the test results in light of their disparate impact on African American candidates for promotion. The consultants explained the process they had used to construct the

57. *See* Ricci v. DeStefano, 557 U.S. 557, 565–66.
58. *See Ricci*, 557 U.S. at 566.

exam. Firefighters spoke for and against certifying the test results. Three outside experts discussed the exam and the results. The mayor, the human resources director, and the city attorney all spoke against certifying the test results. When it finally voted, the civil service commission deadlocked 2-2 (the fifth member had recused himself). Because a majority of the commission had not voted to certify the results, they were, in effect, thrown out, because under the city charter, they could not be used as the basis for promotion without certification.[59]

6.5.4 The Lawsuit

Seventeen white firefighters (including the named plaintiff, Frank Ricci) and one Latino firefighter, all of whom would have been promoted based on their test scores, sued the city and some of its officials (including the mayor, John DeStefano, the named defendant), alleging that by discarding the test results, the city and the named officials discriminated against the plaintiffs based on their race in violation of Title VII. New Haven and its officials defended their actions, arguing that they had a good-faith belief that if they had certified the results, they would have violated Title VII's prohibition on disparate impact. The crux of the city's argument was that it could not be held liable for having violated Title VII's prohibition against disparate treatment by attempting to comply with Title VII's provisions on disparate impact. The district court granted the city's motion for summary judgment and denied that of the plaintiffs, finding that the attempt to avoid liability for disparate impact did not constitute discriminatory intent within the meaning of Title VII's ban on disparate treatment. It further found that the mere fact that the city had neither identified the flaw in the testing procedure nor found an alternative with less disparate impact did not compel the conclusion that the city had to certify the results and proceed with promotions in accordance with those results.[60]

One has to feel sorry for the city of New Haven and its consultants. The city and the consultants did everything they were supposed to do in designing a test to avoid disparate impact. While African American and white firefighters differed in their views of the validity of the tests, none of the three experts from whom the civil service commission heard testimony

59. *See Ricci*, 557 U.S. at 567–74.
60. *See Ricci*, 557 U.S. at 574–76.

faulted the test or the way it was constructed.[61] It simply had disparate impact.

6.5.5 The Legal Analysis: The Majority Opinion

The Supreme Court began its analysis by observing that the city's actions in deciding not to certify the test results and not to make the promotions that would have resulted from them was based on the fact that too many whites and not enough African Americans would have been promoted had the results been used. This, the Court found, was race-based decision making in violation of Title VII.[62] The issue was whether or not the city had some lawful justification for making this decision:

> Whatever the City's ultimate aim—however well intentioned or benevolent it might have seemed—the City made its employment decision because of race. The City rejected the test results solely because the higher scoring candidates were white. The question is not whether that conduct was discriminatory but whether the City had a lawful justification for its race-based action. We consider, therefore, whether the purpose to avoid disparate-impact liability excuses what otherwise would be prohibited disparate-treatment discrimination.[63]

The key to answering this question, the Court said, was to interpret Title VII so as to give effect to both the prohibition against disparate treatment and the prohibition against disparate impact, if possible.[64]

The Court reached into its affirmative action jurisprudence to fashion what it called an "appropriate balance" between the competing demands of Title VII. In its 1986 decision in the case *Wygant v. Jackson Board of Education*, the Court had held that a public school district's affirmative action plan that required the school district to lay off white employees with greater seniority before black employees with less seniority violated the Equal Protection Clause. It rejected the school district's defense that black students needed black teachers as role models to overcome the effects of long-term societal discrimination. In order to justify remedial affirmative

61. *See Ricci*, 557 U.S. at 567–72.
62. *See* Ricci v. DeStefano, 557 U.S. 557, 579 (2009).
63. *See Ricci*, 557 U.S. at 579–80.
64. *See Ricci*, 557 U.S. at 580.

action such as this, the Supreme Court said, an employer must have a "strong basis in evidence" that it previously engaged in discrimination and that remedial action is necessary.[65] The Court reaffirmed this standard three years later in its public contracting decision, *City of Richmond v. J.A. Croson Co.*[66] The Court saw a parallel in the conflict between the race-blind premise of the equal protection principle and the need for government action to remedy past race discrimination, on one hand, and the tension between an employer's competing legal responsibility not to consider race in making employment decisions and not to use selection procedures that have disparate impact on a minority group, on the other.[67] It accordingly adopted "the strong-basis-in-evidence standard as a matter of statutory construction to resolve any conflict between the disparate-treatment and disparate-impact provisions of Title VII."[68]

The Court noted that the strong basis in evidence standard was consistent with the two provisions of Title VII that explicitly address the use of scored testing as a selection device. The first is 42 U.S.C. § 2000e-2(h), which holds that employers may "act upon the results of any professionally developed ability test provided that such test, its administration or action upon the results is not designed, intended or used to discriminate because of race."[69] The second provision is 42 U.S.C. § 2000e-2(l), which prohibits employers from race-norming scored tests; that is, adjusting employment test scores on the basis of race. "If an employer cannot rescore a test based on the candidates' race . . . then it follows *a fortiori* that it may not take the greater step of discarding the test altogether to achieve a more desirable racial distribution of promotion-eligible candidates," the Court said, "absent a strong basis in evidence that the test was deficient and that discarding the results is necessary to avoid violating the disparate-impact provision."[70]

---

65. *See Ricci,* 557 U.S. at 582–83. *See also* Wygant v. Jackson Bd. of Educ., 476 U.S. 267, 277–78 (1986). Also see Appendix 2, Section App. 2.3.2.

66. *See Ricci,* 557 U.S. at 582–83. *See also* City of Richmond v. J.A. Croson Co., 488 U.S. 469, 499 (1989). Also see Appendix 2, Section App. 2.3.3.

67. *See* Ricci v. DeStefano, 557 U.S. 557, 582–83.

68. *See Ricci,* 557 U.S. at 584.

69. *See Ricci,* 557 U.S. at 583.

70. *See Ricci,* 557 U.S. at 584.

6.5.5.1 What Constitutes a Strong Basis in Evidence That an Employer Will Be Liable for Disparate Impact Discrimination?

One might think that given the clear disparate impact that the New Haven firefighter tests had, the city would have easily met the strong basis in evidence standard and would have prevailed on its defense that, had it not thrown the test results out on the basis of race, it would have been liable for disparate impact. That is precisely what the city argued. Indeed, the Court itself said, "the racial adverse impact here was significant, and petitioners [that is, the white firefighters] do not dispute that the City was faced with a prima facie case of disparate impact."[71] The Court also noted that had the city certified the exams, it could not have considered African American applicants for any of the lieutenant or captain positions that were vacant at the time the test was administered.[72] But the Court nevertheless set the bar for establishing a strong basis in evidence defense very high. It rejected the notion that a prima facie case of disparate impact liability constituted a strong basis in evidence, calling it only "a threshold showing of a significant statistical disparity . . . and nothing more."[73]

That is a startling statement on first consideration. The Court explained, however, that under Title VII's disparate impact provisions, an employer is liable only if the exams were not job related and consistent with business necessity, or if there was an equally valid but less discriminatory alternative that accomplished the same thing but which the city refused to adopt.[74] In other words, if the city had used the test results as they were and its black and Latino firefighters had brought a disparate impact lawsuit, the firefighters would have to have shown that the test did not measure what it was supposed to measure in order to prevail. So to establish a strong basis in evidence to support its decision to discard the test results, the city in this lawsuit would have to show the same thing.[75] Citing both the process by which the consultants designed the exams and the testimony

---

71. *See Ricci*, 557 U.S. 586.

72. *See* Ricci v. DeStefano, 557 U.S. 557, 587 (2009).

73. *Ricci*, 557 U.S. at 587.

74. *See Ricci*, 557 U.S. at 587, *citing* 42 U.S.C. §§ 2000e-2(k)(1)(A), (C).

75. *See* Jason Szanyi and Katarina Guttmannova, *Presenting a "Strong Basis in Evidence": How Lawyers Should Use Statistics to Shape the Impact of Ricci v. DeStefano on Title VII Litigation*, Harv. L. & Pol'y Rev. (publication of the American Constitution Society for Law & Policy) (Feb. 4, 2010), http://hlpronline.com/2010/02/szanyi-guttmannova/.

offered by various witnesses in connection with the civil service commission's hearings on whether to certify the exam results, the Court concluded that there was "no genuine dispute that the examinations were job-related and consistent with business necessity."[76]

The Court then considered and rejected the city's arguments that there was a less discriminatory alternative. The first proposal, that the city weight the written and oral examinations differently, was no more than a suggestion without any evidence to support that such a change would have produced different results (the weighting was a function of the city's collective bargaining agreement with the firefighter's union). The second proposal, that the city band the test scores, would be a change in scoring based on race and prohibited by Title VII. The final suggestion, that the city use assessment centers, was made by an expert witness whose testimony supported certifying the test results. The Court concluded that there was not, therefore, a strong basis in evidence for the city's claim that it would have faced disparate impact liability had it certified the tests and made promotions in accordance with its results.[77]

Another way of interpreting the Court's holding would be to say that there was a strong basis for thinking that had New Haven defended itself against a disparate impact lawsuit, it would have prevailed.

6.5.6 Legal Analysis: The Dissent

The Court's decision was far from unanimous: it was a 5-4 decision. The dissent, in contrast to the majority opinion, stressed the context against which the promotional examinations should be viewed, noting the history of discrimination in municipal police and fire departments generally and in New Haven in particular. At the time the examinations were given, African Americans made up between 30 and 40 percent of the city's population but only 9 percent of the New Haven fire department's officer ranks.[78] The dissent also gave different weight to certain facts than did the majority opinion. For example, the dissent questioned the city's commitment to an examination that would fairly evaluate candidates for the positions of lieutenant and captain because it "simply adhered to the testing regime outlined in its two-decades-old-contract with the local firefighters' union"—

---

76. *See Ricci*, 557 U.S. at 587–88.

77. *See* Ricci v. DeStefano, 557 U.S. 557, 589–92 (2009).

78. *See Ricci*, 557 U.S. at 608–09 (Ginsburg, J., dissenting).

namely, the written and oral examination format with its 60/40 weighted scoring ratio.[79] Justice Ginsburg took notice of a 1996 study that found that approximately two-thirds of municipalities surveyed used assessment centers or real-world work simulations as part of their promotional process and that those still using written examinations assigned a median weight of 30 percent of the final score to them, in contrast to New Haven's 60 percent. The courts, her dissent notes, have generally given "unfavorable appraisals to written examinations for determining fire service promotions."[80] In its recitation of the relevant facts, the dissent also emphasized testimony before the civil service commission that questioned the relevancy of some of the questions to New Haven's actual firefighting practices, questioned the fairness of asking firefighters to purchase the study materials, and questioned the entire framework of scored testing for promotion.[81]

More to the point, the dissent also rejected the strong basis in evidence standard announced by the majority opinion, describing the equal protection cases from which it derived as "particularly inapt" for comparison.[82] Seeing no conflict between Title VII's disparate treatment and disparate impact provisions, Justice Ginsburg said:

> I would therefore hold that an employer who jettisons a selection device when its disproportionate racial impact becomes apparent does not violate Title VII's disparate-treatment bar automatically or at all, subject to this key condition: The employer must have good cause to believe the device would not withstand examination for business necessity.[83]

The dissent, unlike the majority, did not think that New Haven would prevail in a disparate impact challenge to the exam, pointing to multiple flaws in the examination process and the existence of better tests with less disparate impact in other cities.[84]

79. *See Ricci*, 557 U.S. at 610 (Ginsburg, J., dissenting).
80. *See Ricci*, 557 U.S. at 615 (Ginsburg, J., dissenting).
81. *See Ricci*, 557 U.S. at 611–620 (Ginsburg, J., dissenting).
82. *See* Ricci v. DeStefano, 557 U.S. 557, 628 (2009) (Ginsburg, J., dissenting).
83. *See Ricci*, 557 U.S. at 625 (Ginsburg, J., dissenting).
84. *See Ricci*, 557 U.S. at 608–09 (Ginsburg, J., dissenting).

6.6 After *Ricci v. DeStefano*: Should a Local Government Employer Use Written Examinations for Hiring and Promotion?

Regrettably, the *Ricci* decision does not provide clear guidelines for local government and community college employers who wish to use scored tests that are nondiscriminatory. However, the case does tell us two things. First, the process of designing employment examinations is complex, requiring consultation with experts and careful consideration of accepted testing standards. For this reason, local government employers must proactively "test the test"—in other words, they must take measures to ensure that their scored examinations reliably test the relevant knowledge, skills, and abilities needed for any individual position. As one lower court applying the *Ricci* decision to a case involving a scored test for firefighters that had disparate impact noted:

> [T]he use of multiple-choice examinations is typically intended to apply objective standards to employment decisions . . . . it is natural to assume that the best performers on an employment test must be the best people for the job. But, the significance of these principles is undermined when an examination is not fair. As Congress recognized in enacting Title VII, when an employment test is not adequately related to the job for which it tests—and when the test adversely affects minority groups—we may not fall back on the notion that better test takers make better employees.[85]

Second, *Ricci* does not prohibit an employer from using employment tests. It instead encourages employers to consider how to design a test that "provide[s] a fair opportunity for all individuals, regardless of their race" and to seek feedback and comments to that end before the test is finalized and administered.[86] In other words, the *Ricci* case stands for the proposition that employers should be zealously race-conscious while constructing an entry-level or promotional employment examination or process. But once an employer administers the test, it may not disregard the test results

---

85. *See* United States v. Vulcan Soc'y, Inc., 637 F. Supp. 2d 77, 83–84 (E.D.N.Y. 2009).

86. *See Ricci*, 557 U.S. at 585.

and expectations of those who have taken it unless it has a strong basis in evidence to think that it will actually be subject to disparate impact liability as opposed to a mere disparate impact challenge.

The *Ricci* opinion makes clear that it is not enough for an employer to be litigation-adverse to meet the standard of a strong basis in evidence.[87] The standard is objective, rather than subjective, and focuses on the strength of the evidence of actual liability, not on the employer's fear of being liable.[88] Under the well-established theory of disparate impact liability, an employer is not liable even where there is undisputed disparate impact if it can show that the test or other selection device is job related and consistent with business necessity. This has been and continues to be the linchpin on which liability for disparate impact turns.

6.7 A Note about the Americans with Disabilities Act and Employment Testing

The Americans with Disabilities Act defines "discrimination" to include the use of "qualification standards, employment tests or other selection criteria that screen out or tend to screen out an individual with a disability or a class of individuals with disabilities unless the standard, test or other selection criteria, as used by the covered entity, is shown to be job-related for the position in question and is consistent with business necessity."[89] The author has nevertheless been unable to find any written examination scored test cases involving claims of disability discrimination. Because the ADA is structured in such a way that the existence of a disability is evaluated on a case-by-case basis, claims of employment discrimination brought under this statute have focused almost exclusively on the particular circumstances of an individual plaintiff's impairment, his or her ability to perform the job duties in question, and the possibilities of reasonable accommodation by that individual employer.[90]

---

87. *See* Ricci v. DeStefano, 557 U.S. 557, 585, 586, 592 (2009).

88. *See* United States v. Brennan, 650 F.3d 65, 110–11 (2d Cir. 2011) (interpreting meaning of "strong basis in evidence" as used in the majority opinion in the *Ricci* case).

89. *See* 42 U.S.C. § 12112(b)(6).

90. *See* Michael Stein and Michael Waterstone, *Disability, Disparate Impact, and Class Actions*, 56 Duke L. J. 860, 882 (2006) (as of the 2006 publication date, the

Administering pre-employment and promotional tests to persons with disabilities presents unique challenges of which employers should be aware. The ADA's reasonable accommodation requirement applies not only to accommodating employees in the performance of their job duties, but to the test-taking process itself—whether the test is of an applicant for employment or part of a promotional process for existing employees. As a matter of law (and common sense), tests should not be given in formats that require use of the impaired skill, unless it is a job-related skill that the test is intended to measure.[91] For example, it would be unlawful to administer a written employment test to an individual who has dyslexia and is unable to read. In this case, an alternative oral test would need to be administered to that person. By the same token, a written test may need to be substituted for an oral test if the applicant taking the test is an individual with a disability that impairs speaking skills or impairs the processing of auditory information. For persons with vision or hearing disabilities, other alternative or accessible test modes or formats include the administration of tests in large print or braille or via a reader or sign interpreter. Where it is not possible to test in an alternative format, the employer may be required, as a reasonable accommodation, to evaluate the skill to be tested in another manner (for example, through an interview, or through education, license, or work experience requirements).[92]

To continue with the example of a written employment test, where the ability to read is job related and the test *is* designed to measure that skill, an accommodation would *not* be required. Where an examination, whether written or physical, is testing a skill, and the amount of time it takes to complete the test is not job related, an applicant with a disability may be entitled to an extension of time in which to complete the test. On the other hand, where the test is designed to measure speed and speed *is* an essential function of the job, no reasonable accommodation would be necessary for the test—although the employer would be required to consider whether some other form of reasonable accommodation would permit the applicant

---

authors found not a single federal decision that analyzed a failure to accommodate claim under disparate impact analysis).

91. *See* 29 C.F.R. § 1630.11.

92. *See* Appendix to 29 C.F.R. Part 1630—Interpretive Guidance on Title I of the Americans with Disabilities Act, comment on 29 C.F.R. § 1630.11.

to perform the job.[93] A change in the way a test is administered would not require reconsideration of test validity, although a change in test content would.

93. *See* Appendix to 29 C.F.R. Part 1630—Interpretive Guidance on Title I of the Americans with Disabilities Act, comment on 29 C.F.R. § 1630.11. An employer is generally required to provide testing accommodations only if it knows in advance that an applicant has a disability that requires such accommodations. Usually, it is the responsibility of the individual with a disability to request any accommodation for a test. The employer can be helpful by informing applicants in advance about any tests to be administered as part of the application process so that the applicant may request an accommodation if needed.

Chapter 7

Testing of Applicants and Candidates for Promotion: Physical Ability Tests and Assessment Centers

Chapter 7

Testing of Applicants and Candidates for Promotion: Physical Ability Tests and Assessment Centers

The previous chapter focused on written tests. This chapter turns to two other kinds of pre-employment and promotional testing for skills and abilities—physical ability tests, such as timed runs, obstacle courses, and tests of weight-lifting capacity; and assessment centers, in which candidates are asked to simulate tasks and react to situations they are likely to encounter on the job. Chapter 5 discussed the potential for physical ability testing to become an unlawful medical examination prohibited by the Americans with Disabilities Act when heart-rate and blood pressure readings were taken in conjunction with the test. This chapter, in contrast, focuses on the Title VII discrimination issues raised by physical ability tests and assessment centers.

7.1 Physical Ability Tests

Physical ability tests are subject to the same type of challenge as written examinations when the results of the tests show a disparate impact on a protected class. The primary difference between cases involving disparate impact stemming from written tests and those involving disparate impact stemming from physical ability testing is that the former tend to impact racial and ethnic minority groups, while the latter tend to impact women.[1] In the public sector, both types of testing occur most frequently in the context of public safety hiring. Like written examinations, physical ability tests that result in disparate impact are unlawful unless they can be shown to be job related and consistent with business necessity. As is the case with written examinations, employers must make this showing through professional validation studies carried out in accordance with the Uniform Guidelines. But once an employer shows that a physical ability test is job related and consistent with business necessity, it will be found liable for disparate impact discrimination only if the applicant or employee can show that an alternate method of testing or selection exists that can accomplish the employer's objectives with less adverse impact. Two issues in the area of physical ability testing are worth special mention: the use of tests validated for another employer or agency and the problems involved in validating cutoff scores.

7.1.1 Using Physical Ability Tests Validated for Other Employers

Many local government employers use physical ability tests that have been designed and validated for other local governments, either within or outside the state, rather than constructing and validating tests of their own. The reason for this is clear: it is expensive to hire a consultant to put together a physical ability test from scratch. And why do so, when someone else has already paid for a test that selects out candidates for a position much like the local government's own position? In North Carolina, this is particularly true among law enforcement agencies. Most North Carolina police departments and sheriff's offices require applicants to pass what is known as the Police Officers Physical Abilities Test or POPAT. The POPAT was designed by the North Carolina Justice Academy under the auspices of the Criminal Justice Education and Training Standards Commission and the Sheriffs' Education and Training Standards Commission of the North Carolina Department of Justice as a test of the basic physical fitness required to be a law enforcement officer. It is administered as part of the state-designed Basic Law Enforcement Training (BLET) course. The POPAT administered as of this writing is given at the end of the 19 weeks of BLET training and must be completed in 7 minutes and 20 seconds. The POPAT consists of the following tasks in the following sequence:

---

1. *See* Lanning v. Se. Pa. Transp. Auth., 308 F.3d 286 (3d Cir. 2002) (physical fitness screening test with adverse impact on female applicants for transit officer positions).

1. Applicant is seatbelted in the driver's seat of a vehicle with his or her hands on the steering wheel. He or she is given two street names.
2. On instructor's command, "Go," the timed event begins.
3. Applicant removes seatbelt and exits the vehicle.
4. Applicant runs 100 yards and returns 100 yards to the front passenger's side door of the vehicle.
5. Applicant opens the vehicle door, removes seatbelted passenger from the vehicle, and drags subject 50 feet to a staircase, placing the subject on the ground. (Body drag must be done walking backwards while grasping subject under both arms.)
6. Applicant then scales and circles a staircase three times, touching every step traveling up and down.
7. Applicant runs from staircase for 25 feet to a 50-pound weighted door.
8. Applicant pushes through the door using the entire side of his or her body.
9. Once through the door, applicant drops to the ground and performs 20 military style push-ups and sit-ups.
10. Applicant runs back to the staircase to scale and circle the staircase three times, touching every step traveling up and down.
11. Applicant runs from staircase (25 feet) to a culvert and crawls through the culvert.
12. Once out of the culvert, applicant drops to the ground and performs 20 military style push-ups and sit-ups.
13. Applicant then runs 100 yards and returns 100 yards to the passenger's side of the vehicle where a subject is standing next to the vehicle.
14. Applicant grasps and drags subject 50 feet to a staircase, placing subject on ground.
15. Applicant must recite the two street names provided at the beginning of the test precisely in the order they were given.
16. Time is stopped.[2]

2. As of May 1, 2012, the North Carolina Justice Academy is developing and validating a new version of the POPAT.

Most local law enforcement departments administer the POPAT to applicants for sworn positions in their department, regardless of whether an applicant passed the POPAT in the BLET course or as administered by another department elsewhere in the state. This is a seemingly sensible approach, as the POPAT was developed and validated as a test of the minimum physical abilities necessary to perform the duties typical of patrol officers statewide. The EEOC recognizes that this is a valid strategy, noting that a test can be a valid predictor of performance on a job in one location and be valid for predicting success on a similar job in a different location if four conditions are met:

1. The evidence from the other studies clearly demonstrates that the test was valid when used elsewhere.
2. The job for which the test will be used closely matches the original job for which the validation study was performed, as shown by a comparison of major work behaviors in each position's job analysis.
3. Evidence of fairness from the other study is considered for those groups constituting a significant factor in the labor market of the new user.
4. The new user takes proper account of variables that might affect the applicability of the study in the new setting—such as different performance standards, work methods, applicant-pool experience, or other factors—and takes account of how recently the validation study was performed.[3]

These conditions also apply when an employer uses a test developed by a company that develops and sells tests for profit or when it uses a test described in professional literature.[4]

---

3. *See* 29 C.F.R. § 1607.7(B). *See also* Rivera v. City of Wichita Falls, 665 F.2d 531, 537 (5th Cir. 1982) (affirming validation of test that had been developed and used at another Texas police academy but making no mention of Uniform Guidelines standards for use of a test validated for use elsewhere).

4. *See* 29 C.F.R. § 1607.7(B). *But see* Lanning v. Se. Pa. Transp. Auth., 181 F.3d 478, 493 n.18 (3d Cir. 1999) (relying on study done for test of Maryland county police officer for validation of Philadelphia transit police test is "misplaced"); Harless v. Duck, 619 F.2d 611, 616 (6th Cir. 1980) (rejecting police officer test, portions of which were taken from a manual published by the Public Personnel Association and had been used in other cities but had never been validated).

Some local law enforcement departments, however, require applicants to pass a modified version of the POPAT—in some instances, a shorter version, in others a version in which the sequence of actions has been changed. This is more problematic, because the POPAT was validated as a test with these particular 13 actions in this particular sequence and the validation study cannot be transferred. Physical ability tests for which the only requirement is that the candidate complete the test within a specified amount of time are considered single, unitary tests for validation purposes. They cannot be split up into component pieces because they are not structurally independent—the length of time that a candidate spends on one part of the test determines how much time the candidate has to complete other parts of the test.[5] As one court put it in discussing a law enforcement physical abilities test in another state:

> [T]he length of time necessary to complete the push-ups determines how much time the candidate would have to complete the sit-ups portion. As an example, a candidate who takes 50 seconds to complete the obstacle course/run then has 40 seconds to complete the required numbers of push-ups and sit-ups, while a candidate who takes 70 seconds to finish the obstacle course/run has only 20 seconds for the push-ups and sit-ups. Similarly, how much of the 20 (or 40) seconds the candidate would have left to complete the required number of sit-ups depends upon how long the candidate took to complete the push-ups. Thus, if each component of the PAT were to be considered separately, the "passing standard" would be different for every candidate who took the PAT, and it would therefore be unclear exactly what the City was attempting to justify as job-related and consistent with business necessity.[6]

Similarly, using the POPAT as a selection device for applicants for all positions in a given law enforcement agency is unlikely to satisfy the standard of job related and consistent with business necessity as it is a test validated for entry-level positions. The duties of a detective, on one hand,

---

5. *See, e.g.*, United States v. City of Erie, Pa., 411 F. Supp. 2d at 553 (physical ability test was unitary test for validation purposes since passing score consisted of one requirement, that the applicant complete the entire test within 90 seconds).

6. *City of Erie, Pa.*, 411 F. Supp. 2d at 544.

or a captain, on the other, will be different from those of patrol officer, and the use of the POPAT for promotional tests or lateral hires will not satisfy the second condition necessary for using a test validated elsewhere because the jobs are different.[7]

7.1.2 Validating Cutoff Scores for Physical Ability Testing That Have a Disparate Impact on Women

As with written examinations, cutoff scores on physical ability tests will rarely meet the standard of job related and consistent with business necessity unless they have been professionally validated. Sometimes, methods that have first-blush common-sense appeal look amateurish under the harsher light of disparate impact analysis. In a case involving a physical agility test for volunteer firefighters, a fire department determined the cutoff score for a test requiring that applicants drag a 280-pound water-filled hose over a distance of 150 feet to be four minutes; this was determined by taking the average of all test scores and then arbitrarily adding some extra time. When challenged, the fire department could not point to any objective evidence that the minimum standard for the hose-drag was four minutes.[8] The cutoff score had a disparate impact on women applicants, and in the absence of a validation study, the court found that it was unlawful under Title VII. In another firefighter case, a city unsuccessfully attempted to persuade the court that it was correct in choosing one standard deviation above the mean as the cutoff point simply because one standard deviation above the mean was frequently used to determine cutoff scores in other situations. The court observed that this meant that the passing score would depend on the average performance of those applicants who happened to take the test. This was inconsistent with showing business necessity because "the ability to perform firefighting tasks adequately depends not on relative but on absolute test performance."[9] This method of determining the cutoff score could result in a city or county hiring people who are,

---

7. *See, e.g.,* U.S. Equal Employment Opportunity Commission, *Adoption of Questions and Answers to Clarify and Provide a Common Interpretation of the Uniform Guidelines on Employee Selection Procedures,* 44 Fed. Reg. 6570 at Q and A 43 (March 2, 1979), www.eeoc.gov/policy/docs/qanda_clarify_procedures.html.

8. *See* Pietras v. Bd. of Fire Comm'rs of Farmingville Fire Dist., 180 F.3d 468, 474 (2d Cir. 1999).

9. *See* Evans v. City of Evanston, Ill., 881 F.2d 382, 384 (7th Cir. 1989).

in fact, unable to perform the job of firefighter successfully in any year or recruiting period where there was a substandard applicant pool.

Another issue in scoring physical ability tests is the correct way to determine the minimum aerobic capacity needed for a position. This issue arises frequently in testing for law enforcement officer positions. Few would argue that law enforcement officers need a certain amount of physical strength and aerobic capacity to function effectively. Most officers, at some time or another, are likely to engage in a foot chase of a suspect—in some places more frequently, in others less frequently. But the fact that some amount of running or sprinting is likely—and the implications that has for public safety—does not absolve the government employer from its responsibility to design a test that measures that ability without discriminating against women applicants.[10] As physical ability tests frequently have disparate impact on female applicants, public employers sometimes attempt to mitigate this problem by establishing a lower cutoff score for women. However, even after adopting a newer, lower cutoff score, employers sometimes find that the test still results in disparate impact liability if the test has not been validated. Where the state of Connecticut adopted different cutoff times for a 1.5 mile run based on the age and gender of corrections applicants, there was nonetheless a disparate impact on women applicants. A group of women who had been rejected based on their inability to meet the standard for the run brought suit. The court rejected outright the notion that different cutoff times could ever represent a minimum measure of aerobic capacity necessary to do the job, which is the standard against which business necessity is measured.[11] Like a firefighter's ability to drag a hose, a law enforcement officer's ability to engage in pursuit must be measured by a single minimum standard for there to be a showing that the test is job related and consistent with business necessity, as a defense to a disparate impact claim must prove.

---

10. *See* Lanning v. Se. Pa. Transp. Auth., 308 F.3d 286, 289 (3d Cir. 2002), *citing* and *quoting* Lanning v. Se. Pa. Transp. Auth., 181 F.3d 478, 490–91 n.16 (3d Cir. 1999) (the business necessity standard takes public safety into consideration); Harless v. Duck, 619 F.2d 611, 616 (6th Cir. 1980) (job description did not establish what physical capacities were necessary); Easterling v. State of Conn., 783 F. Supp. 2d 323, 342 (D. Conn. 2011) (comparing need for transit officer to run significant distances with that of correctional officer).

11. *See Easterling*, 783 F. Supp. 2d at 342.

The single minimum standard must be clearly identified in order to be validated as necessary for successful job performance. In one case, an Alabama correctional facility attempted to justify its minimum height and weight requirements—which had a disparate impact on women—by asserting that a "sufficient" but unspecified amount of physical strength was essential to effective performance as a correctional officer. When the case reached the U.S. Supreme Court, the Court held that this kind of imprecise standard could never justify any form of physical ability testing or cutoff scoring because the correlation between the requirement and the position's duties could never be established.[12]

7.2 Assessment Centers

Assessment centers are another form of scored testing that North Carolina public employers use in evaluating applicants for entry-level or promotional positions. Assessment centers simulate key parts of the job for which a candidate is being considered. They give an employer the opportunity to evaluate an applicant's knowledge of standard operating procedures and, perhaps more importantly, to see the applicant take action without the benefit of prompts (as opposed to having an applicant identify the correct option on a multiple-choice test or merely describe it in an oral examination).

Assessment centers are frequently used to evaluate applicants' decision-making abilities and interpersonal skills. Candidates are evaluated by panels of three to five persons on the basis of a set of criteria or standards that the designer of the assessment center has developed. The panels are usually composed of supervisors and other upper-level managers from the department and employer in question and/or persons in similar positions from other jurisdictions of similar size and needs. The employer typically gives training or instruction to the assessors in what the employer's measures of evaluation are and in what particular abilities or qualities the employer is interested in identifying among the candidates. Types of assessment center exercises include those in which the employer gives a group of job candidates a job-related task to perform that requires them to come to a consensus about how to achieve a goal; so-called in-basket exercises where

12. *See* Dothard v. Rawlinson, 433 U.S. 321, 331–32 (1977).

candidates are asked to read and respond to a series of memos and reports in a limited amount of time (to assess candidates' ability to prioritize tasks and manage time); role-playing exercises; fact-finding exercises; and short presentations. In exercises where individuals other than job candidates participate or play roles, those persons also receive instruction from the team running the assessment center.[13]

7.2.1 An Example of a Valid Law Enforcement Assessment Center

The following is an example of an assessment center used for promotion to lieutenant in a metropolitan police force. The assessment center was the subject of a disparate impact claim, but the court ultimately found it to be job related and consistent with business necessity:

> Based on the job analysis, ADI [*the consultants designing the assessment center*] suggested that candidates be assessed on the basis of performance on three simulation exercises designed to reflect the duties, tasks, and responsibilities encountered by lieutenants—an administrative exercise, a coordination exercise, and a training and directing exercise. In the administrative or "in-basket" exercise, the participant is asked to assume the role of a lieutenant in a hypothetical police department. The candidate is given a set of materials consisting of bulletins, reports, letters, and other communications from superiors, coworkers, subordinates, and citizens and is directed to handle as many of the items as possible in a given time period. Some of the items are routine and require no immediate action, while others require prompt and decisive action. It is up to the candidate to decide, based upon the information available, how to treat each item. The candidate is then required to communicate his or her decisions to other members of the department through written memoranda. In the coordination, or problem-

---

13. On assessment centers generally, see C. R. Swanson & Mark R. Foster, *Conducting Assessment Centers*, *in* Handbook of Human Resource Management in Government 615–34 (Stephen E. Condrey, ed., 3d ed. 2010); James A. Buford, Jr. & James R. Lindner, Human Resource Management in Local Government: Concepts and Applications for HRM Students and Practitioners 207–08 (2002); Dennis M. Daley, Strategic Human Resouce Management: People and Performance in the Public Sector 120–21 (2002).

> analysis exercise, the candidate is asked to assume the role of a lieutenant in charge of the redeployment of manpower within the district to which he or she is assigned. The redeployment may be a result of an anticipated civil disturbance, a political rally, or any other typical occurrence faced by an on-the-job lieutenant. The candidate is given a set of materials describing the need for redeployment, then meets with role players who assume the part of persons affected by the redeployment, e.g., a sergeant under the lieutenant's supervision or a sergeant from another police department involved in the redeployment. Following a review of the written materials and a discussion with the role players, the candidate is required to prepare a brief written summary of the problem and a proposal for its resolution. The training and directing, or complaint-review exercise, is designed to analyze the candidate's skills at dealing with subordinates. In this exercise, the candidate is faced with a subordinate who has had recent performance problems. The candidate is required to review the subordinate's file and related materials, then meet with the sergeant (a role player) to discuss the problem. The candidate is analyzed on his ability to provide guidance to the subordinate.[14]

The opinion also describes the scoring system:

> For each exercise, the drafters developed an assessment guide listing the behaviors to be observed. . . . For example, on the 1985 coordination exercise, the assessor checklist for the organizing and planning dimension requires the assessor to evaluate the candidate on twelve different behaviors ranging from whether the candidate "attempted to keep the discussion organized by verbally summarizing the role player's comments on a given topic," to whether the candidate "completed the task of writing a plan of action within the time allotted" as opposed to "submitted an incomplete report" . . . . Performance at the assessment center is evaluated by teams of three assessors. The

14. *See* Progressive Officers Club, Inc. v. Metro. Dade Cnty., 1990 WL 270786 at *7 (S.D. Fla. 1990).

> assessors base their scores on their observance of the candidate's performance and the checklist provided in the assessor guides. The assessors are required to reconcile their final scores with their checklist and notes. The ratings of the three assessors on each dimension in each exercise must be within one point of each other. If the assessors' scores are more than one point apart on any dimension in any exercise, the assessors are required to discuss the candidate's performance and reach consensus about the appropriate score. Only when the assessors have resolved their differences is the score considered final.
>
> Before an individual can serve as an assessor, he or she must be trained to accurately observe and record behavior. . . . The training process took one week and included introduction into the assessment center method, instructions on the proper method to evaluate behavior, and specific instructions about the exercises the assessors were assigned to observe. During the training process, instructors evaluate the assessors to ensure that the assessors are able to observe and assess behavior in accordance with written guidelines. If the assessors do not reach a sufficient level of proficiency, they are not allowed to proceed to the actual assessment process.[15]

For those unfamiliar with assessment centers, the description quoted above both gives some concrete examples demonstrating how assessment centers differ from written examinations and physical agility tests and shows the complexity of a valid assessment center.

Generally, human resources scholars and professionals consider assessment centers to be accurate predictors of an individual candidate's future success in a position.[16] Studies have also shown that properly constructed assessment centers predict success equally well for whites and African Americans and for men and women, a finding that seems to be correlated by the relatively few disparate impact cases challenging assessment center

---

15. *See Progressive Officers Club*, 1990 WL 270786 at *8.

16. *See* C. R. Swanson & Mark R. Foster, *Conducting Assessment Centers, in* Handbook of Human Resource Management in Government 616 (Stephen E. Condrey, ed., 3d ed. 2010) and sources cited therein.

results.[17] In some instances, courts have ordered the use of assessment centers to increase the numbers of minority groups or women likely to be hired or promoted.[18]

7.2.2 An Example of a Firefighter Assessment Center That Could Not Be Validated

Assessment centers must nevertheless still be validated in accordance with the Uniform Guidelines if they result in disparate impact. A process that has not been professionally designed may fall into some of the traps that resulted in a finding of unlawfulness for a firefighter captain's assessment center administered by the city of Saint Louis, Missouri. The St. Louis assessment center consisted of three parts: a fire-scene simulation, in which the candidates were shown slides of a large fire and were asked to respond in writing to questions regarding their observations and what orders they might give; a training simulation, in which candidates prepared and presented informational lectures from printed materials given to them, similar to training that they might give at the firehouse; and an interview simulation, in which each candidate, playing the role of a fire captain, interacted with a person playing the role of a firefighter involved in a personal confrontation with another firefighter. In each of the second two simulations,

17. *See* C. R. Swanson & Mark R. Foster, *Conducting Assessment Centers, in* HANDBOOK OF HUMAN RESOURCE MANAGEMENT IN GOVERNMENT 617 (Stephen E. Condrey, ed., 3d ed. 2010) and studies cited therein. *See also* Rudder v. Dist. of Columbia, 890 F. Supp. 23, 39 (D.D.C. 1995) *aff'd*, 99 F.3d 448 (D.C. Cir. 1996) ("It is undisputed that the Assessment Center produced no disparate impact on African Americans. Indeed, African Americans scored higher than their white colleagues on this portion of the examination"); *Progressive Officers Club*, 1990 WL 270786 at *24 ("assessment center has not produced any adverse impact against Blacks and was created in a fashion that ensured it was job related"); Belfield v. Chesapeake & Potomac Tel. Co., 1980 WL 88 at *3 (D.D.C. Jan. 31, 1980) (plaintiff did not introduce any evidence showing use of an assessment center as a selection criterion resulted in a disparate impact).

18. *See, e.g.*, United Black Firefighters Ass'n v. City of Akron, 976 F.2d 999, 1004 (6th Cir. 1992). *See also* Bazile v. City of Houston, 2012 WL 573633 at *54 (S.D. Tex. 2012) (approving of agreement to use assessment center in proposed consent decree because ". . . incorporating situational-judgment tests and assessment centers diminishes the risk of disparate impact and increases the validity of the City's promotional processes").

the candidates were physically observed by three assessors who later conferred to evaluate the candidates.[19]

In response to a disparate impact challenge, the city attempted to show that the assessment center had content validity—in other words, that the exercise reflected the important skills or knowledge required by the job. The focal point of the challenge was the city's use of the fire simulation slides and related questions. Unfortunately for the city's defense, the Uniform Guidelines expressly question the ability of a paper-and-pencil test to replicate work behaviors that are not managerial or administrative in nature. Interpreting the Uniform Guidelines, the court found that paper-and-pencil tests of effectiveness in interpersonal relations (for example, supervision), of physical activities (for example, machine or automobile repair), or of ability to function properly under danger (for example, firefighting) are generally not close enough approximations of work behaviors to show content validity.[20] The court described the problem with the fire scene simulation as follows:

> The fire scene simulation was a paper-and-pencil test that required written answers to questions about a slide presentation. It was intended to replicate the work behaviors which a fire captain would undertake in response to the scenes depicted in the slides. The test sought to measure the candidate's ability to observe the situation depicted in the slides and to decide on the correct course of responsive action, including his projected physical actions, his supervision of the firefighters under his command and his ability to deal with the dangers of the situation. It seems to fall squarely within the scope of [EEOC Interpretive] Question and Answer No. 78 as a test which is not a close enough approximation of a work behavior to show content validity. Once again, this outcome is supported by logic and reason. The fire scene simulation, like the multiple choice examination, cannot avoid testing the candidate's proficiency in the written exercise

---

19. *See* Firefighters Inst. for Racial Equality v. City of St. Louis, Mo., 616 F.2d 350, 360–61 (8th Cir. 1980).

20. *See Firefighters Inst. for Racial Equality*, 616 F.2d at 361; Q and A No. 78 at 44 Fed. Reg. 12,007 (1979).

> of verbal skills which is certainly not a critical or necessary job behavior for a fire captain. The candidates may be very proficient at assessing the scene of a fire and issuing the appropriate oral orders but ineffectual in communicating those orders in writing.[21]

The St. Louis case also illustrates one of the other ways in which an assessment center may fail the validity test. Unlike other forms of scored evaluations, the scoring of candidates by assessors leaves room for a large degree of subjectivity. While not unlawful in and of itself, the use of subjective criteria in the hiring process gets much closer scrutiny when there is a claim of disparate impact. Well-designed assessment centers provide highly structured guidance and extensive training to their assessors to counter hidden or unintentional discrimination that subjective evaluation may mask. Contrast the original week-long training given to assessors by the Metro Miami-Dade police department with the assessor training offered by the city of St. Louis: St. Louis gave those assessing the fire simulation exercise a mere one day of training and those assessing the interview and training simulations two days of training. An exercise performed with the assessors to demonstrate the reliability of their scores actually showed substantial variance in the scores they gave.[22]

7.2.3 Assessment Centers in Sum

Public employers should not be discouraged from using assessment centers to assess both entry-level and promotional candidates: as noted above, they have a good record of providing accurate and race- and gender-neutral results. But as with any scored test, employers should design assessment centers with the validity strategies of the Uniform Guidelines in mind and should validate any process that results in disparate impact when used.

---

21. *See Firefighters Inst. for Racial Equality*, 616 F.2d at 361.
22. *See Firefighters Inst. for Racial Equality*, 616 F.2d at 361–62.

Chapter 8

Background Investigations of Applicants for Employment: Criminal Records, Credit History, Reference, and Internet Checks

Chapter 8

Background Investigations of Applicants for Employment: Criminal Records, Credit History, Reference, and Internet Checks

With a few exceptions, North Carolina public employers are not generally required to conduct background investigations of potential employees.[1] Nevertheless, most public employers perform some mix of criminal history, credit history, and reference checks on those applicants to whom they intend to extend a job offer. Employers are increasingly adding a fourth type of background check to their arsenal, as well—the Internet background check. Each type of background investigation raises distinct legal issues, and this chapter therefore discusses each category of background check individually. The chapter concludes with a discussion of the Fair Credit Reporting Act, which imposes very specific obligations on employers who

1. There are a small number of exceptions to this rule, which are set forth in the North Carolina General Statutes (hereinafter G.S.). For example, employees of area mental health authorities and licensed providers of mental health, developmental disability, and substance abuse services who are not licensed professionals must submit to a criminal records history check under G.S. 122C-80(b). So must providers of adult home care services and employees of home care agencies, pursuant to G.S. 131D-40 and G.S. 131E-265, respectively. This is different from the requirement of many licensing agencies that persons pass a criminal records history check before they may be licensed to practice a profession. For example, G.S. 131E-159(g) requires emergency medical technicians and paramedics to undergo a criminal background check before they can be certified. Under G.S. 84-24, attorneys must undergo a criminal records check before they will be licensed to practice law in North Carolina. Similarly, G.S. 90-224(c) requires a criminal background check as part of the process of licensing dental hygienists.

use third party, for-profit companies to conduct any form of background check. Notwithstanding the statute's name, the Fair Credit Reporting Act governs an employer's use of third parties to conduct criminal history, credit, reference, and Internet checks.

8.1 Reasons for Conducting Background Investigations

Why do employers go to the time and expense of conducting background checks when they are not required to do so? Some employers conduct background investigations to make sure that a person has the qualifications, skills, and personal characteristics that they have claimed in the application process. Others do so to make sure that the person does not pose any threat to coworkers, members of the community, or the employer's property. Still others are trying to get a read on an applicant's sense of responsibility, values, and personal integrity. For many employers, a powerful motivation for conducting background investigations of job applicants is a fear that the employer may find itself liable for an employee's wrongful on-the-job acts if it has not sufficiently looked into that employee's background. In North Carolina, such fear is misplaced, as the law of negligent hiring is not very strong.

8.1.1 Fear of Negligent Hiring Claims Not a Reason to Conduct a Background Check

What is negligent hiring? North Carolina common law recognizes negligent hiring as a tort in which an employer is responsible for an injury caused by the negligent or intentional conduct of one its employees. In a negligent hiring case, the injured plaintiff must show that the employer knew or should have known that the employee was not fit to be hired for the particular job because it was foreseeable that the employee might harm someone like the plaintiff. The plaintiff must also show that the employee's employment in that position was the proximate cause of the plaintiff's injury.[2]

---

2. *See, e.g.*, Medlin v. Bass, 327 N.C. 587, 592 (1990); White v. Consol. Planning, Inc., 166 N.C. App. 283, 292–93 (2004); Hogan v. Forsyth Country Club Co., 79 N.C. App. 483, 495–95 (1986).

In North Carolina, claims of negligent hiring have rarely been successful. The North Carolina courts have consistently held that employers do not have any general duty to check the criminal history of an applicant or employee, even where the position requires the employee to go into other people's homes and the chance for theft is great.[3] In a 1990 North Carolina Supreme Court case, the court did not directly address the issue of whether there is a general duty to obtain a criminal history of a job applicant, but it found that a school system could not reasonably have foreseen a school principal's pedophilia absent any mention of inappropriate sexual behavior by his references.[4]

North Carolina public employers need not, therefore, invest the time and resources needed to conduct background investigations simply because they fear liability for negligent hiring. Nevertheless, most employers will continue to perform background checks because of the positive benefits they believe background checks offer.

8.2 Criminal History Record Checks

North Carolina employers do not have any affirmative duty to conduct criminal background checks,[5] but they are not prohibited from doing so, either. Checking the criminal history of both job applicants and current employees is lawful, provided that employers follow the guidelines set forth by the Equal Employment Opportunity Commission (EEOC) to guard against the disparate impact that criminal background checks frequently cause.[6] Nothing prohibits North Carolina local government employers

---

3. *See, e.g.*, Westerhold v. Designer's Way, Inc., 167 N.C. App. 657, 657 (2004) (painting company); Moricle v. Pilkington, 120 N.C. App. 383, 387 (1996) (painting company). *See also* Neal v. Elec. Data Sys. Corp., 1999 WL 1939976, *5 (E.D.N.C. 1999) (sexual harassment claim brought against data company).

4. *See Medlin*, 327 N.C. at 592.

5. *See* Stanley v. Brooks, 112 N.C. App. 609, 612–13 (1993).

6. *See* U.S. Equal Employment Opportunity Commission, *Enforcement Guidance on the Consideration of Arrest and Conviction Records in Employment Decisions Under Title VII of the Civil Rights Act of 1964,* as amended, 42 U.S.C. § 2000e *et seq.*, No. 915.002 (April 25, 2012) (hereinafter *Enforcement Guidance on the Consideration of Arrest and Conviction Records*), www.eeoc.gov/laws/guidance/arrest_conviction.cfm. *See also* Gregory v. Litton Sys. Inc., 472 F.2d 631 (9th Cir. 1972) (finding unlawful

from requiring applicants to provide information about arrest or conviction records. What the law prohibits is imposing a blanket disqualification on any applicant who has an arrest record or a conviction.

8.2.1 Blanket Disqualification of Applicants with Criminal Records Prohibited

Employers may not adopt a policy prohibiting the employment of anyone with a criminal record—policies referred to as "blanket disqualifications" or "absolute bans." No statute expressly sets forth the prohibition on blanket disqualification of applicants with criminal records. The EEOC and the federal courts, however, have found that such policies exclude a disproportionate number of African Americans from consideration for employment. As discussed in Chapter 2, Section 2.1.6, even if an employment practice is facially neutral, when the practice excludes a disproportionate percentage of African Americans—or of any minority group or protected class—it violates Title VII unless the employer can establish that the practice is justified as a business necessity.[7] In other words, because statistics show that the practice of using arrest and conviction records as absolute bars to employment has a disproportionate impact on African Americans, it is a form of unintentional discrimination (disparate impact discrimination) on the basis of race. As such, it violates Title VII unless the employer can show that a blanket disqualification of any person with a criminal record from any position—or from a specific position—is job related and consistent with business necessity.[8]

Recognition that blanket disqualification of applicants with arrest and conviction records caused disparate impact on minority applicants came early in the history of Title VII race discrimination litigation. In the cases *Gregory v. Litton Systems, Inc.* (1972) and *Green v. Missouri Pacific Railroad* (1975), national arrest statistics demonstrated that African Americans suffered a disproportionately high percentage of arrests and criminal convic-

---

discrimination from employer's policy of blanket disqualification of any applicant with an arrest record but denying injunctive relief to forbid the employer from continuing to collect such information). *Gregory* remains one of the leading cases in this area.

7. Griggs v. Duke Power Co., 401 U.S. 424, 431 (1971); Green v. Mo. Pac. R.R. Co., 523 F.2d 1290, 1293 (8th Cir. 1975).

8. *See Enforcement Guidance on the Consideration of Arrest and Conviction Records,* at 8.

tions and that a policy of not hiring anyone with an arrest or conviction led to a rejection rate for African Americans that was two and one-half times the rejection rate for whites.[9] In 1987 and 1990, the EEOC issued official policy statements on the use of conviction records and arrest records, making clear that national statistics showing that African Americans and Latinos were convicted at a rate disproportionate to their representation in the population made the use of a criminal record as a blanket bar to employment unlawful under Title VII unless the employer could demonstrate business necessity.[10]

Given that the EEOC's original policy statements were issued in 1987 and 1990 and the cases cited in the paragraph above date to the 1970s, the question naturally arises: is the racial and national origin breakdown of arrest and conviction records disproportionate enough *today* to make the use of criminal records as an absolute bar to employment unlawful under Title VII? The answer to this question is yes. The EEOC issued a new, comprehensive policy guidance on the use of criminal records in 2012 to replace the original 1987 and 1990 guidances, titled *Enforcement Guidance on the Consideration of Arrest and Conviction Records in Employment Decisions Under Title VII of the Civil Rights Act of 1964, as amended, 42 U.S.C. § 2000e et seq* (hereinafter, the 2012 Guidance).[11] In the 2012 Guidance, the EEOC reports that in 2010, 28 percent of all arrests were of African Americans, who comprised only 14 percent of the general population.[12] In 2008, non-Hispanic blacks made up approximately 12 percent

---

9. *See* Gregory v. Litton Systems, Inc., 316 F. Supp. 401, 403 (C.D. Calif. 1970), *aff'd*, 472 F.2d 631 (9th Cir. 1972); *Green*, 523 F.2d at 1293–95.

10. *See* U.S. Equal Employment Opportunity Commission, *Policy Guidance on the Consideration of Arrest Records in Employment Decisions under Title VII of the Civil Rights Act of 1964, as amended, 42 U.S.C. §2000e et seq. (1982),* No. 915.061 (September 7, 1990) (hereinafter *EEOC Policy Guidance on the Consideration of Arrest Records*), www.eeoc.gov/policy/docs/arrest_records.html, and *EEOC Policy Statement on the Issue of Conviction Records under Title VII of the Civil Rights Act of 1964, as amended, 42 U.S.C. § 2000e et seq. (1982)* (February 4, 1987), www.eeoc.gov/policy/docs/convict1.html.

11. The full citation is EEOC, *Enforcement Guidance on the Consideration of Arrest and Conviction Records in Employment Decisions Under Title VII of the Civil Rights Act of 1964, as amended, 42 U.S.C. § 2000e et seq.*, No. 915.002 (April 25, 2012), www.eeoc.gov/laws/guidance/arrest_conviction.cfm.

12. *See EEOC Enforcement Guidance on the Consideration of Arrest and Conviction Records,* at 9.

of the estimated total U.S. population of 304,060,000. Hispanic residents comprised approximately 15.5 percent of the population and non-Hispanic whites approximately 65.5 percent of the population.[13] Statistics from the FBI show that in 2008, approximately 28 percent of the total number of persons arrested nationwide were black—more than double their representation in the population—while 69 percent of the total number of persons arrested were white, a number more in line with their representation in the population.[14] In terms of inmate population, in 2010, African American men were imprisoned at a rate seven times higher than white men and three times higher than Hispanic men.[15] In 2008, a startling 38.4 percent of the federal prison population was African American and 58.3 percent was white—a significantly lower percentage than the percentage of whites in the population as a whole.[16] A statistical analysis of the nationwide jail population in 2008 shows that non-Hispanic blacks made up approximately 39 percent of that population, non-Hispanic whites 42 percent, and Hispanics 16 percent.[17] Thus, even today, policies that use arrest and conviction records to automatically disqualify applicants will likely have a disparate impact on African Americans and, to a lesser extent, Hispanics.

In the 2012 Guidance, the EEOC says that in assessing claims of disparate impact caused by the use of criminal records, the EEOC will now use national data about arrests and convictions in investigating such claims. It will fall to the employer to rebut the claim that its criminal record policy

---

13. American Indian and Alaskan Native, Asian, and Native Hawaiian and other Pacific Islander were the remaining categories. For population figures, see U.S. Census Bureau, Statistical Abstract of the United States: 2010 (129th Edition 2009), Table 6, "Resident Population by Sex, Race, and Hispanic-Origin Status: 2000 to 2008," www.census.gov/compendia/statab/2010/tables/10s0006.pdf.

14. *See* U.S. Dep't of Justice, Federal Bureau of Investigation, 2008 Crime in the United States, Table 43, www2.fbi.gov/ucr/cius2008/data/table_43.html. The percentages for Hispanics were not listed in this table.

15. *See EEOC Enforcement Guidance on the Consideration of Arrest and Conviction Records,* at 10.

16. *See* Office of Justice Programs, Bureau of Justice Statistics, Mark Motivans, Federal Justice Statistics, 2008—Statistical Tables, Statistical Table 7.10, "Characteristics of federal prison population, October 1, 2007–September 30, 2008," http://bjs.ojp.usdoj.gov/index.cfm?ty=pbdetail&iid=1745.

17. See U.S. Census Bureau, Statistical Abstract of the United States: 2010 (129th Edition 2009), Table 337, "Jail Inmates by Sex, Race, and Hispanic Origin: 1990 to 2008," www.census.gov/compendia/statab/2010/tables/10s0337.pdf.

causes disparate impact by presenting "regional or local data showing that African American and/or Hispanic men are not arrested or convicted at disproportionately higher rates in the employer's particular geographic area." An employer may also present evidence from its own applicant data to show that its criminal record policy did not cause disparate impact.[18] As is the case with charges that a scored test has caused disparate impact, an employer cannot defend itself by showing that it has a racially balanced workforce. As the 2012 Guidance and the cases that preceded it make clear, the purpose of Title VII is to ensure that individuals have the opportunity to compete equally on the basis of job-related criteria. A focus on racial balance in the workforce ignores the opportunity denied to individuals when the criminal history check is not job related and arbitrarily selects out members of a protected class.[19]

8.2.1.1 When Convictions May Disqualify Applicants from Certain Jobs

Few employers can make the case that business necessity dictates that no person with an arrest or conviction can hold any of their jobs. Employers can and do, however, make the case that convictions for certain offenses are sufficiently related to certain jobs or categories of jobs as to warrant an absolute disqualification. Two cases illustrate the difference.

In the 1975 case *Green v. Missouri Pacific Railroad*, an African American job applicant had served 21 months in prison for refusing to serve in the military during the Vietnam War. The employer railroad put forth a number of reasons for claiming that exclusion of any applicant with a conviction greater than a minor traffic offense was a business necessity. It claimed that it feared cargo theft, could not trust persons with convictions to handle company funds, would not be able to bond a person with a criminal conviction, could not put such an employee on the witness stand if need be because the person's credibility could be impeached by the fact of his conviction, and that it might be liable for negligent hiring if the person engaged in a violent act in the workplace. The company also claimed that the workplace might be disrupted by the person's return to criminal behavior, and cited the alleged lack of moral character of persons with

18. *See EEOC Enforcement Guidance on the Consideration of Arrest and Conviction Records,* at 10.

19. *See EEOC Enforcement Guidance on the Consideration of Arrest and Conviction Records,* at 10. See also Chapter 6, note 50 and cases cited therein.

convictions. The railroad did not, however, validate its policy with respect to those reasons, nor did it provide any evidence that there was no less restrictive alternative with a lesser racial impact that would serve as well.[20]

The court in the *Green* case observed that the reasons the employer gave for its policy could serve as "relevant considerations in making individual hiring decisions," but that they "in no way justify an absolute policy which sweeps so broadly":

> We cannot conceive of any business necessity that would automatically place every individual convicted of any offense, except a minor traffic offense, in the permanent ranks of the unemployed. This is particularly true for blacks who have suffered and still suffer from the burdens of discrimination in our society. To deny job opportunities to those individuals because of some conduct which may be remote in time or does not significantly bear upon the particular job requirements is an unnecessarily harsh and unjust burden.[21]

A conviction for embezzlement, for example, might justify exclusion from jobs that handle company funds. A scientifically validated study showing that antiwar protestors were more likely than others to engage in violence in the workplace might have justified an absolute disqualification of all those convicted of antiwar protests from all positions involving interaction with other people. But an absolute ban on all persons with criminal convictions of any sort from all jobs with a company cannot be justified.

Thirty-two years later in another disparate impact case, the Third Circuit granted summary judgment to a public transit employer that could validate its disqualification of applicants who had been convicted of a violent crime. In *El v. Southeastern Pennsylvania Transportation Authority (SEPTA)*, the plaintiff applied for a job as a paratransit operator when he was 47 years old. He had been convicted of second-degree murder when he was 15 and had served a three and a half year prison term. SEPTA, the employer, presented expert testimony to the effect that persons with a conviction for violent crime present a significantly higher risk of danger to passengers than do those without such a conviction. SEPTA argued that its policy was consistent with business necessity because (1) the job of a

20. *See* Green v. Mo. Pac. R.R., 523 F.2d 1290, 1293–95 (8th Cir. 1975).

21. *See Green*, 523 F.2d at 1298.

paratransit driver required that the driver be in very close contact with passengers, (2) the job required that the driver often be alone with passengers, (3) paratransit passengers are vulnerable because they typically have physical and/or mental disabilities, (4) disabled people are disproportionately targeted by sexual and violent criminals, (5) violent criminals recidivate at a high rate, (6) it is impossible to predict with a reasonable degree of accuracy which criminals will recidivate, (7) someone with a conviction for a violent crime is more likely than someone without one to commit a future violent crime irrespective of how remote in time the conviction is, and (8) SEPTA's policy was the most accurate way to screen out applicants who presented an unacceptable risk.[22]

Did the Third Circuit's decision in the *El* case represent a move away from the holding in the *Green* case and from the EEOC's 1987 guidance on the use of conviction records, which incorporated the court's finding in *Green*? Not necessarily. There are two significant differences between the two cases. First, the applicant in the *Green* case was applying for an office job with the railroad corporation, one that did not require the employee to be alone with and in close proximity to vulnerable members of society as did the paratransit position in the *El* case. Second, the disqualification policy in the *Green* case was much more extensive than that in *El*: in the *Green* case, the employer excluded from consideration anyone with any kind of criminal conviction, while in the *El* case, the policy eliminated anyone with a conviction for a crime of violence from consideration for employment as a paratransit driver.

Note that in the *El* case, the plaintiff had urged the court to hold that Title VII prohibited any bright-line rules about criminal convictions such as SEPTA's disqualification of persons with convictions for violent crime. The court, however, rejected that suggestion, saying:

> If a bright-line policy can distinguish between individual applicants that do and do not pose an unacceptable level of risk, then such a policy is consistent with business necessity. Whether a policy can do so is most often a question of fact that the district courts – and juries – must resolve in specific cases.[23]

---

22. *See* El v. Se. Pa. Transp. Auth. (SEPTA), 479 F.3d 232, 245 (3d Cir. 2007).

23. *See El*, 479 F.3d at 245. *See also* McCraven v. City of Chicago, 109 F. Supp. 2d 935 (N.D. Ill. 2000) (use of arrest records to per se disqualify applicant for police officer position is lawful because of the "awesome responsibilities" of law enforcement).

What the *Green* and *El* cases teach employers is that they must be able to justify any policy that would exclude persons with an arrest or conviction record from consideration from any class or type of job. This holds true for policies that bar persons with convictions generally or persons with convictions for particular types of offense. The requirement that employers prove the validity of using conviction records as a selection device is consistent with the approach of both the EEOC and the courts to other employment practices, tests, and qualifications that screen out candidates, as discussed more fully in Chapters 6 and 7. The only difference here is that the arrest and conviction policies are meant to disqualify those who pose too much risk rather than those lacking certain skills.[24]

In some cases, employers have adopted policies precluding persons with criminal convictions from consideration for employment in a particular job because another law or regulation prohibits them holding such a job or because a third party will not issue the applicant a certification, credential, or coverage necessary for the job because of the conviction. Whether a law or regulation is a valid reason for disqualifying an applicant, however, depends on whether it is a federal or state requirement.

If a federal law or regulation prohibits the employment of persons with criminal convictions in a particular kind of position, a blanket disqualification of all applicants with such a conviction from the position will be considered job related and consistent with business necessity. For example, 18 U.S.C. § 1829(a)(1)(A) prohibits a federally insured bank from employing a person convicted of an offense involving fraud, dishonesty, breach of trust, or money laundering for a period of 10 years. Similarly, 5 U.S.C. § 7371 prohibits the employment of any person with a felony conviction as a federal law enforcement agent.[25]

State laws and regulations and local ordinances that prohibit the employment of persons with certain convictions, however, do not receive the same deference, because state and local law is preempted by Title VII, which is

---

24. *See El,* 479 F.3d at 243–44.

25. Persons convicted of certain offenses are also barred from airport jobs that grant unescorted access to secured areas. *See* 49 U.S.C. § 44936(b)(1); United States v. Baer, 324 F.3d 282 (4th Cir. 2003) (FAA has authority to add additional offenses to list set forth in statute). In addition, the federal Labor-Management Reporting and Disclosure Act prohibits persons convicted of certain felonies from being employed by unions and other labor organizations. *See* 29 U.S.C. § 504.

a federal law. This means that an employer who disqualifies persons with convictions from certain positions in accordance with a state law to that effect will still have to show that the exclusion is job related and consistent with business necessity. In North Carolina, for example, the Criminal Justice Education and Training Standards Commission will not certify for employment as a law enforcement officer anyone who has been convicted of a felony or of certain specified misdemeanors,[26] and accordingly, local government law enforcement agencies will not hire anyone with such a record. Theoretically, if the requirement caused a disparate impact on African Americans or Latinos wishing to become law enforcement officers and rejected applicants brought suit for race or national origin disparate impact discrimination, the North Carolina Department of Justice (of which the Criminal Justice Education and Training Standards Commission is a part) and the local government employer would have to show that the requirement is job related and consistent with business necessity. To the author's knowledge, however, this has never happened, presumably because the requirement seems to meet the standard so clearly. In contrast to the large number of cases involving absolute bans on hiring persons with criminal convictions, there are hardly any reported cases involving criminal conviction exclusions that are adopted with respect to particular positions.[27]

This finding bears out the advice that the EEOC gives in the 2012 Guidance. There, the EEOC says that it believes that employers will "consistently" meet the business necessity defense to a claim that a criminal record exclusion has resulted in disparate impact when the employer has developed what the EEOC calls a "targeted screen."[28] The targeted screen is the development of specific, narrowly tailored exclusionary criteria (such as an exclusion

---

26 *See* 12 N.C. Admin. Code 09B .0111.

27. In one of the few cases involving a targeted disqualification, a Mississippi telephone company showed a business need to exclude persons with conviction records for crimes involving dishonesty or fraud from consideration for "positions of trust" that handle money, material, property, or sensitive information because its fidelity bond would not cover such persons. *See* Avant v. S. Cent. Bell Tel. Co., 716 F.2d 1083, 1086 (5th Cir. 1983).

28. According to the 2012 Guidance, employers will also prove the business necessity defense when they have validated the criminal conviction exclusion for the particular position in accordance with the Uniform Guidelines on Employee Selection Procedures. The Commission recognizes, however, that employers will be unlikely to be able to validate a criminal record disqualification using this traditional method as

for financial crimes, or drug-related crimes, or crimes of violence) for a particular position based on a consideration of those factors identified in the *Green* case. An integral part of the EEOC's targeted screen exception is the notification of those who have been selected out by the exclusionary criteria that they have been screened out and the opportunity for them to demonstrate to the employer that the screen is misapplied in their particular circumstances. The *Green* factors, as incorporated into the targeted exclusion exception, are

1. the nature and gravity of the offense or conduct—in other words, how much harm it caused, what kind of behavior it involved (dishonesty versus violence, for example), and whether it was a felony or a misdemeanor;
2. the time that has passed since the offense or conduct or since the completion of the person's sentence; and
3. the nature of the job applied for based on an analysis of the job's duties, essential function, circumstances under which it is performed (under close supervision or not, interacting with coworkers or the public or not), and where the job is performed (out in public, in an office, in a client's home).

8.2.2 How to Construct a Targeted Screen

The rules governing how an employer may use the fact of an arrest differ from those governing how it may use a conviction. This difference stems from the fact that an arrest record in and of itself does not constitute evidence that an individual committed a crime or engaged in the behavior underlying the arrest. In addition, the arrest record frequently does not include the final disposition of the matter, which may be a dismissal or a finding of not guilty.[29] A conviction record, on the other hand, "may be considered reliable evidence that a person engaged in the conduct alleged since the standard of proof for a criminal conviction is 'beyond a reasonable doubt.'"[30]

---

there is a paucity of studies evaluating whether and in what way criminal convictions may be predictive of specific future behavior or conduct in a workplace.

29. *See EEOC Enforcement Guidance on the Consideration of Arrest and Conviction Records,* at 12.

30. *See EEOC Enforcement Guidance on the Consideration of Arrest and Conviction Records,* at 13.

8.2.2.1 Using Arrest Records

Employers must be exceedingly careful in using the fact of an arrest as a factor in an employment decision. If an employer is going to reject an applicant on the basis of an arrest, it must be able to show not only that the alleged conduct is related to the job in question but that it has also made a reasonable effort to determine whether or not the applicant did, in fact, engage in the underlying conduct. This investigation must include giving the applicant an opportunity to explain the circumstances of the arrest. A decision to exclude someone from consideration for employment based on the fact of an arrest, with nothing more, will not be considered job related and consistent with business necessity, even if the alleged conduct is related to the job in question.[31]

8.2.2.2 Using Conviction Records

When using a conviction record in making a hiring decision, an employer does not have to undertake an investigation into whether or not the applicant actually engaged in the alleged conduct. It may rely on the fact of the conviction itself as evidence that the applicant did so. Even in the case of a conviction, however, an employer must consider each set of circumstances *individually*, taking into account the nature and gravity of the offense, the amount of time that has passed since the conviction or the completion of the sentence, and the relationship of the offense to the nature of the job the applicant seeks.[32]

8.2.2.3 Assessing the Relationship between the Job and the Alleged Offense

Although the EEOC instructs employers to consider the nature and gravity of the offense and the amount of time that has passed since an arrest or conviction when using criminal history records in making an employment decision, the author has not found any cases that have turned on these factors. Instead, the determining factor seems to be the relationship between the conduct underlying the offense and the duties of the position. This is

---

31. *See EEOC Enforcement Guidance on the Consideration of Arrest and Conviction Records*, at 12.

32. *See EEOC Enforcement Guidance on the Consideration of Arrest and Conviction Records*, at 13.

true even with respect to the examples that the EEOC gives. The EEOC considered the following conduct to be job related:

- driving while intoxicated where the job is that of bus driver;[33]
- commission of burglary where the job is that of police officer;[34]
- sexual activity with an 18-year-old student (that is, conduct that was not statutory rape) where the job is that of high school teacher;[35] and
- credit card fraud where the job involves accepting credit card payment for room rentals and having supervised access to the personal belongings of those using the facility, although here the criminal conduct occurred 18 months earlier and the employer's screen targeted financial crimes that had occurred within the previous four years.[36]

In contrast, the EEOC did not consider fraudulent receipt of unemployment insurance benefits to be related to the job of bus driver.[37] In another example, it found that a conviction five years previously for misdemeanor fraud for exaggerating the cost of repairs covered by insurance was not relevant to a position with a company that disposed of sensitive files and documents for businesses, where the applicant had held the job for five years.[38]

Court cases provide somewhat more guidance. Courts have found that a conviction for dishonesty or fraud is related to the job of telephone

---

33. *See EEOC Policy Guidance on the Consideration of Arrest Records* Section III, Example 1.

34. *See EEOC Policy Guidance on the Consideration of Arrest Records,* Section III, Example 3. But compare that with Example 4, in which the EEOC does not find an arrest for burglary followed by dismissal of charges to be related to the job of police officer where there applicant explains that the arrest was a case of mistaken identity.

35. *See EEOC Policy Guidance on the Consideration of Arrest Records,* Section III, Example 5. In Example 6, however, the EEOC states that the rejection of a teacher arrested for statutory rape would not be justified as job related without further investigation where evidence showed that the teacher had only befriended a student who became pregnant by another student.

36. *See 2012 EEOC Enforcement Guidance on the Consideration of Arrest and Conviction Records,* at 18–19.

37. *See EEOC Policy Guidance on the Consideration of Arrest Records,* Section III, Example 2.

38. *See 2012 EEOC Enforcement Guidance on the Consideration of Arrest and Conviction Records,* at 19–20.

lineman when that conviction would prevent the applicant from coverage under a fidelity bond;[39] that independent of any criminal record, an applicant's known involvement in drug activity rendered him unqualified to be a police officer;[40] that a conviction for refusing military induction during the Vietnam War was not related to employment with a railroad as an office clerk;[41] that 14 arrests (without corresponding convictions) for reasons other than minor traffic violations do not automatically disqualify a person from employment as a sheet metal mechanic;[42] and that multiple convictions for violent crimes was relevant to a person's application to be a retail sales clerk.[43]

8.2.3 The Catch-22 for Applicants

It is highly likely that many applicants with criminal records do not know that it is unlawful under Title VII to disqualify applicants from employment on the basis of an arrest or conviction. What they do know is that an arrest or conviction will probably raise questions in employers' minds. For this reason, some job applicants do not mention their criminal history records unless directly asked, and many who are asked simply lie. But employers who are cognizant of their responsibilities under Title VII and who will give appropriate consideration to applicants with a criminal record will usually not condone lying and misrepresentation. As a result, applicants with undisclosed criminal records who would have been hired in spite of their criminal history may end up fired for falsifying their employment application. An employer may reject an applicant or terminate an employee who is untruthful on their employment application without fear that it is violating Title VII—unless, of course, the employer rejected or discharged African American applicants or employees who falsified their applications at a higher rate than whites who did so.[44]

---

39. *See* Avant v. S. Cent. Bell Tel. Co., 716 F.2d 1083, 1086 (5th Cir. 1983) (company refused to hire applicants with convictions of dishonesty or fraud because its fidelity bond would not cover such individuals).

40. *See* McCraven v. City of Chicago, 109 F. Supp. 2d 935, 943 (N.D. Ill. 2000).

41. *See* Green v. Mo. Pac. R.R., 523 F.2d 1290, 1298 (8th Cir. 1975).

42. *See* Gregory v. Litton Sys., Inc., 316 F. Supp. 401, 403 (C.D. Calif. 1970).

43. *See* Naugles v. Dollar Gen., Inc., 2010 WL 1254645 (E.D. Mo. 2010).

44. *See, e.g.*, Osborne v. Cleland, 620 F.2d 195, 198 (8th Cir. 1980) (employee of psychiatric hospital terminated for lying about conviction of offense of sexual procurement and not on account of racial animus); Redden v. Wal-Mart Stores, Inc.,

8.2.4 Litigating the Criminal Record Exclusion Disparate Impact Discrimination Claim

For an applicant who has been rejected on the basis of an arrest or conviction to succeed in a disparate impact claim, he or she must show that the employer has a practice or policy of rejecting applicants with criminal records generally (or with criminal records of a particular kind) and that this practice has in fact caused applicants belonging to a protected class to be excluded from jobs (or a subset of jobs) with the employer. It is not sufficient for the applicant to show only that there are statistical disparities in the employer's workforce. The applicant must show "statistical evidence of a kind and degree sufficient to show that the practice in question has caused the exclusion of applicants for jobs or promotions because of their membership in a protected group."[45] The courts have made clear that it is not enough to say that African Americans are arrested at a higher rate than Caucasians in the general population and that an employer who employs a lower percentage of African Americans than exist in the general population is discriminating. The fact that there are no or few members of minority groups holding certain positions within a given employer's workforce may be due to factors other than the employer's selection practices, such as a lack of qualified nonwhite applicants in the labor market. A plaintiff must show that it is *the challenged practice* that disproportionally disqualifies a minority group.[46]

Take the case of an applicant for a position as a Pennsylvania State Police cadet. The applicant's official criminal record had been expunged, but he

---

832 F. Supp. 1262, 1266–68 (N.D. Ind. 1993); Redd v. Fisher Controls, 814 F. Supp. 547, 552–53 (W.D. Texas 1992); Horton v. Nicholson, 435 F. Supp. 2d 429, 438–39 (E.D. Pa. 2006) (employee of VA Hospital terminated for lying about conviction for entering military base using false ID and terms of forced resignation from previous employment); Jimerson v. Kisco Co., Inc., 404 F. Supp. 338 (D.C. Mo. 1975); King v. Girard Bank, 1978 WL 79 (E.D. Pa. 1978). *Cf.* Cross v. U.S. Postal Serv., 483 F. Supp. 1050, 1052 (E.D. Mo. 1979) (court noted with approval language on the application that encouraged disclosure of criminal records by saying, "NOTE a conviction does not automatically mean you cannot be appointed. What you were convicted of, and how long ago, are important. Give all of the facts so that a decision can be made.").

45. *See* Foxworth v. Pa. State Police, 402 F. Supp. 2d 523, 534 (E.D. Pa. 2005), *quoting* Watson v. Fort Worth Bank & Trust, 487 U.S. 977, 994–95 (1988), *aff'd*, 228 F. App'x 151, 156–57 (3d Cir. 2007).

46. *See, e.g.*, McCraven v. City of Chicago, 109 F. Supp. 2d 935, 944 (N.D. Ill. 2000).

truthfully answered on his application that he had stolen from a previous employer. The Pennsylvania State Police had a policy of automatically rejecting any applicant who had engaged in criminal behavior, regardless of whether or not the applicant had been arrested or convicted. The plaintiff's application was therefore rejected. His disparate impact claim failed because his proffer of statistics showing racial disparity in the makeup of the Pennsylvania State Police force was not linked in any way to the criminal behavior policy. In fact, of the other 43 applicants disqualified on the basis of criminal behavior, 41 were white and two were African American.[47] In another case, the Fourth Circuit held that an applicant who refused to answer a questionnaire that included an inquiry about family criminal history could not maintain a disparate impact claim where all she offered was speculation that African American employees would tend to have less favorable answers and would likely be rejected or terminated.[48]

If a rejected applicant does make a prima facie case, the burden shifts to the employer. The employer must now show that the practice in question is justified by business necessity.

8.2.5 A Note on Criminal History Checks and Disparate Treatment Claims under Title VII

The business necessity defense applies only when an applicant claims that a facially neutral policy against hiring persons with an arrest or conviction record has an adverse impact on African American or Latino candidates. This is a disparate impact claim. It is different from one based on a theory of disparate treatment, where an applicant claims, for example, that the employer has rejected African American applicants with conviction records but not white applicants with conviction records.

Perhaps because the standards for the use of arrest and conviction records in employment decisions are now well established, many of the more recent cases alleging unlawful discrimination based on an employer's consideration of an arrest or conviction have been brought as intentional discrimination (disparate treatment) cases rather than under a disparate impact theory. In one Oklahoma case, for example, the human resources director of a community agency was dismissed after her employer learned

---

47. *See Foxworth*, 402 F. Supp. 2d at 529, 534–35.
48. *See* Walls v. City of Petersburg, 895 F.2d 188, 191 (4th Cir. 1990).

that she had a prior arrest and deferred sentence for obtaining money by means of a false and bogus check. The employee charged that the arrest was a pretext for race discrimination, claiming that the employer had not fired other employees with criminal histories. The court found that it was true that the employer treated other employees with criminal histories differently but that this was because none of them were in management, as the plaintiff was, and none had access to sensitive personal information of other employees, such as Social Security and bank account numbers, as a human resources director does. Accordingly, the employer had not violated Title VII.[49] In an Indiana case, a manager for a company that provided claims processing and customer service to Medicare beneficiaries was fired after she pleaded guilty to a charge of felony drug possession. The company's policy was not to employ felons. The plaintiff claimed, however, that she was treated differently than other employees convicted of crimes because of her age and gender. The Seventh Circuit found for the employer because the other employees convicted of crimes were not similarly situated but had been convicted of misdemeanor charges.[50]

---

49. Davis v. Cent. Okla. Cmty. Action Agency, Inc., 2010 WL 56142 at **5 (W.D. Okla. 2010).

50. Miller v. Adminastar Fed., Inc., 179 F. App'x 967, 970, 2006 WL 1233099 at **2 (7th Cir. 2006). *See also* Riley v. Sch. Bd. Union Parish, 2010 WL 2008150 (5th Cir. 2010) (African American substitute English teacher terminated when white teacher certified in English applied for position sued under Title VII and 42 U.S.C. § 1981, claiming that real reason was b/c of marijuana conviction. Her claim that white teachers with criminal convictions were not dismissed did not hold up as circumstances were not the same); Ramos v. Equiserve, 146 F. App'x 565, 567–68, 2005 WL 1981781 at **2–**3(3d Cir. 2005) (Employee dismissed after background check revealed arrests for theft and grand larceny; employer offered to reinstate employee upon proof that charges were dismissed. Employee claimed arrest was pretext for Title VII race and national origin disparate treatment. Court found (1) only evidence that use of arrest record had adverse impact was dismissal of plaintiff and (2) no evidence that employer used hiring policies about arrest and conviction records in a way that favored similarly situated non-minorities); Naugles v. Dollar Gen., Inc., 2010 WL 1254645 (E.D. Mo. 2010) (retailer not liable for Title VII discrimination against applicant with multiple convictions for violent crimes and theft where it applied its criminal history policy in a consistent and nondiscriminatory way).

8.2.6 Best Practices for Employers Who Do Criminal Records Checks

The bottom-line rule about using an applicant's criminal history in making a hiring decision is this: the use of absolute bars or blanket disqualifications of persons with an arrest or conviction record is prohibited, but an employer *may* consider arrest and conviction records in deciding whether to hire a *given* individual for a *particular* position.

The use of criminal record background checks of job applicants is widespread in North Carolina local government. Most North Carolina public employers, however, do not narrowly tailor the questions that they ask applicants about their criminal history. While they may be aware of the EEOC's prohibition on using arrest and conviction records as absolute bars to employment, they nonetheless continue to ask applicants to disclose either all arrests and convictions or all convictions. With that information in hand, they assess whether or not any of the candidate's previous encounters with the justice system merit his or her disqualification from the particular position. After the issuance of the EEOC's 2012 Guidance, this will no longer suffice. Exclusions on the basis of criminal history should now be individualized for each position before the recruitment and selection process begins, and candidates should only be asked about convictions for particular offenses identified as relevant for the particular position. Not only should the exclusionary criteria be limited to offenses relevant to the particular job duties, but employers should remember that a targeted screen will include a reasonable time limitation. A lesser offense should be the basis for exclusion for a shorter period than a more serious offense. No candidate should be turned away without being given the opportunity to explain the particular circumstances of his or her conviction and to show how exclusion would be mistaken in the candidate's case.

In the 2012 Guidance, the EEOC includes some additional best practices that employers should adopt. In developing the targeted exclusionary criminal history screen, employers should keep a record of the rational and justifications for identifying particular criminal offenses as relevant and for determining the exclusion period, including records of any research or legal consultations considered in drafting its policies. City and county managers and their human resources professionals should not forget the importance of educating everyone involved in the hiring process about the way in which criminal history inquiries may violate Title VII.[51]

Finally, employers must remember that if they are going to make an inquiry into an applicant's criminal history, they should not do so lightly and without clear purpose, because the mere gathering of such information poses risks for an employer. As with pre-offer inquiries into medical conditions, the EEOC will presume that even in the absence of other evidence of discrimination, the employer has asked the question because it intends to use the information in making the hiring decision. *For this reason, employers would be wise not to ask questions about criminal history on their application forms but to wait instead until the candidate progresses further in the selection process.*

8.3 Credit History Checks

Public employers do relatively few credit history checks compared with their use of criminal record checks. For the most part, governmental employers limit the investigation of an applicant's credit history to those positions that involve the handling of money or access to confidential information. A 2010 Society for Human Resource Management survey of public and private member employers found that 91 percent of those employers surveyed who conduct credit checks do so only for job candidates for positions with fiduciary and financial responsibility, whether it is handling cash, doing accounting, or overseeing compliance or technology. Forty-six percent of those surveyed conduct credit checks on applicants for senior management positions, while 34 percent do so for positions that have access to confidential information about other employees. In contrast, only 13 percent of employers surveyed conduct credit background investigations on all applicants. Three percent conduct credit checks on those who work in health care and will have access to drugs, and 8 percent conduct credit checks on those working in security.[52]

---

51. *See EEOC Enforcement Guidance on the Consideration of Arrest and Conviction Records,* at 25–26.

52. See Society for Human Resource Management Survey, *Background Checking: the Implications of Credit Background Checks on the Decision to Hire* (SHRM Poll), September 22, 2010, www.shrm.org/Research/SurveyFindings/Articles/Pages/

8.3.1 Reasons Why Employers Perform Credit History Checks

Some employers believe that a person's credit history is a window into an applicant's judgment, at least as it relates to decision making about the spending of money. When an applicant's credit history reveals significant indebtedness, employers are typically interested to know whether the debt is the result of a single event, such as a serious medical condition, or whether there are multiple causes and instances of indebtedness. Where there are multiple instances, employers may look at whether all of the transactions occurred during a single time period or whether the applicant has been in debt for a significant period of his or her adult life. Employers also examine credit history to guard against hiring persons who may be tempted to engage in fraudulent financial activity—embezzlement, for example—at the employer's expense. In support of this theory, the Association of Certified Fraud Examiners has reported that those who commit fraud tend to exhibit certain behavior prior to the fraud—36 percent live beyond their means, and 27 percent have been experiencing financial difficulties.[53]

Others, however, argue that for most positions, credit scores have little or no relevance to a job's requirements and thus are poor predictors of any given applicant's success in a position. A bankruptcy, for example, results in a very negative credit score. But studies show that 85 percent of bankruptcy filings occur due to income loss, serious medical conditions, and divorce, circumstances that are not job related with respect to any position.[54] Even a representative of the TransUnion credit bureau has admitted in testimony before Congress that there is no research that shows a statistical correlation

---

BackgroundCheckingImplications.aspx. Note that the membership of the Society for Human Resource Management is primarily from the private sector.

53. *See* Association of Certified Fraud Examiners, *Report to the Nations on Occupational Fraud and Abuse, 2012*, at 5, www.acfe.com/rttn.aspx.

54. *See* Elizabeth Warren, *The Over-Consumption Myth and Other Tales of Economics, Law, and Morality*, 82 WASH. U.L.Q. 1485, 1510 (2004), *citing* the Consumer Bankruptcy Project 2001 in notes 98 and 27. See also the testimony of Adam Klein, Esq., Outten & Gold, LLP, before the U.S. House of Representatives Committee on Financial Services and Consumer Credit, September 23, 2010; Statement of Chi Chi Wu, Esq., National Consumer Law Center, before the United States Equal Employment Opportunity Commission Meeting of October 20, 2010, on the Employer Use of Credit History as a Screening Tool, www.eeoc.gov/eeoc/meetings/10-20-10/wu.cfm.

between what is in a person's credit report and the person's likely job performance or the likelihood that he or she will commit fraud.[55]

A study of the use of credit checks for employment purposes found that credit history information does not even reflect an applicant's likely success in positions related to financial services and the handling of money. The study, funded by a large employer, compared each of the specific categories of credit information in employees' credit reports with performance evaluations and termination data. The study showed that the performance evaluations of employees with poor credit were not statistically different from those of employees with better credit scores except in one situation: those employees who were more frequently reported as being 30-days late on a payment had *better* performance evaluations than those who had fewer or no late payments.[56]

Citing reasons such as these, both federal and state lawmakers have introduced legislation to prohibit the use of credit histories for employment purposes except in connection with positions that involve the handling of money or sensitive information. As of May 2012, seven states—California,[57] Connecticut,[58] Hawaii,[59] Illinois,[60] Maryland,[61] Oregon[62] and Washington[63]—had laws limiting the use of credit information in employment. The National Council of State Legislatures reports that as of May 1, 2012, 38 bills limiting the use of credit information in employment had been

---

55. See Andrew Martin, *As a Hiring Filter, Credit Checks Draw Questions,* N.Y. Times, April 10, 2010, at B1, www.nytimes.com/2010/04/10/business/10credit.html, on the testimony of Eric Rosenberg, Director of State Government Relations, TransUnion, LLC .

56. See Shawn Fremstad, *Discrediting Workers: How Credit Reports are Distorting the Job Market, Prolonging Unemployment, and Denying Equal Opportunity to Workers,* Demos, 2010, at 1–2, www.demos.org/publication/discrediting-workers-how-credit-reports-are-distorting-job-market-prolonging-unemploymen, citing Jerry K. Palmer and Laura L. Koppes, Investigation of Credit History Validity at Predicting Performance and Turnover, paper presented at meeting of Society for Industrial and Organizational Psychology, Chicago, Illinois, April 3, 2004.

57. *See* Cal. Lab. Code § 1024.5.

58. *See* Conn. Gen. Stat. § 31-51tt.

59. *See* Hawaii Rev. Stat. § 378-2.7.

60. *See* 820 Ill. Comp. Stat. § 70/1.

61. *See* Md. Code, Lab. & Empl. § 3-711.

62. *See* Or. Rev. Stat. § 659A.885

63. *See* Rev. Code. Wash. § 19.182.020.

introduced in the 2012 legislative sessions of 20 states and the District of Columbia.[64] In the 111th Congress (2009–2011), U.S. Representative Steve Cohen of Tennessee introduced House Bill 3149, the Equal Employment for All Act, which would have prohibited employers from using consumer credit checks of applicants and current employees in making employment decisions. The House Financial Services Committee held hearings on the bill, but it did not move out of committee before the end of the session and is now dead.

8.3.2 The Legal Status of Credit Checks for Employment Purposes

Under Title VII, it is unlawful to use credit history as an employment screening tool where its use will have an adverse impact on a protected group, mostly likely a minority group or women. In other words, where the use of credit histories—like the use of criminal records—will have a disparate impact on a protected group, that practice will violate Title VII unless the employer can show that investigation into applicants' credit scores is job related and consistent with business necessity. The law, therefore, falls between the positions of employers and consumer advocates, allowing the use of credit history in hiring decisions but only where the need for a good credit history is closely tied to a particular job's duties.

It is likely that the use of credit scores in making hiring decisions will have a disparate impact on minority groups and women. In general, African Americans, Latinos, single women who are heads of households, and persons who reside in low-income or predominately minority census tracts have lower credit scores than other segments of the population.[65] One study by the federal government showed an average credit risk score for Asians to be 54.8, for non-Hispanic whites 54.0, for Hispanics 38.2, and for African Americans 25.6. For those younger than age 30, the average score was

---

64. *See* National Council of State Legislators, *Use of Credit Information in Employment 2012 Legislation*, updated November 16, 2012, www.ncsl.org/issues-research/banking/use-of-credit-info-in-employ-2012-legis.aspx.

65. *See* Statement by Sandra F. Braunstein, Director, Division of Consumer and Community Affairs, Board of Governors of the Federal Reserve System, before the Subcommittee on Financial Institutions and Consumer Credit, Financial Services Committee, U.S. House of Representatives, March 24, 2010, at 10–11, www.federalreserve.gov/newsevents/testimony/braunstein20100324a.pdf.

34.3, while the average score for those aged 62 or older was 68.1.[66] In light of the foregoing statistics, employers should avoid any use of credit history to screen applicants for employment unless the employer is confident that credit information is necessary to evaluate applicants for a particular job. As the EEOC advises:

> Inquiry into an applicant's current or past assets, liabilities, or credit rating, including bankruptcy or garnishment, refusal or cancellation of bonding, car ownership, rental or ownership of a house, length of residence at an address, charge accounts, furniture ownership, or bank accounts generally should be avoided because they tend to impact more adversely on minorities and females. Exceptions exist if the employer can show that such information is essential to the particular job in question.[67]

There have been relatively few reported cases addressing the question of when a credit history is job related and necessary. Courts have found the practice of investigating credit histories justified where

- the position involved in the sentencing and disposition of criminals required that the employer guard against the potential for corruption,[68]

66. *See* Board of Governors of the Federal Reserve System, *Report to the Congress on Credit Scoring and Its Effects on the Availability and Affordability of Credit,* August 2007, at O-13, www.federalreserve.gov/boarddocs/RptCongress/creditscore/creditscore.pdf.

67. U.S. Equal Employment Opportunity Commission, *Pre-Employment Inquiries and Credit Rating or Economic Status,* www.eeoc.gov/laws/practices/inquiries_credit.cfm. *See also* Wallace v. Debron Corp., 494 F.2d 674, 677 (8th Cir. 1974) (company's policy of terminating employees whose wages were garnished more than once in a 12-month period had disproportionate effect on numbers of African American employees discharged and would violate Title VII unless company showed that its policy fostered employee productivity and that there was no acceptable alternative); Johnson v. Pike Corp. of Am., 332 F. Supp. 490, 494–95 (C.D. Calif. 1971) (employer's practice of discharging employees whose wages had been garnished had disparate impact on minority groups). *Cf.* Friend v. Leidinger, 588 F.2d 61 (4th Cir. 1978) (small sample size precluded finding that fire department's policy of reprimanding firefighters when their paychecks were garnished adversely affected African American firefighters).

68. *See* Walls v. City of Petersburg, 895 F.2d 188, 194 (4th Cir. 1990) (note that this is a privacy rather than a Title VII issue, in this case).

- the state's interest in deterring corruption and conflicts of interest was substantial enough to justify requiring all city employees with annual salaries over $25,000 to disclose financial information, [69]
- the job was with a bank and would involve handling large amounts of cash,[70]
- the position of superintendent of schools incorporated the duties of the chief fiscal officer of the school system.[71]

The EEOC's interest in the potential adverse impact of credit checks has increased recently. In 2009, the EEOC filed a class action lawsuit against the Freeman Companies (a convention and corporate events marketer) alleging that the company violated Title VII by engaging in a pattern and practice of rejecting job applicants on the basis of their credit histories. The EEOC alleged that the Freeman Companies' use of credit histories has had an adverse impact on African American applicants.[72] In October 2010, the EEOC held a special meeting on employers' use of credit histories as screening tools and solicited testimony from employer and employee stakeholders and advocates. Two months later, in December 2010, the EEOC filed a lawsuit against Kaplan Higher Education Corporation (a for-profit university) on the same basis as its suit against the Freeman Companies.[73]

---

69. *See* Barry v. City of New York, 712 F.2d 154(2d Cir.), *cert denied*, 464 U.S. 1017 (1983) (also a privacy case). *See also* Fraternal Order of Police, Lodge 5 v. Philadelphia, 812 F.2d 105, 112–13 (3d Cir. 1987) (strong public interest in avoiding corruption made reasonable required disclosure of all debts over $1,000 and all gifts and income by police officers applying for positions to investigate intra–police department corruption) (privacy case).

70. *See* EEOC v. United Va. Bank/Seaboard Nat'l, 1977 WL 15340 (E.D. Va. 1977).

71. *See* Thomas v. Troy City Bd. of Educ., 302 F. Supp. 2d 1303, 1308 (M.D. Ala. 2004).

72. *See* EEOC Press Release, EEOC Files Nationwide Hiring Discrimination Lawsuit Against Freeman (October 1, 2009), www.eeoc.gov/eeoc/newsroom/release/10-1-09b.cfm. The federal district court subsequently granted the Freeman Companies' partial motion to dismiss with respect to all claims of a discriminatory failure to hire that occurred more than 300 days before the individual claimants filed a charge with the EEOC and partial motion for summary judgment dismissing all claims not included in the original charge made more than 300 days before notice was provided of the expanded investigation. *See* EEOC v. Freeman, 2011 WL 337339 (D. Md. 2011), *and* EEOC v. Freeman, 2010 WL 1728847 (D. Md. 2010).

73. *See* EEOC Press Release, EEOC Files Nationwide Hiring Discrimination Lawsuit Against Kaplan Higher Education Authority (December 21, 2010), www.eeoc.gov/eeoc/newsroom/release/12-21-10a.cfm. Here, too, the court granted the employer's

At approximately the same time, a private law firm, in conjunction with the Lawyers' Committee for Civil Rights, filed a class action lawsuit against the University of Miami and its School of Medicine, alleging that the medical school's use of credit histories to reject job applicants without establishing their job relatedness and the business necessity for their use has resulted in disparate impact on African Americans in violation of Title VII.[74]

8.3.2.1 Bankruptcy as a Basis for Rejecting an Applicant

Although an applicant might be disqualified on the basis of a bankruptcy filing under Title VII if the employer could show a nexus between the circumstances resulting in the bankruptcy and the job in question, the U.S. Bankruptcy Code would not allow it. Section 525(a) of Title 11 of the United States Code (Title 11 contains the U.S. Bankruptcy Code) provides:

> . . . *a governmental unit may not* . . . deny employment to, terminate the employment of, or discriminate with respect to employment against, a person that is or has been a debtor under this title or a bankrupt or a debtor under the Bankruptcy Act, or another person with whom such bankrupt or debtor has been associated, solely because such bankrupt or debtor is or has been a debtor under this title . . . or has not paid a debt that is dischargeable in the case under this title or that was discharged under the Bankruptcy Act.[75]

---

partial motion to dismiss with respect to decisions made more than 300 days prior to the filing of a discrimination charge with the EEOC. *See* EEOC v. Kaplan Higher Educ. Corp., 790 F. Supp. 2d 619 (N.D. Ohio 2011).

74. *See* Appolon v. Univ. of Miami and Leonard M. Miller Sch. of Med., Case 1:10-CV-24166-XXXX, United States District Court for the Southern District of Florida, Miami Division, filed November 22, 2010. For a copy of the complaint, go to www.creditdiscrimination.net/images/stories/documents/Appolon_v._University_of_Miami_complaint_cv-24166.pdf. The district court subsequently dismissed the case with respect to Mary Olivera, the second named plaintiff and class representative for Latinos claiming adverse impact discrimination in hiring on the basis of credit checks and thus to the entire class of Latinos. *See* Appolon v. Univ. of Miami and Leonard M. Miller Sch. of Med., Case No. 1:10-cv-24166-CIV-UNGARO/SIMONTON, United States District Court for the Southern District of Florida, Miami Division, Defendant's Motion to Dismiss Granted in Part, March 14, 2011 (Ungaro, U., J.). For a copy of the memorandum of decision, go to www.workplaceclassaction.com/credit%20check%20blog%20post.pdf.

75. *See* 11 U.S.C. § 525(a). *See also* Potter v. City of Hanceville, 354 B.R. 301 (N.D. Ala. 2006) (denying defendants' motions for summary judgment because it was a

Note that private employers are not bound by this prohibition. Like Section 525(a), which governs public employers, Section 525(b) prohibits private employers from discriminating in employment against someone who has filed for bankruptcy. But it omits the language "deny employment to" found in Section 525(a). The courts have concluded that the Bankruptcy Code makes it unlawful for a public employer to refuse to hire someone because of bankruptcy but allows private employers to refuse to hire such persons, although they too are prohibited from discriminating against current employees in personal bankruptcy. In so holding, the courts have applied traditional rules of statutory construction. They do not attempt to explain why Congress would have made such a distinction between the public and private sectors.[76]

8.3.3 Another Catch-22 for Applicants

Fearing that some employers might reject them on the basis of their poor credit histories, applicants sometimes lie on their employment applications, declaring that they have never defaulted on a loan or declared bankruptcy when in fact they have. Others refuse to explain delinquencies or answer other questions raised by their credit histories when asked. These applicants would serve themselves better if they were honest and forthright about their financial circumstances. In almost all instances where an applicant lies or refuses to explain negative credit reports, the employer rejects the applicant because of his or her lack of honesty. While employers may not reject applicants on the basis of poor credit history, it is clear that they may reject applicants who have not been truthful about their credit history.[77]

---

question of material fact as to whether city council fired police chief based on his filing for personal bankruptcy).

76. *See* Rea v. Federated Investors, ___ F.3d ___, 2010 WL 5094250, *2–*3 (3d Cir. 2010); Burnett v. Stewart Title, Inc., 431 B.R. 894, 897–99 (S.D. Tex. 2010); Myers v. TooJay's Mgmt. Corp., 419 B.R. 51, 56–59 (M.D. Fla. 2009); *In re* Stinson, 285 B.R. 239, 240–43 (W.D. Va. 2002); Fiorani v. Caci, 192 B.R. 401, 404–07 (E.D. Va. 1996). *Contra* Leary v. Warnaco, Inc. 251 B.R. 656, 658 (S.D.N.Y. 2000).

77. *See* Terry v. Elec. Data Sys. Corp., 940 F. Supp. 378, 385–87 (D. Mass. 1996) (in race discrimination case, defendant employer's motion for summary judgment granted where employer showed that it did not reject plaintiff because of his credit problems per se but because when asked, plaintiff refused to explain why he was delinquent on a loan). *See also* Delgado v. Ashcroft, 368 F. Supp. 2d 3, 8 (D.C. Cir. 2004) (genuine issue of material fact existed in disparate treatment case as to whether employer's

Employers who want to use credit histories in making employment decisions should ask themselves the following questions.

1. Is there a clear relationship between a strong credit history and the good financial practices it presupposes and the job in question? Is the need for a person with a good credit history to fill the position dictated by business necessity?

Unless investigation into applicants' credit scores is job related and consistent with business necessity, it will violate Title VII.

2. Is the inquiry into credit history done consistently (that is, for all applicants for the position and not just for African American or Latino applicants)?

If an employer assumes that whites tend to have good credit histories while African Americans do not, and the employer only runs credit checks on African American applicants, it will violate Title VII's prohibition on disparate treatment, as well.

3. Where a rejected applicant has a bad credit score, is the decision to reject an applicant being made on the application as a whole or only on the basis of the credit report? Where an applicant has a poor credit history, does the employer give the applicant an opportunity to explain his or her individual circumstances before rejecting the applicant on this basis?

Because there is so little demonstrated correlation between credit history and job performance and because credit problems may be caused by so many factors outside an applicant's control (layoffs and medical conditions, for example), it is important that employers give applicants an opportunity to explain the circumstances giving rise to credit issues. This is true even where investigation of the applicant's credit history is job related and consistent with business necessity, since as a statistical matter, the credit inquiry will still likely have an adverse impact on African Americans and Latinos. Giving applicants an opportunity to explain their individual circumstances should allow some individuals with poor credit to remain competitive for the position in question.

---

articulated nondiscriminatory reason for not hiring applicant—that he was not candid about financial situation or debts—was pretext for discrimination).

8.4 Reference Checks

Although the law does not require North Carolina public employers to do reference checks, almost all do. And why wouldn't an employer follow up on an applicant's professional and personal references? Checking references can not only help an employer distinguish among applicants but can also provide a legitimate, nondiscriminatory reason as to why an employer rejected a particular applicant when someone challenges a decision as discriminatory and in violation of Title VII, the ADA, the Age Discrimination in Employment Act (ADEA), or the Uniformed Services Employment and Reemployment Rights Act (USERRA).[78] Conversations with an applicant's professional references can provide a defense in the event that the person commits an act that harms another employee or a member of the public during the course of employment.[79] Although as of the date of this book no North Carolina court has found that employers have a general duty to check the references of an applicant or employee, other states have done so. In those states, employers who have conducted reference checks have fared better defending themselves against claims of negligent hiring than those who did not.

---

78. *See* Motley v. Donovan, 319 F. App'x 168, 170–71 (3d Cir. 2009) (employee's receipt of lowest job performance rating among applicants and receipt of "no response" to question about whether evaluator would recommend employee for position he applied for were legitimate, nondiscriminatory reasons for not selecting employee for vacant position of community builder); Danzl v. N. St. Paul-Maplewood-Oakdale Indep. Sch. Dist., 706 F.2d 813, 813–16, 817 (8th Cir. 1983) (school district's reasons for not hiring female candidate as high school principal were legitimate and nondiscriminatory where the male candidate who was hired was better qualified and female candidate had received unfavorable reference checks); Tamez v. Chertoff, 2009 WL 242306 at **5–**7 (S.D. Tex. 2009) (employer's legitimate, nondiscriminatory reasons for not selecting an applicant were not pretextual where other applicants demonstrated better capabilities, were better qualified, and received higher marks on reference checks than the applicant); Wheatley v. Baptist Hosp. of Miami, Inc., 16 F. Supp. 2d 1356, 1361 (S.D. Fla.,1998) (hospital's proffered nondiscriminatory reasons for refusing to hire male applicant as medical-surgical/gynecology nurse—lack of experience, extremely negative references from past employers, and his inappropriate behavior during the interview—were not pretexts for gender discrimination). *Cf.* King v. N.H. Dep't of Res. and Econ. Dev., 562 F.2d 80, 83 (1st Cir. 1977) (single negative reference was not real reason for refusal to hire plaintiff female job applicant).

79. On negligent hiring, see Section 8.1.1, above.

8.4.1 No Liability for Defamation for Employers Who Give Honest Evaluations of Former Employees

Unfortunately for employers, however, reference checks are frequently of minimal use. Fearing that former employees may sue them for defamation if they provide anything other than a stellar job reference, many former employers will provide no more than a confirmation of the fact that a given individual worked for them in a particular capacity for a specified period of time and will omit any kind of evaluative or descriptive information about that person's performance in the job. This fear is misplaced. North Carolina law limits the liability of an employer for defamation when it discloses information to a prospective employer about a current or former employee's job history or job performance.[80] Section 1-539.1 of the North Carolina General Statutes (hereinafter G.S.) defines the term "job performance" to include the suitability of the employee for reemployment; the employee's skills, abilities, and traits as they relate to suitability for future employment and in the case of former employees, the reason for separation. Public employers have additional authority to share information about current or former employees' job performance among themselves through an exception to the municipal and county personnel privacy statutes. G.S. 160A-168(c)(5) and G.S. 153A-98(c)(5) both allow disclosure of otherwise confidential personnel information—such as that related to performance and evaluations—to any "official of an agency of the State or federal government, or any political subdivision of the State" when that information is "necessary and essential to the pursuance of a proper function of the inspecting agency." Checking an employee's suitability for employment in a particular position is just such a proper function.[81]

8.4.2 Reference Checks and the Right to "Informational Privacy"

Very few applicants or employees have ever mounted a legal challenge to an employer's right to ask former employers and others who know an applicant questions about his or her personal qualities or suitability for employment, generally or for a particular type of job. In one 1994 case, a union representing employees of the Internal Revenue Service (IRS) challenged an

80. *See* G.S. 1-539.1.

81. *See* David M. Lawrence, Public Records Law for North Carolina Local Governments 175–76 (2d ed. 2009).

IRS employee questionnaire about personal drug and alcohol use on the grounds that it violated the employees' constitutional right to privacy. The Fifth Circuit held that the employees did not have a reasonable expectation of privacy in that information not being disclosed to their government employer, given that they held positions of trust and that the information would not be publicly disclosed.[82]

In 2011, the United States Supreme Court addressed this issue in a case brought by employees of a federal contractor. The plaintiffs in *National Aeronautics and Space Administration v. Nelson* were employees of the federal government contractor that manages the Jet Propulsion Laboratory (JPL).[83] JPL is a federally funded research facility owned by the National Aeronautics and Space Administration (NASA) and operated by the California Institute of Technology (Cal Tech) under a contract with NASA. None of the people who work at JPL are NASA employees; all are employees of Cal Tech. Prior to 2004, Cal Tech did not have a uniform background check policy in place for JPL employees. In 2004, however, the federal government adopted a requirement that employees of government contractors who have long-term access to federal facilities complete the U.S. Government's standard background check for federal employees in non-sensitive positions. Twenty-eight JPL employees brought suit against NASA, claiming that the background check process violated their constitutional right to what they deemed "informational privacy."

At issue before the Supreme Court were two sets of questions, both of which are frequently asked in both the public and private sectors as part of employment applications and reference checks. The first set asked the employee whether they have used, possessed, supplied, or manufactured illegal drugs during the previous year and, if the answer is yes, to explain and to include information about "any treatment or counseling received." The second set involved questions asked of an employee's references and former landlords. The references are asked whether they have any reason to question the employee's honesty or trustworthiness and, if so, to explain. The references are also asked whether they know of any adverse information concerning the employee's violations of the law, financial integrity,

---

82. Nat'l Treasury Emps. Union v. U.S. Dep't of the Treasury, 25 F.3d 237, 244–45 (5th Cir. 1994).

83. *See* Nat'l Aeronautics and Space Admin. v. Nelson, 2011 WL 148254 (U.S. Sup. Ct. January 19, 2011).

abuse of alcohol and/or drugs, mental or emotional stability, general behavior or conduct, or other matters and, if so, to explain.

Although the case was brought by employees of a private-sector federal contractor, its holding directly applies to public employees, as the Supreme Court rejected the plaintiffs' claim that they had a greater expectation of privacy in the information sought because they were private citizens and not government employees. NASA and the federal government were acting as proprietors and managers of operations, and the work done by JPL employees was the same as work done by federal employees in other NASA facilities. Thus, the standard that applied to federal employees also applied to JPL employees.

The Court assumed without deciding that citizens have a constitutional right to "informational privacy" and held that questions such as those that ask an employee about his or her own illegal drug use and questions posed to an applicant's or an employee's references about an individual's honesty, trustworthiness, financial integrity, mental or emotional condition, or the like are reasonable for the government to ask when acting as a manager of operations or employer—provided, however, that the information gathered is protected by a statute regulating public disclosure.

In the *NASA* case, the information collected by the government was protected against unwarranted disclosures and publication by the federal Privacy Act (5 U.S.C. § 552a), which authorizes the federal government to keep records pertaining to an individual only when relevant and necessary to an end required to be accomplished by law and which gives individuals the right to access their records and request amendments. The Privacy Act also provides that with certain limited exceptions, the government may not disclose records pertaining to an individual without that individual's consent. The Privacy Act, the Court held, provided sufficient safeguards against public disclosure to render the background investigation reasonable.

North Carolina local governments are not covered by the federal Privacy Act. But the provisions of the state's various personnel privacy statutes provide local government employees and applicants with protections similar to those offered by the federal Privacy Act. G.S. 160A-168 and G.S. 153A-98, the respective municipal and county personnel privacy statutes, provide that any information gathered by the city or county relating to the application, selection, or non-selection of an employee is confidential and not open to the public except in certain limited circumstances, such as when another government agency can show that the information is "necessary and essential to the pursuance of a proper function of the inspecting agency" or in response to a court order. Similar provisions may be found in the statutes governing access to the personnel files of area mental health authority employees (G.S. 122C-158), water and sewer authority employees (G.S. 162A-6.1), community college employees (G.S. 115D-27–115D-30), public health authority employees (G.S. 130A-45.9) and public hospital employees (G.S. 131E-257.2).[84]

8.5 Internet Background Checks

Employers are turning to the Internet for supplemental information about job applicants with increasing frequency. Some employers enter applicant names into Internet search engines such as Google and see what turns up; others go to social media sites such as Facebook and LinkedIn to view applicants' profiles. Neither federal and state employment laws nor general privacy laws prohibit an employer from using an Internet search engine to find online information about a job applicant, and it is lawful for an employer to view information that is publicly posted on a job applicant's social networking profile. But such a search will most likely disclose certain types of information about an applicant, and simply having that information could put the employer at risk. As discussed at length elsewhere in this book, antidiscrimination laws protect individuals from discrimination by employers on the basis of personal characteristics such as race, gender, religion, disability, and age.[85] In addition, a North Carolina law protects individuals from discrimination in employment on the basis of the individual's lawful use of a lawful product. The risk for an employer that uses the Internet or social media sites to access information about an applicant is that the EEOC or a jury in a discrimination lawsuit may consider the fact

---

84. There are no statutes and no case law governing access to the personnel records of employees of local Alcohol Beverage Control boards or employees of councils of government. Those agencies may follow the personnel privacy provisions of G.S. 160A-168 and G.S. 153A-98, the respective statutes governing access to municipal and county employee personnel records.

85. These laws include Title VII of the Civil Rights Act of 1964, the Age Discrimination in Employment Act (ADEA), the Americans with Disabilities Act (ADA), the Genetic Information Nondiscrimination Act (GINA), and the Uniformed Services Employment and Reemployment Rights Act (USERRA).

that the employer learned protected-class information through an Internet search as evidence that its hiring decision was discriminatory.[86] The remainder of this section discusses some of the risks that employers run in using the Internet to find information about job applicants.[87]

8.5.1 Some Kinds of Information an Employer May Want to Avoid Acquiring

8.5.1.1 Information about a Disability

The Internet in general and social media sites in particular—with their often intimate look into members' personal lives—may reveal information about an applicant's medical condition or personal or family medical history. The ADA effectively prohibits employers from asking pre-employment medical questions. That prohibition extends to asking a third party any question that it could not directly ask the applicant.[88] It is reasonable, therefore, to interpret the ADA to prohibit an employer from doing an Internet search *designed* to elicit information about disabilities. The ADA does not, however, address the question of whether an Internet search that inadvertently uncovers information relevant to the existence of a disability violates the ADA's prohibition on pre-employment medical inquiries. The safer course remains to avoid coming into possession of such information.

8.5.1.2 Genetic Information

Like the ADA, the Genetic Information Nondiscrimination Act (GINA) not only prohibits employers from discriminating in hiring—it also prohibits employers from requesting or requiring medical or genetic information

---

86. The EEOC considers the mere fact that an employer asks for information that should not be used in making employment decisions a significant red flag. *See* U.S. Equal Employment Opportunity Commission, *Pre-Employment Inquiries and Race,* www.eeoc.gov/laws/practices/inquiries_race.cfm and U.S. Equal Employment Opportunity Commission, *Pre-Employment Inquiries and Religious Affiliation or Beliefs,* www.eeoc.gov/ laws/practices/inquiries_religious.cfm.

87. A more in-depth discussion of this issue may be found in Diane M. Juffras, *Using the Internet to Conduct Background Checks on Applicants for Employment,* Public Employment Law Bulletin No. 38, October 2010, http://sogpubs.unc.edu/electronicversions/pdfs/pelb38.pdf.

88. U.S. Equal Employment Opportunity Commission, *ADA Enforcement Guidance: Preemployment Disability-Related Questions and Medical Examinations* (October 10, 1995), at 12, www.eeoc.gov/policy/docs/preemp.html.

from an applicant.[89] Unlike the ADA, GINA makes clear that an employer is not liable for obtaining information that is commercially or publicly available. The statute itself refers to newspapers, magazines, periodicals, and books as permissible public sources for genetic information about applicants and employees.[90] The GINA regulations adopted by the EEOC include genetic information obtained from publicly accessible electronic media, such as the Internet, television, and movies, as public sources for genetic information whose acquisition will not render an employer automatically liable.[91] But because GINA prohibits employers from making decisions based on genetic information, however learned, possession of genetic information may lend itself to the assumption that the information was used to discriminate. The wise employer will actively seek to avoid acquiring any such information.

8.5.1.3 Information about Tobacco and Alcohol Use

Another category of information that a social media search is likely to turn up is an applicant's use of tobacco or alcohol. Although employers may lawfully regulate employee use of both substances on the job, G.S. 95-28.2 prohibits employers, both public and private, from refusing to hire or otherwise engaging in employment discrimination against a person because the prospective employee ". . . engages in or has engaged in the lawful use of lawful products if the activity occurs off the premises of the employer during nonworking hours and does not adversely affect the employee's job performance or the person's ability to properly fulfill the responsibilities of the position in question or the safety of other employees." Tobacco remains a lawful product, and applicant or employee use of cigarettes in private life cannot form the basis of any employment decision.[92] The same is true of the use of alcohol off-duty, unless the applicant or employee were to arrive at the employer's premises while still under the influence.[93]

---

89. *See* 42 U.S.C. § 2000ff-1(b).

90. 42 U.S.C. § 2000ff-1(b)(4).

91. *See* 29 C.F.R. § 1635.8(b)(4).

92. An employer who violates G.S. 95-28.2 may be liable for lost wages and benefits and subject to an order to offer employment to the rejected applicant. *See* G.S. 95-28.2(e)(1) and (3).

93. An employer may face a more serious risk of a claim of disability discrimination if it makes an employment decision based on awareness of the fact that the applicant

8.5.1.4 *An Applicant's Opinions about Politics and Other Matters of Public Concern*

The sheer variety of material that an Internet search might turn up makes it difficult to generalize about the legal dangers such material poses for employers. There is no question, however, that a *private employer* could refuse to hire an applicant because the persons charged with hiring did not like the contents of that applicant's online communications, whether the subject matter was personal or political. That is because private employers have no duty to respect the free speech rights of their applicants and employees. *Public employers,* on the other hand, must tread very carefully if they propose to use an applicant's online expression as a basis for rejecting the person for employment. That is because the First Amendment to the U.S. Constitution prohibits the government from abridging citizens' rights to freedom of expression. In this respect, electronic expression is no different from speech voiced out loud or from communication in the form of printed words or photographs in a newspaper. The same First Amendment tests apply to *all* public applicant and public employee speech and communication.

Thus, whether a North Carolina local government employer can refuse to hire an applicant because of an Internet posting depends on the nature of the applicant's posting. Only speech on matters of public concern is constitutionally protected.[94] If the applicant's Internet posting or speech

---

uses alcohol in his or her private life. Applicants could claim that the employer refused to hire them because it perceived them as alcoholics based on Facebook postings about their behavior while drinking alcohol. Alcoholism is a covered disability under the ADA. *See* 42 U.S.C. § 12114(c). The ADA also protects applicants and employees whom an employer regards as having a disability even when they do not. *See* 42 U.S.C. § 12112(a).

94. *See* Mt. Healthy City Sch. Dist. Bd. of Educ. v. Doyle, 429 U.S. 274, 283–84 (1977) (teacher's claim that he was not rehired because of his public criticisms of dress code was cognizable First Amendment retaliation claim; burden on school district to show that it would have reached the same decision even in the absence of the speech at issue); Perry v. Sindermann, 408 U.S. 593, 597–98 (1972) (First Amendment prohibited state college from not renewing a professor based on his public criticisms of the college administration). Matters of public concern usually involve charges of illegal action, abuse of authority or power, and fraud, corruption, or waste; matters suitable for legislative attention; allegations of pervasive racial discrimination in a government agency; or questions regarding public safety. *See* Hughes v. Bedsole, 913 F. Supp. 420, 428 (E.D.N.C. 1994) (citing Jurgensen v. Fairfax Cnty., Va., 745 F.2d 868, 871 (4th

does not address a matter of public concern, the communication is not entitled to First Amendment protection and the employer is free to reject the applicant on the basis of what he or she has said.[95] Sometimes employers find photographs of the applicant engaged in questionable behavior or in suggestive poses[96] or complaints about the applicant's current job, supervisor, or coworkers.[97] These are not matters of public concern but are purely private in nature and may be the basis for rejecting an application for employment.

8.5.1.5 Balancing the Interests of the Public Employer against the Applicant's Right to Free Speech

As discussed above, if the applicant's speech does address a matter of public concern—such as unlawful discrimination—the question of whether or not it may form the basis of a rejection is determined by application of what

---

Cir. 1984)); Lewis v. Blackburn, 734 F.2d 1000, 1004–05 (4th Cir. 1984); Love-Lane v. Martin, 355 F.3d 766 (4th Cir. 2004) (allegedly discriminatory practices by school board are always a matter of public concern).

95. Although most First Amendment public employment cases arise in circumstances where a public employee has been terminated on the basis of his or her speech, the U.S. Supreme Court has made clear that the same protections and analysis apply in cases involving a failure to hire an applicant because of something that the applicant said or wrote. *See Perry*, 408 U.S. at 597–98 (1972) (First Amendment prohibited state college from not renewing a professor based on his public criticisms of the college administration). *See also* Rutan v. Republican Party of Ill., 497 U.S. 62, 79 (1990) (hiring based on party affiliation and support violates First Amendment rights to free speech and association); Hubbard v. Adm'r, Envtl. Prot. Agency, 735 F. Supp. 435, 437–38 (D.D.C. 1990) (evidence demonstrated that applicant was rejected for exercise of First Amendment rights).

96. *See* City of San Diego, Cal. v. Roe, 543 U.S. 77, 83–84 (2004) (police officer who had been terminated for offering sexually explicit videos—featuring him in a generic "police" uniform—for sale online was not terminated for speech on a matter of public concern and his termination was not in violation of the First Amendment). *See also* Marshall v. Mayor and Alderman of City of Savannah, Ga., 2010 WL 537852 (11th Cir. 2010) (not for publication in the *Federal Reporter*) (plaintiff was terminated from her position as a city firefighter after posting pictures of herself with the fire and rescue squad on the same page as pictures showing her bare-shouldered and with a bare backside. The district court found that this speech was not entitled to First Amendment protection).

97. *See* Connick v. Myers, 461 U.S. 138 (1983); *Hughes*, 913 F. Supp. at 428 (personal grievances concerning working conditions do not qualify as matters of public concern).

is known as the *Pickering* balancing test. The *Pickering* test (first set forth by the U.S. Supreme Court in the case *Pickering v. Board of Education*)[98] requires a court to weigh an applicant's interest in speaking out about a matter of public concern and the government employer's legitimate and substantial interests in providing public services efficiently.[99] An employer may reject an applicant who has spoken on a matter of public concern if it would have reached the same decision in the absence of the protected speech.[100]

8.5.2 Asking Applicants to Display Their Social Media Pages and Posts

Suppose an employer does an Internet search of an applicant's name and the search does not produce any results. Further suppose that the applicant has the strictest privacy settings on his or her social networking pages and, as a result, no information is public. Can an employer ask an applicant to pull up his or her private social media pages as part of the in-person interview process? *There are no reported cases with jurisdiction over North Carolina addressing whether such a practice is unlawful.* Certainly, it does not violate any antidiscrimination law. Is such a request a coercive invasion of privacy on the part of the government? An analogy from the law governing public employer pre-employment drug testing suggests that the practice does not impinge on an employee's constitutional right to privacy. In the Fourth Amendment drug-testing context, the courts have found that the threat of taking away a job that an employee already has is more coercive than the threat of not considering an applicant for a job absent the test. For example, asking a public employee to undergo drug testing in the absence of reasonable suspicion to believe that the employee is using illegal narcotics is a violation of the Fourth Amendment's protections against unreason-

---

98. 391 U.S. 563, 568 (1968).

99. *See Pickering*, 391 U.S. at 568; *Mt. Healthy City Sch. Dist.*, 429 U.S. at 284 (1977). Factors that the courts will consider include the effect of the applicant's speech on the employer's ability to maintain discipline and harmonious working relationships, whether the applicant's speech would adversely affect a working relationship in which personal loyalty and confidence were especially required, and whether the applicant's statements would impede the proper performance of his or her prospective duties or interfere with the regular operation of the employing agency. *See Pickering*, 391 U.S. at 569–70.

100. *See* Mt. Healthy City Sch. Dist. Bd. of Educ. v. Doyle, 429 U.S. 274, 287 (1977).

able searches and seizures, and the courts will reinstate any employee who refuses to take a drug test under these circumstances. But public employers routinely ask all job *applicants* to undergo drug testing regardless of whether there is reason to think that an individual applicant is under the influence of illegal drugs. No federal court of appeals has ever found such practices coercive or unconstitutional. Under the Fourth Amendment, the same analysis would likely apply to applicants who are asked to disclose their private Internet postings. If applicants do not want to reveal their private social media pages, they can withdraw (or be rejected) as an applicant. They do not have any legally cognizable interest in or right to be considered for a particular opening with a government employer.

8.5.2.1 Proposed Legislation Prohibiting Employer Access to Personal Social Media Pages

Employers should note that notwithstanding the fact that North Carolina has no prohibitions against employers requiring their employees to disclose the content of their personal social media pages, there is increasing interest in preventing such practices elsewhere in other states. Legislation that would prohibit employers from requiring applicants and employees to disclose their personal accounts on social media sites has been adopted by two states, Maryland[101] and Illinois,[102] and introduced in eleven other states.[103] To date, such legislation has not even been introduced into the North Carolina General Assembly.

The interest in controlling employer access to applicant and employee social media accounts is increasing among members of the U.S. Congress, as well. In April 2012, U.S. Representative Eliot Engel of New York and U.S. Senator Jan Schakowsky of Illinois introduced into the U.S. House and Senate, respectively, the Social Networking Online Protection Act,

---

101. *See* Maryland Senate Bill 433, enacted May 2, 2012, and effective October 1, 2012 (history and text available online at http://mlis.state.md.us/2012rs/billfile/sb0433.htm).

102. *See* Illinois Public Act 097-0875, enacted August 1, 2012, and effective January 1, 2012 (history and text available online at www.ilga.gov/legislation/BillStatus.asp?DocNum=3782&GAID=11&DocTypeID=HB&SessionID=84).

103. Legislation has been introduced into the Minnesota State Legislature (H.F. No. 2963), the Ohio General Assembly (S.B. 351), Michigan (HB 5523), as well as into the California, New Jersey, New York, Pennsylvania, South Carolina, and Washington legislatures.

which would prohibit employers from requiring or even requesting that applicants and employees disclose their user names, passwords, or other means for accessing their personal accounts on any social networking website.[104] Violations would be punishable by fines of up to $10,000. In May 2012, U.S. Representative Martin Heinrich of New Mexico and Senator Richard Blumenthal of Connecticut introduced the Password Protection Act of 2012, which would amend the Computer Fraud and Abuse Act (18 U.S.C. § 1030) by making it unlawful for an employer to compel or coerce applicants and employees into giving the employer access through a password or similar login information to data stored on a computer that is not the employer's.[105] The difference between the two proposed acts was technical: one makes the request for a password unlawful while the other makes accessing information stored on another computer unlawful if the access is procured by coercion of an employee. Neither bill passed before the new Congress was sworn in in January 2013, but similar bills are likely to be introduced in the future.

8.5.3 Using the Internet to Learn More about Applicants while Protecting against Liability for Unlawful Employment Practices

How might a North Carolina public employer best protect itself against the risks posed by Internet background searches? The best way would be to delay conducting Internet searches until the end of the hiring process—after a conditional offer of employment has been made. Wherever in the hiring process an Internet search is conducted, however, the employer should adopt a clear policy outlining the kinds of information for which those involved in the hiring process may search. For example, the search could be limited to educational information or to information and comments made by the applicant about former employment. The search could include or be limited to information suggesting current drug use. Any set of search guidelines should direct searchers to omit information revealing the applicant's Title VII personal characteristics, age, or disability. The policy should also make clear what may and may not be considered in the decision-making process when information is inadvertently acquired. As

104. For the text of the Social Networking Online Protection Act (HR 5050), go to www.govtrack.us/congress/bills/112/hr5050/text.

105. For the text of the Password Protection Act of 2012 (HR 5684) go to www.govtrack.us/congress/bills/112/hr5684/text.

is the case with all employment selection practices, it is important that employers use Internet searches in a consistent way. If an Internet search will be used, it must be used on all applicants who meet the requirements for a position, or all candidates who make the first cut, or all who will be granted an interview. The policy should also make clear who is to conduct the search. Without exception, the best practice would be to have someone who is not involved in the evaluation and decision-making process (human resources, when the employer has such a department) conduct the Internet search and protect decision makers from information they should not have.

8.6 Using Outside Agencies to Conduct Background Checks: The Fair Credit Reporting Act

All four types of background check—criminal history, credit history, reference, and Internet checks—have at least this one element in common: if the employer uses a third party consumer reporting agency to conduct the check and report on the results, it must abide by the requirements of the federal Fair Credit Reporting Act (FCRA) by obtaining prior written permission from job applicants to conduct background investigations and by providing notice to those persons whose applications are being rejected based on information disclosed through the background investigation. An employer that uses its own staff or uses government resources such as the State Bureau of Investigation's criminal history database to check job applicants' backgrounds is not subject to the FCRA.

8.6.1 The FCRA's Authorization and Disclosure Requirements

The Fair Credit Reporting Act,[106] a part of the federal Consumer Protection Act, regulates the use of "consumer credit reports" that are provided for a fee by "consumer reporting agencies." The act defines those terms broadly, bringing employer use of for-profit businesses to investigate applicants within its scope. Under the FCRA, a "consumer reporting agency" is any person or business that for a fee

> regularly engages in whole or in part in the practice of assembling or evaluating consumer credit information *or other*

106. 15 U.S.C. § 1681–1681x.

> *information* on consumers for the purpose of furnishing consumer reports to third parties"[107] [emphasis added].

A "consumer credit report" is defined as

> any written, oral or other communication by a consumer reporting agency relating to a consumer's credit worthiness, credit standing, credit capacity, *character, general reputation, personal characteristics, or mode of living* which is . . . collected . . . for the purpose of serving as a factor [emphasis added]

in establishing the person's eligibility for employment purposes, as well as for credit or insurance purposes.[108]

Three sections of the FCRA—15 U.S.C. §§ 1681b, 1681d, and 1681m—detail an employer's responsibilities in using consumer reports for employment purposes. In brief, the FCRA requires employers to

1. certify to a consumer reporting agency *before obtaining a consumer report* that the employer is in compliance with the FCRA and will not misuse any information contained in the report in violation of the law;[109]
2. disclose to applicants in writing, *before the report is obtained,* that a consumer report may be obtained and used in making employment decisions. The disclosure must be made in a document that contains no other information other than the disclosure;[110]
3. obtain written permission from applicants to obtain a consumer credit report *before the report is obtained.* This authorization is the only other material that may be included with the pre-report disclosure mentioned above in (b);[111]
4. *provide an applicant with a pre-adverse action disclosure* that includes a copy of the individual's consumer report and a description of the applicant's rights under the FCRA *before making a*

---

107. *See* 15 U.S.C. § 1681a(f).
108. *See* 15 U.S.C. § 1681a(d)(1).
109. *See* 15 U.S.C. §§ 1681d(a)(2) and (d)(1).
110. *See* 15 U.S.C. § 1681b(b)(2)(i).
111. *See* 15 U.S.C. § 1681b(b)(2)(ii).

decision not to hire the applicant based on the information in the consumer report;[112] and

5. *after the decision not to hire or other adverse action*, provide an applicant either orally, in writing, or electronically with the name, number, and address of the consumer reporting agency that supplied the report, a statement saying the reporting agency that supplied the report did not make the decision or take the adverse action and cannot give specific reasons for it, and a notice of the individual's right to dispute information contained in the report, as well as the right to obtain a free copy of the report from the reporting agency within 60 days.[113]

Somewhat more stringent requirements apply to "investigative consumer reports," which are defined as

> a consumer report . . . in which information on a consumer's character, general reputation, personal characteristics, or mode of living is obtained through personal interviews with neighbors, friends, or associates of the consumer reported on or with others with whom he is acquainted. . . .[114]

In the case of investigative consumer reports, the disclosure that a report will be obtained must clearly state that the employer is ordering *an investigative report that will include information as to character, general reputation, personal characteristics, and mode of living.* This disclosure must be made in writing and mailed to the job applicant within three days after the date on which the report was requested from a consumer reporting agency.[115] Employers using investigative consumer reports must also disclose to applicants the nature and scope of the investigation within five days of the applicant's request for such information.[116] Employers who violate the employment provisions of the FCRA may be liable to the job

---

112. *See* 15 U.S.C. § 1681b(b)(3). An example of the summary of consumer rights may be found in Appendix 4.

113. *See* 15 U.S.C. § 1681m(a).

114. *See* 15 U.S.C. § 1681a(e).

115. *See* 15 U.S.C. § 1681d(a).

116. *See* 15 U.S.C. § 1681d(b).

applicant for actual damages if the violation was negligent and for punitive damages in the case of a willful violation.[117]

8.6.2 No Obligation for Employers to Reconsider Applicants Rejected on the Basis of Incorrect Information Supplied by a Third-Party Consumer Reporting Agency

Employers should note, however, that in no case does the FCRA give an applicant appeal rights with respect to a decision not to hire. Nor are there any circumstances in which a reporting mistake by the consumer reporting agency will result in an obligation on the part of the employer to hire the applicant. As Congress explained in the introductory section of the FCRA:

> [I]t is the purpose of this subchapter to require that consumer reporting agencies adopt reasonable procedures for meeting the needs of commerce for consumer credit, personnel, insurance, and other information in a manner which is fair and equitable to the consumer, with regard to the confidentiality, accuracy, relevancy, and proper utilization of such information in accordance with the requirements of this subchapter.[118]

In the case of consumer reports used for employment purposes, it is the employer, and not the consumer reporting agency, that has direct contact with the applicant. The FCRA has accordingly given responsibility for obtaining permission and giving disclosure information to the employer. The employer's legal responsibility is limited to disclosure.[119]

If the information that the consumer reporting agency has given to the employer is incorrect, there is no requirement that the employer reconsider its decision or reopen its search. Employers are required to give applicants information about the background check results so that applicants can work with consumer reporting agencies to clarify and correct any errors

---

117. *See* 15 U.S.C. § 1681o for negligent noncompliance and 15 U.S.C. § 1681n for willful noncompliance. *See also* Mathews v. Gov't Emps. Ins. Co., 23 F. Supp. 2d 1160 (S.D. Calif. 1998) (denying summary judgment to employer that admitted violating the Fair Credit Reporting Act (FCRA) by not informing affected applicants that their rejection was based on information in their credit reports; also holding that there was genuine issue of material fact as to whether employer's conduct was willful).

118. *See* 15 U.S.C. § 1681(b).

119. *See* Drury v. TNT Holland Motor Express, Inc., 885 F. Supp. 161, 165–66 (W.D. Mich. 1994).

for the future. Ultimate responsibility for the accuracy and relevancy of the information remains with the consumer reporting agency.

Occasionally, an applicant may refuse to grant an employer authorization to conduct a third party background check. In that case, the employer may reject the application.[120]

120. *See, e.g.*, Kelchner v. Sycamore Manor Health Ctr., 135 F. App'x 499, 502 (3d Cir. 2005) (FCRA did not prohibit employer from taking adverse action against an employee who refused to authorize a consumer report). *Cf.* G.S. 7A-349, which gives the N.C. Department of Justice authorization to terminate any employee who refuses to consent to a criminal history check.

Chapter 9

Hiring Employees versus Engaging Independent Contractors

Chapter 9

Hiring Employees versus Engaging Independent Contractors

Public employers are continually challenged to cut and to stretch the amount of money in their budgets allocated to personnel costs. One way of doing this is to outsource some of the work done by employees to outside businesses or individuals. These outside service providers are referred to as "independent contractors." Independent contractors can be attractive to employers in that they perform their services for a set fee and are not provided with employee benefits or any other form of compensation, such as overtime. Fees paid to independent contractors are not subject to employment taxes to which the employer must make a contribution, such as FICA (Federal Insurance Contributions Act) or FUTA (Federal Unemployment Tax Act) taxes.

When a public employer contracts with an outside *company* to provide a service, whether that service is payroll preparation, janitorial work, or providing nurses for a county health clinic, it is clear that the worker providing the service is an employee of the outside company: the worker's wages, employment taxes, and benefits are paid by that company. This is true even though day-to-day assignments and supervision of the worker may be done by the public employer.[1] When a public employer contracts with an outside *individual* to provide services, maintaining the legal distinction between

1. For tort and employment discrimination law liability purposes, the public employer and the outside company would likely be considered joint employers of the worker, but they would not be joint employers for compensation purposes.

a worker who is an employee and one who is an independent contractor can be tricky.[2] Why? Because not just any worker can be classified as an independent contractor. Independent contractor is a distinct legal status determined by factors that go beyond an employer and employee's mutual desire to contract for work on that basis. For example, both the United States Department of Labor (which administers federal overtime law) and the Internal Revenue Service (which oversees employee federal income tax withholding and Social Security and Medicare payroll contributions) have specific tests for determining whether a worker is an employee or an independent contractor for overtime and tax purposes. Federal and state antidiscrimination laws and state statutes governing who qualifies for workers' compensation and unemployment benefits use similar tests.

Very few hiring relationships meet the legal test for independent contractor status. Employers who misclassify workers as independent contractors may incur significant (and unbudgeted) liabilities, such as liability for back overtime, Internal Revenue Service (IRS) penalties, and liability for the value of lost benefits. This chapter summarizes the factors that a public employer should consider in determining whether a worker legally qualifies for independent contractor status or must be classified as an employee.[3] Each of the relevant legal factors is discussed through the example of a hypothetical North Carolina county that has just engaged the services of three new workers. The chapter concludes with a discussion of certain government positions whose correct classification is sometimes difficult.

---

2. Sometimes, employers contracting with outside individuals refer to them as "contract employees." The latter term—contract employee—is a misnomer, as all employees have an employment contract. Most employees do not have a written employment agreement, however, which may be why the term contract employee is sometimes used to refer to a relationship that is really one of hiring organization and independent contractor.

3. This chapter draws heavily from two articles the author has published on this topic: Diane M. Juffras, *Independent Contractor or Employee? The Legal Distinction and Its Consequences*, Public Employment Law Bulletin No. 32, May 2005, www.iog.unc.edu/pubs/electronicversions/pdfs/pelb32.pdf, and Diane M. Juffras, *Determining Whether a Worker Is an Independent Contractor or an Employee*, Popular Government, Fall 2006, at 25–34, http://sogpubs.unc.edu/electronicversions/pg/pgfal06/article3.pdf.

9.1 Employee or Independent Contractor: A Hypothetical

Paradise County needs an additional sanitation worker in the public works department, an additional visiting nurse in the health department, and an additional accounting technician in the finance department. In each case, the new position would have the same job duties as other employees. The county commissioners do not think it possible to fund all three requests. Rather than choose among them, they allocate enough money for each of the three departments to add an additional worker on what the commissioners call an "independent contractor" basis: the workers are to be paid at an hourly rate, and they will not receive any employee benefits. The public works, health, and finance departments advertise for and hire workers, who sign agreements stating that they understand that they are hired as independent contractors and that, as such, they will not receive benefits. The payroll office, seeing that the workers are not receiving benefits, does not withhold income or Social Security and Medicare (FICA) taxes or make employer-required FICA contributions.

After the new workers have been on the job for several months, one of them approaches the payroll office and complains that she often works more than 40 hours per week, but she does not receive overtime. She also complains that the county has not withheld Social Security and Medicare taxes from her paycheck. The worker is concerned that she is not receiving credit with the Social Security Administration for her time working for Paradise County and that she will not receive all of the Social Security benefits to which she would otherwise be entitled at retirement.

The payroll office tells the worker that because she was classified as an independent contractor, (1) she is not covered by the Fair Labor Standards Act and is not entitled to overtime, and (2) the county is not required to withhold Social Security and Medicare taxes. Dissatisfied with this answer, the worker complains to her supervisor. The supervisor reminds her that she agreed to work as an independent contractor and tells her that if she doesn't like it, she can quit.

The worker files complaints with the United States Department of Labor and the Internal Revenue Service. They each begin an investigation into Paradise County's worker classifications. Are Paradise County's three new workers legitimately classified as independent contractors? Or will the Department of Labor and the IRS determine that they are employees, regardless of what label the county puts on them?

9.2 An Agreement to Work as an Independent Contractor Has No Legal Significance

The Paradise County hypothetical illustrates one of the most common misconceptions about who is and is not an independent contractor. Many employers believe that so long as a worker wants or agrees to be paid as an independent contractor, the employer is not responsible for paying overtime or for withholding taxes for that worker. That simply is not so. All of the workers that Paradise County has hired as "independent contractors" are—as far as the law is concerned—employees.

Although the various tests for determining whether a worker is an employee or an independent contractor go by different names, they differ only slightly: all are variants of the common law test for determining whether or not someone is an "employee." Thus, the tests share common principles. Under all of the tests, the essence of the relationship between a hiring organization and an *independent contractor* is the agreement by the independent contractor to do a discrete job according to the independent contractor's own judgment and methods, without supervision by the hiring organization. The hiring organization retains approval only as to the results of the work. In contrast, an employer may require an *employee* to perform his or her duties in particular ways using particular methods at particular times even if, in fact, the employer gives assignments only occasionally. An employee may be disciplined—even discharged—for failing to follow the employer's instructions about how to perform a task. An independent contractor may not.

9.2.1 The Classic Independent Contractor

A classic example of an independent contractor is the swimming pool contractor. Imagine that a city wants to build a swimming pool. Officials of the city have opinions about what features they want in a swimming pool, but they do not know how to construct a swimming pool, and no one in the city's regular employ has experience in swimming pool construction. So the city engages a swimming pool contractor to construct the pool.

The city will tell the swimming pool contractor what result it wants: a swimming pool of a particular size, in a particular layout, with specified depths, and with certain accessories such as diving boards, stairs, and ladders. The city and contractor will agree upon a price for the final product. While the city may negotiate with the contractor—and even have a price above which it will not go—the city will not be able to set the price unilaterally. The contractor, who will supply all of the materials, equipment, and workers needed to construct the swimming pool, will estimate how much time it will take to construct the pool and how much it will cost. It will then determine how much or how little profit it is willing to make to take this job.

Contrast this with the Paradise County hypothetical set forth above. The county did not set out to hire someone with specialized skills for a discrete job with respect to the sanitation worker, the accounting technician, or the visiting nurse. What each department head asked for was funding to hire one additional employee. What each got was permission to hire someone to perform the job functions of an employee under an alternate compensation arrangement.

9.2.2 The Fair Labor Standards Act Test to Determine Whether a Worker Is an Employee or an Independent Contractor

The Fair Labor Standards Act (FLSA) defines "employee" broadly as "any individual employed by an employer."[4] It defines "employer" as "any person acting directly or indirectly in the interest of an employer in relation to an employee,"[5] while to "employ" someone is "to suffer or permit [them] to work."[6] On its face, it is hard to see what sort of worker would

4. *See* 29 U.S.C. § 203(e)(1).
5. *See* 29 U.S.C. § 203(d).
6. *See* 29 U.S.C. § 203(g).

not fall within the FLSA's definition of employee—it would seem to cover everybody.

The U.S. Department of Labor and the courts nevertheless recognize that there are people who perform work who simply cannot be called employees of the organization. To determine whether or not a worker is an employee for FLSA purposes, courts have developed what is called an "economic reality" test.

9.2.2.1 The Economic Reality Test

The economic reality test looks at whether a worker is economically dependent upon the organization for which he or she renders services.[7] To put it another way, the courts ask whether a worker depends upon an employer for the opportunity to render service or whether the worker is in business for himself or herself. To make this determination, the courts use a six-factor test that asks:

1. What is the nature and degree of control that the hiring organization has over the way in which the worker is to perform the work? The more control that the hiring organization has over the worker, the more likely it is that the worker is an employee.
2. Does the worker have an opportunity to make a profit or a loss? The ability to make a profit or sustain a loss on a job is the hallmark of an independent contractor.
3. Does the worker have an investment in the materials, equipment, or other personnel required to perform the work? When a worker supplies the materials or equipment needed for the job or directly hires others to assist him or her in performing the work, this factor will weigh heavily in favor of independent contractor status.
4. Does the work require skill and independent initiative? Independent contractors usually have a special skill and exercise initiative in seeking out assignments or clients.
5. What is the expected duration of the working relationship? The independent contractor relationship is usually for a limited duration. Where a hiring organization engages a worker indefinitely, or where the worker has performed services for the hiring organiza-

7. *See* Rutherford Food Corp. v. McComb, 331 U.S. 722, 726–28, 730 (1947).

tion for a long period of time, the courts are more likely to find that the worker is an employee.

6. To what extent is the work an integral part of the hiring organization's operations? Independent contractors usually perform work that is peripheral to the hiring organization's operations. Where a worker is doing a job that is essential to the organization's operations, this factor will weigh in favor of employee status.

No single factor is dispositive in making the determination of worker status, and some of them overlap. Each situation is evaluated in light of all of the circumstances of the hiring organization–worker relationship.[8]

9.2.3 The Internal Revenue Code Test to Determine Whether a Worker Is an Employee or an Independent Contractor

The Internal Revenue Service also has an interest in seeing that employers who classify workers as independent contractors or contract employees are legally entitled to do so. Under the Internal Revenue Code (the Code), an employer is required to withhold estimated federal income taxes from an employee's wage payments. In addition, the Code imposes Social Security and Medicare taxes on the wages of employees, both of which an employer must remit to the IRS through payroll deduction. Employers themselves also pay Social Security and Medicare taxes on each person they employ.

In contrast, an organization is not required to withhold income or FICA taxes from its payments to an independent contractor, nor does it pay any Social Security or Medicare taxes on the independent contractor's fee. A hiring organization's legal responsibilities end with the filing of annual information returns (form 1099) with both the worker and the IRS that show the money paid to the contractor during the tax year. An independent contractor is responsible for directly paying both income and FICA taxes to the IRS.[9]

---

8. *See* Chao v. Mid-Atl. Installation Servs., Inc., 16 F. App'x 104, 106, 2001 WL 739243 **1 (4th Cir. 2001); Dubois v. Sec'y of Def., 161 F.3d 2, 1998 WL 610863 **1 (4th Cir. 1998) (unpublished disposition); Donovan v. DialAmerica Mktg., Inc., 757 F.2d 1376, 1382–83 (3d Cir.), *cert. denied*, 474 U.S. 919 (1985); Brock v. Superior Care, Inc., 840 F.2d 1054, 1059 (2d Cir. 1988).

9. The IRS has stepped up its efforts to identify employees incorrectly classified as independent contractors in recent years: independent contractors tend to understate their income—sometimes erroneously, sometimes consciously—resulting in

Thus, the federal government stands to lose potentially significant amounts of revenue when hiring organizations misclassify employees as independent contractors. Not only are employer contributions to Social Security and Medicare completely lost, but independent contractors may underreport income and remit less in the way of income tax and FICA contributions than they actually owe. This is true even where the hiring organization properly reports the amount paid to the independent contractor to the IRS.

9.2.3.1 The Right to Control Test

The Code does not formally define the term "employee" for the purposes of determining federal income tax liability but instead provides that the usual common law rules apply in determining the employer–employee relationship.[10] The common law test, sometimes known as the "right to control" test, looks at whether the organization for which the worker is performing services has the right to control or direct the worker. In a 1987 Revenue Ruling, the IRS compiled and set out a list of 20 factors that the courts had considered over the years in applying the right to control test. Those factors are:

1. whether the worker must comply with another person's instructions about the work;
2. whether the worker requires training in order to do the work;
3. whether the work performed by the worker is integrated into the hiring organization's operations;
4. whether the worker must perform the services personally;
5. who hires, supervises, and pays the worker's assistants, if any;
6. whether the worker and hiring organization have a continuing relationship;

---

revenue loss for the federal government from underpayment of both federal income and employment taxes. Thus, when an employer is both withholding an employee's share and contributing its own share, federal tax revenues are both greater and more predictable.

10. *See* 26 U.S.C. § 3121(d)(2). *See also* Weber v. Commissioner, 60 F.3d 1104, 1110 (4th Cir. 1995); Eren v. Commissioner, 180 F.3d 594, 596–97 (4th Cir. 1999) (because foreign earned income tax exclusion section of Internal Revenue Code does not define employee, common law rules apply in distinguishing employees and independent contractors under federal tax law), *citing* Nationwide Mut. Ins. Co. v. Darden, 503 U.S. 318, 322–23 (1992).

7. whether the work must be performed during set hours;
8. whether the worker must devote most of his or her time to the work for the hiring organization;
9. whether the work must be performed on the employer's premises or can be done elsewhere;
10. whether the worker must perform services in an order or sequence set by the hiring organization;
11. whether the worker must submit reports;
12. whether the worker is paid by the hour, week, or month;
13. whether the worker's business or traveling expenses are paid by the hiring organization;
14. whether the worker furnished the tools, material, and equipment needed to perform the work;
15. whether the worker has a significant investment in facilities needed to do the work;
16. whether the worker can make a profit or suffer a loss as a result of performing the services for the hiring organization;
17. whether the worker can work for more than one firm at a time;
18. whether the worker makes his or her services available to the general public;
19. whether the hiring organization can discharge the worker;
20. whether the worker has the right to terminate the relationship with the hiring organization.[11]

Both the IRS and the courts emphasize that no single factor is controlling and that the importance of a factor will vary depending on the occupation at issue and the circumstances under which the services are rendered.[12]

---

11. *See* Rev. Rul. 87-41 (1987), 1987-1 C.B. 296. Most of these factors appear in the summary of the common law test set forth by the United States Supreme Court in *Darden*, 503 U.S. at 323–24 (applying common law test to determine who qualifies as an employee under Employee Retirement Income Security Act (ERISA)) and Cmty. for Creative Non-Violence v. Reid, 490 U.S. 730, 751–52 (1989) (applying common law test to determine who is an employee for purposes of the Copyright Act). *See also* Clackamas Gastroenterology Assocs., P.C. v. Wells, 538 U.S. 440 (2003) (EEOC focus on common law test is appropriate for determining who is employee for purposes of Americans with Disabilities Act).

12. *See* Rev. Rul. 87-41 (1987), 1987-1 C.B. 296. *See also Weber*, 60 F.3d at 1110 (looking at seven of the 20 factors to determine whether minister was employee of church); Hosp. Res. Pers., Inc. v. United States, 68 F.3d 421, 427 (11th Cir. 1995) ("Although

In *Weber v. Commissioner*, for example, the Fourth Circuit looked at seven factors in determining whether a minister was an employee of his church: (1) the degree of control exercised by the church over the details of the work; (2) which party—church or minister—had invested in the facilities used in the work; (3) the opportunity of the minister for profit or loss; (4) whether the church had the right to discharge the minister; (5) whether the work was part of the church's regular business; (6) the permanency of the relationship; and (7) the relationship the parties believed they were creating.[13] With respect to the first factor—the right to control—the Fourth Circuit noted that it is not only actual control exercised by the hiring organization that is relevant, but also the extent to which the organization has the right to intervene to assert control.[14]

Because the Department of Labor and the IRS use nominally different tests to determine worker status—the economic reality test versus the right to control test—it is theoretically possible that in a particular case a worker could be found to be an employee under one test and an independent contractor under the other—that is, it is possible that the same worker could be an employee for FLSA purposes and an independent contractor for tax purposes, or vice versa. But in fact, the two tests look to the same factors, and a worker whom a hiring organization has a right to control is also one who is economically dependent upon the hiring organization. The author has found no fact pattern set forth in case law, Department of Labor Wage and Hour Opinion Letters, or IRS Revenue Rulings that would lead to different conclusions under the two tests. For that reason, the factors indicative of worker status under both the FLSA economic reality test and the IRS right to control test will be discussed together in the following sections.

---

no one factor is definitive on its own, collectively the factors define the extent of an employer's control over the time and manner in which a worker performs. This control test is fundamental in establishing a worker's status."); Gen. Inv. Corp. v. United States, 823 F.2d 337, 341 (9th Cir. 1987); REAG, Inc. v. United States, 801 F. Supp. 494, 501 (W.D. Okla. 1992); Critical Care Register Nursing, Inc. v. United States, 776 F. Supp. 1025, 1028–29 (E.D. Pa. 1991).

13. *See Weber*, 60 F.3d at 1110.

14. *See Weber*, 60 F.3d at 1110.

9.3 Five Key Factors

The legal test for independent contractor status looks at a number of different factors that may be grouped into five general categories: (1) the nature and degree of the hiring organization's control over the worker, (2) the worker's opportunity for profit or loss, (3) whether the work performed is itself an integral part of the hiring organization's business, (4) the duration of the relationship between the hiring organization and the worker, and (5) the hiring organization's right to discharge the worker. No single factor is always the determining factor. Instead, the importance of a given factor will vary depending on both the occupation at issue and the circumstances under which the services are rendered.[15]

A closer look at these five factors will make clear that unlike the swimming pool contractor, the Paradise County workers in the hypothetical set forth above cannot be classified as independent contractors. They must be classified as employees.

9.3.1 The Nature and Degree of the Employer's Control over the Worker

The more control that the hiring party has over a worker, the more likely it is that the worker is an employee. A hiring party has control over a worker when it has *the right* unilaterally to assign the worker a task or to require something of the worker at any given time. The hiring party *does not have to exercise that right* to have control over the worker for that worker to be an employee as a matter of law.[16]

---

15. *See* Rev. Rul. 87-41 (1987), 1987-1 C.B. 296 (listing 20 factors that courts have considered over the years in applying the right to control test). *See also Weber*, 60 F.3d at 1110 (looking at seven of the 20 factors to determine whether minister was employee of church); Hosp. Res. Pers., Inc., 68 F.3d at 427 ("Although no one factor is definitive on its own, collectively the factors define the extent of an employer's control over the time and manner in which a worker performs. This control test is fundamental in establishing a worker's status.").

16. *See* 26 C.F.R. § 31.3401(c)-1(b) (employment tax regulations); Weber v. Commissioner, 60 F.3d 1104, 1110 (4th Cir. 1995). *See also* Cromwell v. Driftwood Elec. Contractors, Inc., 348 F. App'x 57, 60 (5th Cir. 2009) (cable installer an employee where employer had control over schedules and work assignments, among other things). *Cf.* Freund v. Hi-Tech Satellite, Inc., 185 F. App'x 782, 784–85 (11th Cir. 2006) (where home satellite system installer was independent contractor because although company scheduled all appointments, the installer could reschedule them, installer was

Working conditions that indicate employer control include the following:

- *Training* in the actual methods the worker is to use or, more generally, in the hiring party's policies and procedures.[17]
- *Requiring that the worker submit written or oral reports.* These may be reports of time spent on certain tasks or on the project as a whole. The worker may be required to give a detailed description of the work performed or of clients or patients seen in a given time period. A hiring party does not have to monitor a worker's performance on a daily basis in order to exercise control.[18]

---

unsupervised and determined how to do the work and installer worked for multiple companies).

17. Where an architect (1) was required to follow the procedures and directives in the hiring organization's handbook, (2) could not exceed budget, and (3) had his hours, leave, and pay set by employer, the court found that (1) the hiring organization had the right to control the architect's activities, and (2) the architect was an employee for tax purposes. *See* Eren v. Commissioner, 180 F.3d 594, 597 (4th Cir. 1997). Similarly, the IRS held that a park attendant hired on a seasonal basis by a government agency was an employee, in part because the agency provided training and instructions on methods to be used and set specific hours. *See* I.R.S. Priv. Ltr. Rul. 200323023 (Feb. 24, 2003). In the context of medical professionals, the right of the hiring organization to require compliance with its general policies is indicated by whether or not a physician or registered nurse is subject to the direction and control of a chief of staff, medical director, or some other authority. *See* Rev. Rul. 66-274 (1966), 1966-2 C.B. 446 (physician director of hospital pathology department not subject to direction and control of any hospital representative such as chief of staff is independent contractor). *See also* Rev. Rul. 73-417, 1973-2 C.B. 332 (physician director of hospital laboratory is employee, in part because he must comply with all rules and regulations of hospital); Richardson v. Genesee Cnty. Cmty. Mental Health Servs., 45 F. Supp. 2d 610, 614 (E.D. Mich. 1999) (employing agency that provided nurses with patient care guidelines, as well as with work rules governing "employee conduct," exercised supervisory control for purposes of determining whether nurses were "employees" within the meaning of the FLSA).

18. *See* Brock v. Superior Care, Inc., 840 F.2d 1054, 1057, 1060 (2d Cir. 1988) (where nurses work off-site with individual patients needing home or specialized care, the employer will still exercise control and supervision where it visits job sites even as infrequently as once or twice a month and requires nurses to keep and submit to it patient care notes required by federal and state law). *See also* Donovan v. DialAmerica Mktg., Inc., 757 F.2d 1376, 1383–84 (3d Cir.), *cert. denied*, 474 U.S. 919 (1985); Mathis v. Hous. Auth. of Umatilla Cnty., 242 F. Supp. 2d 777, 783 (D. Or. 2002) (Section 8 housing coordinator was subject to housing authority's control where she worked at housing authority offices, was subject to direction of executive director, and housing

- *Payment of any kind of regular wage*—whether by the hour, week, or month. In contrast, payment by the job or on a commission basis is evidence of an independent contractor relationship.[19] Courts also consider the fact that the hiring party has unilaterally set a worker's hourly wage as evidence that the hiring party controls the worker.[20]

9.3.1.1 Paradise County's Control over Its New Workers

Think again about the construction of the swimming pool. While the city will no doubt be curious about how the work is progressing and city officials may well visit the job site, the city will not be telling the contractor how to excavate the earth or what method to use in mixing the concrete. Nor does the city have the right to tell the contractor that when the contractor is done with this swimming pool, the city has another one for him or her to construct at the same price on the other side of town—although the city and the contractor may well come to some agreement on a second job. The city may worry that the contractor is not working fast enough, but until the contractor misses a contractual deadline, there is nothing the city can do.

---

authority reserved right to change or reassign job duties). On the IRS side, *cf. Weber*, 60 F.3d at 1110.

19. See *Cromwell*, 348 F. App'x at 60 (cable company had complete control over installer's pay); I.R.S. Priv. Ltr. Rul. 9320038 (Feb. 22, 1993) (department of corrections medical director paid hourly rate is employee). See also I.R.S. Priv. Ltr. Rul. 200339006 (June 9, 2003) (accounting technician paid hourly wage was employee); I.R.S. Priv. Ltr. Rul. 9728013 (April 9, 1997) (part-time lifeguard paid hourly wage is employee); I.R.S. Priv. Ltr. Rul. 9326015 (March 31, 1993) (physician in university health clinic). *See also Eren*, 180 F.3d at 597 (payment of architect on salary basis is evidence of employee status); *Weber*, 60 F.3d at 1111 (payment of minister on salary basis weighs in favor of employee status).

20. *See* Ruffin v. New Destination, 800 F. Supp. 2d 262, 268 (D.D.C. 2011) (social worker and reverend were employees of agency where employer set rate and method of payment); LeMaster v. Alternative Healthcare Solutions, Inc., 726 F. Supp. 2d 854, 861 (M.D. Tenn. 2010); *Brock*, 840 F.2d at 1060. *See also* U.S. Dep't of Labor Wage and Hour Opinion Letter dated Dec. 7, 2000, 2000 WL 33126542 (fact that company controlled rate at which package-delivery drivers were compensated factor leading to conclusion that drivers were employees, rather than independent contractors). *See also Eren*, 180 F.3d at 597 (architect whose pay and leave were set by hiring party is employee). *Cf. Freund*, 185 F. App'x at 784–85 (independent contractor installer of satellite systems paid by the job, not by the hour).

Now think about Paradise County's "independent contractors." The sanitation worker, visiting nurse, and accounting technician would each work under the supervision of another county employee. The sanitation worker will not choose his own routes but will have a route, truck, and coworkers assigned to him by a supervisor. The visiting nurse will have to follow the health department's patient care guidelines and will be required by the county to adhere to applicable state and federal regulations governing the treatment and billing of patients—all of which are evidence of employer control.[21] The accounting technician will be told how the county tracks and records accounts payable and will have to use the software program already in place.[22]

All three workers will have to abide by county work rules governing personal behavior. All three will be expected to work scheduled hours. They will not be allowed to take care of personal or other business while working for Paradise County. They will be held to the same workplace standards for job performance and personal conduct as employees working for the county.

The conditions under which Paradise County's so-called independent contractors work make clear that in each case, the county has the right to control the performance of their work.

9.3.1.2 Control over Professional Employees

The degree of control necessary to find employee status varies in accordance with the nature of the services the worker provides. Professionals such as physicians, certified public accountants, lawyers, dentists, registered nurses, and building and electrical contractors (to name just a few examples) require specialized skills to do their work. The methods that

---

21. *See* U.S. Dep't of Labor Wage and Hour Opinion Letter dated Aug. 24, 1999, 1999 WL 1788146 (hospital is likely joint employer of private duty nurses with nurse registry).

22. *See* I.R.S. Priv. Ltr. Rul. 200339006 (June 9, 2003) (accounting technician who was paid an hourly wage; given all necessary supplies, equipment, and materials needed to perform her services; and received assignments from a supervisor who determined the methods by which the services were to be performed was employee rather than independent contractor); I.R.S. Priv. Ltr. Rul. 200222005 (Feb. 15, 2002) (clerical worker hired because she submitted lowest bid but who worked under similar conditions to accounting technician, described above, was employee).

these skilled professionals use are frequently dictated by the standards of their individual professions, rather than by the hiring organization. The high level of knowledge and skill needed to perform their respective services often precludes direct supervision of their work. Nevertheless, when skilled workers such as these are hired under conditions in which they are paid a set salary and follow prescribed routines during set hours, they lose some of the independence that characterizes the practice of their profession and their usual status as independent contractors and they become employees.[23]

Such is the situation of Paradise County's new visiting nurse. Registered nurses are considered skilled professionals, and the IRS generally recognizes them as independent contractors when they perform private-duty nursing services for individual patients. In a private-duty nursing setting, nurses typically have full discretion in administering their professional services and are not subject to enough direction and control by the hiring party (usually the patient or the patient's family member) to establish an employment relationship. But when registered nurses are part of a medical staff of a hiring organization, they are usually subject to the control of a physician or another nurse. Under these conditions, the registered nurse is an employee. The IRS makes a distinction between registered nurses, on one hand, and licensed practical nurses (LPNs), nurse's aides, and home health aides, on the other. LPNs and aides who assist patients with personal and domestic care do not generally render professional care and are usually subject to almost complete direction and control regardless of the setting in which they perform their services: they are almost always employees.[24]

---

23. *See* Eren v. Commissioner, 180 F.3d 594, 596 (4th Cir. 1997) (architect); Weber v. Commissioner, 60 F.3d 1104, 1111 (4th Cir. 1995) (minister); Kentfield Med. Hosp. Corp. v. United States, 215 F. Supp. 2d 1064, 1070 (N.D. Calif. 2002) (psychologists). *See also* Rev. Rul. 87-41, 1987-1 C.B. 296 (the IRS's 20-factor discussion); Rev. Rul. 58-268, 1958-1 C.B. 353 (dental hygienist); I.R.S. Priv. Ltr. Rul. 9323013 (March 11, 1993) (psychiatrist at state psychiatric facility who serves as court-appointed examiner charged with examining individuals who have been involuntarily committed to the facility is an employee); I.R.S. Priv. Ltr. Rul. 9201033 (Jan. 3, 1992) (x-ray technician).

24. *See* Rev. Rul. 61-196, 1961-2 C.B. 155. This is similar to the distinction made by the Department of Labor in its regulations governing the classification of exempt and nonexempt employees: RNs may be classified as exempt professionals, while LPNs may not. *See* 29 C.F.R. § 541.301(e)(2). *See also LeMaster*, 726 F. Supp. 2d at 861 (fact

9.3.2 Opportunity for Profit or Loss

Consider once again the construction of the city swimming pool. The contractor will come to work having already purchased everything that is needed to do the job. The city is unlikely to supply anything. Since the construction of a pool usually requires more labor than that of a single worker, the contractor will typically supply and pay his or her own assistants. The contractor will factor the cost of the material, the equipment, and the helpers into the price of the job. Whether the contractor accurately assesses these direct and indirect costs determines whether he or she makes a profit or takes a loss on the job.

Where a worker has the opportunity to make a profit or take a loss on a job—either by completing the work faster or more slowly than the worker anticipated or at greater or lesser cost than estimated—the courts are more likely to find that the worker is an independent contractor. Employees do not typically have the possibility of making a profit or loss because they are usually paid a straight salary or an hourly wage and do not usually supply their own materials, equipment, and personnel. A worker who has no investment in the work cannot incur a loss or make a profit.[25]

---

that LPNs do not generally have the skills necessary to locate and manage discrete work projects characteristic of independent contractors, and that their skills are of task-specific, specialized kind that form piece of larger enterprise, suggests employee status).

25. *See* Bruecher Found. Servs., Inc. v. United States, 383 F. App'x 381, 390 (5th Cir. 2010) (where foundation repair company paid its workers by the hour at the end of the week regardless of whether job was completed and provided the necessary tools and supplies, the workers were employees); *LeMaster*, 726 F. Supp. 2d at 862 (nurses whose compensation was not tied to performance and who had no opportunity for profit or loss other than their set wage were employees); Donald G. Cave, a Prof'l Law Corp. v. C.I.R., 2012 WL 975044 at *4 (5th Cir. 2012) (law clerk was employee where firm paid his salary regardless of the amount of work he completed, clerk could neither increase his profit through skill and initiative nor sustain risk of losses, and firm provided him with all amenities needed to complete his work); Richardson v. Genesee Cnty. Cmty. Mental Health Servs., 45 F. Supp. 2d 610, 614 (E.D. Mich. 1999) (FLSA case; nurses at mental health crisis clinic who had no opportunity for profit or loss were employees); *Eren*, 180 F.3d at 597 (IRC case; salaried architect who was not paid commission or percentage of profits had no opportunity for profit or loss); *Weber*, 60 F.3d at 1111 (IRC case; minister paid a salary and provided with a parsonage, a utility expense allowance, and a travel allowance had no opportunity for profit or loss); Clincy v. Galardi S. Enters., Inc., 808 F. Supp. 2d 1326, 1345–47 (N.D. Ga. 2011)

The facts of *Chao v. Mid-Atlantic Installation Services, Inc.,* a Fourth Circuit Court of Appeals case, illustrate a real-world application of this factor. At issue in this case was whether cable installers were independent contractors or employees entitled to overtime. The cable installers' opportunity for profit or loss manifested itself in a number of ways. First, the hiring company could charge the installers if they failed to comply with either the technical requirements of an installation or with local ordinances regulating cable installation. Second, the fact that the installers supplied their own trucks and tools and had responsibility for their own liability and automobile insurance showed that the installers incurred expenses of a type not normally borne by employees that affected the amount they ultimately earned from a set of jobs. So too did the fact that the installers had responsibility for paying any assistants they hired and for reporting payments made to the assistants to the IRS. These factors weighed heavily in the court's conclusion that the cable installers were independent contractors.[26]

In contrast, when a hospital provided psychologists with staff, office space, and all of the supplies necessary for them to see patients, the court found that the psychologists were employees, not independent contractors. Similarly, nurses who worked at a crisis clinic at an hourly rate but

---

(exotic dancers had little opportunity for profit or loss where nightclub operator made decisions about advertising and promotion and dancers made minimal investments in materials compared to that of operator); Thompson v. Linda And A., Inc., 779 F. Supp. 2d 139, 148–49 (D.D.C. 2011) (where exotic dancers were paid by the shift and had no investment stake in the club, arrangement weighed heavily in favor of employee status). *See also* Rev. Rul. 70-309, 1970-1 C.B. 199 (oil-well pumpers who work in field who assume no business risks are employees); I.R.S. Priv. Ltr. Rul. 9251032 (Sept. 21, 1992) (nurse in state tuberculosis outreach program who assumed no risk of profit or loss is employee). *See also* Cromwell v. Driftwood Elec. Contractors, Inc., 348 F. App'x 57, 60 (5th Cir. 2009) (workers who restored damaged telecommunications lines in wake of hurricane were employees within meaning of FLSA even though nature of the work was temporary, and workers invested a substantial amount in their trucks, equipment, and tools but nevertheless worked on a steady and reliable basis over approximately 11 months exclusively for company that had complete control of their schedule and pay, which limited opportunity for profit or loss by workers).

26. *See* Chao v. Mid-Atl. Installation Servs., Inc., 16 F. App'x 104, 107, 2001 WL 739243 **3 (4th Cir. 2001); *See also* U.S. Dep't of Labor Wage and Hour Opinion Letter dated Sept. 5, 2002, 2002 WL 32406602.

supplied nothing beyond their own expertise were found not to have any investment in their work.[27]

Sometimes a worker has an opportunity to make a profit or incur a loss even where all of the tools, equipment, and personnel needed to do the job are supplied by the hiring organization, as in the case of certain kinds of service providers who control how many clients or patients they may see in a given day (physicians, for example) and thus how much the hiring organization may bill third party payors like insurance companies. In two contrasting cases, the IRS found that a hospital physician whose compensation consisted *solely* of a percentage of his department's gross receipts was an independent contractor, while a hospital physician whose compensation was also a percentage of charges attributable to his department but who was also *guaranteed a minimum salary* was an employee.[28] The distinction here was that the first physician ran a risk that his salary might not be enough to cover his expenses, while the second physician ran no such risk.

In Paradise County, none of the so-called contract employees will bring tools of their trade to work with them. The sanitation worker, the visiting nurse, and the accounting technician will each use the employer's supplies and equipment. To the extent that the work requires collaboration, they will each work with other workers hired by the employer, rather than going out and seeking assistants themselves. Their individual lack of investment in the resources needed to perform their respective jobs also weighs in favor of employee status for each of these workers, as does the fact that their compensation will be entirely a function of the number of hours worked. They have no opportunity for profit or loss.[29]

---

27. *See Richardson*, 45 F. Supp. 2d at 614. *See also Weber*, 60 F.3d at 1111 (when a church provided a minister with an office, this factor weighed in favor of employee status).

28. *See* Rev. Rul. 66-274, 1966-2 C.B. 446 (independent contractor); Rev. Rul. 73-417, 1973-2 C.B. 332 (employee).

29. *See* I.R.S. Priv. Ltr. Rul. 200339006 (June 9, 2003) (accounting technician who was paid by the hour and could not hire assistants or substitutes had no opportunity for profit or loss).

9.3.3 Integral Part of the Employer's Business

Where the work that an individual does is an integral part of the employer's operation, the worker is more likely to be an employee than an independent contractor.[30] How do the courts measure whether a specific job is integral to an organization? One measure is whether the worker provides services that the employing organization exists to provide. Workers who perform the mission work of an agency are an integral part of the employer's business. For example, nurses hired by a crisis clinic to provide mental health crisis intervention and referral services to the public were an integral part of the clinic's operation.[31] Similarly, a Section 8 housing coordinator who supervised one of three programs administered by the employer housing authority was an integral part of the housing authority's organization.[32] Treating patients was an integral part of the professional practice of a group of psychologists.[33] None of the positions in these examples were entitled to independent contractor status; all of the workers were employees.[34]

Another question the court may ask includes whether the worker performs the same work as others who are classified as employees. Where independent contractors perform the same work as employees, they are considered integrated into the employer's hierarchy and more likely to be employees.[35] Similarly, where workers are independent contractors after-hours for their regular employers but perform the same job duties as they do during regular hours, they are most certainly going to be determined to be employees.[36] Indeed, for FLSA purposes, even where regular employees

30. *See* Thomas v. Brock, 617 F. Supp. 526, 535 (W.D.N.C. 1985), *aff'd in part, modified in part and remanded by* 810 F.2d 448 (4th Cir. 1987).

31. *See* Richardson v. Genesee Cnty. Cmty. Mental Health Servs., 45 F. Supp. 2d 610, 614 (E.D. Mich. 1999). *See also* U.S. Dep't of Labor Wage and Hour Opinion Letter dated Aug. 24, 1999, 1999 WL 1788146 (hospital is likely joint employer of private duty nurses with nurse registry).

32. *See* Mathis v. Hous. Auth. of Umatilla Cnty., 242 F. Supp. 2d 777, 785 (D. Or. 2002).

33. *See* I.R.S. Priv. Ltr. Rul. 9320038 (Feb. 22 1993).

34. For additional examples from the private sector, see *Solis v. International Detective and Protective Service, Ltd.*, 819 F. Supp. 2d 740, 749–53 (N.D. Ill. 2011) (security guards were integral part of commercial security company's business and were thus employees); *Thompson v. Linda And A., Inc.*, 779 F. Supp. 2d 139, 150–51 (D.D.C. 2011) (exotic dancers were an integral part of adult entertainment nightclubs business); *Clincy v. Galardi South Enterprises, Inc.*, 808 F. Supp. 2d 1326, 1348–49 (N.D. Ga. 2011).

35. *See* Brock v. Superior Care, Inc., 840 F.2d 1054, 1057–58 (2d Cir. 1988); *Mathis*, 242 F. Supp. 2d at 785.

36. *See Richardson*, 45 F. Supp. 2d at 614.

are hired to perform different jobs afterhours, they almost always must be treated as employees. As the U.S. Department of Labor advised one company that desired to hire an employee (the lead designer of its monthly magazine) as an independent contractor (to do the typesetting and laying out of books) through her private business:

> [I]t is our opinion that the graphic designer when performing work for your company in her freelance graphic design capacity would also be an employee of your company and not an independent contractor. This is so even though the work that she would perform as a freelance artist would be different than her normal job responsibilities at the company. *It has long been the position of the Wage and Hour Division that it is unrealistic to assume that an employment and "independent contractor relationship" may exist concurrently between the same parties in the same workweek* [emphasis added].[37]

In the case of the swimming pool contractor, it is clear that the contractor does not provide services that are basic to the employer's mission (because even if providing recreational services is basic to a city's business, building swimming pools is not). Nor does the contractor do work similar to that done by employees—indeed, the whole point of bringing in the swimming pool contractor was to tap into expertise and experience that is both lacking in the city's workforce and unlikely to be needed again.

The situation of the Paradise County workers is markedly different. Two perform some of the mission work of the county (sanitation work, provision of public health services); one performs work essential to the county's business operations (paying its bills). All three perform the same work as others hired as employees. A court would likely find all three to be an integral part of the county's operations. This factor also weighs heavily in favor of employee status.

9.3.4 Exclusivity and Duration of the Relationship

Independent contractors usually have a special skill and exercise initiative in seeking out assignments or clients. For example, electricians, carpenters, and construction workers, like swimming pool contractors, have special

---

37. *See* U.S. Dep't of Labor Wage and Hour Opinion Letter dated July 5, 2000, 2000 WL 33126569.

skills.[38] Registered nurses are also skilled workers.[39] But the mere fact of having a special skill is not in and of itself indicative of independent contractor status. What counts is whether the worker exercises significant initiative in locating work opportunities or clients. Thus, electricians and carpenters who serve the needs of a single hiring organization (such as a city or county) over a long period of time will likely be employees, rather than independent contractors. But when a worker advertises his or her services to the public on a regular and consistent basis and performs services for a number of unrelated persons or businesses at the same time, that fact generally indicates that the worker is an independent contractor.[40] The swimming pool contractor is a case in point: the relationship between the city and the contractor will not be exclusive. It lasts only as long as it takes to construct the pool: once payment is made for the finished product, the relationship ends, although the contractor will continue to construct swimming pools for others.

Neither the job of sanitation worker nor that of accounting technician requires any special skill or initiative. Individual sanitation workers do not generally offer their services to the public: trash collection is usually a municipal service or one provided by a company under contract. If an accounting technician provided services to a variety of different clients at the same time, the clerk could be an independent contractor. Here, however, the fact that the clerk works a regular 40-hour week for the county under direct supervision argues against such status.[41]

---

38. *See* Chao v. Mid-Atl. Installation Servs., Inc., 16 F. App'x 104, 107, 2001 WL 739243 **3 (4th Cir. 2001). *See also* Richardson v. Genesee Cnty. Cmty. Mental Health Servs., 45 F. Supp. 2d 610, 614 (E.D. Mich. 1999) (nurse working after regularly scheduled hours at crisis clinic run by same employer does not locate clients independently), *citing Brock*, 840 F.2d at 1060 (where nurses are paid hourly rate by employing organization, rather than directly by patient, they are likely to be employees). *See also* Mathis v. Hous. Auth. of Umatilla Cnty., 242 F. Supp. 2d 777, 784 (D. Or. 2002) (special skills factor weighs toward employee status where Section 8 housing coordinator's work and client contact took place at housing authority during regular business hours; coordinator did not use skills in any independent way).

39. *See Richardson*, 45 F. Supp. 2d at 614.

40. Performing services for two or more persons or businesses simultaneously, however, is not conclusive evidence of independent contractor status: a person can work for two organizations or persons as an employee of each.

41. *See, e.g.*, Donald G. Cave, a Prof'l Law Corp. v. C.I.R., 2012 WL 975044 at *2–*4 (5th Cir. 2012) (attorneys were employees and not independent contractors of law firm

The visiting nurse does have a special skill. This factor will not weigh heavily in favor of independent contractor status, however, because the nurse does not seek out client service opportunities on her own but is assigned patients by the health department and is paid by the county, rather than by the patient.

The fact that Paradise County expects to have a continuing relationship with its three newest workers further indicates that these workers should be classified as employees.

9.3.5 The Right to Discharge the Worker

An employer exercises control over an employee through the threat of dismissal, which causes the employee to obey the employer's instructions. A true independent contractor, however, cannot be fired so long as the independent contractor produces a result that meets the hiring party's specifications. So when a hiring party has the right to fire the worker, it is usually treated as evidence that the worker is an employee, rather than an independent contractor.[42]

The right of the *worker* to terminate his or her services at any time without incurring any liability is also characteristic of an employment relationship. In contrast, an independent contractor who quits without completing the job for which he or she was hired might have to forfeit some of the contract price. The hiring party could also sue the independent contractor either for specific performance (an order from the court to the worker to do the work agreed upon) or for breach of contract, provided that the

---

where they maintained continuous and exclusive relationships with firm and were not specialists called in to perform specific tasks).

42. *See* Weber v. Commissioner, 60 F.3d 1104, 1111, 1113 (4th Cir. 1995) (although minister could not be fired at will, his failure to follow the Book of Discipline could have resulted in termination by fellow members of the clergy); Ruffin v. New Destination, 800 F. Supp. 2d 262, 268 (D.D.C. 2011) (social worker and reverend were employees of group counseling provider where provider had power to hire and fire them and they were subject to supervision of provider's clinical director); Clincy v. Galardi S. Enters., Inc., 808 F. Supp. 2d 1326, 1343–45 (N.D. Ga. 2011) (exotic dancers were employees of club where it retained the right to fine and otherwise discipline them); Rev. Rul. 75-41, 1975-1 C.B. 323 (physicians working for physician services corporation who can be fired at will are employees); I.R.S. Priv. Ltr. Rul. 9320038 (Feb. 22, 1993) (medical director who can be fired with 30-days' notice is employee).

hiring party can show damages resulting from the failure to complete the work as agreed.[43]

9.4 The Conclusion: Paradise County Has Three New Employees

In engaging the services of the sanitation worker, visiting nurse, and accounting clerk, Paradise County has taken on three new employees, notwithstanding how the county or the workers describe the relationship. Why is that the case? Because Paradise County has (1) retained the right to control the work of the sanitation worker, visiting nurse, and accounting clerk; (2) has the right to fire each of them; and (3) has not provided the workers with the opportunity to make a profit or suffer a loss.

The workers, for their part, (1) individually have made no investment in the performance of their services for the county and (2) do not seek out client opportunities on their own. Finally, with respect to each of the workers, (1) both Paradise County and the worker envision a continuing relationship, and (2) the work done is an integral part of the business of county government.

As a matter of law, the workers are employees, not independent contractors.

9.5 Some Difficult Cases

9.5.1 Positions Funded through Grants

Almost all North Carolina government employers—state agencies, local governments, community colleges, and four-year colleges—have positions whose salaries are funded through grants from federal or private sources. Because these positions are generally created outside of the organization's usual classification and budgeting process, employers may be tempted to engage the workers as independent contractors. An IRS Revenue Ruling on the status of a professor and a clerical worker whose salaries were funded

---

43. *See* Rev. Rul. 70-309, 1970-1 C.B. 199 (oil-well pumpers can quit at any time); I.R.S. Priv. Ltr. Rul. 9320038 (Feb. 22, 1993) (department of corrections medical director who could be fired with 30-days' notice and could quit at any time was employee); I.R.S. Priv. Ltr. Rul. 200339006 (June 9, 2003) (accounting tech who could quit without incurring liability or penalty was employee).

through a grant to a college makes clear that for *all* grant-funded positions, employers should continue to do economic reality and right to control analyses. The ruling shows that most workers hired to fill grant-funded positions will be employees rather than independent contractors.

In Revenue Ruling 55-583, the IRS found that a professor who was responsible for conducting research and supervising support staff under a grant from a private foundation to a state college was an employee of the college with respect to both that portion of his salary that was paid out of the college's budget *and* the portion paid out of grant funds. Although the professor had discretion with respect to the means and methods of performing the research, as well as over the hours during which research was performed, the college had broad general supervision over the way the grant money was spent and had a right to exercise direction and control. The professor had hired a clerical assistant to work with him exclusively on grant-related research and her salary was also paid from grant funds. The IRS found that she had been hired with the implied consent of the college and held that where one employee (here, the professor) hires other individuals in connection with the first employee's work with either the express or implied consent of the employer, those other individuals are also employees of the employer.[44]

Two points are worth emphasizing here. Except perhaps in the case of certain kinds of scientific research, most grants are made to the organization—sometimes to the individual who will carry out the project *and* to the organization, but rarely to the individual alone. This means that the hiring organization will usually have the right to exercise direction and control over the activities funded by the grant. As explained above, the right to control a worker's activities weighs heavily in favor of employee status, even where the hiring organization does not exercise that right.

Second, the individual in charge of administering the grant may well prefer that workers hired under the grant not receive the benefits paid to other employees in the organization. This may be because the positions are for a defined, short-term duration or because the grant money is not sufficient to cover the cost of the benefits. Even if grant-funded workers do not receive benefits, they are likely to be employees if the organization or an employee of the organization is directing them in the performance of

44. *See* Rev. Rul. 55-583, 1955-2 C.B. 405.

their duties. While the duration of the relationship is a distinct factor to be considered in determining worker status, the fact that a job is temporary will not turn the worker into an independent contractor where other factors weigh in favor of employee status.

9.5.2 Adjunct or Part-Time Instructors in Colleges, Recreation and Parks Departments, or Employee Training and Development Programs

While educational institutions make the greatest and most obvious use of adjunct or part-time instructors, local government recreation and parks departments also frequently hire part-time workers to teach physical education and activity classes and other subjects. Similarly, employers offering employee training and development programs are likely to make use of outside, adjunct workers to lead training sessions. Use of adjunct instructors such as these would, on its face, appear to be a textbook example of the proper classification of a worker as an independent contractor for the following reasons:

- adjunct instructors are engaged for a limited duration to do a defined job;
- adjunct instructors typically have a particular expertise for which they are hired and typically perform similar or related services for other organizations or individuals;
- for colleges and local government recreation programs, the hiring organization charges a fixed fee for the courses or sessions that adjunct instructors teach and typically pays the instructors some percentage of that as a fixed fee for their services.

The IRS, however, takes a different view. In a series of revenue rulings, private letter rulings, and technical advice memoranda, the IRS has held that part-time instructors are employees where the hiring organization

- determines the courses that are offered,
- determines the content and hours of each course,
- enrolls the students, and
- provides the facilities at which the instruction is offered,

and the instructor

- is required to perform his or her services personally,
- has no investment in the facilities, and

- does not bear a risk of profit or loss (that is, the instructor is paid the same amount whether or not tuition and fee payments cover the hiring organization's expenses).

The IRS takes this position even if the instructor provides teaching services or services related to the subject of expertise to others and may devote only a small percentage of work time to the instruction performed for the hiring organization.[45] The IRS analysis focuses on the fact that the hiring organization controls everything about the way in which the "teaching services" are performed—that is, in each of the cases the IRS considered, the hiring organization controlled everything except the actual delivery of the material.

Would the FLSA economic reality test provide a different result? Probably not. As discussed above, the FLSA economic reality test and the IRS right to control test consider essentially the same factors. Research for this book has not revealed any cases that address the issue of an adjunct instructor's status as employee or independent contractor under the FLSA. This lack of cases is not surprising. Most instructors would have little reason to bring an FLSA claim. Many instructors would qualify as FLSA-exempt professionals and few nonexempt part-time instructors are likely to work in excess of 40 hours such that overtime is an issue.

9.5.3 Physicians

Correctly classifying physicians hired to staff health clinics, on-site occupational health offices, or public hospitals presents some of the same challenges as classifying registered nurses, discussed above in the section on professionals. Given their very high level of specialized training, physicians generally exercise almost complete discretion in their treatment of patients and are subject to relatively little day-to-day supervision. Where there is such supervision, it is generally provided by another physician.

As discussed earlier, an important factor in determining whether a worker is an employee or independent contractor is the extent to which the services the worker performs are an integral part of the hiring organization's regular business. As the IRS has noted in Revenue Ruling 66-274, a

---

45. *See* Rev. Rul. 70-308, 1970-1 C.B. 199; I.R.S. Tech. Adv. Mem. 91-05-007 (February 1, 1991); I.R.S. Tech. Adv. Mem. 89-25-001 (June 23, 1989); I.R.S. Priv. Ltr. Rul. 8728022 (April 10, 1987).

hiring organization that engages a physician usually does so because providing medical services is necessary to its operation. More important than the question of whether the physician's services are integral to the organization, therefore, is the way the services of the physician are integrated into the hiring organization. Significant factors here are (1) the manner in which the physician is paid for his services—that is, whether the physician is paid on a percentage basis, a salary basis, or a percentage basis with a guaranteed minimum; (2) whether the physician is permitted to employ associate physicians or to engage substitutes when he or she is absent from work; (3) if the physician is permitted to engage substitutes, whether the physician or the hiring organization is responsible for compensating them; and (4) whether the physician is permitted to engage in the private practice of medicine or to perform professional services for others.[46] In other words, in the case of physicians, the right to control is a less important set of factors for IRS purposes than is the extent to which the physician is economically independent of the hiring organization.

Applying these factors, the IRS found that a physician director of a hospital pathology department was an independent contractor where the physician received a percentage of the department's gross receipts as his only compensation; personally paid his associates or substitutes; was permitted to engage in the private practice of medicine; and was not subject to the direction and control of any hospital representative, such as a chief of staff.[47] But a physician director of a hospital laboratory was an employee where he was guaranteed a minimum salary in addition to a specified percentage of charges attributable to his department, and he could not pursue outside business or provide pathology services to others without written consent.[48]

46. *See* Rev. Rul. 66-274, 1966-2 C.B. 446. *See also Weber*, 60 F.3d at 1112 (minister's work clearly part of regular work of United Methodist Church); I.R.S. Priv. Ltr. Rul. 9320038 (Feb. 22, 1993) (department of corrections medical director paid hourly rate is employee); I.R.S. Priv. Ltr. Rul. 8937039 (Sept. 15, 1989) (psychologists treating patients for professional firm are employees).

47. *See* Rev. Rul. 66-274, 1966-2 C.B. 446.

48. *See* Rev. Rul. 73-417, 1973-2 C.B. 332.

9.6 A Price to Pay

An employer that misclassifies workers as independent contractors when those workers do not meet the legal test for independent contractor status may be subject to significant penalties under both the Fair Labor Standards Act and the Internal Revenue Code. For workers covered by the FLSA, penalties include

1. liability for overtime compensation going back for a period of two years—three years if the employer has reason to know it has misclassified the worker; and
2. liquidated damages in an amount equal to the amount of overtime owed.[49]

When the Internal Revenue Service determines that a worker previously classified as an independent contractor does not meet the right to control test and is legally an employee, the employer will be liable for

1. 1.5 percent of each worker's federal income tax liability where the misclassification was unintentional,
2. both the employer's share of FICA contributions and up to 20 percent of the employee's missing FICA contributions, and
3. interest on the under-withheld amounts and other IRS penalties.

---

49. *See* 29 U.S.C. §§ 216(b) and 255(a). *See also* Brock v. Superior Care, Inc., 840 F.2d 1054, 1061 (2d Cir. 1988). Note that conduct that is merely unreasonable or negligent with respect to ascertaining an employer's obligations under the FLSA is not considered to be willful. *See* McLaughlin v. Richland Shoe Co., 486 U.S. 128, 131, 133–35 (1988), *overruling* Donovan v. Bel-Loc Diner, Inc., 780 F.2d. 1113 (4th Cir. 1985). *See also* Troutt v. Stavola Bros., Inc., 905 F. Supp. 295, 302 (M.D.N.C. 1995), *aff'd*, 107 F.3d 1104 (4th Cir. 1997) (mere failure to seek legal advice, standing alone, is insufficient to establish willfulness where there is no pattern of complaints to employer or in the industry that could establish knowledge or recklessness on part of employer). But an employer's failure to investigate whether its policies violate the FLSA where employees have questioned those policies would be reckless. *See* Davis v. Charoen Pokphand (USA), Inc., 302 F. Supp. 2d 1314, 1327 (M.D. Ala. 2004); LaPorte v. Gen. Elec. Plastics, 838 F. Supp. 549, 558 (M.D. Ala. 1993). In the Fourth Circuit, the determination of whether a violation was willful or not under 29 U.S.C. § 255(a), and thus whether the employer's liability for back overtime extends back three or merely two years, will be determined by a jury. *See* Fowler v. Land Mgmt. Grp., Inc., 978 F. 2d 158, 162–63 (4th Cir. 1992); Soto v. McLean, 20 F. Supp. 2d 901, 913 (E.D.N.C. 1998) (denying defendants' motion for summary judgment).

The employer may not seek reimbursement from the worker for taxes, penalties, or fines imposed by the IRS.[50] These liabilities make illusory those projected savings that caused the organization to engage workers as independent contractors in the first place.

In certain limited circumstances, employers may avail themselves of a defense against liability for their failure to withhold employee federal income taxes. For a discussion of this defense (known as the Section 530 safe harbor), see the author's article, "Independent Contractor or Employee? The Legal Distinction and Its Consequences."[51]

9.7 Worker Classification and Employee Benefits

In several private sector cases, workers engaged as independent contractors have successfully sued their hiring organizations, claiming that they are common law employees and that they are therefore entitled to participate in the hiring organization's employee benefit plans.[52] In some cases, the employees have sought the value of benefits retroactively. Could such a suit be successful against a North Carolina public employer?

The answer to this question is unclear. There are no reported cases involving claims of this kind against a public employer from North Carolina state or federal courts. But public employers should consider the following: Although the Teachers and State Employees Retirement System (TSERS), the Local Government Employee Retirement System (LGERS), the North Carolina Workers' Compensation Act, and the North Carolina Employment Security Act require workers to be employees before they are entitled to benefits, the North Carolina Supreme Court has defined "employee" in the context of workers' compensation and unemployment benefits by recourse to the common law right of control test for employee status.[53] It would likely do the same in the case of TSERS and LGERS, as

---

50. *See* 26 U.S.C. §§ 3509, 6601, 6651, 6662, and 6721.

51. *See* Diane M. Juffras, *Independent Contractor or Employee? The Legal Distinction and Its Consequences*, Public Employment Law Bulletin No. 32, May 2005, at 16–18, http://sogpubs.unc.edu/electronicversions/pdfs/pelb32.pdf.

52. *See, e.g.*, Vizcaino v. Microsoft Corp., 120 F.3d 1006 (9th Cir. 1997), *cert. denied*, 522 U.S. 1098 (1998).

53. *See* N.C. Gen. Stat. (hereinafter G.S.) §§ 135-3(1) and 135-1(10) (TSERS); G.S. 128-21(10) (LGERS); G.S. 97-2(2), McGown v. Hines, 353 N.C. 683, 686 (2001);

A Model Checklist to Help Determine Independent Contractor or Employee Status

Employers should modify this checklist as is appropriate to the nature of their organization as a whole or to a particular department. Every proposal to engage a worker as an independent contractor must be assessed individually. Whether that worker legally qualifies as an independent contractor will depend on the fact and circumstances of the individual situation.

PART I: The answer "yes" indicates that the factor weighs in favor of employee status, while the answer "no" indicates that the factor weighs in favor of independent contractor status.

Factor	Yes	No
1. Does the hiring organization have the right to control when, where and how the worker will do the job, or the order and sequence in which the worker will perform services? (Check "yes" even if the organization does not intend to exercise that right).		
2. Does the hiring organization set the worker's hours and schedule?		
3. Must the work be performed personally by the worker (as opposed to the worker subcontracting it out or furnishing his or her own substitute)?		
4. Is the hiring organization providing training of any kind?		
5. Does the hiring organization provide the worker with the tools, supplies, and/or equipment needed to do the job (as opposed to requiring the worker to bring his or her own tools, equipment and supplies to the job)?		
6. Does an employee of the hiring organization supervise the worker?		
7. Does the worker have to submit written or make oral reports?		
8. Is the work performed on the hiring organization's premises or at a site controlled or designated by the hiring organization?		
9. If the worker is performing services off-site, does the hiring organization have the right to send supervisors to the site to check up on the worker? (check "yes" even if the organization has no intention of exercising that right)		
10. Can the worker be fired at the will of the hiring organization?		

11. Can the worker quit the job at will without incurring any liability?		
12. Will the hiring organization hire, fire and pay the worker's assistants?		
13. Will the worker be paid by the hour, week or month (as opposed to being paid for the successful completion of the job or piece)?		
14. Has the hiring organization unilaterally set the worker's rate of pay?		
15. Does the hiring organization reimburse the worker for expenses and travel?		

Factor	Yes	No
16. Is the relationship between the hiring organization and the worker going to be a continuing relationship?		
17. Does anyone else perform the same or similar services for the organization as an employee?		
18. Are the services performed by the worker part of the core or day-to-day operations of the hiring organization?		
19. Is the worker a current employee in another capacity?		
20. Was the worker an employee at any time during the past year and did the worker provide the same or similar services as an employee?		

PART II: Here, the answer "yes" indicates that the factor weighs in favor of independent contractor status, while the answer "no" indicates that the factor weighs in favor of employee status.

Factor	Yes	No
21. Does the worker perform similar services for others as an independent contractor?		
22. Does the worker advertise his or her services to the public?		
23. Has the worker made any investment in facilities or equipment needed to do the work?		
24. Does the arrangement between hiring organization and worker allow the worker to make a profit or suffer a loss?		

it would in interpreting a promise of retiree health benefits to employees meeting certain eligibility requirements.

For a detailed discussion of the arguments workers might make for the value of benefits they should have received if they had been properly classified as employees rather than as independent contractors, see the author's article "Independent Contractor or Employee? The Legal Distinction and Its Consequences."[54]

9.8 Most Public Sector Workers Are Employees, Not Independent Contractors

Most people performing services for a public sector organization are employees within the common law definition of that term. True independent contractors are few. Government employers can unwittingly accrue substantial unfunded liabilities in the form of unpaid overtime, unpaid employer FICA contributions, and penalties for violating the FLSA and Internal Revenue Code, as well as liability for unpaid benefits, when they misclassify employees as independent contractors. For this reason, it is crucial that each public employer establish a procedure whereby it does an individualized analysis of any proposed relationship with a worker it plans to engage on an independent contractor basis. Few will so qualify.

Every proposal to engage a worker as an independent contractor must be assessed individually. Whether that worker legally qualifies as an independent contractor will depend on the particular facts and circumstances of the arrangement. Employers may consider using a checklist to help guide their evaluations of individual positions. A model checklist is provided on pages 342–43.

Hughart v. Dasco Transp., Inc., 606 S.E.2d 379, 385 (N.C. App. 2005) (NC Workers' Compensation Act); G.S. 96-8(6)a; Emp't Sec. Comm'n v. Huckabee, 120 N.C. App. 217, 219 (1995), *aff'd*, 343 N.C. 297 (N.C. Employment Security Act). For the right of control test under North Carolina law, see *Hayes v. Elon College*, 224 N.C. 11, 15 (1944).

54. *See* Diane M. Juffras, *Independent Contractor or Employee? The Legal Distinction and Its Consequences*, PUBLIC EMPLOYMENT LAW BULLETIN No. 32, May 2005, at 20–25, http://sogpubs.unc.edu/electronicversions/pdfs/pelb32.pdf.

Chapter 10

Applicant Records: Confidentiality and Retention

Chapter 10

Applicant Records: Confidentiality and Retention

Under the Americans with Disabilities Act (ADA) and the Genetic Information Nondisclosure Act (GINA), all employers, public and private, have obligations both to keep certain portions of applicant records confidential and to retain those records for designated periods of time. Those statutes, as well as Title VII of the Civil Rights Act of 1964, also require employers to maintain aggregate statistics about the race, gender, national origin, and disability status of their applicant pools and their workforces. North Carolina public employers have additional duties imposed on them by the General Statutes and the Archives Division of the North Carolina Department of Cultural Resources. This chapter sets forth these obligations, surveying them by category rather than by statute.

10.1 Confidentiality of Applicant Records

Two sets of rules govern a North Carolina public employer's duty of confidentiality when it comes to applications and the documents related to an application. The first set governs disclosure of applicant information to the public; the second set governs who within the employer organization has access to which parts of the applicant's file.

10.1.1 Disclosure of Applicant Information to the Public

Section 132-6 of the North Carolina General Statutes (hereinafter G.S.) gives the public the right of access to and the right to copy documents made in the transaction of business by state and local governments.[1] G.S. 160A-168 exempts the personnel files of city employees from the provisions of G.S. 132-6, the statute that requires that public records be made available for inspection and copying, and G.S. 153A-98 exempts the personnel files of county employees from G.S. 132-6. Under both G.S. 160A-168 and G.S. 153A-98, certain information in personnel files is open to the public and other information is not to be disclosed except under special circumstances. The same holds true for the statutes governing access to the personnel files of area mental health authority employees,[2] community college employees,[3] water and sewer authority employees,[4] district health department employees,[5] public health authority employees,[6] and public hospital employees.[7] The statutes cover the personnel files of three groups: current employees, former employees, and applicants for employment. *None of the statutes allows public access to any portion of an applicant's file.* This includes the name of the applicant.[8] The statutes generally allow employees to see their own personnel files, but local government employers do not have to allow applicants to see their own files. Alone among the personnel

1. *See* N.C. Gen. Stat. (hereinafter G.S.) §§ 132-1 and 132-6.

2. *See* G.S. 122C-158.

3. *See* G.S. 115D-27.

4. See G.S. 162A-6.1.

5. *See* G.S. 130A-42, which subjects district health department employee records to the same rules of confidentiality and public disclosure as those of county employees as set forth in G.S. 153A-98.

6. *See* G.S. 130A-45.9.

7. *See* G.S. 131E-257.2. Absent from the foregoing list are employees of councils of government, local alcohol and beverage control boards, and soil and water conservation districts, among others, for whom the North Carolina General Assembly has not enacted personnel privacy statutes. Those organizations may follow the rules set forth in G.S. 160A-168 and G.S. 153A-98. *See* David M. Lawrence, Public Records Law for North Carolina Local Governments 142–45 (2d ed. 2009).

8. *See* Elkin Tribune v. Yadkin Cnty. Bd. of Cnty. Comm'rs, 331 N.C. 735 (1992) (disclosure of applications for position of county manager, which were governed by statute imposing conditions on disclosure of county employee personnel files, rather than by Public Records Act, was erroneous).

records statutes, the community college statute gives the right of access to their own files to applicants for community college positions.[9]

10.1.2 Disclosure of Applicant Information within the Hiring Organization

The personnel privacy statutes do not address the question of who within the employer's organization may see an applicant's file, but the general rule should be that only the human resources department and those involved in the hiring decision may see the file. This would include the city or county manager (or city council in a mayor–council form of government), a county health or social services director, the area mental health or water and sewer authority director, or any other person with hiring authority within a local government entity. In a community college this would include the board of trustees or, where the board has delegated hiring authority, the president. Depending on the position, others involved in the decision may include department heads and immediate supervisors and other organization employees who are part of the interviewing and evaluation process. Anyone who is not involved in the hiring decision would fall into the category of the public, to whom no disclosure is authorized.

10.1.2.1 Application of Current Employee for a Different Job

When a current employee of a local government or community college applies for a different job with the same employer, the employer should open a new, separate applicant file for that employee in order to give that application the same protection from public disclosure that other applicants receive. Not only will the application be confidential with respect to the general public and the press, but the applicant file will not be open to the employee's current supervisor. As with persons applying for jobs outside their current organization, the current employee who is an applicant for a different job may not wish to jeopardize the relationship with his or her current supervisor by letting the supervisor know that the employee is seeking another position. For city and county employees, area mental health authority employees, and water and sewer authority employees, personnel files, unlike applicant files, are open for inspection by the employee's supervisor.[10]

---

9. *See* G.S. 115D-29(a)(1).

10. *See* G.S. 160A-168(c)(3), G.S. 153A-98(c)(3), G.S. 122C-158(c)(3), and G.S. 162A-6.1, respectively. G.S. 115D-29(a)(2) opens community college employee files to "the

10.1.3 Confidentiality of Applicant Medical and Genetic Information

Under the Americans with Disabilities Act, employers may only obtain medical information from applicants once they have made a conditional offer of employment.[11] Sometimes it is obtained through a medical questionnaire, through the employee's provision of his or her own medical records, or through a medical examination performed by an employer physician. Under the Genetic Information Nondiscrimination Act, employers may never actively seek genetic information, although it can and does happen that an employer inadvertently acquires genetic and family medical information because a physician provides it without being asked, the employee volunteers it, or coworkers discuss it.[12] How should an employer treat the medical and genetic information of its job applicants?

The ADA provides that any medical information obtained by an employer about an applicant or employee must be collected on a separate form, kept in a separate medical file, and treated as a "confidential medical record."[13] Similarly, if an employer has somehow obtained genetic information about an applicant, it must also keep this information separate from the rest of the applicant file and treat it as a confidential medical record. This information may be maintained in the same file as medical information obtained under the ADA. GINA does not require that covered entities maintain a separate medical file for genetic information.[14] Unlike the Health Insurance Portability and Accountability Act (HIPAA) regulations that health care providers must observe, neither the ADA nor GINA requires employers to use encryption, password authorization, and other security safeguards for any electronic medical records they maintain. Nevertheless, the confidentiality provisions of the ADA and GINA apply not only to an employer's paper records that contain medical and genetic

---

president and other supervisory personnel," so opening an applicant file for a current community college employee applying for a different job may not protect the application from disclosure to the employee's current supervisor.

11. *See* 29 C.F.R. §§ 1630.13(a) and 1630.14(b).

12. Thus, when an employer has an applicant fill out a post-offer medical questionnaire or undergo a post-offer medical examination consistent with the ADA, it must direct the applicant and the physician performing the examination not to collect genetic information—that is, not to collect medical history. *See* 29 C.F.R. § 1635.8(d).

13. *See* 42 U.S.C. § 12112(d)(3)(B); 29 C.F.R. § 1630.14(b)(1).

14. *See* 29 C.F.R. § 1635.9.

information but to any information that it keeps electronically, as well.[15] Segregation of medical information is an absolute rule. An employer should not place *any* medical-related material in an applicant's or employee's non-medical file. If an employer needs to put a document that has some medical information in it in an applicant or personnel file, the employer must remove the medical information from the document before putting it in the regular file.

Medical information may be given to those persons involved in the hiring process if they have a need to know. For example, medical information may be relevant to department heads and supervisors if the applicant will need a reasonable accommodation either of the hiring process itself or in order to do the job and these members of the management team will be involved in devising or implementing an accommodation. On the other hand, a physical examination that has revealed a condition or physical anomaly unrelated to the performance of the job should not be shared with anyone. Within a human resources department in which people have distinct roles, medical information should be seen only by those persons whose responsibilities require them to see it, and not by anyone else.[16]

10.2 Aggregate Information about Applicants Required for Equal Employment Opportunity Commission Reporting Purposes

Employers with 15 or more employees—that is, those subject to Title VII and the ADA—are required to keep those records and statistics that would enable them to complete the Equal Employment Opportunity Commission (EEOC) Report EEO-4, which asks for aggregate and not personally identifiable data on the composition of an employer's workforce. A copy of the Report EEO-4 form may be found in Appendix 5. Local government employers with 100 or more employees and a rotating sample of local

15. *See* EEOC Informal Discussion Letter dated May 31, 2011, from Peggy R. Mastroianni, Legal Counsel, www.eeoc.gov/eeoc/foia/letters/2011/ada_gina_confidentrequre.html.

16. *See* U.S. Equal Employment Opportunity Commission, *ADA Enforcement Guidance: Preemployment Disability-Related Questions and Medical Examinations*, No. 915.002 (October 10, 1995), at 20–21, www.eeoc.gov/policy/docs/medfin5.pdf.

government employers with 15–99 employees are required to file Report EEO-4 every two years.[17] Community colleges must report similar information on the Higher Education Staff Information Report EEO-6.[18]

Given that there is a risk of liability for unlawful discrimination where an employer simply knows something about an applicant's or employee's race, color, gender, religion, national original, or disability, one might rightfully wonder how to go about collecting such information. The EEOC advises using so-called tear-off sheets with the application. The tear-off sheet, and not the application, should have information about an applicant's membership in various protected classes. Upon receipt of the application, the human resources department separates or tears off the sheet and files it or records the information separately for statistical purposes. No information about the applicant's protected class status should be seen by anyone involved in the selection process, from the initial screener to the final decision maker.[19]

10.3 Retention of Applicant Records

North Carolina public employers are subject to two sets of recordkeeping requirements related to applicant records: those of the individual federal antidiscrimination statutes and those of the Government Records Branch of the North Carolina Department of Cultural Resources Division

---

17. *See* 29 C.F.R. § 1602.30–1602.32. Note that this requirement is separate and distinct from the requirement set forth in 29 C.F.R. § 1607.4 that each employer "should maintain and have available for inspection records or other information which will disclose the impact which its tests and other selection procedures have upon employment opportunities of persons by identifiable race, sex, or ethnic group . . . ."

18. *See* 29 C.F.R. §§ 1602.48 and 1602.50.

19. *See* EEOC Informal Discussion Letter dated August 5, 2002, from Dianna B. Johnston, Assistant Legal Counsel, www.eeoc.gov/eeoc/foia/letters/2002/titlevii_ada_inquiries.html, *citing* Robinson v. Adams, 847 F.2d 1315 (9th Cir. 1987) (Title VII is not violated where the screener is unaware of the plaintiff's race, which was noted only on a separate sheet from the applications), *cert. denied*, 490 U.S. 1105 (1989). *See also* EEOC Informal Discussion Letter dated October 15, 2008, from Reed L. Russell, Legal Counsel, www.eeoc.gov/eeoc/foia/letters/2008/titlevii_question_gender_race.html; EEOC Informal Discussion Letter dated October 27, 2005, from Peggy R. Mastroianni, Associate Legal Counsel, www.eeoc.gov/eeoc/foia/letters/2005/internet_hiring.html.

of Archives and Records. Fortunately, their requirements with respect to applicant records are the same.

10.3.1 Retention of Applicant Records under Federal Antidiscrimination Statutes

Pursuant to its authority under Title VII, the ADA, and GINA, the EEOC has issued regulations relating to the preservation of applicant and employee records. Both local governments and community colleges must preserve applicant records for a period of two years after the decision on whether to hire or reject the applicant (or for two years after the document was created, whichever is later).[20] Where an applicant has filed a charge of discrimination under Title VII, the ADA, or GINA, the employer must retain all application forms, test papers, and other relevant material related to the unsuccessful applicant and *to all other applicants for the same position* until the statute of limitations for filing a charge or filing an action in U.S. district court has run or until the EEOC charge or the litigation has been resolved.[21] The regulation governing recordkeeping for community colleges contains an exception that the regulation applicable to local government employers does not: applicant records need not be maintained where the applicant is a non-student applying for a position that is known to be of a temporary or seasonal nature.[22] The EEOC's Age Discrimination in Employment Act regulations require employers to keep applicant files only for a period of one year, unless a claim of discrimination is filed, in which case they are to be retained until the matter is resolved.[23]

10.3.1.1 Internet Searches and the Uniform Guidelines on Employee Selection Procedures

The use of Internet background checks is a selection procedure governed by Title VII and the EEOC's Uniform Guidelines on Employee Selection Procedures (Uniform Guidelines).[24] This means that North Carolina public employers who are doing Internet background checks must meet the recordkeeping requirement of the Uniform Guidelines with respect to their

20. *See* 29 C.F.R. §§ 1602.31 and 1602.49(a).
21. *See* 29 C.F.R. §§ 1602.31 and 1602.49(a).
22. *See* 29 C.F.R. § 1602.49(b).
23. *See* 29 C.F.R. § 1627.3.
24. 29 C.F.R. § 1607 *et seq.*

Internet background searches and must ensure that their use of Internet searches does not result in disparate impact on Title VII–protected classes. The employment regulations issued by the EEOC under the authority of Title VII include a requirement that employers maintain records that will disclose the impact that tests and other selection procedures have had on employment opportunities for persons of different races, genders, or ethnic groups:

> Each user should maintain and have available for inspection records or other information which will disclose the impact which its tests and other selection procedures have upon employment opportunities of persons by identifiable race, sex, or ethnic group as set forth in paragraph B of this section, in order to determine compliance with these guidelines.[25]

This recordkeeping regulation was designed to provide a way of ensuring that no selection device disproportionately excludes (that is, has a disparate impact on) any particular protected class. The Uniform Guidelines recordkeeping regulation is in addition to the more general requirement that employers keep for a period of one year "application forms submitted by applicants and other records having to do with hiring. . . ."[26]

10.3.2 Retention of Applicant Records under North Carolina Law

G.S. Chapter 121, the North Carolina Archives and History Act, confers upon the North Carolina Department of Cultural Resources the legal responsibility for developing a records management program for state agencies, giving advice and assistance to the state and local public officials and agencies about the maintenance and preservation of public records and regulating the disposition and destruction of state and local government documents and records that are public records under G.S. Chapter 132.[27] To that end, the Archives Division of the Department of Cultural Resources has developed separate records retention schedules for state agencies, local governments, the University of North Carolina system, community colleges, and local boards of education. The records retention schedules may be found on the website of the Government Records Branch of the Archives

25. *See* 29 C.F.R. § 1607.4(A).
26. *See* 29 C.F.R. § 1602.14.
27. *See* G.S. 121-4(2) and 121-5(b).

Division. There are links to individual schedules for municipalities, county government management, local ABC boards, county boards of elections, county departments of social services, county health departments, offices of the register of deeds, offices of the county sheriff, local management entities, public hospitals, local public transportation systems, water and sewer authorities, public libraries, and regional councils of governments.[28]

While each schedule has a standard for personnel records, all of the personnel records standards are the same. The EEOC's reporting regulations take precedence over state law relating to the retention of applicant records,[29] but the Government Records Branch staff has incorporated the EEOC's record retention requirements into its personnel records standard, so public employers need only consult the state schedule to be in compliance with both state and federal law. For applicant material, the personnel records standard provides as set forth in the following paragraphs.

Employment applications and resumes, including records submitted by job applicants for vacant positions or by current employees for promotion, transfer, or training opportunities, as well as applications, transcripts, resumes, and letters of reference, should be transferred to the personnel file of the successful applicant. Any remaining records of successful applicants may be destroyed two years from the date the record was created or received or the person was hired. For applicants not hired, employment applications, resumes, and similar records should be retained until two years after the date the record was received, if no charge of discrimination has been filed. If a charge of discrimination has been filed, the records must be retained for one year after the resolution of the charge. Unsolicited applications and resumes and those received after the posted closing date should be kept for two years after they are received.

Records about the selection of applicants for a given position, including interview documentation, rosters, eligibility lists, test ranking sheets, justification statements, background and criminal history checks, health or physical examinations, and similar records should be transferred to the personnel file where the applicant has been hired. For applicants who are

---

28. The main page for Government Records Branch's local government records retention and disposition schedules may be found at www.records.ncdcr.gov/local/default.htm.

29. *See* 29 C.F.R. §§ 1602.38 and 1602.55.

not hired, records should be kept until two years after the resolution of any discrimination charge.

Aptitude and skills testing records, including records concerning aptitude and skills tests required of job applicants or of current employees to qualify for promotion or transfer should be kept for two years after the date the record was created. Validation studies and copies of the tests themselves, as well as records relating to the planning and administration of tests, should be kept for two years after the time the employer stops using the test.

In addition, *position description records*, including information on job title, grade, and duties and responsibilities should be retained for two years after the date the position description is superseded by a new one. *Job advertisements and postings* should be kept for two years.[30]

---

30. For these standards, see North Carolina Department of Cultural Resources, Division of Historical Resources, Archives and Records Section, Government Records Branch, *Municipal Records Retention and Disposition Schedule*, May 19. 2009, Standard 15—Personnel Records, pp. 95–107, www.records.ncdcr.gov/local/default.htm. As noted in the text, the schedule with respect to applicant records is the same for all local government entities.

Appendix 1

Application of Employment Laws to Small Employers

Federal Employment Law	Applies To
Fair Credit Reporting Act (FCRA) 15 U.S.C. §§ 1681–1681x	All local government and community college employers regardless of size
Title VII of the Civil Rights Act of 1967	All employers with 15 or more employees
The Americans with Disabilities Act of 1990 (ADA)	All employers with 15 or more employees
The Rehabilitation Act of 1973 (similar to the ADA)	Any local government or community college employer who receives federal funds for any purpose
The Genetic Information Nondiscrimination Act (GINA)	All employers with 15 or more employees
The Age Discrimination in Employment Act (ADEA)	All local government and community college employers (courts divided on whether statute applies to all public employers or only to those with 20 or more employees, which is the minimum for private sector employers)
Uniformed Services Employment and Reemployment Rights Act (USERRA)	All local government and community college employers regardless of size
Immigration Reform and Control Act (IRCA)	All local government and community college employers regardless of size
Equal Protection Clause of the Fourteenth Amendment to the U.S. Constitution	All local government and community college employers regardless of size

North Carolina Employment Law	Applies To
The North Carolina Equal Employment Practices Act G.S. 143-422.1 through 143-422.3	All employers with 15 or more employees
The North Carolina Persons with Disabilities Protection Act	All employers with 15 or more employees
G.S. 95-28.2. Discrimination against persons for lawful use of lawful products during nonworking hours prohibited	All local government and community college employers regardless of size
G.S. 143B-421.1. Selective Service registration	All local government and community college employers regardless of size
G.S. 1-539.12. Immunity from civil liability for employers disclosing information	All local government and community college employers regardless of size
G.S. 127B-12 through 127B-14. Discrimination against members of the military forces prohibited	All local government and community college employers regardless of size
G.S. 126-7.1(i) (requirement to use E-Verify)	All community colleges regardless of size
G.S. 160A-169.1 and G.S. 153A-99.1 (requirement to use E-Verify)	All cities and counties regardless of size
G.S. 95-28.1A (discrimination based on genetic testing or genetic information prohibited)	All local government and community college employers regardless of size

Appendix 2

Affirmative Action Today in North Carolina Government Employment

Many employers, both public and private, advertise themselves as Affirmative Action/Equal Employment Opportunity employers. This claim is usually meant to convey to applicants and others that the employer does not discriminate and provides a welcoming environment for workers of every race, color, gender, religion, national origin, age, and disability status. Does it mean, however, that the employer has an affirmative action program? Should an applicant or the general public assume that such an employer will take race, gender, or other protected status into consideration in making an employment decision? The continued widespread use of the AA/EEO label suggests that many employers are unclear about the distinction between the concepts of affirmative action and equal employment opportunity and about the current state of the law governing affirmative action plans. Indeed, despite the use of this term by a number of North Carolina public employers, to the author's knowledge there are no North Carolina local government or community college employers who have formal affirmative action plans. Understanding what affirmative action is and is not and what form of affirmative action a public employer may take is crucial for any local government or community college that wants to pursue a diverse workforce.

APP. 2.1 What Is Affirmative Action?

Affirmative action is a legal concept separate and distinct from the concepts of equal employment opportunity (EEO) and workplace diversity. The term *affirmative action* is generally understood to mean the deliberate use of preferences based on race or gender in selection or promotion. The federal Equal Employment Opportunity Commission (EEOC), however, defines affirmative action more narrowly as "actions appropriate to overcome the effects of past or present practices, policies, or other barriers to equal employment opportunity."[1] In contrast, the phrase *equal employment opportunity* means simply extending equal opportunities for hiring, training, and promotion to all applicants and employees without regard to their membership in a protected class. *An equal opportunity employer* (EOE) is an employer that says it makes hiring, training, and promotion decisions without reference to race, color, gender, religion, national origin, age, disability, or military status. The EEOC defines *workforce diversity* as "a business management concept under which employers voluntarily promote an inclusive workplace" by creating a culture of respect for individual differences in order to "draw talent and ideas from all segments of the population."[2]

The legal status of affirmative action has changed over time, beginning—as the EEOC's definition suggests—as a broad set of deliberate actions and plans to bring more African Americans and women into areas of the workforce from which they had been traditionally excluded. Some employers voluntarily adopted affirmative action plans. Others were directed to adopt affirmative action plans by court order or as part of the settlement of a Title VII discrimination lawsuit. Still others adopted affirmative action plans to comply with Executive Order 11246, which prohibits federal contractors and subcontractors from discriminating in employment decisions on the basis of race, color, religion, sex, or national origin and requires covered contractors to take affirmative action to ensure that equal opportunity is provided in all aspects of their employment. From the start, affirmative action plans have been challenged by applicants and employees in majority groups who saw such programs as depriving them of the opportunity to be

1. *See* 29 C.F.R. § 1608.1(c).

2. *See* U.S. Equal Employment Opportunity Commission, *Compliance Manual*, No. 915.003 (April 16, 2006), at at 15–31, www.eeoc.gov/policy/docs/race-color.pdf.

hired, to be promoted, or to avoid layoff based on their merits. Title VII's prohibition against using race and gender has provided the basis for challenging affirmative action plans in both the private and public sectors. In public sector employment, the Equal Protection Clause of the Fourteenth Amendment has offered an additional basis for challenging affirmative action because government affirmative action plans, by their very nature, treat different classes of persons differently.

Over time, the United States Supreme Court has narrowed the confines of what constitutes lawful affirmative action, and some affirmative action practices that were initially considered lawful are now prohibited. Today, there are only two circumstances under which it is clearly lawful for local government employers and community colleges to adopt formal affirmative action hiring plans. The first is where the government employer has made a finding that the effects of past discriminatory practices taken by that organization persist in its workplace in the present. The second is where the government employer has been ordered to adopt an affirmative action plan by a court or as part of a court-approved settlement. A few courts have recognized the operational need for diversity in certain segments of the public workforce, such as public safety, as a lawful reason to adopt an affirmative action plan. However, neither the United States Supreme Court nor the Fourth Circuit Court of Appeals has addressed this issue.

APP. 2.2 Title VII Challenges to Affirmative Action

Voluntary affirmative action would seem to violate Title VII's basic rule that no employment action is to be taken on the basis of race, color, gender, religion, or national origin. Nevertheless, Title VII *seems* to say that voluntary affirmative action is permissible. Within Title VII, Section 2000e-2, the very section that prohibits the use of race, color, and gender in employment decisions, also says that Title VII does not *require* employers to give preferential treatment to any protected class because of any imbalance in its workforce when compared to the number of persons in that class in the employer's geographic area or in the available workforce:

> Nothing contained in this subchapter shall be interpreted to require any employer . . . to grant preferential treatment to any individual or to any group because of the race, color, religion,

> sex, or national origin of such individual or group *on account of an imbalance* which may exist with respect to the total number or percentage of persons of any race, color, religion, sex, or national origin employed by any employer . . . in comparison with the total number or percentage of persons of such race, color, religion, sex, or national origin in any community, State, section, or other area, or in the available work force in any community, State, section, or other area [emphasis added].[3]

The implication of this section is that while preferential treatment to correct racial or other imbalances is not required, it is permitted. In other words, this section of Title VII appears to say that employers may adopt voluntary affirmative action plans.

App. 2.2.1 The Four Criteria That an Affirmative Action Plan Must Meet to Satisfy Title VII

In 1979, the U.S. Supreme Court decided its first affirmative-action-in-employment case, *United Steelworkers of America v. Weber*.[4] In that case a white employee sued his employer and his union, challenging a voluntarily adopted job training program that reserved 50 percent of the program's openings for African American employees until the percentage of African American craftworkers became commensurate with their percentage in the local workforce.[5] Both the federal trial court and the court of appeals found that the affirmative action plan violated Title VII, holding that all employment preferences based on race, even those that resulted from a bona fide affirmative action plan, violated Title VII's prohibition against race discrimination in employment.[6] The Supreme Court reversed that decision and upheld the affirmative action program, ruling that Title VII's ban on racial discrimination did not forbid voluntary affirmative action plans.[7] To prohibit all race-conscious affirmative action, the Court said, would be at odds with the very purpose of Title VII: to break down old patterns of racial segregation and hierarchy and to open opportunities to

3. *See* 42 U.S.C. § 2000e-2(j).
4. 443 U.S. 193 (1979).
5. *See* United Steelworkers of Am. v. Weber, 443 U.S. 193, 198–99 (1979).
6. *See Weber*, 443 U.S. at 200.
7. *See Weber*, 443 U.S. at 208.

African Americans and other minority groups in occupations that had been traditionally closed to them.[8]

The Supreme Court set forth four criteria which employers must meet for an affirmative action plan to be lawful under Title VII. First, there must be a showing of a conspicuous racial imbalance in traditionally segregated job categories. Second, the plan must be reasonably related to remedying the imbalance. Third, the plan must not trammel the rights of the majority-race workers by requiring their termination and replacement with African American employees or serve as a complete bar to the advancement of majority-race workers. Fourth, the plan must be a temporary measure to eliminate an existing racial imbalance and must not seek to maintain racial balance indefinitely into the future.[9] Although the *Weber* case involved a collective bargaining agreement between a private employer and a labor union, its holdings were equally applicable to public sector employers and the non-union workplace and to affirmative action plans involving gender, as the Court's decision one year later in *Johnson v. Transportation Agency, Santa Clara County, California*, shows.

In the *Johnson* case, a county transportation agency voluntarily adopted an affirmative action plan that allowed race and gender to be considered as one factor in making promotions within traditionally segregated job classifications in which women and African Americans were still significantly underrepresented when compared to the local workforce. Here, no specific number of positions was set aside for women or African Americans. The plan instead provided for annual evaluation and readjustment of short-range goals.[10] A white male employee who was equally qualified but passed over for promotion in favor of a female employee brought suit challenging the affirmative action plan.[11] The Supreme Court held that the county agency had not violated Title VII when it took the female employee's gender into consideration in making its hiring decision, because the county's affirmative action plan satisfied the factors set forth in the *Weber* decision.[12] First, the plan was created in response to a manifest imbalance

---

8. *See Weber*, 443 U.S. at 201–07.

9. *See Weber*, 443 U.S. at 208–09.

10. *See* Johnson v. Transp. Agency, Santa Clara Cnty., Cal., 480 U.S. 616, 620–22 (1987).

11. *See Johnson*, 480 U.S. at 623–25.

12. *See Johnson*, 480 U.S. at 620, 623–24.

in the number of women in a traditionally segregated job—that of road dispatcher—when compared to the number of women in the available labor force.[13] Second, the plan was reasonably related to the imbalance. Third, there was no numerical standard or quota for the hiring of women, only a long-term goal, and gender was only one factor in the decision-making process. Thus, the rights of male employees were not "trammeled" and there was no absolute bar to their advancement.[14] Fourth and finally, the plan's purpose was to attain a balanced workforce, not to maintain one.[15] The Supreme Court also made clear in the *Johnson* case that under Title VII, it was not necessary for an employer to show that it had itself committed discrimination in the past for it to adopt an affirmative action program.[16]

The Supreme Court's decisions in *Weber* and *Johnson* still govern consideration of whether an affirmative action plan is lawful under Title VII today. Title VII challenges to affirmative action are like other claims of race or gender discrimination in that they are analyzed under the *McDonnell Douglas* burden shifting framework. Here, as with other disparate treatment or intentional discrimination claims, once a plaintiff establishes a prima facie case that race or gender has been taken into account in an employment decision, the burden shifts to the employer to articulate a nondiscriminatory rationale for its decision. The existence of an affirmative action plan is a legitimate, nondiscriminatory reason for an employment decision as long as the plan in question satisfies the requirements set forth in the *Weber* and *Johnson* cases.[17] Title VII affirmative action litigation, therefore, today focuses on whether a particular affirmative action plan satisfies each of those criteria.

Post-*Johnson* challenges to affirmative action plans have made clear that rectifying general societal discrimination and providing role models for minorities and women will not satisfy the *Weber-Johnson* requirement that there be a manifest imbalance in race or gender in an occupation or job

---

13. *See Johnson*, 480 U.S. at 631–36.

14. *See Johnson*, 480 U.S. at 637.

15. *See Johnson*, 480 U.S. at 638.

16. *See* Johnson v. Transp. Agency, Santa Clara Cnty., Cal., 480 U.S. 616, 630 (1987), *citing* United Steelworkers of Am. v. Weber, 443 U.S. 193, 212 (1979).

17. *See* United States v. Brennan, 650 F.3d 65, 94, 104 (2d Cir. 2011) (drawing a distinction between affirmative action plans and make-whole relief and finding that affirmative action plans are intended to provide *ex ante* benefits to all members of a racial or gender class).

when compared to the labor pool. In a 1996 case from the federal Third Circuit Court of Appeals, a local board of education adopted a policy that provided that where job candidates were equally qualified, applicants meeting the criteria of the affirmative action program would be hired. When budget issues forced the school district to lay off teachers, it turned to the affirmative action plan for guidance. The school district chose plaintiff Sharon Taxman for layoff instead of another teacher of equal seniority and equal qualifications because Taxman was white. The other teacher was the only African American teacher in the high school's business department and the school board thought it important to have a role model within that department for the school's African American students.[18] Taxman sued under Title VII.

The Third Circuit found that the affirmative action policy did not satisfy the *Weber* and *Johnson* criteria. The plan was not remedial because there was no manifest imbalance between the numbers of black and white teachers in the school district as a whole. Indeed, both sides agreed that there was no time during which African American teachers were underrepresented or underutilized in the school district. The court held:

> The affirmative action plans at issue in *Weber* and *Johnson* were sustained only because the Supreme Court, examining those plans in light of congressional intent, found a secondary congressional objective in Title VII that had to be accommodated—i.e., the elimination of the effects of past discrimination in the workplace. Here, there is no congressional recognition of diversity as a Title VII objective requiring accommodation. . . . While the Court in *Weber* and *Johnson* permitted some deviation from the antidiscrimination mandate of the statute in order to erase the effects of past discrimination, these rulings do not open the door to additional non-remedial deviations.[19]

The court also found that the plan unnecessarily trammeled the rights of the plaintiff in that it caused her to lose a tenured job. Finally, the Court

18. *See* Taxman v. Bd. of Educ. of Twp. of Piscataway, 91 F.3d 1547, 1550 (3d Cir. 1996).

19. *See Taxman*, 91 F.3d at 1557–58.

found that the plan was one of unlimited duration, in that it was to be resurrected from time to time whenever the board perceived a need for it.[20]

Other Title VII challenges to affirmative action have focused on whether there was a racial imbalance in the workforce,[21] whether a plan that reset its goals every year trammeled the rights of white applicants,[22] the lack of a formal set of goals that would mark the end of the plan,[23] whether there was a manifest imbalance in compensation between male and female employees,[24] and whether remedial pay increases were more than remedial.[25]

There have been no recent challenges to any North Carolina public employer affirmative action plans most likely because, to the author's knowledge, no formal plans exist.

App. 2.2.2 Title VII and Affirmative Action: A Summary

Both public and private employer affirmative action plans are subject to challenge under Title VII. The rules that can be derived from the Supreme Court's cases in this area may be summarized as follows:

1. To be lawful under Title VII, plans with race or gender preference must be designed to correct manifest imbalances reflecting underrepresentation of minority groups in traditionally segregated job categories.

---

20. *See Taxman*, 91 F.3d at 1564.

21. *See, e.g.*, Humphries v. Pulaski Cnty. Special Sch. Dist., 580 F.3d 688, 695–96 (8th Cir. 2009) (question of material fact as to whether the workforce was racially imbalanced).

22. *See, e.g.*, Sharkey v. Dixie Elec. Membership Corp., 262 F. App'x 598, 603 (5th Cir. 2008) (affirmative action plan satisfied all of the *Weber* and *Johnson* criteria).

23. *See, e.g.*, Lilly v. City of Beckley, W. Va., 797 F.2d 191 (1986) (informal affirmative action plan adopted to avoid loss of funding for all-white and all-male city police department did not satisfy *Weber* and *Johnson* criteria).

24. *See, e.g.*, Maitland v. Univ. of Minn., 155 F.3d 1013, 1016 (8th Cir. 1998) (question of material fact as to whether there was manifest imbalance between male and female faculty salaries at time of adoption of affirmative action plan); Smith v. Va. Commonwealth Univ., 84 F.3d 672 (4th Cir. 1996) (same).

25. *See, e.g.*, Rudebusch v. Hughes, 313 F.3d 506, 520–21 (9th Cir. 2002) (faculty pay adjustments did not trammel the rights of male professors, but whether the pay increases were more than remedial was a disputed issue of material fact).

2. It is not necessary that a public employer admit past discrimination to adopt an affirmative action plan under Title VII. However, societal discrimination or the role model theory will not support race-conscious plans.
3. Race or sex may be considered as one factor among many under Title VII in a decision to promote or hire.
4. An affirmative action plan may not unnecessarily trammel the rights of majority-race or majority-gender employees or applicants or create an absolute bar to their advancement.
5. Plans must be temporary and must be aimed only at attaining a balanced workforce, not at maintaining a permanent race or gender balance.

APP. 2.3 Equal Protection Challenges to Affirmative Action

App. 2.3.1 The First Case: *Regents of University of California v. Bakke*

The affirmative action plans of government employers are subject to challenge under the Equal Protection Clause of the Fourteenth Amendment as well as under Title VII. The first U.S. Supreme Court case to examine the status of affirmative action under the Equal Protection Clause was the 1978 case *Regents of University of California v. Bakke*.[26] The *Bakke* case arose out of university admissions practices rather than employment practices, but its principles were applied in the employment context thereafter. The *Bakke* case involved the express use of quotas as a form of affirmative action: the medical school at the University of California at Davis set aside 16 of 100 seats in the entering class for minority applicants. The equal protection question before the Supreme Court was whether a race-based classification such as the medical school's set-aside for minority applicants was subject to strict scrutiny, as earlier decisions on race-based classifications had held, or to a less demanding standard.[27]

The Court's decision in the *Bakke* case did not give clear direction to universities or government employers, as there was no one opinion that

---

26. *See* Regents of Univ. of Cal. v. Bakke, 438 U.S. 265 (1978).

27. *See Bakke*, 438 U.S. at 287–89 (1978). See the discussion of the Equal Protection Clause, rational basis, and intermediate and strict scrutiny in Chapter 2, Section 2.10.

had a majority of votes. Five justices—a majority—did agree that "[g]overnment may take race into account when it acts not to demean or insult any racial group, but to remedy disadvantages cast on minorities by past racial prejudice, at least when appropriate findings have been made by judicial, legislative, or administrative bodies with competence to act in this area."[28] The same five agreed that some uses of race in university admissions were permissible.[29] Only one *Bakke* justice, however, Justice Powell, concluded that race-based government affirmative action programs must satisfy strict scrutiny—that is, (1) the government must make a showing that the race-based classification is *necessary* to promote a *compelling* government interest, and (2) the race-conscious plan must be *narrowly tailored* to further that interest.[30]

In Justice Powell's opinion, the medical school's program failed this test.[31] The medical school identified four government interests that its plan was designed to serve:

1. "reducing the historic deficit of traditionally disfavored minorities in medical schools and in the medical profession,"[32]
2. countering the effects of societal discrimination,
3. increasing the number of physicians who would practice in underserved communities, and
4. obtaining the educational benefits that flow from an ethnically diverse student body.[33]

In this case, Justice Powell said, there was no judicial, legislative, or administrative finding of discrimination in the medical school or the medical profession,[34] and the medical school faculty was not an appropriate body to determine the groups and boundaries of societal discrimination.[35] Even if improving medical care in underserved communities was a compelling government interest, Justice Powell found, there was no evidence showing

---

28. *See Bakke*, 438 U.S. at 325.
29. *See Bakke*, 438 U.S. at 325–26.
30. *See Bakke*, 438 U.S. at 359 (opinion of Justice Powell).
31. *See* Regents of Univ. of Cal. v. Bakke, 438 U.S. 265, 320 (1978).
32. *Bakke*, 438 U.S. at 306.
33. *See Bakke*, 438 U.S. at 305–06.
34. *See Bakke*, 438 U.S. at 307.
35. *See Bakke*, 438 U.S. at 309.

that the admissions quota furthered that interest.[36] Justice Powell did find that the attainment of a diverse student body was a constitutionally permissible goal for an institution of higher education.[37] He did not, however, find the use of an explicit number of set-aside seats for minority applicants to be a narrowly tailored way of furthering that goal, and he suggested that it might stand in the way of "genuine diversity."[38]

Four other justices concurred in the judgment that the government can sometimes make racial classifications and joined Justice Powell in reversing the decision of the court below, which had prohibited the university from ever adopting race-conscious admissions measures. These justices, however, defined "strict scrutiny" differently than Justice Powell, using a definition that would later come to be deemed "intermediate scrutiny." The four justices would have required racial classifications designed to further remedial purposes to serve *important* governmental objectives and be *substantially related* to achievement of those objectives.[39] They found the medical school's affirmative action plan satisfied this standard.[40]

App. 2.3.2 The Only Affirmative Action Employment Case to Come before the Supreme Court: *Wygant v. Jackson Board of Education*

To date, the Supreme Court has heard only one equal protection challenge to affirmative action that involved employment.[41] In the 1986 case *Wygant v. Jackson Board of Education*, the Court held that a public school district's affirmative action plan that required that white employees with greater seniority be laid off before African American employees with less seniority violated the Equal Protection Clause. Four justices concurred in the judgment that the plan was unconstitutional, but only three joined in the plurality opinion, which—like the opinion in the *Bakke* case—was written

36. *See* Regents of Univ. of Cal. v. Bakke, 438 U.S. 265, 310 (1978).

37. *See Bakke*, 438 U.S. at 311–15 (1978).

38. *See Bakke*, 438 U.S. at 315–18.

39. *See Bakke*, 438 U.S. at 359 (opinion of Justices Brennan, White, Marshall, and Blackmun).

40. *See Bakke*, 438 U.S. at 369–70.

41. *See* Wygant v. Jackson Bd. of Educ., 476 U.S. 267 (1986) (teacher employment); City of Richmond v. J.A. Croson Co., 488 U.S. 469 (1989) (minority set-aside program for local government contracting); Metro Broad. v. FCC, 497 U.S. 547 (1990) (minority set-aside program for broadcast licenses); Adarand Constructors, Inc. v. Pena, 515 U.S. 200 (1995) (minority set-aside program for federal contracting).

by Justice Powell. The plurality opinion rejected the justification that the school district offered for the plan; namely, that black students needed black teachers as role models in order to alleviate the effects of societal discrimination. Justice Powell's opinion said:

> This Court never has held that societal discrimination alone is sufficient to justify a racial classification. Rather, the Court has insisted upon some showing of prior discrimination by the governmental unit involved before allowing limited use of racial classifications in order to remedy such discrimination.[42]

Instead, Justice Powell said, the employer must demonstrate convincing evidence to justify the conclusion that it engaged in prior discrimination and that remedial affirmative action is necessary.[43]

In its arguments before the Court, the school district acknowledged past discrimination in which it had itself engaged, but because the school district had not pursued that argument in the courts below, the Supreme Court declined to consider that justification.[44] Nevertheless, in dicta Justice Powell's plurality opinion said that even if there were evidence to the effect that the board of education had engaged in racially discriminatory practices in the past, the layoff plan was not specifically and narrowly tailored to remedy such past discrimination. Justice Powell distinguished between hiring plans and layoff plans: hiring plans would have only a diffuse effect on white applicants, because such plans would foreclose only one opportunity among others for white applicants, while layoff plans entailed the loss of an existing job and would place the burden of achieving racial equality on specific individuals. The opinion concluded that although the school district's layoff plan was not narrowly tailored to remedy any past discrimination it may have engaged in, other policies, such as the adoption of hiring goals, could be.[45]

42. *See Wygant*, 476 U.S. at 274.
43. *See Wygant*, 476 U.S. at 277–78.
44. *See Wygant*, 476 U.S. at 277–78.
45. *See Wygant*, 476 U.S. at 284.

App. 2.3.3 The Adoption of Strict Scrutiny as the Test for Racial and National Origin Classifications

Three years later, in *City of Richmond v. J.A. Croson Co.*, a public contracting case, a majority of the Supreme Court finally agreed that any racial classification by a state or local government was subject to strict scrutiny. The city of Richmond, Virginia, had adopted a requirement that all contractors with whom it did business give a specified percentage of their subcontracts to minority contractors. The city offered no evidence of past discrimination in the Richmond area construction industry and sought to justify its use of racial classifications by pointing to generalized discrimination that, it claimed, everyone knew had existed. The Court again rejected the premise that remedying general societal discrimination could ever be a compelling government interest that justified the use of race-based classifications.[46] In emphasizing the necessity for a showing of real past discrimination, the Court pointed out the impossibility of determining whether a remedial plan was narrowly tailored when there was no identifiable discrimination against which to measure the remedies.[47] The purpose of the strict scrutiny test, the Court said, was to ensure "that the means chosen 'fit' this compelling goal so closely that there is little or no possibility that the motive for the classification was illegitimate racial prejudice or stereotype."[48] The Court also emphasized the necessity of considering whether there are any race-neutral means to remedy discrimination before a local government turns to other, race-based remedies.[49]

For a time the Supreme Court had held that the Fifth Amendment, which guarantees that the federal government will give equal protection of the laws to its citizens, required that congressional actions satisfy only intermediate scrutiny when Congress's purposes were benign and sought to remedy discrimination.[50] But in its 1995 decision in *Adarand Constructors, Inc. v. Pena*, the Court held for the first time that all government actions

46. *See Croson*, 488 U.S. at 497–505.

47. *See* City of Richmond v. J.A. Croson Co., 488 U.S. 469, 507 (1989).

48. *See Croson*, 488 U.S. at 493.

49. *See Croson*, 488 U.S. at 507, *citing* United States v. Paradise, 480 U.S. 149, 171 (1987).

50. *See* Metro Broad., Inc. v. FCC, 497 U.S. 547, 564–65 (1990), *overruled by* Adarand Constructors, Inc. v. Pena, 515 U.S. 200 (1995). *See also* Fullilove v. Klutznick, 448 U.S. 448, 480–83, 490–92 (1980).

involving race-based classifications, whether taken by federal, state, or local government, must satisfy the strict scrutiny standard.[51]

App. 2.3.4 Diversity as a Compelling Government Interest: The *Grutter* and *Gratz* Decisions

Twenty-five years separate the Supreme Court's first decision on affirmative action and equal protection in the *Bakke* case from its most recent decision in the paired cases of *Grutter v. Bollinger* and *Gratz v. Bollinger*. In the *Grutter* and *Gratz* cases, the Court affirmed that strict scrutiny—a showing that the plan was narrowly tailored to further a compelling government interest—was the appropriate standard for all government race- and national origin-based classifications.[52] The *Grutter* and *Gratz* cases were, like the *Bakke* case, university admissions cases: *Grutter* and *Gratz* challenged the University of Michigan's law school affirmative action plan and the University of Michigan's undergraduate college affirmative action plan respectively. The compelling government interest identified by the university in both cases was obtaining the educational benefits that flow from a diverse student body. The law school's affirmative action plan did not make use of a quota or give numeric values to race or national origin but instead looked at the "whole candidate," with contribution to the diversity of the incoming class only one of many factors considered.[53] The Supreme Court held that the law school's plan passed strict scrutiny and did not violate the Equal Protection Clause. It found that the law school's policy was narrowly tailored to further the school's interest in diversity: admissions officials were to consider grades and test scores but were also directed to look beyond grades and tests to all the ways in which an applicant might contribute to a diverse educational environment. While the policy did not limit what characteristics and experiences might be considered as a contribution to diversity, it did reaffirm the law school's commitment to racial and ethnic diversity.[54]

Michigan's undergraduate admissions affirmative action policy, in contrast, did not survive strict scrutiny. The undergraduate affirmative action policy automatically distributed 20 points, or one-fifth of the points needed

51. *See Adarand*, 515 U.S. at 224–27.

52. *See* Grutter v. Bollinger, 539 U.S. 306 (2003); Gratz v. Bollinger, 539 U.S. 244 (2003).

53. *Grutter*, 539 U.S. at 315–16.

54. *See Grutter*, 539 U.S. at 307–309, 315–16.

to guarantee admission, to every single "underrepresented minority" applicant solely because of race.[55] In practice, the policy of "automatic distribution of 20 points had the effect of making 'the factor of race . . . decisive' for virtually every minimally qualified underrepresented minority applicant."[56] The Court found that, in contrast to the law school's policy, the undergraduate admissions policy was not narrowly tailored to achieve the benefit of a diverse student body.

App. 2.3.5 Equal Protection after *Grutter* and *Gratz*

The *Grutter* and *Gratz* cases involved student admissions to public institutions of higher education. The Supreme Court did not indicate one way or another whether its holdings were applicable in the context of public employment. To date, there have been relatively few cases in which public employers have cited the need for diversity as the compelling government interest that justified the adoption of an affirmative action plan. Instead, most cases have continued to turn on the issue of whether there was evidence that a government employer had discriminated in the past and on whether the affirmative action plan's particular remedies were narrowly tailored to compensate for that discrimination.

For example, in the 2006 case *Kohlbek v. City of Omaha, Nebraska,* the affirmative action plan governing promotions within the city fire department was found to violate the Equal Protection Clause because there was no evidence of past discrimination. Under Omaha's plan, whenever the minority representation in a particular position was less than its stated goal (which was based on the minority population in the area and within the fire department ranks), candidates on the promotion-eligible list were promoted out of rank order, based on their race. The city contended that the affirmative action plan was developed to remedy past discrimination within the fire department. The Eighth Circuit Court of Appeals held, however, that before a remedial racial classification could be justified, there must be identifiable past discrimination. In this case, there was neither a statistically significant difference between the actual and expected number of minorities in the relevant fire officer ranks nor any other evidence of past or continuing discrimination. Thus, the plan could not be considered

55. *See Gratz,* 539 U.S. at 270.

56. *See Gratz,* 539 U.S. at 272, *quoting* Regents of Univ. of Cal. v. Bakke, 438 U.S. 265, 317 (1978).

"narrowly tailored to further the goal of remedying past discrimination," as the strict scrutiny test required.[57] At trial, the city had also argued in the alternative that it had a compelling interest in developing and retaining a diverse workforce—an argument that sounds much like the University of Michigan's successful argument in the *Grutter* case—but the trial court did not decide the issue and it was therefore not considered by the Eighth Circuit.[58]

One local government employer's argument that it needs a diverse workforce received a positive reception before a federal appeals court. In *Petit v. City of Chicago,* the city adjusted the scores on a police promotional examination to bring the lower scores of African Amercian officers in line with those of white officers. It took this action because under the terms of a federal court order, the city was prohibited from promoting officers in test rank order unless the test had been validated. Here, the city believed that the test scheme in question would be difficult to validate. It reasoned that a score adjustment would bring some African American officers within the higher-scoring pool from which the officers who receive promotions would come. White patrol officers who were not promoted to sergeant after the exam scores were standardized based on race challenged the city's practice on equal protection grounds. Based on the expert testimony of several witnesses, the court found that the city had an operational need for a diverse workforce—in another words, in order for the city to provide services effectively, it needed a sufficient number of racial minority employees to be among those providing those services:

> . . . a visible presence of minorities in supervisory positions is critical to effective policing in a racially diverse city like Chicago because supervisors "set the tone for the department." Equally important, the presence of minority supervisors is an impor-

57. *See* Kohlbek v. City of Omaha, Neb., 447 F.3d 552, 555–57, 557–58 (8th Cir. 2006). *See also* Lomack v. City of Newark, 463 F.3d 303 (3d Cir. 2006) (race-based transfer and assignment policy in city fire department did not pass strict scrutiny test where racial imbalance in fire houses was not the result of past discrimination).

58. *See Kohlbek*, 447 F.3d at 557–78. *Cf.* Reynolds v. City of Chicago, 296 F.3d 524, 528, 530 (7th Cir. 2002) (jury's finding of past discrimination against African Americans in the Chicago police department was neither erroneous nor unreasonable; remedying past discrimination was a compelling government interest and out of rank promotion of black, female, and Latino officers did not violate the Equal Protection Clause).

> tant means of earning the community's trust . . . which in turn increases police effectiveness in protecting the city.[59]

Having a diverse workforce in the police department, the court held, was therefore a compelling government interest. The court further found that the particular manner in which the test was administered and scored was narrowly tailored to meet that interest, and thus the city's race-based score standardization and promotional process satisfied the strict scrutiny test.[60]

Does the result in the *Petit* case mean that local government employers may adopt affirmative action programs in their public safety departments where the employer can show that a diverse workforce better serves the community? Perhaps it does. Whether an affirmative action program can survive strict scrutiny may depend upon the strength of the evidence that a city or county brings forth in support of its claim. In the *Petit* case, the city presented the testimony of an academic expert in criminal justice and police–community relations, the former chief of police of a city on the West Coast, and a number of high-ranking Chicago police officials.

In contrast to the *Petit* case, though, is the Fourth Circuit case *Hayes v. North State Law Enforcement Officers Association*.[61] In the *Hayes* case—which was decided in 1993, long before the Supreme Court's decisions in *Grutter* and *Gratz*—the Charlotte police department gave preference to African American candidates for promotion to sergeant both pursuant to a consent decree and because of the police chief's belief that the department needed a racially diverse police force in order to be an effective law enforcement agency. The Fourth Circuit declined to address whether or not achieving racial diversity in the police department was a compelling state interest because it found that the evidence offered by the city to establish the benefits of diversity was not even sufficient to create an issue of material fact. The city's evidence consisted of the testimony of the Charlotte police chief—based on his experiences as a police officer—and of three reports issued 33 years earlier in response to race riots in the city of Detroit, Michigan.[62] As the Fourth Circuit explained:

> . . . while these reports may express legitimate opinions about the need for diversity in effective law enforcement, in

59. *See* Petit v. City of Chicago, 352 F.2d 1111, 1115 (7th Cir. 2004).
60. *See Petit*, 352 F.2d at 1114–18.
61. *See* Hayes v. N. State Law Enforcement Officers Ass'n, 10 F.3d 207 (1993).
62. *See Hayes*, 10 F.3d at 214.

> themselves they contain no *factual* support for the City's position that diversity at all ranks, or specifically at the rank of sergeant, was essential to effective law enforcement in Charlotte, North Carolina, in February 1991, when the City made these promotions.[63]

Four years later, in the case *Alexander v. Estepp*, the Fourth Circuit again sidestepped the question of whether having a diverse workforce and remedying statistical but general evidence of past discrimination in county fire departments could qualify as a compelling government interest.[64] In this case, a Maryland county fire department ranked candidates for firefighter positions based on performance examinations, written examinations, and interviews as well as on the basis of express preferences based on characteristics such as current employment with the county, status as a volunteer firefighter, veteran status, and county residency.[65] Each year, fire department management set an informal cap on the number of whites and the number of males that could be offered employment. Once a cap was reached, a lower-ranking, uncapped applicant (that is, a minority applicant or a woman) was offered employment instead of the higher-ranking, capped applicant. Even if it were to assume that the need for a diverse workforce and for remedying past discrimination were compelling government interests, the court said, the program was not narrowly tailored because the means chosen by the fire department to address these interests were not closely enough related to remedying the problem.[66] The evidence showed that a non-race-based alternative, the elimination of the preference for volunteer firefighters, would have increased the hiring of African Americans and women. In addition, the county's program was not narrowly tailored in that it passed over whites to the benefit of Latino Americans and Asian Americans, two minority groups about whom the county had introduced no evidence of prior discrimination.[67]

The U.S. Supreme Court is once again considering the role of race in an undergraduate admissions process in the case *Fisher v. University of*

---

63. *See Hayes*, 10 F.3d at 215.
64. *See* Alexander v. Estepp, 95 F.3d 312, 316 (4th Cir. 1996).
65. *See Alexander*, 95 F.3d at 314.
66. *See Alexander*, 95 F.3d at 316.
67. *See Alexander*, 95 F.3d at 316.

Texas at Austin. The issue before the court is whether the Equal Protection Clause, as interpreted by the Supreme Court in the *Grutter* and *Gratz* cases, permits the University of Texas to use race as a factor in admissions in a process where the top 10 percent of each high school's graduating class is automatically admitted to the University of Texas and the remaining seats are filled by considering each application individually and race is one factor that is considered. The Court heard oral argument in the *Fisher* case on October 10, 2012, but as this book goes to press, it has not yet handed down its decision.[68]

App. 2.3.6 A Narrowly Tailored Plan

Much of the focus in the Supreme Court's affirmative action cases has been on whether or not strict scrutiny is the appropriate standard of review for race-based classifications and on what constitutes a compelling government interest. Only one Supreme Court case set forth in one place a comprehensive set of factors to be considered in evaluating whether an affirmative action plan is narrowly tailored to meet the government's compelling interests. That case was *United States v. Paradise*, a 1987 decision in which the Court held that a district court's order that the Alabama Department of Public Safety adopt a race-conscious promotion procedure satisfied the Equal Protection Clause.[69] In the *Paradise* case, the Supreme Court identified the following four factors as relevant:

1. the necessity of the particular relief and the efficacy of alternative remedies;
2. the flexibility and duration of the relief, including the availability of waiver provisions;
3. the relationship between the numerical goal of the relief and the relevant labor market; and
4. the impact of the relief on the rights of third parties.[70]

---

68. Fisher v. Univ. of Tex. at Austin, Docket No. 11-345.

69. *See* United States v. Paradise, 480 U.S. 149 (1987).

70. *See Paradise*, 480 U.S. at 171 (requirement that 50 percent of promotions in state trooper ranks go to African Americans was justified by compelling government interest in eradicating past discrimination). *See also* Hayes v. N. State Law Enforcement Officers Ass'n, 10 F.3d 207, 216 (1993).

Or, as one court of appeals phrased it, "three distinct inquiries fuel the narrow tailoring analysis: (1) the prior consideration of race-neutral alternative measures, (2) the relationship between the degree of preference and the effects of prior discrimination, and (3) the severity of the burden placed upon third parties."[71] These factors are similar to those used to evaluate whether affirmative action programs comply with Title VII.

App. 2.3.7 Affirmative Action and the Equal Protection Clause: A Summary

It took the United States Supreme Court more than 25 years to develop the standards against which an affirmative action plan must be measured for compliance with the Equal Protection Clause. A few rules are now clear:

1. Remedying demonstrated past discrimination by a government employer is almost always a compelling government interest that justifies the adoption of race-conscious measures.[72] A local government need not make a formal finding of past discrimination when it adopts a race-conscious remedy for an imbalanced, non-diverse workforce. But if its race-conscious practices were to be challenged, the employer would have to show that there was strong evidence of past discrimination that warranted the race-conscious policy it adopted.[73] The employer must also show that

---

71. *See* Kohlbek v. City of Omaha, Neb., 447 F.3d 552, 556 (8th Cir. 2006); Dean v. City of Shreveport, 438 F.3d 448, 458 (5th Cir. 2006) (summary judgment precluded by factual issues in dispute relevant to narrowly tailored analysis); Rutherford v. City of Cleveland, 179 F. App'x 366, 377–78 (6th Cir. 2006) (affirmative action plan for city police department was narrowly tailored and did not violate the Equal Protection Clause); Peightal v. Metro. Dade Cnty., 26 F.3d 1545, 1557 (11th Cir. 1994) (affirmative action plan for county fire department satisfied strict scrutiny and the Equal Protection Clause).

72. *See, e.g.*, City of Richmond v. J.A. Croson Co., 488 U.S. 469, 504 (1989); Wygant v. Jackson Bd. of Educ., 476 U.S. 267, 274 (1986); H.B. Rowe Co., Inc. v. Tippett, 615 F.3d 233, 241 (4th Cir. 2010) (upholdng North Carolina's minority highway contractor program but not its gender participation goals); Cotter v. City of Boston, 323 F.3d 160, 171 (1st Cir. 2003).

73. *See Croson*, 488 U.S. at 500; *Wygant*, 476 U.S. at 277; *Dean*, 438 F.3d, at 455 (city made adequate showing of past discrimination justifying its entering into a consent decree); *Kohlbek*, 447 F.3d at 555–57. Strong evidence does not mean conclusive proof. *See H.B. Rowe Co., Inc.*, 615 F.3d at 241.

there are present effects of the past discrimination that necessitate a race-conscious employment policy.[74]

2. Correcting general societal discrimination is never a compelling government interest.
3. It is unclear whether the Supreme Court or the Fourth Circuit would find a need for diversity in the workforce to be a compelling government interest. Those few cases in which a government employer has made this argument show that, at a minimum, the public employer must be prepared to offer contemporaneous studies and expert opinions.
4. To show that a plan is narrowly tailored to meet a government employer's compelling interest, a local government or community college must show that the particular plan is necessary and that there are no alternative, equally effective remedies; that the plan is limited in duration and designed only to achieve and not to maintain racial proportionality; and that the plan will not unduly interfere with the right of third-party applicants or employees.

APP. 2.4 Court-Ordered Affirmative Action

App. 2.4.1 Court-Ordered Affirmative Action under Title VII

The previous discussions of Title VII and Equal Protection Clause challenges to affirmative action plans have involved voluntary affirmative action programs. Courts have sometimes ordered the adoption of affirmative action plans as remedies in cases where plaintiffs have proven race or gender discrimination in violation of Title VII or to enforce the terms of a consent decree. Title VII explicitly authorizes courts to order affirmative action where there is a finding that the employer has intentionally engaged in discrimination:

> If the court finds that the respondent has intentionally engaged in or is intentionally engaging in an unlawful employment practice charged in the complaint, the court may enjoin the

74. *See Dean*, 438 F.3d at 456–57; *Kohlbek*, 447 F.3d at 557–58. *See also* Lomack v. City of Newark, 463 F.3d 303, 303 (3d Cir. 2006).

> respondent from engaging in such unlawful employment practice, and *order such affirmative action as may be appropriate,* which may include, but is not limited to, reinstatement or hiring of employees, with or without back pay . . . , or any other equitable relief as the court deems appropriate . . . .[75] (emphasis added)

Like voluntary affirmative action programs, court-ordered affirmative action has also been challenged both as violative of the Equal Protection Clause and as going beyond the bounds of Title VII.

App. 2.4.2 The Limits of Affirmative Action as a Title VII Remedy

Initially, in a 1984 case, the United States Supreme Court found that a court could order affirmative action as a remedy in a Title VII case only for those who have been actual victims of illegal discrimination.[76] But two years later, in 1986, the Supreme Court changed its mind, holding that affirmative race-conscious relief might be ordered by a court under Title VII to remedy past discrimination even if it benefited individuals who were not themselves identified victims of past discrimination.[77]

App. 2.4.3 Court-Ordered Affirmative Action and Equal Protection

Although the Supreme Court rejected the medical school's minority set-aside program in the 1976 *Bakke* case and the University of Michigan's undergraduate admissions practice of awarding extra points to candidates based on race in the 2003 *Gratz* case, it has allowed the use of quotas as a remedy after a finding of unlawful discrimination in public employment cases where the history of racial discrimination has been pervasive and continuing. In its 1987 decision in the case *United States v. Paradise,* the Court found that a district court's order for a one-black-for-one-white promotional requirement for the Alabama Department of Public Safety

---

75. *See* 42 U.S.C. § 2000e-5(g)(1).

76. *See* Firefighters Local Union No. 1784 v. Stotts, 467 U.S. 561 (1984).

77. *See* Local 28, Sheet Metal Workers Int'l Ass'n v. EEOC, 478 U.S. 421 (1986). *See also* Local 93, Int'l Ass'n of Firefighters v. City of Cleveland, 478 U.S. 501 (1986) (Title VII does not prohibit parties from entering into consent decrees that benefited individuals who were not actual victims of discrimination).

was permissible under the Equal Protection Clause.[78] The race-conscious relief in this case was justified, the Court said, by a compelling government interest in eradicating Alabama's "pervasive, systematic, and obstinate discriminatory exclusion of blacks"[79] within the ranks of its state troopers and by the federal government's interest in compliance with federal court orders: at the time of the decision, Alabama had been resisting and failing to implement court orders with respect to the integration of the upper ranks of its state troopers for almost ten years.[80] Consistent with other affirmative action decisions, the decision held that the one-for-one requirement did not disproportionately harm the interests of innocent white Alabama troopers in that it did not require the layoff or discharge of any white employees. Moreover, because it required the promotion only of qualified African American candidates and was limited in scope and duration, the order merely postponed the promotions of qualified white candidates. The one-for-one requirement existed to fulfill a promotional goal and, said the Court, like a hiring goal, imposed only a diffuse burden on white employees.[81]

In holding that the affirmative action plan in the *Paradise* case was narrowly tailored to achieve the government's interest in remedying past discrimination and promoting compliance with court orders, the Court gave deference to the district court's firsthand experience with the parties and with Alabama's refusal to comply with its previous orders.[82] It also noted that the district court's decree was effective, temporary, and flexible in that it applied only if there were qualified African American candidates available, if there was a need for promotions within the department, and if the department failed to implement a promotional procedure that did not have an adverse impact on African Americans, as it had previously been ordered to do.[83]

In subsequent decisions of the federal courts of appeals, affirmative action court orders and consent decrees have continued to be challenged. Analyses

78. *See* United States v. Paradise, 480 U.S. 149, 186 (1987).
79. *See Paradise*, 480 U.S. at 166.
80. *See Paradise*, 480 U.S. at 171–76.
81. *See Paradise*, 480 U.S. at 182–83.
82. *See Paradise*, 480 U.S. at 184–85.
83. *See Paradise*, 480 U.S. at 185.

of the validity of court orders involving public employers have tended to focus on whether there is a strong basis in evidence for concluding that discrimination took place in the past and has continuing present effects—as required for an affirmative action plan to satisfy both the Equal Protection Clause and Title VII[84]—and on whether the remedy is narrowly tailored.[85]

84. *See, e.g.,* Maryland Troopers Ass'n, Inc. v. Evans, 993 F.2d 1072, 1077 (4th Cir. 1993) (no strong basis in evidence of continuing discrimination where there was no gross statistical disparity in percentage of African American troopers to percentage of African Americans in relevant qualified labor pool after state adopted affirmative action plan in accordance with consent decree and eliminated disparities in workforce). *See also* Brunet v. City of Columbus, 1 F.3d 390, 409 (6th Cir. 1993) (fire department affirmative action plan in consent decree that gave hiring preference to women was not supported by strong basis in evidence where discrimination against women occurred more than 10 years ago).

85. *See, e.g.,* Chicago Firefighters Local 2 v. City of Chicago, 249 F.3d 649, 657–58 (7th Cir. 2001) (remedy is narrowly tailored when as few as possible white employees have promotions delayed to make way for African American and Hispanic employees; modest delay in promotion is not an undue hardship on white employees); Black Fire Fighters Ass'n of Dallas v. City of Dallas, Tex., 19 F.3d 992, 996–97 (5th Cir. 1994) (consent decree's use of "skip promotion" system to promote African Americans over whites who scored higher on promotion exams not narrowly tailored to remedy prior discrimination where change in exam to eliminate disparate impact was alternative remedy).

Appendix 3

Validation of Employment Selection Devices That Cause Disparate Impact

In lawsuits in which rejected applicants allege that a particular selection device has had a disparate impact on a protected class, the plaintiffs typically make their prima facie case the introduction of statistical evidence.[1] There are several different methods that may be used to measure adverse impact. The best known is the Equal Employment Opportunity Commission's so-called four-fifths rule, which finds adverse impact when members of a protected class are selected for positions at a rate less than four-fifths (80 percent) of that of another group. The EEOC gives the following example of how the rule works: if 50 percent of white applicants receive a passing score on a test but only 30 percent of African American applicants pass, the ratio of protected-class applicants (African Americans) to that of white applicants (the other group) would be 30/50, which is equal to 60 percent, which violates the four-fifths rule.[2] But courts frequently find a disparate impact if the difference between the number of members of the protected

1. *See, e.g.*, Watson v. Fort Worth Bank & Trust Co., 487 U.S. 977, 987 (1988).

2. See Equal Employment Opportunity Commission, Uniform Guidelines on Employee Selection Procedures, 29 C.F.R. § 1607 *et seq.* (hereinafter Uniform Guidelines) generally and 29 C.F.R. §§ 1607.4(D) and 1607.16(R) for examples. In *Ricci v. DeStefano*, the Supreme Court assumed the validity of the Uniform Guidelines. See *Ricci*, 557 U.S. 557, 632 n.11, 634 n.13 (2009).

class selected and the number that would be anticipated in a random selection system is more than two or three standard deviations.[3]

Employers may demonstrate that a challenged practice is job related and consistent with business necessity by showing that the practice, test, or process used has been validated. To validate a selection device or criterion—whether it is a written examination, a physical agility test, or the use of an educational qualification—means to establish through objective evidence that the practice or criterion accurately predicts who will be successful in the position in question. Typically, employers use formal validation studies, but the use of a formal study is not required. There are three types of validation studies: (1) studies that show the challenged practice has content validity, (2) studies that show the challenged practice has construct validity, and (3) studies that show the challenged practice is criterion related.[4] In the Uniform Guidelines, which govern analysis of disparate impact, the Equal Employment Opportunity Commission describes the differences between the three types of validation as follows:

> *Content validity* entails showing that the test measures the job or adequately reflects the skills or knowledge required by the job. A typing test for secretaries is an example of this kind of test. A showing of content validity does not require empirical evidence but instead "should consist of data showing that the content of the selection procedure is representative of important aspects of performance on the job."[5]
>
> *Construct validity* assesses the degree to which the test or evaluation tool measures identifiable characteristics that are important for successful performance of the job in question.[6] A construct validity study is most appropriate where the evaluation procedure seeks to identify abstract qualities that may be important characteristics for proper job performance but can-

3. *See* 1 Barbara Lindemann & Paul Grossman, Employment Discrimination Law 90–91 (4th ed. 2007) and cases cited therein.

4. *See* Uniform Guidelines, 29 C.F.R. § 1607.5(B). *See also Watson*, 487 U.S. at 998; Albemarle Paper Co. v. Moody, 422 U.S. 405, 431 (1975); Banos v. City of Chicago, 398 F.3d 889, 892 (7th Cir. 2005).

5. *See* 29 C.F.R. § 1607.5(B); *Banos*, 398 F.3d at 893.

6. *See* 29 C.F.R. §§ 1607.5(B) and 1607.14(D). *See also* United States v. City of New York, 731 F. Supp. 2d 291, 306 (E.D.N.Y. 2010).

> not be measured directly, such as creativity. Construct validity studies are usually not appropriate for validating physical exams because these physical qualities and abilities may be readily observed and quantified.[7]
>
> *Criterion-related validity* looks at whether a test is adequately correlated with future job performance and is constructed to measure traits thought to be relevant to future job performance. An IQ test is an example of this kind of test. A showing of criterion-related validity requires "empirical data demonstrating that the selection procedure is predictive of or significantly correlated with important elements of job performance.[8]

The law does not require that an employer conduct a formal validation study before using a given applicant evaluation tool. But an employer's chances of prevailing in litigation challenging its use of the procedure are better if it does. For example, where a state police exam was based on a "content validity *strategy*" not in accordance with professional standards or with the EEOC's selection guidelines and where this non-job-related selection procedure had a negative impact on African Americans, Latinos, and women, the state was enjoined from using the exam.[9] Validation studies can be expensive, however. A validation study may be unnecessary if the employer demonstrates that the procedure is sufficiently related to safe and efficient job performance.[10]

If the point of a selection device or test is to identify those applicants who are best able to perform particular tasks or otherwise function best in carrying out a specific set of responsibilities, it is crucial that an employer understand what knowledge, skills, and abilities and what personal characteristics are needed for a person to be successful in that particular job. In other words, an employer must look beneath the job description and identify those specific things that enable persons who are successful in the job

---

7. *See* Williams v. Ford Motor Co., 187 F.3d 533, 540 (6th Cir. 1999); Zamlen v. City of Cleveland, 906 F.2d 209, 218 (6th Cir. 1990).

8. *See* 29 C.F.R. § 1607.5(B); *Banos*, 398 F.3d at 893.

9. *See* United States v. State of New York, 475 F. Supp. 1103, 1110 (N.D.N.Y. 1979).

10. *See* EEOC v. Dial Corp., 469 F.3d 735, 742 (8th Cir. 2006).

to perform the functions set forth in the job description.[11] For this reason, the Uniform Guidelines require that a study of the content or construct validity of a scored test include a job analysis.[12]

For a test or selection device to have *content* validity (that is, the content of the test is representative of important aspects of performance on the job), it must be based on a job analysis that

> includes an analysis of the important work behavior(s) required for successful performance and their relative importance and, if the behavior results in work product(s), an analysis of the work product(s). Any job analysis should focus on the work behavior(s) and the tasks associated with them. If work behavior(s) are not observable, the job analysis should identify and analyze those aspects of the behavior(s) that can be observed and the observed work products. The work behavior(s) selected for measurement should be critical work behavior(s) and/or important work behavior(s) constituting most of the job.[13]

One judge translated this regulation as requiring a job analysis to be "a thorough survey of the relative importance of the various skills involved in the job in question and the degree of competency required in regard to each skill."[14]

For a test or selection device to have *construct* validity (that is, the test measures a trait or characteristic important for successful performance in the job), it must be based on a job analysis that shows

> the work behavior(s) required for successful performance of the job, or the groups of jobs being studied, the critical or important work behavior(s) in the job or group of jobs being studied, and an identification of the construct(s) believed to underlie successful performance of these critical or important work behaviors

---

11. *See* United States v. Cnty. of Fairfax, Va., 629 F.2d 932, 943 (4th Cir. 1980); Vanguard Justice Soc'y, Inc. v. Hughes, 592 F. Supp. 245, 258 (D. Md. 1984); M.O.C.H.A. Soc'y, Inc. v. City of Buffalo, 2009 WL 604898 (W.D.N.Y. Mar. 9, 2009). *See also* 29 C.F.R. §§ 1607.14(C)(2) and (4).

12. *See* 29 C.F.R. § 1607.14(A).

13. *See* 29 C.F.R. § 1607.14(C)(2).

14. *See* Vulcan Soc'y of the New York City Fire Dep't v. Commission, 360 F. Supp. 1265, 1274 (S.D.N.Y. 1973).

> in the job or jobs in question. Each construct should be named and defined, so as to distinguish it from other constructs. If a group of jobs is being studied the jobs should have in common one or more critical or important work behaviors at a comparable level of complexity.[15]

Examples of constructs include integrity, adaptability, inductive and deductive reasoning, and spatial orientation.[16]

Criterion-related validity, the most complex type of study, also requires analysis of work activities and behaviors.

---

15. *See* 29 C.F.R. § 1607.14(D)(2).

16. *See* United States v. City of New York, 731 F. Supp. 2d 291, 303–04 (E.D.N.Y. 2010).

Appendix 4

Model Summary of Employee Rights for Fair Credit Reporting Act Compliance

This form must be enclosed with the pre-adverse action disclosure that must be sent to an applicant before making a final decision not to hire the applicant based on information in the consumer report prepared by the third party agency. The form was developed by the Federal Trade Commission. Copies may be found at www.consumer.ftc.gov/articles/pdf-0096-fair-credit-reporting-act.pdf.

Para informacion en espanol, visite www.ftc.gov/credit o escribe a la FTC Consumer Response Center, Room 130-A 600 Pennsylvania Ave. N.W., Washington, D.C. 20580.

A Summary of Your Rights Under the Fair Credit Reporting Act

The federal Fair Credit Reporting Act (FCRA) promotes the accuracy, fairness, and privacy of information in the files of consumer reporting agencies. There are many types of consumer reporting agencies, including credit bureaus and specialty agencies (such as agencies that sell information about check writing histories, medical records, and rental history records). Here is a summary of your major rights under the FCRA. **For more information, including information about additional rights, go to www.ftc.gov/credit or write to: Consumer Response Center, Room 130-A, Federal Trade Commission, 600 Pennsylvania Ave. N.W., Washington, D.C. 20580.**

- **You must be told if information in your file has been used against you.** Anyone who uses a credit report or another type of consumer report to deny your application for credit, insurance, or employment – or to take another adverse action against you – must tell you, and must give you the name, address, and phone number of the agency that provided the information.
- **You have the right to know what is in your file.** You may request and obtain all the information about you in the files of a consumer reporting agency (your "file disclosure"). You will be required to provide proper identification, which may include your Social Security number. In many cases, the disclosure will be free. You are entitled to a free file disclosure if:
    - a person has taken adverse action against you because of information in your credit report;
    - you are the victim of identify theft and place a fraud alert in your file;
    - your file contains inaccurate information as a result of fraud;
    - you are on public assistance;
    - you are unemployed but expect to apply for employment within 60 days.

  In addition, by September 2005 all consumers will be entitled to one free disclosure every 12 months upon request from each nationwide credit bureau and from nationwide specialty consumer reporting agencies. See www.ftc.gov/credit for additional information.
- **You have the right to ask for a credit score.** Credit scores are numerical summaries of your credit-worthiness based on information from credit bureaus. You may request a credit score from consumer reporting agencies that create scores or distribute scores used in residential real property loans, but you will have to pay for it. In some mortgage transactions, you will receive credit score information for free from the mortgage lender.
- **You have the right to dispute incomplete or inaccurate information.** If you identify information in your file that is incomplete or inaccurate, and report it to the consumer reporting agency, the agency must investigate unless your dispute is frivolous. See www.ftc.gov/credit for an explanation of dispute procedures.
- **Consumer reporting agencies must correct or delete inaccurate, incomplete, or unverifiable information.** Inaccurate, incomplete or unverifiable information must be removed or corrected, usually within 30 days. However, a consumer reporting agency may continue to report information it has verified as accurate.

- **Consumer reporting agencies may not report outdated negative information.** In most cases, a consumer reporting agency may not report negative information that is more than seven years old, or bankruptcies that are more than 10 years old.
- **Access to your file is limited.** A consumer reporting agency may provide information about you only to people with a valid need -- usually to consider an application with a creditor, insurer, employer, landlord, or other business. The FCRA specifies those with a valid need for access.
- **You must give your consent for reports to be provided to employers.** A consumer reporting agency may not give out information about you to your employer, or a potential employer, without your written consent given to the employer. Written consent generally is not required in the trucking industry. For more information, go to www.ftc.gov/credit.
- **You may limit "prescreened" offers of credit and insurance you get based on information in your credit report.** Unsolicited "prescreened" offers for credit and insurance must include a toll-free phone number you can call if you choose to remove your name and address from the lists these offers are based on. You may opt-out with the nationwide credit bureaus at 1-888-5-OPTOUT (1-888-567-8688).
- **You may seek damages from violators.** If a consumer reporting agency, or, in some cases, a user of consumer reports or a furnisher of information to a consumer reporting agency violates the FCRA, you may be able to sue in state or federal court.
- **Identity theft victims and active duty military personnel have additional rights.** For more information, visit www.ftc.gov/credit.

States may enforce the FCRA, and many states have their own consumer reporting laws. In some cases, you may have more rights under state law. For more information, contact your state or local consumer protection agency or your state Attorney General. Federal enforcers are:

TYPE OF BUSINESS:	CONTACT:
Consumer reporting agencies, creditors and others not listed below	Federal Trade Commission: Consumer Response Center - FCRA Washington, DC 20580 1-877-382-4357
National banks, federal branches/agencies of foreign banks (word "National" or initials "N.A." appear in or after bank's name)	Office of the Comptroller of the Currency Compliance Management, Mail Stop 6-6 Washington, DC 20219 800-613-6743
Federal Reserve System member banks (except national banks, and federal branches/agencies of foreign banks)	Federal Reserve Consumer Help (FRCH) P O Box 1200 Minneapolis, MN 55480 Telephone: 888-851-1920 Website Address: www.federalreserveconsumerhelp.gov Email Address: ConsumerHelp@FederalReserve.gov
Savings associations and federally chartered savings banks (word "Federal" or initials "F.S.B." appear in federal institution's name)	Office of Thrift Supervision Consumer Complaints Washington, DC 20552 800-842-6929
Federal credit unions (words "Federal Credit Union" appear in institution's name)	National Credit Union Administration 1775 Duke Street Alexandria, VA 22314 703-519-4600
State-chartered banks that are not members of the Federal Reserve System	Federal Deposit Insurance Corporation Consumer Response Center, 2345 Grand Avenue, Suite 100 Kansas City, Missouri 64108-2638 1-877-275-3342
Air, surface, or rail common carriers regulated by former Civil Aeronautics Board or Interstate Commerce Commission	Department of Transportation , Office of Financial Management Washington, DC 20590 202-366-1306
Activities subject to the Packers and Stockyards Act, 1921	Department of Agriculture Office of Deputy Administrator - GIPSA Washington, DC 20250 202-720-7051

Appendix 5

Equal Employment Opportunity Commission State and Local Government Information (EEO-4)

This form must be completed by local government employers with 100 or more employees and filed with the Equal Employment Opportunity Commission every two years. Local government employers with 15 to 99 employees may be asked to submit this form on a random sampling basis.

EQUAL EMPLOYMENT OPPORTUNITY COMMISSION

STATE AND LOCAL GOVERNMENT INFORMATION (EEO-4)

EXCLUDE SCHOOL SYSTEMS AND EDUCATIONAL INSTITUTIONS
(Read attached instructions prior to completing this form)

APPROVED BY OMB 3046-0008

EXPIRES 12/31/2005

DO NOT ALTER INFORMATION PRINTED IN THIS BOX

MAIL COMPLETED FORM TO:
EEO-4 Reporting Center
PO Box 8127
Reston VA 20195

A. TYPE OF GOVERNMENT (Check one box only)

☐ 1. State ☐ 2. County ☐ 3. City ☐ 4. Township ☐ 5. Special District

☐ 6. Other (Specify)____________________

B. IDENTIFICATION

1. NAME OF POLITICAL JURISDICTION (If same as label, skip to Item C)

2. Address--Number and Street	CITY/TOWN	COUNTY	STATE/ZIP	EEOC USE ONLY A
				B

C. FUNCTION

(Check one box to indicate the function(s) for which this form is being submitted. Data should be reported for all departments and agencies in your government covered by the function(s) indicated. If you cannot supply the data for every agency within the function(s) attach a list showing name and address of agencies whose data are not included.)

	1.Financial Administration. Tax billing and collection, budgeting, purchasing, central accounting and similar financial administration carried on by a treasurer's, auditor's or comptroller's office and GENERAL CONTROL. Duties usually performed by boards of supervisors or commissioners, central administration offices and agencies, central personnel or planning agencies, all judicial offices and employees (judges, magistrates, bailiffs, etc.)		8. HEALTH. Provision of public health services, outpatient clinics, visiting nurses, food and sanitary inspections, mental health, alcohol rehabilitation service, etc.
			9. HOUSING. Code enforcement, low rent public housing, fair housing ordinance enforcement, housing for elderly, housing rehabilitation, rent control.
	2. STREETS AND HIGHWAYS. Maintenance, repair, construction and administration of streets, alleys, sidewalks, roads, highways and bridges.		10. COMMUNITY DEVELOPMENT. Planning, zoning, land development, open space, beautification, preservation.
	3. PUBLIC WELFARE. Maintenance of homes and other institutions for the needy; administration of public assistance. (Hospitals and sanatoriums should be reported as item7.)		11. CORRECTIONS. Jails, reformatories, detention homes, halfway houses, prisons, parole and probation activities
	4. POLICE PROTECTION. Duties of a police department sheriff's, constable's, coroner's office, etc., including technical and clerical employees engaged in police activities.		12. UTILITIES AND TRANSPORTATION. Includes water supply, electric power, transit, gas, airports, water transportation and terminals.
	5. FIRE PROTECTION. Duties of the uniformed fire force and clerical employees. (Report any forest fire protection activities as item 6.)		13. SANITATION AND SEWAGE. Street cleaning, garbage and refuse collection and disposal. Provision, maintenance and operation of sanitary and storm sewer systems and sewage disposal plants.
	6. NATURAL RESOURCES. Agriculture, forestry, forest fire protection, irrigation drainage, flood control, etc., and PARKS AND RECREATION. Provision, maintenance and operation of parks, playgrounds, swimming pools, auditoriums, museums, marinas, zoos, etc.		14. EMPLOYMENT SECURITY STATE GOVERNMENTS ONLY
	7. HOSPITALS AND SANATORIUMS. Operation and maintenance of institutions for inpatient medical care.		15. OTHER (Specify on Page Four)

EEOC FORM 164 FEB 97 (Previous Editions are Obsolete) PAGE 1

D. EMPLOYMENT DATA AS OF JUNE 30

(Do not include elected/appointed officials. Blanks will be counted as zero)

1. FULL-TIME EMPLOYEES (Temporary employees are not included)

		MALE						FEMALE				
JOB CATEGORIES	ANNUAL SALARY (In thousands 000)	TOTAL (COLUMNS B-K)	NON-HISPANIC ORIGIN		HISPANIC	ASIAN OR PACIFIC ISLANDER	AMERICAN INDIAN OR ALASKAN NATIVE	NON-HISPANIC ORIGIN		HISPANIC	ASIAN OR PACIFIC ISLANDER	AMERICAN INDIAN OR ALASKAN NATIVE
			WHITE	Black				White	Black			
		A	B	C	D	E	F	G	H	I	J	K
OFFICIALS ADMINISTRATORS	1. $0.1-15.9											
	2. 16.0-19.9											
	3. 20.0-24.9											
	4. 25.0-32.9											
	5. 33.0-42.9											
	6. 43.0-54.9											
	7. 55.0-69.9											
	8. 70.0 PLUS											
PROFESSIONALS	9. $0.1-15.9											
	10. 16.0-19.9											
	11. 20.0-24.9											
	12. 25.0-32.9											
	13. 33.0-42.9											
	14. 43.0-54.9											
	15. 55.0-69.9											
	16. 70.0 PLUS											
TECHNICIANS	17. $0.1-15.9											
	18. 16.0-19.9											
	19. 20.0-24.9											
	20. 25.0-32.9											
	21. 33.0-42.9											
	22. 43.0-54.9											
	23. 55.0-69.9											
	24. 70.0 PLUS											
PROTECTIVE SERVICE	25. $0.1-15.9											
	26. 16.0-19.9											
	27. 20.0-24.9											
	28. 25.0-32.9											
	29. 33.0-42.9											
	30. 43.0-54.9											
	31. 55.0-69.9											
	32. 70.0 PLUS											
PARA-PROFESSIONALS	33. $0.1-15.9											
	34. 16.0-19.9											
	35. 20.0-24.9											
	36. 25.0-32.9											
	37. 33.0-42.9											
	38. 43.0-54.9											
	39. 55.0-69.9											
	40. 70.0 PLUS											
ADMINISTRATIVE SUPPORT	41. $0.1-15.9											
	42. 16.0-19.9											
	43. 20.0-24.9											
	44. 25.0-32.9											
	45. 33.0-42.9											
	46. 43.0-54.9											
	47. 55.0-69.9											
	48. 70.0 PLUS											

D. EMPLOYMENT DATA AS OF JUNE 30 (Cont.)

(Do not include elected/appointed officials. Blanks will be counted as zero)

1. FULL-TIME EMPLOYEES (Temporary employees are not included)

JOB CATEGORIES	ANNUAL SALARY (In thousands 000)	MALE						FEMALE				
		TOTAL (COLUMNS B-K)	NON-HISPANIC ORIGIN		HISPANIC	ASIAN OR PACIFIC ISLANDER	AMERICAN INDIAN OR ALASKAN NATIVE	NON-HISPANIC ORIGIN		HISPANIC	ASIAN OR PACIFIC ISLANDER	AMERICAN INDIAN OR ALASKAN NATIVE
			WHITE	Black				White	Black			
		A	B	C	D	E	F	G	H	I	J	K
SKILLEDCRAFT	49. $0.1-15.9											
	50. 16.0-19.9											
	51. 20.0-24.9											
	52. 25.0-32.9											
	53. 33.0-42.9											
	54. 43.0-54.9											
	55. 55.0-69.9											
	56. 70.0 PLUS											
SERVICE MAINTENANCE	57. $0.1-15.9											
	58. 16.0-19.9											
	59. 20.0-24.9											
	60. 25.0-32.9											
	61. 33.0-42.9											
	62. 43.0-54.9											
	63. 55.0-69.9											
	64. 70.0 PLUS											
65. TOTAL FULL TIME (LINES 1 - 64)												
2. OTHER THAN FULL-TIME EMPLOYEES (Including temporary employees												
66. OFFICIALS/ADMIN												
67. PROFESSIONALS												
68. TECHNICIANS												
69. PROTECTIVE SERVICE												
70. PARA-PROFESSIONAL												
71. ADMIN. SUPPORT												
72. SKILLED CRAFT												
73. SERVICE/MAINTENANCE												
74. TOTAL OTHER THAN FULL TIME (LINES 66 - 73)												
3. NEW HIRES DURING FISCAL YEAR - Permanent full time only JULY 1 - JUNE 30												
75. OFFICIALS/ADMIN												
76. PROFESSIONALS												
77. TECHNICIANS												
78. PROTECTIVE SERVICE												
79. PARA-PROFESSIONAL												
80. ADMIN. SUPPORT												
81. SKILLED CRAFT												
82. SERVICE/MAINTENANCE												
83. TOTAL NEW HIRES (LINES 75 - 82)												

EEOC FORM 164, FEB 97 (Previous Editions are Obsolete)

REMARKS (List National Crime Information Center (NCIC) number assigned to any Criminal Justice Agencies whose data are included in this report)

LIST AGENCIES INCLUDED ON THIS FORM

CERTIFICATION. I certify that the information given in this report is correct and true to the best of my knowledge and was reported in accordance with accompanying instructions. (Willfully false statements on this report are punishable by law, US Code, Title 18, Section 1001.)

NAME OF PERSON TO CONTACT REGARDING THIS FORM	TITLE
ADDRESS (Number and Street, City, State, Zip Code)	TELEPHONE NUMBER extension: FAX NUMBER

DATE E-MAIL	TYPED NAME/TITLE OF AUTHORIZED OFFICIAL	SIGNATURE

EEOC FORM 164, FEB 97 (Previous Editions Obsolete)

Case Index

A

B

C

D

E

F

G

H

O

P

R

S

T

U

V

W

Y

Z

Statute Index

United States Code

Code of Federal Regulations

North Carolina General Statutes

North Carolina Administrative Code

Subject Index

A

B

D

E

F

H

I

J

M

N

O

P

S

T

U

V